D1160071

BY THE SAME AUTHOR.

THE MENTAL AND PHYSICAL LIFE OF SCHOOL CHILDREN.
With Tables and Diagrams.
Crown 8vo.

EDUCATIONAL PSYCHOLOGY

EDUCATIONAL PSYCHOLOGY

AN OBJECTIVE STUDY

BY

PETER SANDIFORD

PROFESSOR OF EDUCATIONAL PSYCHOLOGY IN THE UNIVERSITY OF TORONTO

WITH 57 ILLUSTRATIONS

LONGMANS, GREEN AND CO.

LONDON ◆ NEW YORK ◆ TORONTO

1930

SANDIFORD

EDUCATIONAL PSYCHOLOGY

LONGMANS, GREEN AND CO.

55 FIFTH AVENUE, NEW YORK

221 EAST 20TH STREET, CHICAGO

TREMONT TEMPLE, BOSTON

128 UNIVERSITY AVENUE, TORONTO

LONGMANS, GREEN AND CO. LTD.

39 PATERNOSTER ROW, E C 4, LONDON

53 NICOL ROAD, BOMBAY

6 OLD COURT HOUSE STREET, CALCUTTA

167 MOUNT ROAD, MADRAS

First Edition June 1928
Reprinted December 1928
June 1929, October 1929
February 1930

PRINTED IN THE UNITED STATES OF AMERICA

TO

MY WIFE AND CHILDREN

THIS BOOK IS AFFECTIONATELY

DEDICATED

PREFACE

At the present time the world of experience can be rather sharply divided into two parts—the world of science and the world of belief. In the former are included physics, chemistry, biology and the other sciences which confine themselves to experimental and verifiable data. In the latter are included religion, philosophy, and the parts of psychology which, of necessity, limit themselves to the subjective data of experience. Formerly, knowledge was mainly subjective. But in the seventeenth and eighteenth centuries certain of the sciences emancipated themselves from the metaphysical speculations which previously characterized them. Their subsequent progress was remarkable and constituted a landmark in the upward advance of the human race. Psychology, unfortunately, persisted in the mediæval tradition. For the most part it continued to revolve around words, definitions and introspections. In recent times, however, a serious attempt to bring it within the field of science has been made. The binding shackles of speculation have not been wholly removed; in fact, the subject has been cleft in two, one part remaining under the banner of the introspective metaphysician, the other boldly unfurling the flag of scientific freedom. Scientific psychology is making rapid advances; and it is merely stating the sober truth to say that in the past half-century more progress has been made than in the previous two thousand years.

This sharp cleavage between the subjective and objective aspects of psychology has not been recognized by most of the writers on the subject They have tried to run with the hares and hunt with the hounds. Consequently, we find in the textbooks of psychology almost as many interpretations of, say, instincts and emotions as there are authors. A physicist of to-day would be very much surprised if, in different texts, he found discordant accounts of the various topics comprising his subject. Similarly, a biologist expects general agreement among the statements found in treatises on biology. Yet psychologists, apparently, are still content to wrangle about unverifiable introspections and beliefs. Unlike the physicist and the biologist, they have not gone back to the laboratory for their facts, and until they do, this confusion will remain.

Few people realize the difficulties which confront the scientific psychologist. Experimentation in the biological sciences is obviously more difficult than in the non-biological ones, simply because of the difficulty of controlling living things. Psychology, which is a branch of biology since it endeavours to bring within experimental control the behaviour of human beings, is the most difficult of all the sciences. Being also new, its verifiable data are few, but they are rapidly increasing.

In this book a serious attempt has been made to confine statements to the objective and verifiable data of carefully controlled observations and experiments. That it has not been wholly successful I am acutely aware, but I feel that in this method lies the way of progress. Later writers will undoubtedly have fuller and better material at their command.

Since the method is comparatively new, considerable space has been devoted to the scientific foundations of the subject. In course of time much of the material dealt with may be taken for granted, and the discussion confined to data more pertinent to the field. But in my opinion that time has not yet arrived. A casual reading of the text will show my indebtedness to Thorndike, Watson, Cattell, Herrick, and Child. The references have been carefully selected and confined to those which will enable a serious student to secure very complete bibliographies in any branch of the subject he is interested in.

The manuscript has been read in part by my colleague, Dr. E. A. Linell, and by my wife. For their generous help and valuable criticisms I am deeply grateful.

PETER SANDIFORD.

TORONTO, 1928.

CONTENTS

INTRODUCTION

The Nature of Educational Psychology

PART I

MAN'S EQUIPMENT FOR LEARNING

CHAPTER I

The Inheritance of Human Traits

CHAPTER II

The Behaviour of Organisms

CHAPTER III

How the Human Body Works

A. Organs of Response: Muscles and Glands

CHAPTER IV

How the Human Body Works

B. Organs of Reception: Sense Organs

CHAPTER V

How the Human Body Works

C. Organs of Connection: The Nervous System

CHAPTER VI

Non-variable Behaviour: Reflexes and Instincts

CHAPTER VII

Non-variable Behaviour: Emotions

CHAPTER VIII

Intelligence: its Nature and Measurement

PART II

THE LEARNING PROCESS

CHAPTER IX

Conditioned Stimuli and Conditioned Reactions

CHAPTER X

The Laws of Learning

CHAPTER XI

Improvement in Learning

CHAPTER XII

The Permanence of Improvement: Remembering and Forgetting

CHAPTER XIII

Continuous Practice: Fatigue in Learning

CHAPTER XIV

Transfer of Training: Reciprocal Improvement in Learning

CHAPTER XV

The Measurement of Improvement: Educational Tests

CHAPTER XVI

Improvement in Special Subjects

A. The Acquirement of Language Habits

PAGE

READING

SPELLING

HANDWRITING

CHAPTER XVII

IMPROVEMENT IN SPECIAL SUBJECTS

B. THE ACQUIREMENTS OF SKILL IN ARITHMETIC

LIST OF TABLES

LIST OF ILLUSTRATIONS AND DIAGRAMS

EDUCATIONAL PSYCHOLOGY

EDUCATIONAL PSYCHOLOGY

INTRODUCTION

THE NATURE OF EDUCATIONAL PSYCHOLOGY

BEFORE one can appreciate the point of view taken by the educational psychologist of to-day, it is necessary first to ascertain the viewpoint generally accepted by the "plain" or general psychologist. For educational psychology, as we shall see later, is nothing more nor less than the application of psychological principles to the problems of the schoolroom. A brief summary of the development of subject-matter and methods in psychology will, therefore, be given.

Old Viewpoints in Psychology.—Psychology as a separate branch of study is more than 2000 years old. Aristotle, the greatest organizer of knowledge and the best text-book writer of all time, is generally regarded as the founder of the subject. His treatise, *De anima* (on the soul), marks the birth of psychology as a separate science. Though the subject is old, its name is fairly new. Apparently we owe it to Rudolf Goeckel [1] (or Goclenius), whose book, published in 1590, bore the title *Psychologia*. This word, built up from *psyche* (soul) and *logos* (word, talk about, science of), fitted the subject so well that it has since been retained.

Speculations about the soul can be traced back to remotest antiquity. Aristotle extended and systematized these speculations. The psyche (soul) of the Greeks was the essence or true being of an organism; it was the cause and principle of its life. Without a soul the body was merely a corpse. To the Greek, therefore, the connotation of the word "soul" was wider than is now accepted, including the modern notions of both mind and soul. By the time the Middle Ages were reached, the mental and spiritual aspects of the soul had become separate subjects of study; the philosopher (or psychologist) emphasizing the one,

[1] Brett, *History of Psychology*, II, p. 150.

the theologian the other. Psychology changed, then, from the study of the soul to the study of the mind.

The problem of the relation between mind and body, between mental and physical phenomena, remained a puzzling and unsolved riddle down to the end of the mediæval period. Descartes (1596–1650), the second founder of psychology, cut the Gordian knot by giving new definitions to matter and mind. He boldly proclaimed that matter and mind were both substances, but between them was no natural connection. Matter was extended substance, that is, was substance capable of filling space. Mind was unextended thinking substance whose essence was consciousness. From this time psychology gradually became the study or the science of consciousness.

Various meanings were given to consciousness, the commonest being that of awareness. Consciousness was that which increased in amount as the individual passed from the deepest of dreamless sleep to the most wakeful of his waking moments. Consciousness could only be studied introspectively; it was a private domain into which no stranger could enter. Later, it was observed that people did things—reacted or behaved—when they were conscious; they did nothing of psychological importance when unconscious. To an observer, a person's behaviour was the index of his consciousness. Why not study his behaviour? This latter was a public affair which could be observed by several at a time; which could even be made the subject of experimental investigation and thus form the subject-matter of a true science. Gradually psychology became an objective science—the study of behaviour. Although there are many interpretations of behaviour (all schools accepting the observable responses to stimuli as the subject-matter of psychology) no psychologist would deny that the objective viewpoint is the one that dominates the subject to-day. And very few of them, even those who are most reluctant to break with an honourable past, would maintain that the subjective or introspective method of study yields data which can be used by science.

Thus, in brief, is the story of psychology. Summing it up we may say with Woodworth[1]: "First psychology lost its soul, then it lost its mind, then it lost consciousness; it still has behaviour of a kind."

The New Viewpoint in Psychology.—Modern psychology is dominated by the scientific attitude and aim. "Science is nothing but trained and organized common-sense," said Huxley. Its data are the facts of experience which are communicable and verifiable. Its aim is the concise description of the know-

[1] Woodworth, *Psychology, a Study of Mental Life*, p. 2.

able universe. Science, therefore, classifies facts, notes their sequences and relationships, judges them and draws conclusions from them which are unbiased by personal feeling. If religion is defined as the world of subjective belief, then science is the world of objective fact. But belief and fact, it must be noted, are independent categories.

The earlier metaphysical or speculative psychology had closer relationship to the world of religion than to the world of science. Science demands objectivity and experimentation. Modern psychology, in contrast with ancient, is, therefore, objective rather than subjective; experimental rather than speculative. Its extreme form, usually called behaviourism, is a purely objective, experimental branch of natural science, more closely related to physiology than to any other of the sciences. Its subject-matter is the behaviour or activities of human beings. With consciousness as subject-matter it will have nothing to do, claiming that consciousness is neither a definable nor a usable concept so far as science is concerned.[1] But some critic might say that physiology also studies behaviour objectively; wherein does it differ from psychology? The answer is simple. Whereas physiology studies the actions of parts of the body—organs and the like—psychology studies the reactions of the body as a whole.

Such a conception of psychology makes a clean break with the past. Especially does it break with consciousness and introspection. Now man's consciousness, as he has long realized, is a very important part of his life. The awareness of himself and the world in which he lives seems, in many ways, to be the most important fact connected with living. Why does behaviourism discard it? Behaviourism discards consciousness because it cannot provide the factual data demanded by a natural science. Modern psychology says, let the individual enjoy conscious experiences as much as he likes; that is his private personal affair; but do not let him impose his introspective speculations on the scientific world. There they have no place at all, nor, so far as can be judged at present, can they ever find a place. They are, however, the legitimate province of the speculative philosopher.

At first glance the limitation of psychology to data which can be used scientifically seems to narrow the field of study unduly. But further consideration shows that the subject gains far more than it loses. Against the losses of introspectionist data, which can only be gleaned from normal and superior adult human beings, can be placed the gains of observational and experimental

[1] Watson, *Lectures in Print: Behaviorism*, p. 3.

data gathered from the scientific study of very young children, of abnormal people such as the feeble-minded and insane, and of animals lower than humans. From these important groups, introspection could gather no data at all, yet it is from the study of them that behaviourism has garnered its finest fruits.

Modern psychology, contrasted with ancient, presents the following characteristics :

(1) It links up the behaviour of human beings with that of lower organisms.

(2) It is objective in its methods ; its conclusions and generalizations are open to verification by other workers.

(3) It is more definitely experimental than the older psychology.

(4) It aims to predict and control behaviour.

The Failure of Introspection.—So long as psychology was regarded as the study of consciousness or mental states, introspection was its only method. The word literally means a looking within ; introspectionists looked into the mind, as it were, and observed its workings. Introspection fails as a scientific method for the following reasons :

(1) In introspection the mind is asked to attend to its own workings. It is as if we asked the kettle of boiling water to describe the boiling, or the zinc and sulphuric acid the fizzing. "The mind in watching its own workings," says Stout,[1] "must necessarily have its attention divided between two objects—on the one hand the mental operation itself which is to be observed, and on the other, the object to which this mental operation is directed."

(2) Before mental states can be described they must first happen. Nobody can describe his feelings of anger until the state of anger has occurred. Introspection is, therefore, always retrospection ; it describes memories of events that either are past or passing away.

(3) If an observation of a state of mind is made, the very act of observing tends to change it. Thus if an observer says to himself : "I am angry, I must observe this anger very carefully," the calmness and deliberation necessary to such observation will inevitably dissipate the anger. It destroys the object it is examining. As James[2] states : "The attempt at introspective analysis in these cases is, in fact, like seizing a spinning-top to catch its motion, or trying to turn up the gas quickly enough to see how the darkness looks."

(4) Mental states change so rapidly that only the slower changes can be observed, the quicker ones elude introspective

[1] Stout, *Manual of Psychology*, p. 18.
[2] James, *Principles of Psychology*, I, p. 244.

observation. For instance, nobody has been able to observe introspectively what really happens when we feel the meaning of a word and then write it. What my mental processes are as I write this sentence are beyond my powers of introspective analysis, and, for that matter, those of everybody else in a similar situation.

(5) It is not given to everybody to introspect either easily or well. Judging from results, introspectionists as a class have analysed and reasoned with ease, hence their over-emphasis of such processes as analysis, reasoning, and judgment, and the comparative neglect of others equally frequent and valuable.

(6) Physiological actions, posture habits and others that have become automatic seldom enter into consciousness at all. They, therefore, escape the introspectionist, although nobody would deny their importance in intellectual life. If modern psycho-analysis is to be believed, many states observed in consciousness are the results of unconscious causes whose actual nature is still obscure and unknown. Man rationalizes his behaviour to a most extraordinary extent; he can find excellent reasons for doing anything he wants to do. Yet introspection failed to discover these twists in mental states. When we do things because "we feel we must" the cause for them is always hidden and never forms part of the "content of consciousness" with which the introspectionist is constrained to deal. The mental states discoverable by introspection, therefore, must give a very one-sided picture of intellectual activity.

(7) The essence of a science is controlled observation under experimental conditions. Scientific results are of such a nature that they are verifiable by the reconstruction of the original conditions. A mental state is a unique event; introspection of a state that can never be repeated can never yield results of indubitable scientific validity. The method of comparing introspections of different skilled observers, regarded by the older psychologists as having scientific validity, is of very doubtful value for science. If I say, "When I am angry I feel so-and-so," and another person says, "No, your description is wrong; when I am angry I feel thus—and—thus," who is to judge of the truth between us?

(8) Introspection, as was suggested earlier, deals solely with the mental states of normal or superior human beings; those of the insane and mental defectives are beyond its ken. Yet objective observation of insanity and hysteria has shown that these abnormalities are but extreme and unbalanced developments of characteristics and functions which form integral parts of normal human behaviour. As for animals, introspection could not possibly have anything to do with them. Yet it is from the field

of animal learning that a new world has been opened up which is proving of the utmost importance for education. Introspection missed the great truth that behaviour in animals is graded on the evolutionary scale. Man at the top of the scale exhibits forms of behaviour differing not in kind but only in degree from those below him.

The foregoing criticisms surely dispose of the claim made by introspectionists that theirs is the only method of psychological observation. Introspection, at its best, only gives relatively uniform results when the observations are of a comparatively simple nature. Apparently all observers agree that when a bright light, say a glowing electric bulb, is looked at for a short time and the eyes then turned upon a dark background, a "positive after-image" of the filament appears. But with "negative after-images" there is far from unanimity of opinion. And the more complex the mental process, the more variable the data of introspection become. It may also be freely granted that certain sorts of information can only be obtained by introspection. The pleasure that one derives from reading a book is largely sealed from the observer, and statements about this pleasure do not yield reliable data for a science. A far better method is to make careful records of what a man reads. In the last analysis we judge of a man's pleasure in reading by the kind and quantity of the reading that he does. He may report that he loves reading Shakespeare, but if his Shakespeare becomes dusty on his shelves, while *Pollyanna* is read and re-read, we are apt to mistrust his statement, although it may have been made in perfectly good faith. If he says, "I can add a column of 100 figures in 10 seconds" he is reporting a self-observation which is easily verified, not an introspection.

Introspection cannot be made to give consistent or verifiable results. For this reason, and also because of the inherent difficulties of introspection summarized above, scientific psychology has abandoned the data of introspection to philosophers and confines itself to objective data obtained from observation and experiment.

The Aim of Scientific Psychology.—The particular aim of scientific psychology is to observe the behaviour of organisms —both human and sub-human. With animals what they do is observed; with humans what they both do and say is dealt with. For saying is only a form of behaviour. In technical language, psychology gathers data about responses or reactions to stimuli or situations. Observing responses, it endeavours to determine the situation which produced them; knowing the situations it endeavours to predict the probable responses to them.

A stimulus as used in psychology is a relatively simple factor influencing the responses of organisms. When these factors are more complex, as they usually are in the social world, the name "situation" is given to them. Thus a green light or the prick of a pin is called a stimulus. But a teacher at work on an arithmetic problem with a pupil would be a situation. Situations are really the sum total of a mass of stimulating factors which lead organisms, including man, to react as a whole. The complete exploration of the situation—response mechanism, usually abbreviated to S→R, is the task of scientific psychology. While this, at first glance, may seem to be absurdly simple, it really involves the investigation of what animals and humans do every moment of their lives.

The Divisions of Psychological Studies.—The diagram given below, which is a modification of one first designed by Yerkes,[1] represents the main divisions of psychology as studied to-day.

Psychology	Normal	Adult	Human	Individual	Pure
	Abnormal	Young Child or Genetic	Animal or Comparative	Group or Social	Applied, Educational, Industrial, and Legal

Each term in the upper line is contrasted with the one immediately below it—Normal with Abnormal ; Human with Animal ; and Pure with Applied. The lines and cross-lines indicate the various combinations which are to be found. Thus normal, young humans can be studied as individuals or in groups so as to develop the principles of pure science. Plain or general psychology is represented by all the words of the upper line—Normal, Adult, Human, Individual, and Pure.

The various branches will now be briefly described so as to make the matter a little clearer.

(*a*) *Normal Psychology* studies the behaviour of normal organisms. Normal organisms exhibit variabilities, but the variations must not be so great as to be readily classed as abnormal. The line of demarcation between normal and abnormal is difficult to draw and is usually a matter of expediency or convenience. The method of normal psychology is description of behaviour as it actually exists in the species, without reference to the way in which it evolved.

(*b*) *Abnormal Psychology* deals with the behaviour of abnormal organisms. Especially is it interested in the study of the feeble-minded (aments)—those suffering from an imperfectly developed

[1] Yerkes, *Introduction to Psychology*, p. 17.

nervous system, and the insane (dements)—those whose nervous system has been normal but is now impaired or diseased in some way.

(*c*) *Adult Psychology* is the study of the behaviour of adult humans. Introspective psychology was, perforce, confined to adult psychology.

(*d*) *Child Psychology* is a branch of genetic psychology Genetic psychology may deal either with the development of behaviour in the individual or in the species. The scientific study of the pre-school child has recently given great impetus to this branch of the subject.

(*e*) *Human Psychology* describes the behaviour of human beings in contrast with the behaviour of sub-human species. When psychology is mentioned alone it always refers to human psychology.

(*f*) *Animal Psychology*, since it is studied mainly from the comparative standpoint, is frequently called comparative psychology. It is a purely experimental branch and has a great and steadily increasing literature. It was from animal behaviour during the learning process that the laws of learning, now applied with such success to pupils in school, were first developed.

(*g*) *Individual Psychology*, or the Psychology of Individual Differences, treats of variations in human behaviour. Individuals differ in their behaviour according to race, sex, intelligence and the like. These differences are of greater psychological significance than the likenesses.

(*h*) *Social or Group Psychology* deals with the behaviour of the individual as he is influenced by the society or group of which he forms a part. It is not to be confused with sociology, which is concerned with the study of human institutions of all sorts.

(*i*) *Pure Psychology* is the science which develops the general principles or laws of behaviour. Many forms of scientific psychology are of the pure type, interested in truths rather than applications of truth.

(*j*) *Applied Psychology*, whose main sub-divisions are educational, industrial, and legal, applies the findings of pure psychology to the practical situations of life. Applied psychology is dependent upon the research of the pure scientist whose only desire is to know and to understand.

Some branches of psychology, such as experimental psychology and physiological or neurological psychology, are methods of psychological study rather than true divisions of the subject-matter of psychology. Others, such as the psychology of advertising, the psychology of religion, the psychology of arithmetic.

algebra, reading, etc., are special sub-topics of the major fields of applied psychology.

The Nature of Educational Psychology.—Educational psychology, as we have seen, is a major branch or subdivision of applied psychology. It utilizes the laws and principles discovered by "Pure" psychology. Its subject-matter is the behaviour of human beings undergoing the process of education Generally speaking, it deals with the young rather than the old, and with the learning situations of the school rather than those of the wider environment. Its main subdivisions are:

(1) *The Original Nature of Man.*—This branch tries to discover what traits, powers, or capacities a child possesses which may be used as the basis of an educational training. The inheritance of these traits, their variability, etc., are topics of interest to the educational psychologist. So also are his bodily mechanisms of behaviour, his equipment of reflexes, instincts and other unlearned or non-variable forms of behaviour, his general intelligence, and, in general, all his native gifts concerned with behaviour.

(2) *The Psychology of Learning*, or, as it is more generally called, *the learning process.*—Given the original nature of man, this second great branch of the subject inquires how the teacher can best arrange educational situations so as to bring about desired responses. The laws of learning are formulated from a study of specific acts of learning. The rate, progress, and limits of improvement are investigated with a view to discovering the factors which underlie the most economical or advantageous forms of learning.

(3) *Psychology of Special Subjects.*—Having discovered the laws underlying learning in general, they are next applied to special subjects such as reading, arithmetic, spelling, algebra, modern languages, etc. It is, therefore, a sub-topic of the "Learning Process," since it deals with the learning process as applied to the various branches of the curriculum.

(4) *Child Study.*—Being a specific application of (1) and (2) above, this branch forms a true subdivision of educational psychology. How do the language responses mature in children? When do the various instincts and emotional responses normally make their appearance? These and other problems having to do with the genesis and development of behaviour in children constitute the subject-matter of child study.

(5) *Educational Statistics.*—Human and animal behaviour is variable. Psychological measurements, therefore, are measures of variable quantities. For their interpretation a statistical technique is essential. The application of statistics to educational

measurements now forms an important branch of educational psychology. For advanced students of the subject it forms an indispensable part of their equipment. Indeed, much of the recent literature in the field remains a sealed book unless a student understands the meaning of some statistical terms and the simpler methods of statistical computation.

The Methods of Psychological Study. — Scientific psychology, like every other science, is dependent upon factual data obtained from observations. Observation is either uncontrolled (general) or controlled (experimental). A scientific experiment, therefore, is nothing more nor less than a device for controlling observations by limiting the field. Casual observation shows that babies sometimes show signs of fear—moving away from objects, puckering up the face and crying. What causes the fear? Experiment limits the field. The blanket on which the baby is lying is jerked suddenly. Does the baby show fear? A loud noise is made by hammering iron near a placid baby. Does the baby show fear? If one baby reacts to insecurity or to noise, will other babies react also? The more carefully the experiment is controlled—that is, the more rigidly extraneous and non-essential factors are excluded—the greater the confidence that can be placed in the results. Psychological science in these respects is like any other science. Compared with experimentation in physics and chemistry, psychological experimentation, since it deals with living organisms, is by far the more difficult.

Secondly, psychology utilizes the *principle of causation*, namely, that every event has a cause, or that every event is the effect of some antecedent cause. Tommy misspelled the word "receive." Why did he do it? What was the cause? Psychology tries to link together cause and effect (the misspelling). If successful, it is said to have explained or found the reason for the misspelling.

Thirdly, like all other sciences, psychology tries to explain as many effects as possible by the same principle. This is in accordance with the *law of parsimony* or the *law of economy in hypotheses*. Of several rival hypotheses or theories, science accepts that which is the simplest and explains the most. Behaviourism states that all forms of human behaviour can be ultimately reduced either to movement of muscles or secretion of glands. It may be that this hypothesis is too simple, but so long as it explains all known phenomena of behaviour, it can be accepted.

Fourthly, psychology uses the steps found in all logical thinking. Noting a certain form of behaviour, the psychologist is puzzled by it. A *problem* is presented. After clearly defining the field, a *tentative hypothesis* is proposed to account for the particular form of behaviour. Observation and experiment are then invoked to provide further *data.* If these data fit the tentative hypothesis more confidence can be placed in it; in fact, it may be elevated into a *theory.* Still further testing out and experimentation may fail to provide a single instance which conflicts with the theory. If this is found to be so, then the theory may become a *law* or *principle.* And by applying the law events can be *predicted.* In the realm of the inorganic such laws are common; at present there are few substantiated laws in the world of organisms. There can be no doubt that they will evolve in course of time; the science of behaviour is still very young and very difficult.

In addition to the usual methods of observation, with and without experimental control, utilized by all sciences, psychology uses some methods of study that are peculiarly its own. The first of these is the *conditioned response* method—the conditioning of reflexes, glandular secretions, and emotional responses. This method is so important as to warrant discussion in a separate chapter. The second is that of *verbal report.* Man is the only animal that uses speech reactions; in fact, speech is his main form of reaction. As far as possible, the psychologist tries to limit verbal reports to those which are obtained under experimental conditions. The third method is that of *tests,* chiefly those of intelligence and of educational achievement. Tests have proved excellent devices for grading human behaviour into various levels. For the interpretation of the results obtained by the third method, a knowledge of statistical technique is essential. *Statistics* is sometimes regarded as a fourth method of psychology, but since psychology shares this technique with economics and a number of other subjects, it is better to regard it as a device rather than a separate method.

References

Brett, G. S. *A History of Psychology.* 3 vols. London, Allen & Unwin, 1912 and 1921. Pp. xx+388, 394, 322.

Dunlap, K. *Elements of Scientific Psychology.* St. Louis, Mosby, 1922. Pp. 368.

Gates, A. I. *Psychology for Students of Education.* New York, Macmillan, 1924. Pp. xvi+489.

Hunter, W. S. *General Psychology.* University of Chicago Press, 1919. Pp. xiii+351.

James, W. *Principles of Psychology.* 2 vols. New York, Holt, 1908. Pp. xii+689, vi+704.

KANTOR, J. R. *Principles of Psychology.* New York, Knopf, 1924. Pp. xix+473.

MOORE, J. S. *The Foundations of Psychology.* Princeton University Press, 1921. Pp. xix+239.

STOUT, G. F. *Manual of Psychology.* London, University Tutorial Press, 1898. Pp. xvi+661.

THOMSON, J. A. *Introduction to Science.* London, Williams & Norgate, 1911. Pp. 256.

WARD, J. *Psychological Principles.* Cambridge, University Press, 1918. Pp. xiv+478.

WARREN, H. C. *Human Psychology.* Boston, Houghton Mifflin, 1919. Pp. xx+460.

WATSON, J. B. *Behaviorism.* New York, People's Institute Publishing Co., 1925. Pp. 251.

WATSON, J. B. *Psychology from the Standpoint of a Behaviorist.* 2nd Ed. Philadelphia, Lippincott, 1924. Pp. xiii+448.

WOODWORTH, R. S. *Psychology: A Study of Mental Life.* New York, Holt, 1921. Pp. x+580.

PART I

MAN'S EQUIPMENT FOR LEARNING

CHAPTER I

THE INHERITANCE OF HUMAN TRAITS

Heredity.—Every teacher should be interested in the hereditary equipment of the pupils he teaches, in what they bring with them to school, for it is on this foundation that he has to build the educational superstructure. Some pupils are naturally clever, some naturally stupid ; some are naturally musical, some naturally unmusical ; some have language ability and some have not. In fact, every talent exhibited in every degree is found in the school population. Teachers have long known this, but the general public still holds him responsible for any shortcomings in his pupils, although the blame ought rightfully to be placed upon Nature. For heredity, rather than the specialized environment called schooling, is mainly responsible. " You can't make a silk purse out of a sow's ear," neither can you " gather grapes of thorns or figs of thistles."

The study of heredity in human beings, therefore, should be one of the first duties of the teacher. About the subject there is, unfortunately, more ignorance than understanding and enlightenment. Heredity to some is a mysterious force which moulds the offspring in the likeness of the parent ; to others it is the antithesis of variation, that is, heredity consists in the resemblances, and variation in the dissimilarities between progenitors and descendants. Heredity is not a force. Neither is it merely the likenesses between offspring and parents ; it includes all traits both like and unlike.

What heredity really is can best be understood by tracing life back to its beginnings. Man, like all the higher organisms, starts life as a single cell—a fertilized ovum or egg-cell, technically called a *zygote*. This zygote is the most wonderful speck of matter in the whole universe, for it contains, potentially, all the characters—mental, moral, and physical—that the adult human being will subsequently display. The two cells from which it is derived are incredibly small, the ovum being only 1/125 of an inch in diameter and the spermatozoön (male generative cell) about 300,000 times smaller than the ovum. Yet when these two cells unite it is then and there determined whether the resultant individual will be male or female, tall or short, blue-eyed or brown-eyed, clever or stupid. Every trait that the individual will later exhibit is potentially present; in other words, his heredity is fixed, nothing can possibly be added to it. Heredity, therefore, can be defined as the sum total of the traits potentially present in the fertilized ovum.

The part that environment plays is similarly misunderstood. There is a widespread belief that a change in environment will lead to a change in heredity, and that these changes are transmissible to offspring. After thirty years of experimentation upon plants, animals, and human beings, science can say with a great deal of assurance that there are no grounds for this popular belief. Environment is simply the correlative of heredity; it merely determines which, and to what extent, hereditary traits shall be developed. Heredity represents the fixed element in the situation, environment the flexible factor. By improving the environment of an individual the better hereditary potentialities will undoubtedly be developed, but this improvement is limited to one generation. If we want to improve the race, the better individuals must become the parents of it. Race remains remarkably constant from generation to generation, despite marked changes in the environment.

If environment is to be regarded as the correlative of heredity, developing only that which is potentially present in heredity, education, which is one of the environmental factors, is distinctly limited in its possibilities. It cannot permanently improve the race, although it may profoundly affect a single generation.

Imagine two equally intelligent children, one of whom is taught to read, the other not. The differences between them due to these different environments will be great, but in the next generation things will even up again. The children of both the reader and the non-reader will be born with the potential ability to read just as their parents were before them.

At first glance this may seem an unduly pessimistic doctrine for the teacher. He cannot change the hereditary possibilities of pupils; he must accept pupils as he finds them and make the most of them. Even if he succeeds in lifting them to the highest plane possible, all the work has to be done over again in the next generation. But it has its hopeful side. Even the most rabid environmentalist would hardly claim that everything that teachers have done in the past has been safe and wise. And the non-transmissible feature of education ensures that our mistakes will not be perpetuated. One hesitates to imagine what the human race would be like to-day if every indent made on the plastic nature of youth in the past had been faithfully transmitted to succeeding generations.

The chief interest in the study of heredity for the teacher should be the discovery of the innate capacities of a pupil as they develop under the influence of the school environment, and especially the comparison of these characteristics with those of his ancestors, both near and remote. But a proper understanding of the subject demands a technical knowledge of the physiological mechanisms by which hereditary traits are handed down from generation to generation. Some knowledge of the variability of hereditary traits is desirable, and also of the laws they appear to obey. The remainder of the chapter, therefore, will be devoted to a discussion of these subjects.

Laws of Heredity.—Even the most casual comparison of the traits of offspring with their parents shows that *like tends to beget like*. This may be regarded as the *first great law of heredity*. Cats give birth to kittens, dogs to puppies, cows to calves, and human beings to human babies. Further, the kittens, puppies, calves, and babies resemble their own particular parents rather than other parents. The young of every kind resemble their species and their parents. Not only is this true in a general way, but in every detail as well. Black-skinned parents generally have black-skinned children, tall parents tall children, clever parents clever children, and stupid parents stupid children. That children are bound to resemble their parents somewhat closely is due to the continuity of the germ-plasm (the essential germinal material, that part of the substance of the parents which does not die with them, but perpetuates itself in their offspring), and to the way the actual mechanism of heredity works. In development, as both Galton and Weismann showed, a part of the germ-plasm contained in the parent egg-cell is not used up in the construction of the body of the offspring, but is reserved unchanged for the formation of germ-cells of the following generation. As a matter of fact, the sex cells, from which the next generation is derived, are separated from the rest of the body at a very early period of embryological development; in the threadworm, at the very first division, one daughter-cell dividing at a very slow rate and producing nothing but germ-cells, the other daughter-cell dividing more quickly and differentiating to form the various parts of the body of the adult worm. This early segregation has been observed in many animals and presumably holds also for man. The child is, therefore, as old as the parent, since while the parent's body was developing from the fertilized ovum, a residue of unaltered germinal material was kept apart to form the reproductive cells, one of which became the starting-point of the child.

> " From another point of view, it has been said that father and son ought to be thought of as half-brothers by two different mothers, each being the product of the same strain of paternal germ-plasm, but not of the same strain of maternal germ-plasm. Biologically, the father and mother should not be thought of as the *producer* of a child, but as the trustee of a stream of germ-plasm which produces a child whenever the proper conditions arise. Or as Sir Michael Foster puts it, ' The animal body is in reality a vehicle for ova or sperm ; and after the life of the parent has become potentially renewed in the offspring, the body remains as a cast-off envelope whose future is but to die.' " [1]

The similarities due to the actual mechanism of heredity will be described in a later section dealing with the " Gene or Factorial Hypothesis."

Illustrations of this first law of heredity are omnipresent. It is at the basis of all plant and animal breeding. In human beings the truth of the law can be demonstrated by the study of any family tree. The inheritance of superior mental traits, especially those leading to scientific eminence, is exemplified in the Wedgwood-Darwin-Galton family. This family tree has been traced back by Karl Pearson [2] for over 1000 years. Persons of great ability abound in it. Some of the members who lived within the past two centuries are shown in Fig. 1. A study of it shows that for five generations in direct descent members of the Darwin family have been elected to fellowship in the Royal Society (England). The younger members living to-day give every indication of upholding the worthy traditions of their forefathers.

Francis Galton, cousin of Charles Darwin, was the first to make a statistical study of the inheritance of talent. His researches, first published as a series of articles in 1865 under the title " Hereditary Talent and Genius," were expanded into a book called *Hereditary Genius* in 1869. He studied the biographies of 977 fairly eminent men, each ranking in his opinion as about one in 4000 of the general population. The classes studied included : judges of England from 1660–1865, the statesmen of the time of George III, the premiers for one hundred years prior

[1] Popenoe and Johnson, *Applied Eugenics*, p. 29.

[2] Pearson, *The Life, Letters, and Labours of Francis Galton*, vol. i. Pedigree Plates.

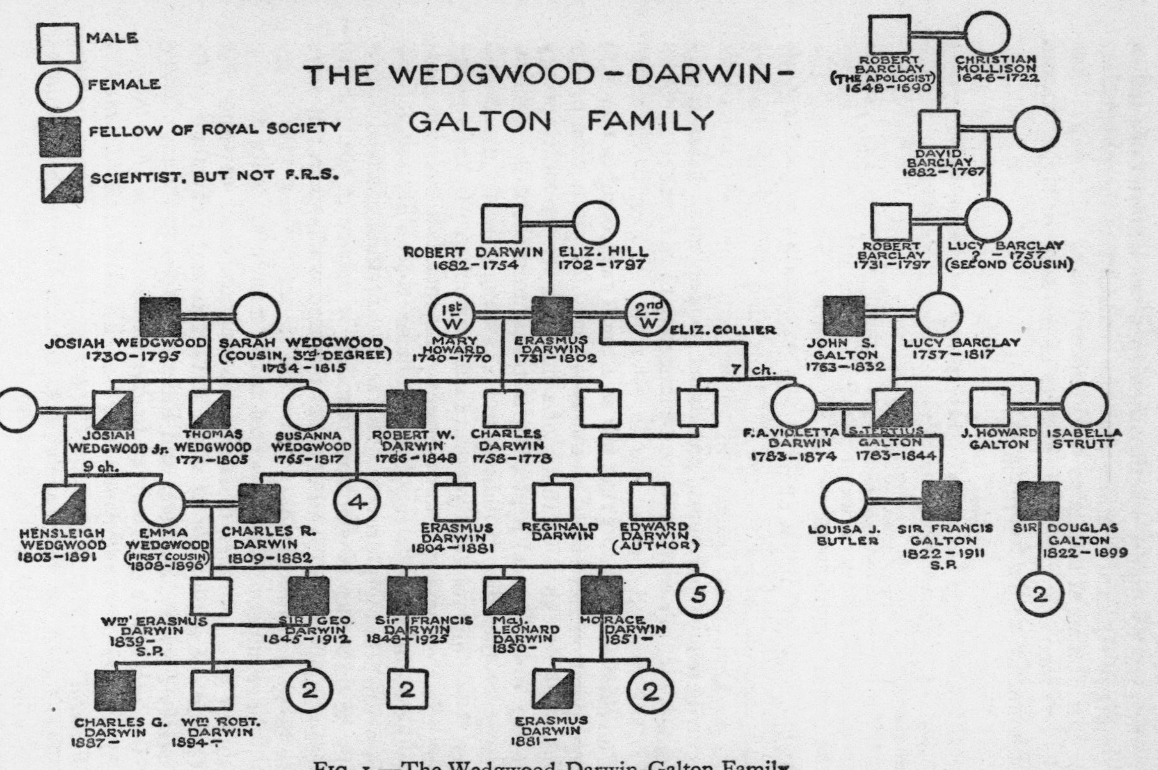

FIG. 1.—The Wedgwood-Darwin-Galton Family.

to 1868, commanders, literary and scientific men, poets, painters, musicians, divines, modern scholars, oarsmen, and wrestlers. His method was to inquire whether these men had a greater or smaller number of eminent relations than the generality of the population or than statistical estimates would accord them. He found that the 977 men examined had relatives of the same or higher degree of eminence to the following extent:

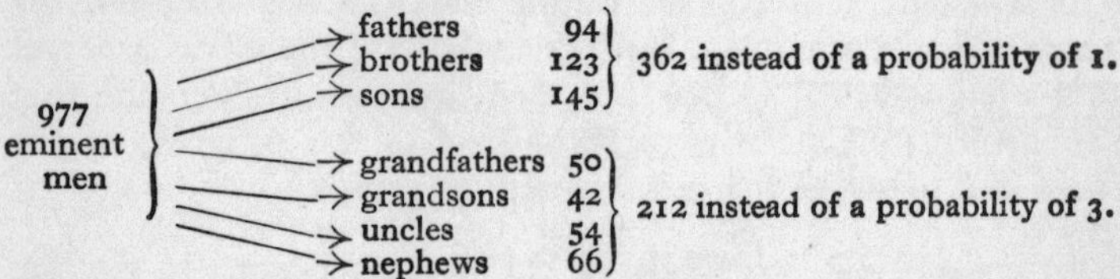

Taking the 286 judges alone, it was discovered that 109 of them had relatives who also rose to distinction. Of these relatives 26 per cent. were fathers and 36 per cent. sons. Grandfathers contributed 7½ per cent., grandsons 9½ per cent., great-grandfathers 0·5, per cent. and great-grandsons 1½ per cent.

The methodology of the investigation is open to criticism. The chief faults are: (1) unfair selection—neglecting to take into consideration the whole of the members of a given group; (2) assuming that the true rating of a man is given by contemporary public opinion; (3) neglecting to take into account the political nature of the office of judge; and (4) assuming that "genius will out"—a contention not yet proven, since there may be the swamping effect of poverty and other environmental factors. Yet, notwithstanding these defects, his main thesis, that ability is inherited, is overwhelmingly proven. His secondary thesis, that ability is due to three factors which are found to be present in nearly every case—intellect, zeal, and capacity for hard work—does not seem to be so well supported.

That superior ability seems to be mainly a family affair is shown by a number of later investigations, chief of which are Galton's *English Men of Science*, Galton and Schuster's *Noteworthy Families*, Schuster and Elderton's *Inheritance and Ability*, Havelock Ellis's *A Study of British Genius*, Woods' *Mental and Moral Heredity in Royalty*, and Cattell's *A Statistical Study of Eminent Men* and *A Statistical Study of American Men of Science*. Space forbids a detailed analysis of these; but the mass of evidence they bring out is most impressive.

Lest it be suspected that only one side of the case is presented, we hasten to mention De Candolle's *Histoire des sciences et des savants depuis deux siècles*. This study, published in Geneva in 1873, was a reply to Galton's *Hereditary Genius*. In it, De

Candolle tried to show that environment was the chief factor in the production of scientific genius. His subjects were the past and present associates and corresponding members of the Academy of Sciences, Paris (founded 1666), the corresponding members of the Royal Society, London (founded 1662), and the foreign members and correspondents of the Royal Academy, Berlin (founded 1700). In all, the members studied were 212 for Paris, 235 for London, and 105 for Berlin. He did not trace out the ancestry of these scientists, but his analysis of the environmental factors which seemed to produce them led him to conclude that the following influences were favourable to the progress of the sciences and hence to the development of genius :

1. A considerable proportion of the people belonging to the rich and leisured classes relative to those who needs must work constantly in order to live, and especially to those who work at unskilled manual labour.
2. A considerable number of intellectual men of easy circumstances who are willing to devote their lives to scientific pursuits.
3. An ancient culture of the spiritual sides of one's nature directed for several generations into right channels.
4. Immigration of intelligent families having a taste for intellectual work.
5. Existence of several contiguous families having favourable traditions towards science and to intellectual occupations of every kind.
6. A good system of education, especially secondary and higher education, organized independently of politics and religion.
7. Abundant material means in the shape of libraries, laboratories, observatories and so forth, for the pursuit of science.
8. Public curiosity for truth rather than fiction.
9. Freedom to express or publish opinion.
10. Public opinion favourable to science and to scientists.
11. Liberty to exercise any profession.
12. Religion not placed upon an authoritative basis.
13. Clergy the friends of education.
14. Clergy not restricted to celibacy.
15. Habitual employment of one of the three principal languages—English, French, German—with as full a knowledge of non-native tongues as possible.
16. Small independent countries or a confederation of the same.
17. Situated in the temperate zone.
18. Proximity to civilized countries.

Switzerland was found at the head of countries producing scientific genius, and De Candolle explains it by saying that she had a greater number of the above favourable conditions than any other country. While he did not disprove Galton's contention that genius was largely a matter of heredity, he did well to draw attention, as Cattell did later in his American studies, to the part that environment plays in securing the best flowering of genius.

In his *Educational Determinism*, Bagley has still more strenuously combated the theory that heredity alone determines what a person will become. The rôle of environment is very clearly shown.

The illustrations showing that " like tends to beget like " have so far been taken from families which showed superior ability. Just as many can be drawn from studies in which mental defects and criminality have been distressingly frequent. The first serious study of a notorious family was made by R. L. Dugdale between 1874–1877.[1] This family, given by him the fictitious name of *The Jukes*, was resident in upper New York State, but later became scattered over fourteen of the United States. The discovery of Dugdale's original manuscript in 1911 provided the starting-point for a new study. Dr. Estabrook continued the investigations between 1912 and 1915, visiting as many members of the family as could then be discovered. *The Jukes in 1915* is the fruit of the investigation.

The founder of the family was Max Jukes, a shiftless hunter and fisher, who was born between 1720 and 1740. Two of his sons married two sisters of a very degenerate family consisting of six sisters. The study traces out the descendants of these two marriages, together with those of three other sisters—Ada, known to the community among whom she lived as " Margaret, the mother of criminals," Bell, a viciously immoral woman, and Clara who married a licentious person known to have shot a man.

The results of the two studies are summarized by Estabrook as follows :

" Dugdale studied 709 persons, 540 being of Juke blood and 169 of " X " blood who had married into the Juke family. He estimated that the Juke family would consist of 1200 persons were it possible to have traced all the lines of descent from the original 6 sisters. Of the 709 whom he studied, 180 had either been in the poorhouse or received outdoor relief to the extent of 800 years. There had been 140 criminals and offenders, 60 habitual thieves, 7 lives sacrificed by murder, 50 common prostitutes, 50 women venereally diseased contaminating 440 persons, and 30 prosecutions in bastardy. The total cost to the state of New York of this one group of mental and social degenerates was estimated, for a period of 75 years beginning in 1800, at $1,308,000.

" In the present investigation, 2820 people have been studied inclusive of all considered by Dugdale ; 2094 were of Juke blood and 726 of " X " blood who married into the Juke family ; of these 366

[1] Dugdale, *The Jukes*, 1877.

were paupers, while 171 were criminals ; and 10 lives have been sacrificed by murder. In school work 62 did well, 288 fairly well, while 458 were retarded two or more years. It is known that 166 never attended school ; the school data for the rest of the family were unobtainable. There were 282 intemperate and 277 harlots. The total cost to the state has been estimated at $2,093,685." [1]

The spreading of the Jukes from their original habitat, forced on them by the closing of the cement works which gave many of them employment, has tended to improve their status. Is this improvement due to heredity or to environment or both ? The best answer, in the light of the facts, seems to be as follows : The Jukes of admittedly bad stock were undoubtedly improved by environment. This enabled them to marry into better families. The blood of the better families has been the main cause of such permanent improvements as are now found in the Juke stock. Dissemination has improved the Juke stock, but at a terrible expense to the communities into which they have migrated. The fact that so many of the 1258 descendants living in 1915 found it impossible to adjust themselves socially to the new environments disposes of the claim that environment alone improves stock ; the responses of the individual are also dependent upon his constitution. " Environment affords the stimulus ; heredity determines largely the nature of the reacting substance ; the reaction, or behaviour, is the resultant or product of the two." [2]

Similar studies of the Nams, Zeros, Dacks, Ishmaels, Sixties, Hickories, Hill Folk, Piney Folk and the rest, show that the bulk of the trouble lies in the fact that " like tends to beget like." All of these families showed hereditary mental defect.

Two instructive genealogies have been worked out, each of which exhibits a common paternal ancestor who left two lines of descendants by different mothers. These are the Kallikak family studied by Dr. H. H. Goddard and the Edwards family studied by Dr. A. E. Winship.

The common ancestor in the Kallikak family was Martin Kallikak (name fictitious), a young soldier of the Revolutionary War. During the campaign Martin had a son by a nameless, feeble-minded girl, from whom 480 individuals have descended in direct line. This line has never been an asset to the world. On the contrary, 143 of these descendants are known to have been feeble-minded, and only 46 are known to have been normal. The rest are unknown or doubtful. Thirty-six have been illegitimate, 33 sexually immoral, 24 confirmed alcoholics, 3 epileptics,

[1] Estabrook, *The Jukes in 1915*, pp. 1 and 2.
[2] Davenport, in Preface to Estabrook's *The Jukes in 1915*.

3 criminals, 8 keepers of houses of ill-fame, and 83 children so feeble that they died in infancy.

After the war Martin married a Quakeress of good stock, and from the union 496 descendants have been traced. All of these, except two, were of normal or super-normal mentality and morality, holding positions as lawyers, doctors, teachers, traders, governors, professors and presidents of colleges and universities. This line of children apparently could not turn out badly in any environment; nobody ever had to build an asylum or prison to accommodate them. The other line, bearing the same name and living on the same soil, apparently could not turn out well; they were a perennial charge on the community in which they lived. After examining all the evidence Dr. Goddard concludes: "The fact that the descendants of both the normal and the feeble-minded mother have been studied and traced in every conceivable environment, and that the respective strains have been true to type, tends to confirm the belief that heredity has been the determining factor in the formation of their respective characters."

Similar evidence is adduced by A. E. Winship in his book *Jukes-Edwards: A Study in Education and Heredity*. Elizabeth Tuthill was a New England woman of great beauty and wonderful intellect. In 1667 she married Richard Edwards to whom she bore a son, Timothy Edwards (the father of Jonathan Edwards), and four daughters. Later, Richard Edwards married again, this time a woman of average mentality by whom he had three sons and two daughters. None of the descendants of this second marriage rose above mediocrity. But the descendants of the first marriage—all of whom carried the reproductive plasm of Elizabeth Tuthill—present a wonderful array of eminent men and women. Besides Timothy Edwards, a pastor of great learning, and his son Jonathan, one of the world's greatest intellects, pre-eminent as a theologian and President of Princeton University, there are among them Jonathan Edwards, Jun., President of Union College; Timothy Dwight, President of Yale; Sereno Dwight, President of Hamilton; Theodore Dwight Woolsey, President of Yale for 25 years; Daniel Tyler, a general in the American Civil War and founder of the iron industries of Alabama; Timothy Dwight 2nd, President of Yale 1886–1898; Theodore William Dwight, founder and head of the Columbia Law School; Merril Edward Gates, President of Amherst; Catharine Maria Sedgwick, the authoress; Charles Sedgwick Minot, the eminent embryologist and biologist of the Harvard Medical School; Winston Churchill, the American novelist; Mrs. Theodore Roosevelt, a woman of great intellect; Aaron Burr, Vice-President of the United States; Morrison R. Waite,

Chief Justice of the United States; Mrs. Eli Whitney, a notable woman, wife of the inventor of the cotton gin; Robert T. Paine, one of the signers of the Declaration of Independence; the Marchioness of Donegal, a distinguished woman of Ireland; the Fairbanks brothers, manufacturers of weighing scales; Bishop Vincent, founder of the Chautauqua movement and father of George Vincent, head of the Rockefeller Foundation; Grover Cleveland and Ulysses S. Grant, Presidents of the United States.

From Jonathan Edwards and his brilliant wife, Sarah Pierrpont, one branch alone, have descended 1394 persons (to year 1900), among whom were 13 college presidents, 295 college graduates, 65 college professors, 60 physicians, 100 clergymen, 75 army or navy officers, 60 prominent authors, 100 lawyers, 30 judges, 80 public officials, 3 congressmen, 2 United States senators, and 1 vice-president of the United States.

It is inconceivable that racial stock has had no influence in these dual records of the Kallikak and the Edwards families.

Common observation, however, shows that although like tends to beget like, the resemblances of parents and offspring are never perfect. Kittens are never exactly like the parent cats, children are never exactly like their parents. Sometimes the differences are most marked, as, for example, when a feeble-minded child is born to normal-minded parents, short children to tall parents, blue-eyed children to brown-eyed parents. Thus we get the *second great law of heredity* that *although like tends to beget like, there are always variations.*

A variation is frequently confused with a modification or, as it is more usually called, an acquired character. Technically defined, a variation is a filial departure from the parental type which is founded on a germinal change. The important part of the definition is that which insists on the germinal change. Variations are inheritable; they are passed on from one generation to another. Being due to potentialities of the cell, variations are expressed from within. Modifications, on the other hand, are impressed on the organism from without and are non-inheritable; they are changes in the structure acquired in the lifetime of the individual as a direct result of environment—chiefly use, injury, or training. In this sense education is an acquired character, and is not directly passed on to the next generation. What is passed on is the potentiality which enables the next generation to receive an education approximately equivalent to that which the parent received. No one denies, either, that injuries are modifications, not variations. The tailless condition of the dog or sheep due to mutilation (docking) is a modification; the progeny of such animals are always born with tails. On the other hand, the tail-less condition of the Manx cat is a true variation (mutation), and as such appears in Manx kittens. Fortunately for mankind, while the gains of variations are capitalized in the offspring, the losses of modifications never involve racial bankruptcy.

The cause of variations is still wrapt in mystery. All that can be said about it at present is that variability is a fact of life, that all living protoplasm has an inherent tendency to vary. Without variation in plants and animals there could be no evolution. Darwin thought that "natural selection," the constant selection of the variations which make for success in the struggle for existence, was the explanation of evolution; the successful variant became the dominant racial type. Whatever the explanation, every reputable scientist believes that evolution has taken, and is taking, place, and that man is the final product of an evolutionary process which has been going on for millions of years.

Laws of Variation.—The *first law of variation* runs: *If a large number of unselected, homogeneous individuals of a given species be measured for a varying trait, the measures are found to be distributed according to the curve of chance or probability curve.* This law will now be illustrated by concrete examples.

First as to the *Curve of Chance.* If ten coins are tossed 1024 times, and the number of heads which turns up counted, a record closely approximating Table I will result.

No. of Heads.	Frequency of Occurrence.
0	1
1	10
2	45
3	120
4	210
5	252
6	210
7	120
8	45
9	10
10	1
Total	1024

TABLE I.—Showing the theoretical frequency of heads that will turn up when 10 coins are tossed 1024 times.

The most frequent number of heads is 5; while 4 and 6, 7 and 3, 8 and 2, 9 and 1, and 10 and 0 appear with equal but decreasing frequency as we pass from the middle to the ends of the table. If now we plot a curve by placing the number of heads on one axis (x axis) and frequency of occurrence on the other axis (y axis) we get a curve, Fig. 2, which if smoothed would resemble a bell in shape. If 100 coins had been tossed 10,000 times the likeness to a bell would have been much closer. Since the number of heads that turns up is obviously the result of chance, the curve so obtained is known as the curve of chance or probability curve. The area or surface the curve of chance

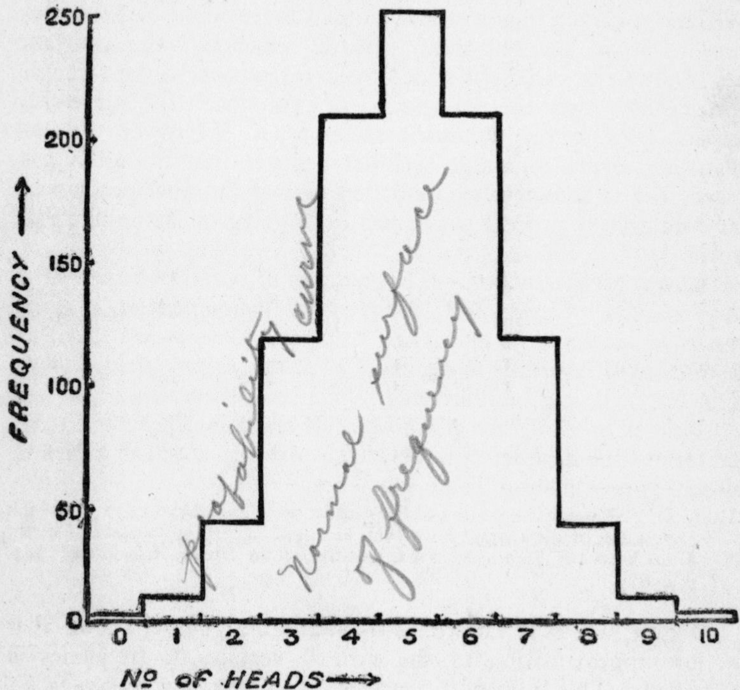

FIG. 2.—Curve showing the theoretical frequency of heads turning up when 10 coins are tossed 1024 times.

encloses is known as the *normal surface of frequency*, since it represents an area that normally appears when chance alone determines it.

That variable traits, like height of adult men in any race, approximate a distribution closely resembling that obtained from tossing coins can be shown from any comprehensive series of records. Common observation shows that men cluster around the average in height, extremely tall or short men being comparatively rare. The following figures, which are taken from the final report of the Anthropometric Committee of the British Association, show this quite plainly.

Height without shoes.		Number of men within said limits of height. Place of birth.				Total.
Inches.	Metres.	England.	Scotland.	Wales.	Ireland.	
57	1·448	1	—	1	—	2
58	1·474	3	1	—	—	4
59	1·499	12	—	1	1	14
60	1·525	39	2	—	—	41
61	1·550	70	2	9	2	83
62	1·575	128	9	30	2	169
63	1·601	320	19	48	7	394
64	1·625	524	47	83	15	669
65	1·653	740	109	108	33	990
66	1·677	881	139	145	58	1223
67	1·702	918	210	128	73	1329
68	1·728	886	210	72	62	1230
69	1·754	753	218	52	40	1063
70	1·779	473	115	33	25	646
71	1·804	254	102	21	15	392
72	1·830	117	69	6	10	202
73	1·855	48	26	2	3	79
74	1·881	16	15	1	—	32
75	1·906	9	6	1	—	16
76	1·931	1	4	—	—	5
77	1·957	1	1	—	—	2
Total ..		6194	1304	741	346	8585

TABLE II.—Showing the stature of 8585 adult males (age from 23 to 50) of the population of the United Kingdom, arranged according to place of birth. *Final Report of Anthropometric Committee of the British Association*, 1883, p. 256.

Fig. 3, which is known as a distribution curve, shows that a close approximation to the normal surface of frequency is obtained. This form of diagram is called a *frequency polygon.*

In the British Columbia School Survey an intelligence test, consisting of 215 items, was given to all the women students attending the Vancouver Normal School. The results are summarized in Table III.

Score (No. of items correct).	Number of students obtaining score.
30–39	1
40–49	0
50–59	2
60–69	11
70–79	20
80–89	37
90–99	44
100–109	49

Score (No. of items correct).	Number of students obtaining score.
110–119	45
120–129	33
130–139	21
140–149	5
150–159	3
160–169	0
170–179	1
Total	272

TABLE III.—Showing the distribution of scores obtained by 272 women students of Vancouver Normal School in an intelligence test consisting of 215 items.

Table III reads: one student obtained a score between 30 and 39; 49 between 100 and 109; 21 between 130 and 139, etc. These results are plotted in Fig. 4. This step-shaped diagram is known as a *histogram* or *column diagram.* It tells the same story as a frequency polygon would do, namely, that its general shape conforms to the normal surface of frequency. A perfect or theoretical normal surface of frequency is shown for comparison in Fig. 5.

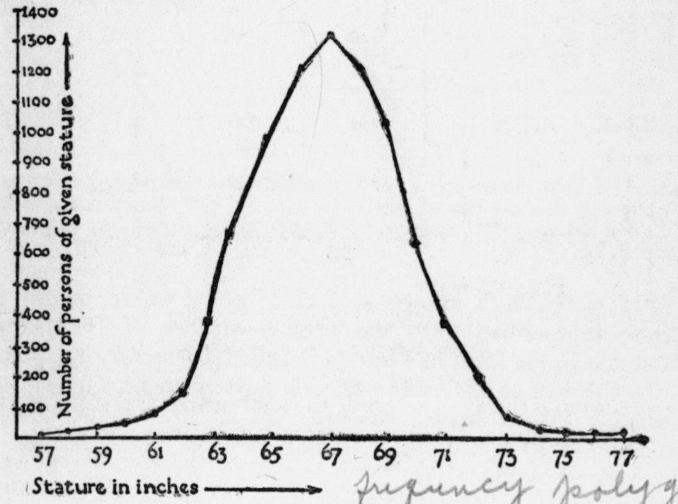

FIG. 3.—Distribution curve for the stature of 8585 adult males in the United Kingdom.

Every known variable trait (speed in addition, ability to memorize, general intelligence, general morality, speed in typewriting, ability in handwriting, sizes of leaves, length of tentacles), whether of human beings, animals, or plants, is found to be distributed among unselected members of any homogeneous group according to the curve of chance. So constantly is this condition found that if a trait, measured over a sufficiently large number of individuals, gives a skew distribution, it is presumptive evidence that selection of some sort has been at work. The curve of chance, enclosing the normal surface of frequency, is thus seen to be the most important known to educators and to naturalists. It demonstrates that the *one* type found in nature and human nature is that which we call medium, average, or mediocre. More people are average or medium in their traits than anything else. People vary, but there is a regularity about their variations. The majority for any trait

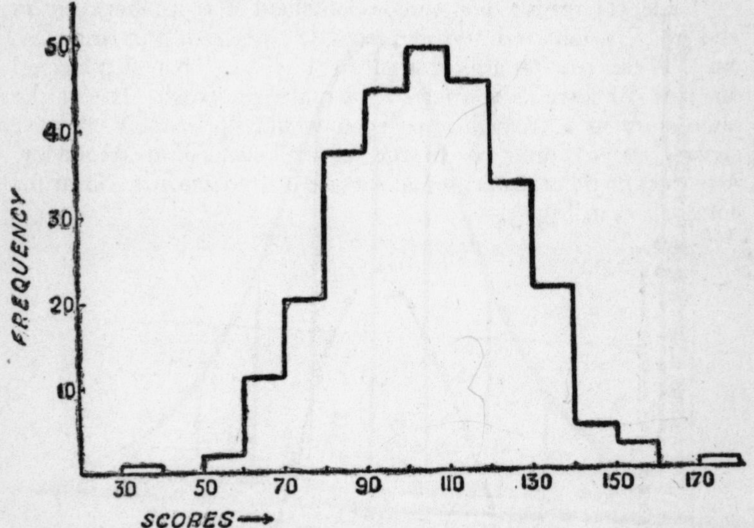

Fig. 4.—Histogram or column diagram showing scores made by 272 women students in an intelligence test.

cluster around the average, while the subnormals and supernormals steadily decrease as the distance from the average increases.

The *second law of variation*, known as the law of regression, is a statistical, not a biological law. *In successive generations variants tend to move towards the average of the species of which they form a part.* As Galton described it:

"Each peculiarity in a man is shared by his kinsmen, but on the *average* in a less degree. It is reduced to a definite fraction of its amount, quite independently of what its amount might be. The fraction differs in different orders of kinship, becoming smaller as they are more remote. When the kinship is so distant that its effects are not worth taking into account, the peculiarity of the man, however remarkable it may have been, is reduced to zero in his kinsmen. This apparent paradox is fundamentally due to the greater frequency of the mediocre deviations than of extreme ones, occurring between limits separated by equal widths."

It seems, therefore, as if Nature abhorred extremes or large variations of any kind, as if the normal were to be preserved at all costs. Taking stature as an illustration, the law of regression tells heavily against the full hereditary transmission of it. Tall parents, on the whole, will have taller children than the average of the population, but shorter than they themselves are. Con-

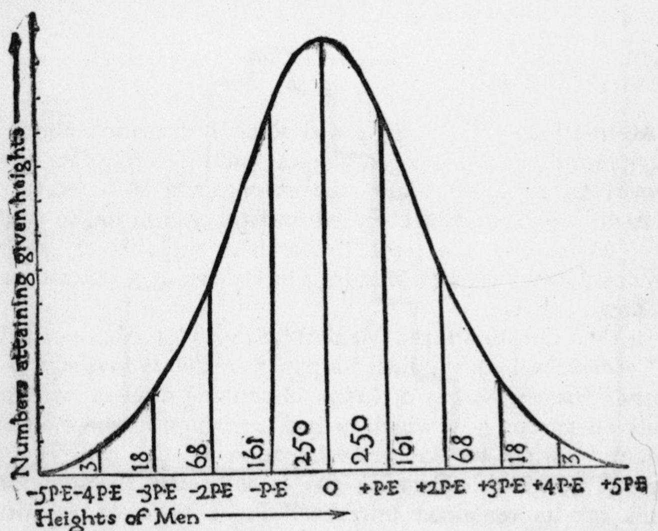

FIG. 5.—A normal distribution curve or a normal surface of frequency. The theoretical distribution of 1000 persons is shown.

versely, short parents, on the whole, will have children shorter than the average of the population, yet taller than their own average. The tall stock moves down and the short stock moves up towards the average. In an actual measurement of adult Englishmen, Galton found that fathers of 72 inches in height had sons of an average stature of 70·8 inches, while fathers of 66 inches had sons whose average height was 68·3. The average height of the English professional class, from which most of the examples were taken, is 69·14 inches. Galton went too far in applying the law to individuals, yet it does seem to apply to all mental and physical traits of groups. Being a statistical law it does not prevent improvement of stock by selection and assortative mating, but it does explain why, under our present system of marriages, races of giants, both intellectual and physical, are not produced.

Galton thought the general amount of regression in heredity was one-half. He thus obtained his law of ancestral heredity, namely, that an individual derived on the average one-half from his parents, one-quarter from his four grandparents, one-eighth from his eight great-grandparents, and so on. The series is thus $\frac{1}{2}$, $\frac{1}{4}$, $\frac{1}{8}$, $\frac{1}{16}$, or for each individual in his ancestry $0{\cdot}5^2$, $0{\cdot}5^4$, $0{\cdot}5^6$ . . . $0{\cdot}5^{2n}$ for an ancestor of the *n*th place. Pearson, however, found in his studies of eye-colour in man and colour-coat in horses the parental contribution to be greater than Galton assumed. His series was:

Parents.	Grandparents.	Great-grandparents.	Great-great-grandparents.
0·6244	0·1988	0·0630	0·0202

Mendelism.—Having gleaned some information about the inheritance of traits from genealogical and biometric data, it now behoves us to inquire into the mechanism of heredity—the means by which traits are passed on from generation to generation. As most of the recent research in the subject has been stimulated by the work of Mendel, a brief account of his discoveries will now be given.

In 1866 Gregor Johann Mendel (1822–1884), Abbot of Brünn (in Czechoslovakia), published a paper in the *Proceedings of the Natural History Society of Brünn*, describing a series of experiments on garden peas which he had carried on in the monastery garden. Owing to the pre-occupation of the scientific and religious world with Darwin's *Origin of Species*, the significance of his results remained unrealized for a third of a century. Nägeli learned of the work from correspondence, but failed to see its importance. Reference to the paper was made by Focke in 1881, but the impression seems to have been general that experiments in hybridization, such as Mendel had carried out, led to no definite conclusions. In 1900 De Vries, Correns, and Tschermak each independently rediscovered Mendel's law. From that time on Mendelism has dominated biology. Experiments at first were confined to plants; they were then extended to quick-breeding animals like mice, rats, rabbits, and guinea pigs; later, observations on man himself were made. Since 1910 the quick-breeding fruit-fly (*Drosophila melanogaster*), a species which exhibits a large variety of new modifications and is easy to breed in the laboratory, in the hands of Morgan and his school has given us more knowledge concerning heredity than had been learned from all experiments before that time

The following may be regarded as a typical Mendelian experiment, in fact it is one that Mendel himself made. References are to Fig. 6. If a pea (WW) which has a wrinkled skin when dried is sown and crossed with a pea (RR) which remains round when dried, the resultant peas of the first filial generation (F_1) are all round (R*w*). Not a single wrinkled pea appears. If now these (F_1) peas are sown and self-fertilized, or crossed indiscriminately among themselves, the resultant crop (F_2), if

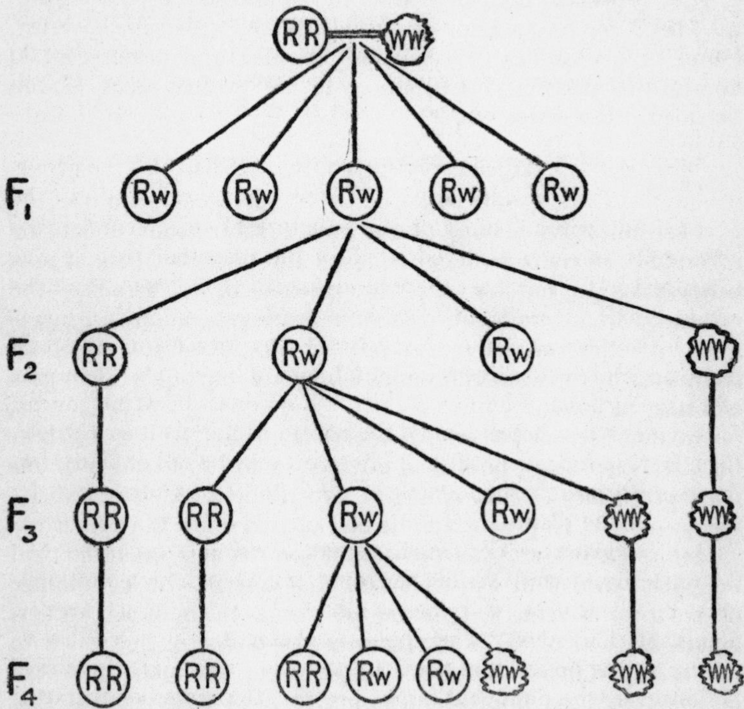

FIG. 6.—Diagrammatic representation of a typical Mendelian experiment with round or wrinkled peas. "Roundness" is dominant and "Wrinkledness" is recessive.

counted, is found to have three times as many round peas as wrinkled ones. The wrinkled peas of this generation are "pure," that is, on sowing and self-fertilizing they produce none but wrinkled peas. But the round peas are of two kinds. One-third of them, or 25 per cent. of the (F_2) crop, breed true with respect to roundness. The other two-thirds, or 50 per cent. of the (F_2) crop, behave exactly as the (F_1) crop did; they produce round and wrinkled peas in the proportion of 3 to 1. Of this (F_3) crop, one-third of the round peas and the whole of the wrinkled peas are "pure"; two-thirds of the round are "impure" as before. So long as the experiment is continued the same kind of results will be obtained.

Mendel discovered that the following pairs of contrasted characters behaved exactly as round and wrinkled peas: (1) Tall and dwarf peas; (2) normal leaved and fasciated peas (leaves and flowers bunched at the top); (3) peas with hard pods and peas with soft pods; (4) green-podded and yellow-podded peas; (5) peas with a grey seed-coat when ripe and peas with a white seed-coat; (6) and peas with yellow cotyledons (seed-leaves) and peas with green cotyledons. The first-named character had the power of obscuring the second in each of the seven cases studied.

Mendel was a skilled experimentalist. He had also the genius to interpret his results aright. Later cytological studies—the detailed microscopic study of the structure of cells, especially of germ cells—have but served to show the essential truth of this interpretation. There are three fundamental elements in Mendel's explanation. These are:

(1) *Independent Unit Characters.*—Any organism, although physiologically a unit, from the standpoint of heredity is a complex of a large number of heritable units. Roundness or wrinkledness, for example, is independent of the nature of the plant as a whole. Each is an independent unit. The plant may be tall or short, but the roundness or wrinkledness of the ripe peas is unaffected by the size of the plant.

(2) *Dominance.*—Certain characters, like roundness or tallness, dominate and become visible when present, even though wrinkledness or dwarfness is present also. They are thus termed dominant characters. The opposing character which recedes, as it were, in the presence of the dominant one, is called the *recessive.* If, however, the dominant is not present, the recessive character shows.

(3) *Purity of the Gametes* (reproductive cells).—A better name for it is *segregation.* The reproductive cell can only contain one of the two alternative characters. It can, for example, contain the character for roundness or wrinkledness, but not both. If two germ-cells, each containing the factor for wrinkledness, unite to form a zygote (fertilized egg), the resultant pea will be wrinkled; if each contain the factor for roundness, the pea will be round; if one contain the factor for roundness and the other the factor for wrinkledness, the pea will be round owing to the dominance of roundness. Alternative characters are segregated in the formation of the germ-cells, and no germ-cell can contain both. Fig. 7,

A and B, illustrates the mechanism of segregation which will be discussed more fully in a subsequent section dealing with the "Gene or Factorial Hypothesis."

If now we take two peas, each of which exhibits two characters (say tall and round, and dwarf and wrinkled), and cross them, instead of the 1, 2, 1 ratio obtained above, we should get a 9, 3, 3, 1

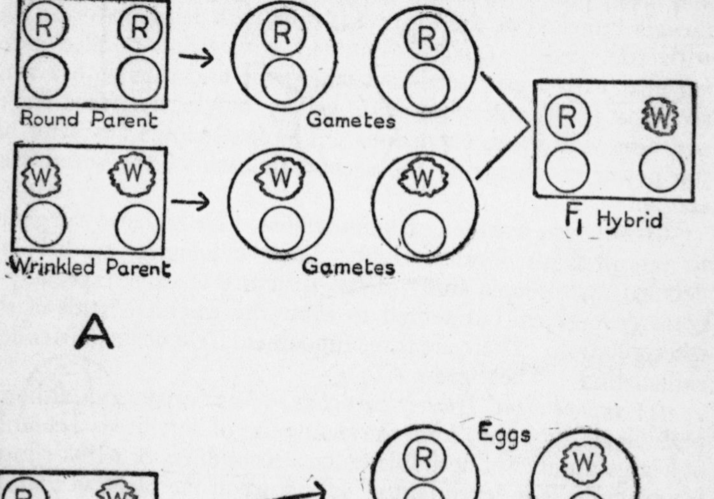

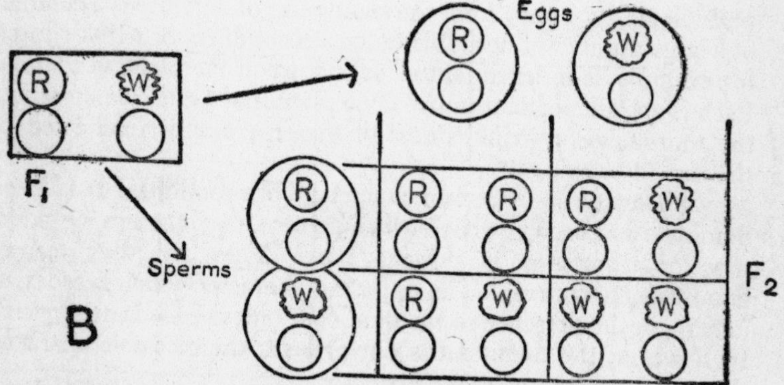

FIG. 7, A and B.—Diagram A illustrating behaviour of chromosomes in Mendel's cross of round and wrinkled peas. Rectangles, nuclei of zygotes; large circles, gametes; small circles, chromosomes. Diagram B illustrating the behaviour of F_1 generation when inbred. Note the 3 : 1 ratio in F_2.

ratio in the (F_2) generation, as can be seen from Fig. 8. Nine will be tall and round, 3 will be tall and wrinkled, 3 will be dwarf and round, and 1 will be dwarf and wrinkled. Further, only Nos. 1, 6, 11, and 16 will breed true; the other twelve would split into various types on further breeding.

Continuing the experiment further by the addition of another pair of unit characters, say yellow and green, the tri-hybrid ratio of 27, 9, 9, 9, 3, 3, 3, 1 would be observed in the (F_2) generation—27 tall round yellow, 9 tall round green, 9 tall wrinkled yellow,

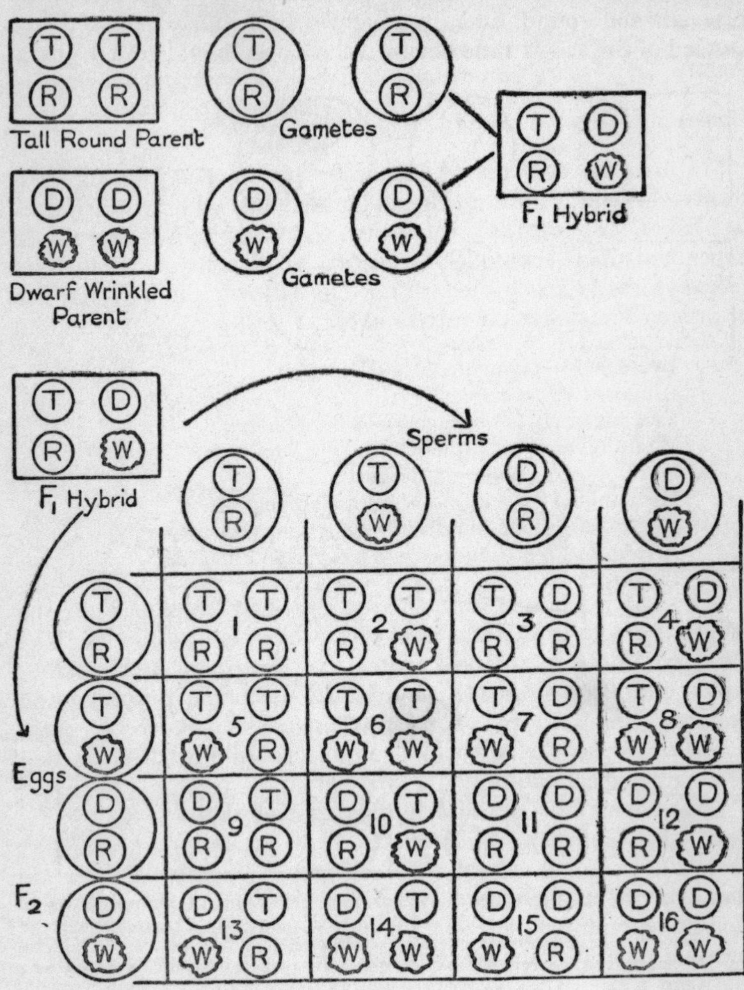

FIG. 8.—Diagram illustrating the dihybrid ratio 9, 3, 3, 1 in the F_2 generation.

9 dwarf round yellow, 3 tall wrinkled green, 3 dwarf round green, 3 dwarf wrinkled yellow, 1 dwarf wrinkled green.

Using a knowledge of Mendelian inheritance breeders can produce almost at will plants and animals exhibiting one or other of the following Mendelian characters :

	Dominant.	Recessive.
Wheat and barley	Beardless ; non-immune to rust	Bearded ; immune to rust
Maize	" Starch " seed	" Sugar " seed
Mice	Coloured coat	Albino coat
Rabbits	Angora fur	Short fur
Cattle	Hornlessness	Horns
Poultry	Brown eggs ; broodiness	White eggs ; non-broodiness
Guinea pigs	Black	Albino

In man, the evidence of Mendelian phenomena is as yet very scanty. While his inheritance is undoubtedly of a factorial kind (see later), it appears as if Mendelian characters in man were each dependent upon a number of factors. Complete dominance or recessiveness is rarely met with. The following is a partial list of proven Mendelian characters in man :

Eye-colour—pigmented eye dominant.
Albinism—a recessive.
Brachydactyly (stub fingers)—a dominant.
White blaze of hair (piebaldism)—a dominant.
Huntington's chorea—a dominant.
Hæmophilia (bleeding)—a sex-linked character.
Red-green colour-blindness—a sex-linked character.
A form of night-blindness—a sex-linked character.

Of more doubtful authenticity are—hair colour, notorious family characteristics such as the Hapsburg lip, woolly hair like a negro's, cataract, enlarged spleen, polydactylism, deaf-mutism, feeble-mindedness, musical ability, artistic ability in writing and painting, some forms of insanity, nomadism, myopia, gout, tendency to produce twins, and some scores of other traits mostly of a pathological nature.

Eye-colour was the first human trait observed to follow the laws of Mendelian inheritance. Eyes are either pigmented (brown), or unpigmented (blue or grey). Pigmented eyes are dominant to unpigmented eyes. Let the factors for pigmentation be represented by (PP) ; for blue or grey by (pp). The (PP) eyes are those of the negro, Italian, Hindu, Chinese, and the like, the (pp) those of some Scandinavians and Anglo-Saxons. The six possibilities are shown schematically below :

Parents.	Offspring.	
(1) PP—PP	4PP	(all brown)
(2) PP—pp	4Pp	(all brown)
(3) PP—Pp	2PP+2Pp	(all brown)
(4) Pp—Pp	PP+2Pp+pp	(¾ brown)
(5) Pp—pp	2Pp+2pp	(½ brown)
(6) pp—pp	4pp	(no brown)

Children of two blue-eyed parents, therefore, are bound to have blue eyes, and it is possible (Case 4) for two brown-eyed parents to have blue-eyed children.

In red-green colour blindness the inheritance of the defect is sex-linked. The defect is transmitted by the female and is inherited by one-half of the males. A colour-blind male marrying a normal female would never have colour-blind offspring, but his daughter marrying a normal man would have on the average half her sons and none of her daughters colour-blind. The scheme of inheritance is, therefore, somewhat as follows :

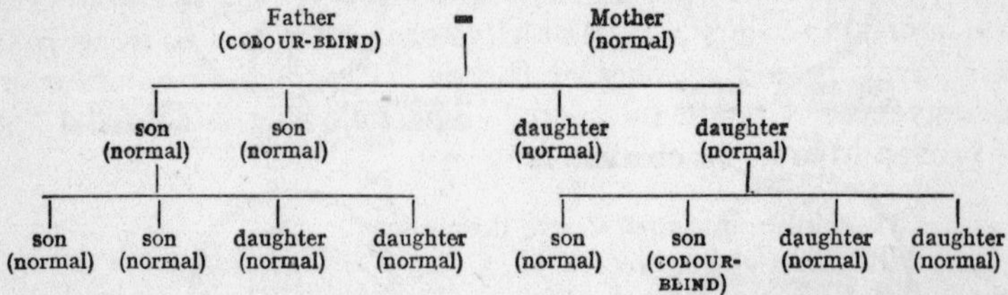

The explanation of the above is that the gene or factor of colour vision is linked with the X chromosome of the male germ-cell, the sex inheritance in man being of the XY type (see next section).

The Gene or Factorial Hypothesis.—Before the factorial hypothesis can be properly understood, the nature of chromosomes must be known. Chromosomes make themselves apparent at the time of the division of a cell (mitosis). A typical cell division of the egg of ascaris, a parasitic roundworm, is illustrated graphically in Fig. 9. Just before the cell divides, the chromatin or the nucleus (an easily stained substance from which chromosomes, the sole bearers of heredity, are derived) collects into a slender ribbon which coils about within the nucleus (A). This band becomes thicker and breaks into four approximately equal segments. These segments are called *chromosomes*. At this stage the nuclear membrane dissolves away (B). These chromosomes next move to the equatorial plane of the cell (C). Each chromosome splits down the centre into two equal parts, resulting in two chromosomes with identical contents (D). The two sets of chromosomes are drawn apart, and the cell begins to divide, one set of chromosomes going to each of the daughter cells (E). The division of the cells is next completed by the growth of a dividing cell wall. The chromosomes then reverse processes (B) and (A), becoming joined to form a chromatin coil which finally dissolves and becomes enclosed once more within a nuclear membrane (F). Thus two new cells have arisen from the old one and each contains the same number of chromosomes as the old one.

"The sperm of every species of animal or plant carries a definite number of bodies called chromosomes. The egg carries the same number. Consequently, when the sperm unites with the egg, the fertilized egg will contain the double number of chromosomes. For each chromosome contributed by the sperm

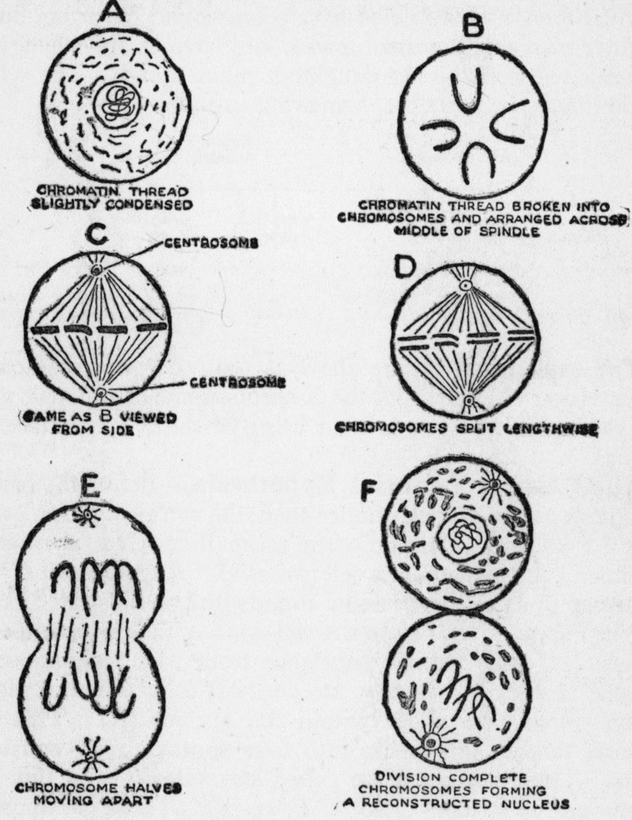

FIG. 9.—Cell division of the egg of Ascaris (a parasitic roundworm).

there is a corresponding chromosome contributed by the egg, *i.e.* there are two chromosomes of each kind which constitute a pair."[1] The fertilized egg then behaves in cell division as described above, so that every cell of the organism contains as many chromosome pairs as there are single chromosomes in the sperm or ova.

Each species of animal or plant has a definite and charac-

[1] Morgan, *The Mechanism of Mendelian Heredity*, pp. 1 and 2.

teristic number of chromosomes in each of its cells, and half this number in each of its sperms or ova. Thus in each cell of the human body there are 48 chromosomes, with 24 each in the sperm and ovum. The body cells of the ox, guinea-pig, and onion each carry 16; salamanders and trout, 24; monkeys, 54; potato

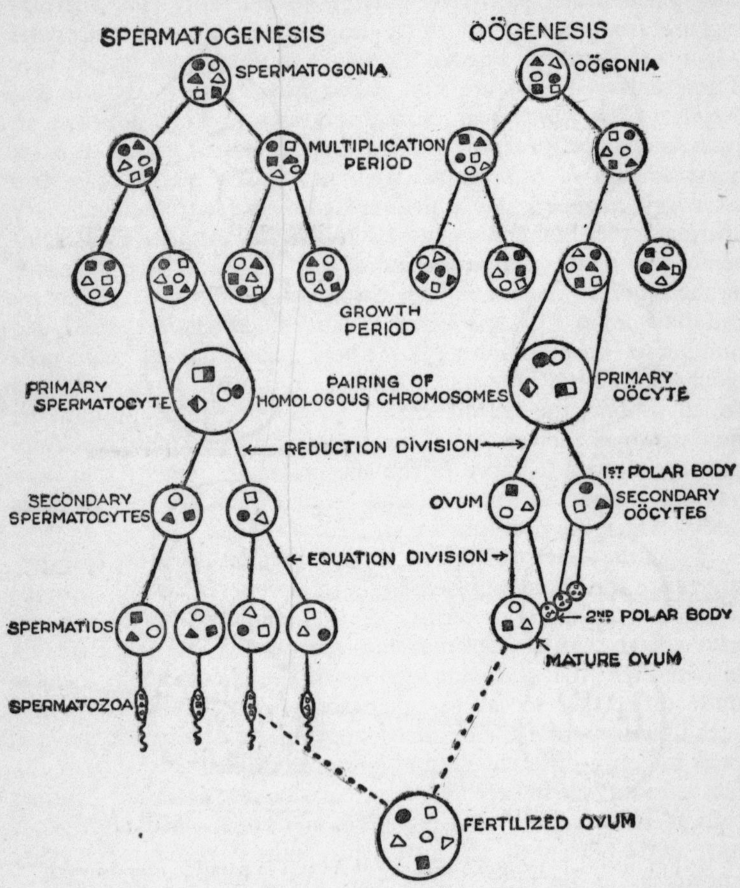

FIG. 10.—Maturation of sperms and ova.

beetle, 36; mouse, 40; cotton, 56; garden pea, 14; corn, 20; evening primrose, 14; nightshade, 72; tobacco, 48; wheat, 16; drosophila, 8; and ascaris, 4.

How does it happen that the sperms and ova only contain one-half as many chromosomes as the cells from which they are derived? The process is somewhat elaborate, but reference to Fig. 10, in which chromosomes contributed by the male parent are shaded, by the female parent unshaded, should make it clear. The germ-cells prior to *maturation* do not differ in any important respect from other cells. They multiply as do other cells and suffer no reduction in the number of chromosomes (see *Spermatogonia* and *Oögonia* in Fig. 10). Just before the final processes take place these germ-cells enlarge considerably, the spermatogonia from twenty to thirty times their original size; the oögonia to hundreds or even thousands of times their former size. These enlarged cells are now called *primary spermatocytes* and *oöcytes*. The *homologous* chromosomes now come together in pairs and unite, probably mixing their contents, and then draw apart again. A *reduction division* now takes place. The two *secondary spermatocytes* which are formed from each primary spermatocyte obtain only one-half the original number of chromosomes (in the diagram, 3 instead of 6). The next step is known as the *equation division*. Each chromosome splits as in ordinary cell division, and the *spermatids* thus formed contain the reduced number of chromosomes (3). These spermatids or male cells elongate, become very much smaller, and grow a whip-like tail which propels the mature male reproductive cells through the fluid in which they swim. The stages through which the oöcytes pass are similar to those of the spermatocytes, except that only one egg instead of four matures. The others are lost as polar bodies which are non-functional.

From the above description it will be realized that the chromosomes are the bearers of heredity; in fact, heredity and chromosomes are synonymous terms. Yet Morgan and his co-workers have shown that the chromosomes are not the ultimate elements in heredity; that different sections of the chromosomes behave quite differently so far as inheritance is concerned. Whether each unit section of the chromosome contains a different enzyme, or is merely a different kind of protoplasm, is unknown, but the fact remains that, in heredity, these parts behave as units. Morgan calls these hereditary elements *genes* or *factors*. Although genes have never been seen, the factorial hypothesis accounts for every known fact in heredity. The genes of the fruit-fly are arranged in a definite position, somewhat like peas in a pod, on one or other of the four pairs of chromosomes (see Fig. 11). Those occurring on the same chromosomes become linked in inheritance. So far, several hundred mutant characters of the fruit-fly have been studied, and to such good purpose that Morgan can now predict with unerring accuracy the results of any particular mating. Genes or factors, therefore, are the true unit-characters in inheritance; the "unit-characters" of Mendelians are simply various combinations of genes. The term "unit-character," therefore, should be given up, for it has proven itself to be a compound character. Up to the present the factorial or gene hypothesis has withstood every critical onslaught of scientific biologists.

By means of the factorial hypothesis we can easily explain the inheritance of quantitative characters and the existence of individual variations in man. When it is remembered (1) that there are 24 chromosomes present in each human sperm and ovum, and that by combination these will give rise to more than a million possible kinds of germ-cells in the (F_1) generation, (2) that the number of combinations which two such sets of germ-cells may produce through fertilization is enormously greater,

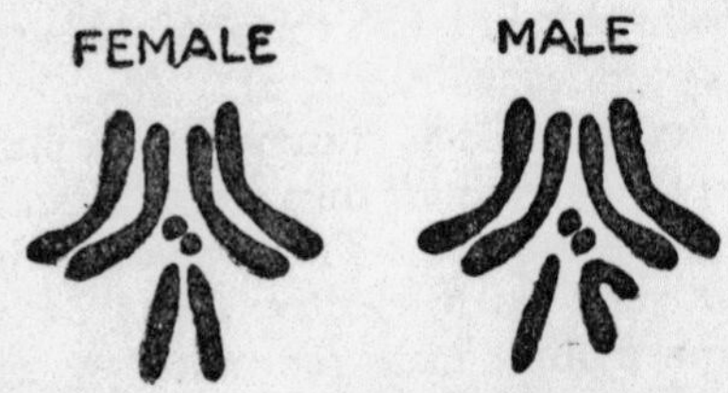

FIG. 11.—Diagram showing the characteristic pairing, size relations, and shapes of the chromosomes of the fruit-fly. In the male an X and a Y chromosome correspond to an XX pair of the females (after Bridges).

and (3) that each chromosome bears a large, although unknown, number of genes or factors, we begin to understand why two identical human beings are unknown and why variations are distributed according to the law of chance.

Studies of Twins.—Since twins possess the nearest approach to identical heredities that is possible among human beings, studies of twins should help to settle some of the vexed problems connected with heredity and environment.[1] Several reputable studies of twins have been made, among the most important for education being those of Galton, Thorndike, Merriman, and Lauterbach.[2] Galton broke new ground, but as he used the

[1] Studies of orphan institutions where the heredities are different, but the environment approximately the same for all would be, in a sense, complementary to those of twins, but so far as the author is aware only one has been made (Wingfield).

[2] Galton, "History of Twins" (1883), in *Inquiries into Human Faculty*, pp. 155–173 of the Everyman Edition.

Thorndike, "Measurement of Twins," *Archives of Philos. Psy. and Scientific Methods*. Science Press, N.Y., 1905 (o.p.).

Merriman, "The Intellectual Resemblances of Twins," *Psy. Mon. Suppl.* 33, 1924, Princeton, N.Y.

Lauterbach, "Studies in Twin Resemblance," *Genetics*, vol. x, No. 6 (Nov. 1925), pp. 525–568.

questionnaire method, his findings, though interesting, have little scientific validity. He, however, drew attention to two kinds of twins, like and unlike, or non-fraternal and fraternal. Like twins are always of the same sex and, as Newman has shown, are probably developed from one ovum. In embryo they have a common placenta and a common chorion (enclosing membrane). Since the placentas of fraternal twins may sometimes fuse together, the touchstone test for non-fraternal or like twins is the common chorion. Unlike or fraternal twins may be of the same or different sexes. They are really multiple births due to the fertilization of two ova. They usually have two placentas and always have two chorions in embryo.

Thorndike's study broke new ground, for he subjected 50 pairs of twins, selected at random from the public schools of New York City, to objective measurement—8 physical and 6 mental measurements. In comparing them he made use of the statistical device of correlation.[1] The following is a synopsis of his argument:

If the resemblances of twins are due to heredity, then—

(1) The resemblances of twins between the ages of 9 and 11 should equal the resemblances of twins between 12 and 14.

(2) The resemblances of twins should be greater than the resemblances of siblings (any children of the same parents)

(3) The resemblances of twins in traits much subject to training should be equal to the resemblances in traits less subject to training.

On the other hand, if the environment is the more potent factor, then:

(1) The resemblances of twins between the ages of 9 and 11 should be less than the resemblance of twins between 12 and 14.

(2) Resemblances of twins should equal the resemblances of siblings.

(3) Resemblances of twins in traits subject to training should be greater than resemblances in traits less subject to training.

Some of his findings are listed in Table IV.

[1] The coefficient of correlation, r, is a measure of resemblance between two series of measures—of the tendency they exhibit to vary together. Weight tends to vary with height, but the relationship is not perfect, or we should always find that the tallest man was the heaviest, the shortest man the lightest, and so forth. This tendency towards concomitant variation, or the tendency of two traits to vary together, is called a correlation. A coefficient of correlation is a measure of this tendency. It varies from $+1$ (perfect correlation) to -1 (perfect inverse correlation).

Test.	Twins.	Siblings.	Younger twins.	Older twins.
Cancellation of A's . .	0·69	0·32	0·66	0·73
Cancellation of *a-t*, and *r-e*	0·71	0·29	0·81	0·62
Mis-spelled words . .	0·80	—	0·76	0·74
Addition	0·75	—	0·90	0·54
Multiplication	0·84	—	0·91	0·69
Opposites	0·90	0·30	0·96	0·88
Averages	0·78	—	0·83	0·70

TABLE IV.—Some correlations of twins and siblings in six mental tests.

Pearson found that coefficients of correlation of mental traits in siblings such as intelligence, vivacity, conscientiousness, popularity, temper, self-consciousness, and shyness—traits in which environment may possibly play a large part—averaged 0·52. In traits such as eye-colour, cephalic index, colour of hair, stature, forearm length, and span of arms, over which environment, except that of food, can exercise little control, these same siblings had an average coefficient of correlation of 0·52 also. Arguing from his own and from Pearson's results, Thorndike concluded: "The nature of the germ-cells causes whatever similarities and differences exist in the original natures of men, that these conditions affect mind and body equally, and that in life the differences in modification of body and mind produced by such differences as obtain between the environment of present-day New York public school children are slight." A better interpretation would be that the potential or hereditary traits of siblings, unlike twins, and like twins represent a series increasing in similarity. Under the influence of environment these potential traits develop into a similar series of increasing likenesses. But environment causes slight differences to appear even when the heredities are identical as in those of like twins.

Merriman in his study of the intellectual resemblances of twins employed three intelligence tests—the Stanford-Binet, Army Beta, and National Intelligence Test—and Teachers' Estimates. His main findings are given in Table V.

Stanford-Binet I.Q.'s.

Pairs compared.	No. of pairs.	Pearson *r*.
All pairs 5–9 years.	47	0·81
,, 10–16 ,, ...	58	0·76

Army Beta.

All pairs 5–9 years	28	0·68
„ 10–16 „	48	0·67

National Intelligence Test.

All pairs 5–9 years	54	0·80
„ 11–18 „	89	0·87

Teachers' Estimates.

All pairs 5–9 years	39	0·67
„ 10–16 „	51	0·37

TABLE V.—Comparison of the resemblances of twins by means of the Pearson coefficient of correlation.

Older twins are less alike than younger twins. Environment has had more time to bring out such differences in the potential heredity as existed when the twins began life.

Lauterbach used twenty-one tests or measurements on 210 pairs of twins. The tests employed were the Terman Group Test of Mental Ability; the N.I.T.; the Thorndike-McCall Reading Scale; the Courtis Standard Research Tests in Arithmetic, Series B; Memory Span for Digits; Discrimination of Lines and Ovals; O-test for Speed of Movement; Kansas City Handwriting Scale; Height, standing and sitting; Weight; Cephalic Index; Colour of Eyes and Hair; Whorl of Head Hair; Handedness; and Palm Patterns.

He was interested in features which would identify like twins—sex, features, texture and coloration of skin, colour of hair and eyes, height, weight, cephalic index, right and left-handedness, friction-ridges of hands, whorl of hair, and birth marks. It has been supposed that those features, like right and left-handedness hair-whorls on crown of head, friction-ridges, etc., which show symmetry reversal, would be reversed in like twins produced from a single ovum, but he was unable to obtain confirmatory evidence.

In the summary of his findings given in Table VI, Lauterbach used *a*, *b* for male; *x*, *y* for female. Thus *ab* and *xy* are boy twins and girl twins respectively, while *ax* are twins of opposite sex.

Test.	Same sex, *ab* and *xy*.	Different sexes, *ax*.
I.Q.	0·77	0·56
Reading Quotient	0·59	0·56
Arithmetic, accuracy	0·69	0·35
,, speed	0·70	0·39
Memory for digits	0·40	0·25
Handwriting, quality	0·69	0·37
,, speed	0·83	0·41
Averages	0·67	0·41
Cephalic index	0·67	0·59
Weight	0·89	0·50
Height, standing	0·80	0·53
,, sitting	0·73	0·59
Averages	0·77	0·55

TABLE VI. Coefficients of correlations found in various tests given to twins of the same and of opposite sexes by Lauterbach.

In physical traits the following facts were found:

	ab.	*xy.*	*ax.*	Younger twins.	Older twins.
Average *r*'s	0·75	0·80	0·55	0·63	0·62

Lauterbach's findings may usefully be compared with Elderton's summaries given below:

	r
Like-sex twins	0·80
Unlike-sex twins	0·50
Siblings	0·50
Parent-child	0·40
Cousins	0·25

Unlike-sex twins are not more alike than siblings.

Some of Lauterbach's conclusions are the following:

1. Older twins show no greater degree of resemblance than younger twins. This is in conformity with the findings of Thorndike (1905) and Merriman (1924), and favours the argument that heredity is more potent than environment.

2. Like-sex pairs of twins show a greater degree of resemblance than unlike-sex pairs. These differences in degree of similarity are attributed by Merriman to the circumstance of origin (mono-zygotic or di-zygotic). The facts seem to favour the theory.

3. Twins show a greater degree of resemblance than other sibs. It has also been shown that single-birth sibs are more nearly alike than parents and children; and parents and children than cousins. The inference follows that the closer the relationship, the greater the resemblance.

4. Unlike-sex pairs show a degree of resemblance about equal to that of single sibs. A fraternal relationship is thus indicated.

5. There is no evidence to warrant the assumption that twins are intellectually handicapped. (*Note.*—Since Merriman's average I.Q. was 96 and Lauterbach's 95, it would seem as if twins were slightly handicapped.)

6. The monozygotic origin of quadruplets among armadillos has been established by Newman. By analogy, twins among other vertebrates, including man, may have a similar genesis.

7. The dissection of conjoined twins, and X-ray examinations of their anatomy, favour the theory of the mono-zygotic origin of twins by fission in the fertilized ovum.

8. An examination of the fœtal membranes of twins at birth has frequently revealed a single placenta and a single chorion. Embryologists maintain that such a condition is the result of genesis from a single ovum.

9. Sex ratios among twins favour the theory of two types of twins, the actual ratio being approximately 1 : 1 : 1, whereas if they were only one type, it ought by the law of chance to be 1 : 2 : 1. (Cf. J. B. Nichols, *Memoirs of the American Anthropological Association*, I, 1907, regarding twin births. He gives the following figures:

♂♂	♂♀	♀♀
234,497	264,098	219,312

which approach the 1 : 1 : 1 ratio.)

10. Merriman has shown statistically that a distribution of the intelligence quotients of a twin population represents two types of population, and he concludes that these two types are determined by one-egg and two-egg genesis.

In his study of *Twins and Orphans*, Wingfield[1] eliminated the following statistical misinterpretations found in previous studies: (1) Failure to eliminate the effect of age on the amount of resemblance found; (2) failure to take into account the variability of measurements. He also increased the reliability of his measurements by giving several tests and by using composite scores for his comparisons.

Tests were given to 102 pairs of twins and to 29 orphans who had spent a minimum of three years and 25 per cent. of their lives in the same orphanage.

[1] Wingfield, A. H., *Twins and Orphans*, 1927.

The tests used were :

1. The National Intelligence Test, Scale A, Form 1.
2. The Multi-mental Scale of McCall.
3. The Stanford Achievement Test—a battery of nine sub-tests.
4. The British Columbia Test in the Fundamentals of Arithmetic.
5. The Morrison-McCall Spelling Scale.

Since in twin data it is impossible to determine which should be considered the X variable and which the Y variable, the Otis formula

$$r=1-\frac{1}{2}\left(\frac{\sigma d^2}{\sigma y^2}\right)$$

was used instead of the Pearson in the calculation of the coefficients of correlation. Further, the standard error of estimate $\sigma\sqrt{1-r^2}$ was used in comparing the resemblances. The smaller this standard of estimate, the greater is the resemblance among the individuals comprising the group.

The following are summaries of the results :

1. Resemblances of Twins in General Intelligence.

Group.	No. of pairs.	Raw r.	r for constant age.	σ	Standard error of estimate.	Mean difference in I.Q.'s.
All twin pairs .	102	0·76	0·75±0·029	13·5	8·92	9·65
Unlike-sex pairs .	26	0·62	0·59±0·086	12·9	10·40	12·00
Like-sex pairs .	76	0·83	0·82±0·025	13·6	7·79	8·50
Fraternal pairs .	57	0·72	0·70±0·045	12·6	9·03	11·74
Identical pairs .	45	0·91	0·90±0·019	14·3	6·23	6·23

2. Resemblance of Younger Twins (45 pairs) and Older Twins (50 pairs).

Twins.	Twins 8–11 years.			Twins 12–15 years.		
	Raw r.	r for constant age.	Standard error of estimate.	Raw r.	r for constant age.	Standard error of estimate.
General Intelligence (I.Q.) .	0·73	0·71±0·047	8·09	0·78	0·77±0·038	9·16
Stanford Achievement (E.Q.) .	0·73	0·64±0·060	8·13	0·90	0·87±0·023	5·35
Stanford Achievement (A.Q.) .	0·82	0·82±0·033	3·95	0·72	0·72±0·046	5·10
Arithmetic . .	0·94	0·89±0·022	2·70	0·85	0·73±0·045	4·00
Spelling . . .	0·89	0·85±0·029	4·18	0·89	0·85±0·026	4·41
Average . .	—	0·742	5·41	—	0·788	5·60

3. Resemblances of all Twin Pairs in Native and Acquired Traits.

1. E.Q.'s (Stanford Achievement) . . .	r=0·76±0·029 (94 pairs)
I.Q.'s (General Intelligence) . . .	r=0·75±0·029 (102 pairs)
Difference	=0·01±0·041
2. A.Q.'s (Stanford Achievement) . . .	r=0·83±0·021 (94 pairs)
I.Q.'s (General Intelligence). . . .	r=0·75±0·029 (102 pairs)
Difference	=0·08±0·036
3. Arithmetic Scores	r=0·78±0·028 (88 pairs)
I.Q.'s (General Intelligence) . . .	r=0·75±0·029 (102 pairs)
Difference	=0·03±0·040
4. Spelling Scores	r=0·85±0·019 (92 pairs)
I.Q.'s (General Intelligence). . . .	r=0·75±0·029 (102 pairs)
Difference	=0·10±0·035

4. Orphans paired at random (15 pairs).

Trait.	Raw r.	Correlation between age and trait.	r for constant age.
I.Q.'s	−0·49	−0·18	−0·54
E.Q.'s	−0·19	−0·62	−0·79
A.Q.'s	−0·54	−0·38	−0·79
Arithmetic	0·14	0·58	−0·30
Spelling	0·08	0·61	−0·49
Average			−0·58

5. Orphans paired to nearest age (15 pairs).

Trait.	Raw r.	Correlation between age and trait.	r for constant age.
I.Q.'s	0·16	−0·18	0·13
E.Q.'s	0·34	−0·62	−0·07
A.Q.'s	0·54	−0·38	0·47
Arithmetic	0·46	0·58	0·18
Spelling	0·59	0·61	0·35
Average			0·21

6. Coefficients of correlation for intelligence among groups exhibiting different degrees of genetic relationship. (The first four and last are from Wingfield's study, the others from researches of other workers.)

Group.	r
Physically identical twins	0·90
Like-sex twins	0·82
Fraternal twins	0·70
Unlike-sex twins	0·59
Siblings	0·50
Parent-child	0·30
Cousins	0·27
Grandparent-grandchild	0·15
Unrelated children	0·00
Orphans	0·00

The following conclusions may be drawn from the data presented :

1. There is no significant difference in the amount of resemblance in mental traits between younger and older twins.

2. Twins are no more alike in those traits upon which the school has concentrated its training than in general intelligence.

3. Hence, considering 1 and 2, environment is inadequate to account for the mental resemblances of twins.

4. Like-sex pairs of twins show a greater degree of resemblance in intelligence than unlike-sex pairs.

5. Unlike-sex pairs of twins have approximately the same degree of resemblance in intelligence as siblings.

6. There are two distinct types of twins because :

(*a*) The like-sex group, which must partly consist of a number of uni-ovular, or identical pairs, shows a higher degree of mental resemblance than the unlike-sex group.

(*b*) Physically identical pairs show a higher degree of resemblance than fraternal pairs.

(*c*) The degree of resemblance of siblings in mental traits is nearer to that of unlike-sex pairs than to that of the like-sex pairs. This bears out the contention that unlike-sex pairs are, from the genetic standpoint, really siblings that are born at the same time.

(*d*) Members of fraternal pairs of twins show, on the whole, greater diversity in school grades than members of physically identical pairs. This latter group is probably composed largely of uni-ovular twins.

7. Orphan children, who have been reared together for a considerable portion of their lives, are no more alike than unrelated children paired at random, either in general intelligence or other intellectual traits.

8. Twins as a group are very slightly below (2 to 3 per cent.) the average of the population in general intelligence, but show about the same degree of variability as unselected children.

9. Orphan children are about 7 per cent. below the average intelligence of unselected children.

10. The amount of resemblance in general intelligence varies from $r=0$ for unrelated individuals to a maximum of $r=0{\cdot}90$ for physically identical twins. Intermediate values are found in accordance with the

genetic relationship of the individuals. Therefore, there is an increasing degree of resemblance in general intelligence among human beings with an increasing degree of blood relationship among them. *Ergo*, general intelligence is an inherited trait.

Social Heredity.—The evidence of the preceding sections can best be interpreted by the phrase, "heredity and environment are correlative factors." Heredity or nature provides whatever potentialities we possess; environment or nurture determines whether or not they shall be realized in actuality. A Beethoven born in the depths of an African forest or in the wilds of Patagonia would never compose beautiful sonatas and symphonies, although he might, and probably would, become the best tom-tom beater of his tribe. A tone-deaf person, on the other hand, though taught by the best teachers of music, would never become a musician. A feeble-minded child can never be educated into normality, although he can and should be trained to do some of a number of economically useful things that lie within the compass of one suffering from this disability. When these limitations of education are widely recognized, teachers will refrain from trying to produce a race of geniuses by education alone; on the other hand, they will see to it that potential ability, wherever found, is never wasted through denial of educational opportunity. Education can and does produce wonders in one generation; its effects, however, are mostly limited to one generation. To improve human stock permanently it must first be bred and then educated.

Yet even casual observation shows that social heredity, a form of educational environment, affects permanently more than a single generation. Children are born *with* a biological heritage; they are born *into* a social heritage. Although parents cannot pass on their knowledge and learning, yet in a very real way the knowledge, laws, customs, and traditions of mankind descend from generation to generation. Mankind through countless generations has stored his acquisitions of knowledge in books, pictures, works of art and utility, laws and traditions. These become environmental stimuli of powerful potency to succeeding generations, providing, of course, that they have the natural intelligence to profit from them. A parent who surrounds his children with good books and good pictures in a tasteful home, provides them with opportunities for travel and converses with them intelligently, is providing them with a social heritage of the highest value. If they do not profit from this good environment it is probably because they cannot. The teacher, likewise, through improved text-books and better methods of teaching, provides a better social heredity for his pupils in that he makes learning more thorough and expeditious. This social inheritance, unlike the biological inheritance which is passed from parent to child through the germ plasm, must be acquired anew by each generation. To some extent a good social heritage can offset a bad biological inheritance, as when a knowledge of health laws helps to overcome the handicap of a bad physical constitution. Even here the possible improvement is comparatively small and is limited to one generation. No social heritage, however good, can replace a sound biological inheritance. Yet it is with education as a social heritage that the teacher concerns himself all the time. It is the one factor under his control by means of which he makes the most of the potentialities each pupil brings with him to school.

References

Bagley, W. C. *Educational Determinism.* Baltimore, Warwick and York, 1925. Pp. 194.

Cattell, J. M. "A Statistical Study of American Men of Science." *Science*, vol. xvi, 1906, pp. 732 ff.

Conklin, E. G. *Heredity and Environment in the Development of Man.* Princeton University Press, 3rd ed., 1920.

Davenport, C. B. *Heredity in Relation to Eugenics.* New York, Holt, 1911. Pp. xi+298.

De Candolle, A. *Histoire des sciences et des savants depuis deux siècles.* Geneva, H. Georg, 1783. 2nd ed., 1888. Pp. xvi+594.

Dugdale, R. L. *The Jukes.* N.Y., Putnam, 1877. Pp. viii+120.

Ellis, H. *A Study of British Genius*, 1904. New ed. Boston, Houghton Mifflin, 1926. Pp. xvi+396.

Estabrook, A. H. *The Jukes in 1915.* Washington, Carnegie Institution, 1916. Pp. vii+85.

Galton, F. *English Men of Science: their Nature and Nature.* N.Y., Appleton, 1890 (Reprint of 1874 edition). Pp. xiii+270.

Galton, F. *Inquiries into Human Faculty and its Development.* London, Dent, 1883. Pp. xviii+261.

Galton, F. *Hereditary Genius: an Inquiry into its Laws and Consequences.* N.Y., Appleton, 1880 (Reprint of 1869 edition). Pp. vi+390.

Galton, F. *Natural Inheritance.* London, 1889. Pp. 259.

Galton and Schuster. *Noteworthy Families.* London, Murray, 1906. Pp. xlii+96.

Goddard, H. H. *The Kallikak Family.* N.Y., Macmillan, 1914. Pp. xv +125.

Lauterbach, C. E. "Studies in Twin Resemblances," *Genetics*, vol. x, No. 6 (Nov. 1925), pp. 525–568.

Merriman, C. "The Intellectual Resemblance of Twins," *Psy. Mon. Suppl.* 33. Princeton, *Psy. Rev.*, 1924. Pp. 58.

Morgan, Sturtevant, Muller and Bridges. *The Mechanism of Mendelian Heredity.* N.Y., Holt, 1923. Pp. xiv+357.

NATIONAL SOCIETY FOR THE STUDY OF EDUCATION. Twenty-seventh Yearbook. Part I. Nature and Nurture: their Influence upon Intelligence. Part II. Nature and Nurture: their Influence upon Achievement. Bloomington, Ill., Public School Publishing Co., 1928. Pp. ix+465; xxv+393.

NEWMAN, H. H. *The Biology of Twinning*. University of Chicago Press, 1917.

NEWMAN, H. H. *Evolution, Genetics and Eugenics*. University of Chicago Press, 1925. Pp. xx+639.

NEWMAN, H. H. *The Physiology of Twinning*. University of Chicago Press, 1923. Pp. 230.

PEARSON, K. "On the Laws of Inheritance in Man, II." "On the Inheritance of the Mental and Moral Characters in Man, etc." *Biometrika*, vol. iii, part ii, 1904, pp. 131–190.

POPENOE AND JOHNSON. *Applied Eugenics*. N.Y., Macmillan, 1918. Pp. xii+459.

SHULL, A. F. *Heredity*. N.Y., McGraw Hill, 1926. Pp. xi+287.

THORNDIKE, E. L. "Measurement of Twins," *Archives of Philosophy, Psychology and Scientific Methods*. N.Y., Science Press, 1905. Pp. 64.

WIGGAM, A. E. *The Fruit of the Family Tree*. Indianapolis, Bobbs-Merrill, 1924. Pp. 369.

WILSON, E. B. *The Cell in Development and Heredity*. N.Y., Macmillan, 1925.

WINGFIELD, A. H. *Twins and Orphans: The Inheritance of Intelligence*. London, J. M. Dent, 1928. Pp. 127.

WINSHIP, A. E. *Jukes-Edwards: A Study in Education and Heredity*. Harrisburg, Pa., Myers, 1900. Pp. 88.

WOODS, F. A. *Mental and Moral Heredity in Royalty*. N.Y., Holt, 1906. Pp. viii+312.

CHAPTER II

THE BEHAVIOUR OF ORGANISMS

The Meaning of Behaviour.—In the Introduction to this book psychology was defined tentatively as the study of the behaviour of organisms, especially the behaviour of human beings—what they do and say. Since behaviour is a key word in psychology there must be no dubiety regarding its significance. A close inquiry into its meaning and use will, therefore, be made.

Let us begin with a number of explicit statements about behaviour :

(1) In the first place, behaviour is the response of an organism to some form of stimulation. The response is an adjustment or regulation of some kind. In the higher organisms the response is a manifestation of an excitation—conduction phenomenon. Responses are generally movements or changes in movements ; or secretions or changes in secretions. The movements may be due either to striped or unstriped muscles, and the secretions to duct or to ductless glands (see Chapter III). Responses, therefore, are frequently hidden from direct observation. The movements of the laryngeal muscles during speaking and thinking (which is mainly silent speech), so important in human behaviour, and the movements of the alimentary canal during digestion, etc., are examples of hidden movements. With the hidden intrinsic, physiological, or vital processes of the body, psychology has little to do ; these are the special province of physiology.

If the adjustments made by the organism in response to environmental stimuli are adequate, the organism lives ; if inadequate, it either lives on a lower plane or dies. As Spencer truly said, " life is the continuous adjustment of internal relations to external relations."

(2) Behaviour always takes place in some environment. Organisms have no meaning except in relation to environment ; an organism without an environment is unthinkable. This does not mean that the differences in the behaviour of organisms are solely determined by environment. In the previous chapter it

was shown that the potentialities of behaviour resided in the genes of the chromosomes. Not all the genes or combinations of them are developed by environment. Each individual represents but a portion, probably a very small portion, of his hereditary possibilities. The selective agency is environment. This determines the particular combinations of genes which shall be realized in actuality. Thus the genes of man determine, for example, that under the stimuli of food and use he grows arms instead of wings, while the genes of a chicken under similar stimulation lead to wings instead of arms. And the behaviour possibilities of arms and wings are totally different. The same stimuli of food and use also determine whether a particular man shall grow big, hard muscles or small, flabby ones. But it is the genes that fix the limits of muscular development for each particular individual. Further, the genes do not start their own development; the starting agency is environment. An organism is no self-starting mechanism; its reactions are always started by some stimulus outside of itself.

Since, as we have seen, each cell of a multicellular organism contains identical chromosomes, there must be some agency determining which cells shall develop into muscle cells, bone cells, and the like. The agency determining this development, and consequently the behaviour patterns of the individual, is, according to Child, the physiological gradient.[1]

(3) The kind of behaviour an organism exhibits is dependent upon its structure and constitution, and upon the nature of the exciting stimulus. Differing organisms will behave differently even when excited by the same stimulus. If one could imagine a situation in which a partridge, sparrow, deer, and man were startled simultaneously by the same noise, the resultant behaviour would be very different. The partridge would freeze, the sparrow fly, the deer run, and the man start.

(4) The grade or level of behaviour is dependent upon the grade or level of biological development of the organism. Behaviour runs from low to high, high being defined as the greater capacity for diversified living. The greater the biological development of the organism, the higher is its behaviour. Plants undoubtedly behave. If Bose's researches are confirmed, they may even have a primitive kind of nervous system. Plants, however, are fixed in location; they may react towards light, heat, winds, and moisture, but such adjustments as they make are necessarily to a narrower environment than the adjustments that animals make. Again, animals of simpler biological structure,

[1] Child, *Physiological Foundations of Behaviour*, chaps. vi, vii, and viii.

like fishes and reptiles, exhibit behaviour patterns of a lower order than animals of more complex biological structure, say, birds and mammals. Increasing complexity of structure is paralleled by increasing complexity of behaviour. Man represents the highest form of biological evolution and he exhibits the most complex forms of behaviour.

The organism's complexity of structure is due to the correlated differentiation of muscles and glands on the one hand, and to the nervous system on the other. Biologists, therefore, are right in maintaining that "what is functionally higher is biologically higher." The lowly earthworm creeping among the roots of a giant tree is biologically higher than the tree. It is the complexity of the behaviour patterns that counts; neither the work done nor the energy transformed is a criterion. As Herrick says, "The energy expenditure of a single calorie in the brain of an engineer may be of more significance in the construction of a cantilever bridge than that of all the muscular work required in its fabrication.[1]

(5) Behaviour, in all but the simplest organisms, shows increasing complexity with age. Adult behaviour in mankind is more complex and elaborate than infantile behaviour. Behaviour in childhood is more directly innate—that is, reflexive or instinctive in character; behaviour in maturity is more intelligent. So true is this generally, that Stanley Hall maintained the thesis that the development of behaviour in the individual paralleled its development in the race. Further researches show that this recapitulatory theory will not bear too close a scrutiny, nevertheless it is indubitably true that throughout childhood and far into maturity behaviour in mankind becomes increasingly complex. And to a lesser degree the same is true of animals lower than man.

(6) Behaviour also shows increasing complexity as we ascend the evolutionary scale. The lowest organisms exhibit little more than tropisms—relative simple, definite responses to external stimulations generally of a physical or chemical character, which lead to the orientation of the body with respect to the stimulus. Both plants and moths are tropic with respect to light; their reactions are said to be positively heliotropic. In higher animals reflexes, instincts, and intelligent behaviour make their appearance. In man and in some gregarious animals social behaviour—behaviour within a group—plays an important, perhaps a dominant, rôle.

(7) Organisms show two major groups of behaviour activities.

[1] Herrick, *Neurological Foundations of Animal Behaviour*, p. 15.

The first group, which includes the metabolic processes of nutrition, respiration, circulation, and excretion, has been variously called *intrinsic*, *visceral*, or *physiological* behaviour. Intrinsic behaviour, therefore, is concerned with the life processes of the body—those which maintain it in health and vigour and secure its reproduction. Psychology has little direct interest in the intrinsic activities of organisms; however, as previously stated, they form the chief province of physiological studies.

The second group is known as *integrative* or *somatic* behaviour. It is with integrative behaviour that psychology is directly concerned, since integrative behaviour represents the immediate adjustments of the organism to its environment. Locomotion and other muscular movements of the body as a whole or of its parts, owing their co-ordination to the action of the central nervous system, are the chief forms of integrative behaviour. But sharp lines of demarcation cannot be drawn between integrative and intrinsic behaviour. Springing from a common root—the inherent irritability of protoplasm—they simply represent two different lines of development which forever remain mutually dependent and interactive.

(8) Since behaviour represents a response to a stimulus it may be symbolized by the formula S → R. The arrow for higher organisms represents the inner co-ordinations of the nervous system between the stimulus and the response. Even the most complex forms of behaviour can be analysed in terms of the S → R formula.

Although the immediate response to a stimulus may be regarded as a convenient unit of behaviour, it must never be forgotten that the arrow represents a number of intermediate, intervening processes. According to Herrick[1] this unit of behaviour in higher animals includes the following processes:

(i) The *stimulus*, a physical agent of some sort which impinges upon excitable protoplasm.

(ii) The *excitation*, or the direct effect of the stimulus upon the specific protoplasm which is affected. A special receptive apparatus is usually provided for each kind of stimulus to which the body is sensitive, namely, the sense organ or receptor. The sense organ is usually regarded as part of the nervous system, though it may contain a very complex assortment of non-nervous accessory tissues.

(iii) The *afferent transmission*. The apparatus is a sensory nervous pathway which transmits the excitation from the receptor to a centre of correlation.

(iv) The *central adjustment*. The adjuster is a nerve centre in which the afferent impulse is transferred to the efferent pathway, with

[1] Herrick, *Neurological Foundations of Animal Behaviour*, p. 121

or without more or less complex modification of the excitation in the centre itself.

(v) The *efferent transmission.* The apparatus is a motor nervous pathway which transmits the excitation to the peripheral organ of response.

(vi) The *response.* The specific apparatus of response is termed the effector, which is usually not a part of the nervous system—muscles, gland, electric-organ, etc.

As we shall see later, the above is a description of a simple reflex-arc, upon which all higher forms of behaviour are built. For the present all that need be noted is that processes (ii)–(v) represent the arrow of S → R, with chief emphasis on process (iv), the central adjustment.

Principles of Organic Behaviour.—From the previous explicit statements about behaviour a number of principles can be derived.[1]

(1) All organisms are active because they are alive, and are continually being subjected to sensory stimulation. Just what life is, still remains a mystery. As far as is known at present the bases of life are the various protoplasms comprising the bodies of plants and animals. Protoplasm is an organic chemical compound of highly complex molecular structure. It exhibits irritability or excitability, and this is the fundamental fact about life. The reactions of protoplasm to sensory stimulations form the bases of behaviour in living things. Apparently protoplasm cannot excite itself, but when stimulated by an external factor changes in some way not yet made out. After such a stimulation it is doubtful if it ever returns to the same condition. Memory and learning are thus concerned with this characteristic of protoplasm.

(2) All sensory stimuli exert some effect on the activity of the organism, not necessarily overt. This principle is really an application of the doctrine of the conservation of energy. If heat, light, sound, or other energies of the external world stimulate sense organs, energy is released and something must result. This something in man is usually the movement of a muscle or the secretion of a gland, which can either be directly observed or, if hidden, can be made apparent by means of a suitable apparatus. It is quite possible, of course, that the energy may be absorbed in the alteration of the internal structures of cells, but it is very difficult to demonstrate this. What must not be forgotten is that the energy released is greater than the exciting stimulus and bears no direct quantitative relation to it; in other words, the cells are magazines of energy which are set off by external stimulation.

[1] See Carr, *Psychology*, chap. iv.

(3) All activity is initiated by some form of sensory stimulus. This principle denies the claim of the vitalist who says that protoplasm is fundamentally capable of self-excitation. But it does not imply that the external objective, environment, is the only starting-point of behaviour reactions. Intra-organic states, such as hunger and thirst, may be very effective in starting a whole series of behaviour reactions. It does imply that neural impulses cannot be spontaneously aroused ; nerve cells require a stimulus before they can function. Not all of the physical energies are sensory stimuli for an organism. The eye is sensitive to light waves of a certain range of lengths only ; the ear to sounds of a certain range of frequency, etc. We are, however, totally insensitive to the Hertzian waves of wireless telegraphy because man has no sensory apparatus for recording them.

(4) Every movement resulting from a sensory stimulation inevitably modifies the situation, and the subsequent response is to the modified situation. This is due to the presence of kinæsthetic sense organs in muscles, tendons, and membranes covering the joints, which automatically record any movement that is made. The movement, therefore, becomes in turn the sensory stimulus for a succeeding movement. In writing, the sensory stimulation obtained from making a particular letter becomes the stimulus for the next one. In walking, the movement of the right leg becomes the stimulus for the left. In speaking, the muscles of the larynx (as well as the sound of the voice) help us to keep the sentence going. People who become stone deaf do not forget how to speak, nor do they mix up their sentences. The balance of the body is preserved automatically through the agency of sensory stimulations from muscles that have previously moved. The importance of this principle has long been overlooked because the mechanism, in its working, does not usually evoke consciousness.

Protoplasmic Behaviour.—Thus far, we have been dealing with organismic behaviour, and chiefly with the behaviour of multicellular organisms. Hints have been given that the inquiry must be pushed further—in fact, into the behaviour of the protoplasms which compose the cells. What are protoplasms ? is a question that naturally arises.

Protoplasms are highly complex chemical compounds, frequently with more than 1000 atoms to each molecule, comprising the bodies of living creatures. Molecules of protoplasm, in the form of a gluey paste (colloid), combine to form cells. Protoplasms are thus the bases of cells, as cells are of organisms. Protoplasms vary in composition from species to species, and from cell to cell within the species. There is every reason for believing that the characteristic differences between species result from the hereditary constitution of their protoplasms. From generation to generation protoplasm is continuous, although changing slowly in the long course of evolution. In this respect protoplasm is remarkably stable.

All protoplasms exhibit irritability, that is, all react in some way to appropriate stimulation. Different sorts of protoplasmic behaviour become integrated into the behaviour of cells ; different forms of cellular behaviour become integrated into the behaviour of multicellular organisms ; and the behaviour of multicellular organisms becomes integrated into the behaviour of the group. In other words, protoplasmic behaviour is colloidal ; organismic behaviour is cellular ; and group behaviour is organismic, the whole forming a continuous series. Differences in behaviour patterns found in organisms rest upon differences in the stable organization of the protoplasmic substratum of cells.

All protoplasm, whatever its variety, can form a plasma membrane. The plasma membrane plays a different part in behaviour from the rest of the protoplasm of the cell. Thus the amœba, consisting mainly of a granular protoplasm, forms a plasma membrane resembling a cell wall, wherever the protoplasm comes in contact with water. The protoplasm at the surface is more rigid than the protoplasm in the interior of the cell. Although there is a continual movement of protoplasm from surface to interior, and *vice versâ*, the plasma membrane remains intact, being formed the instant the interior protoplasm reaches the surface. The plasma membrane exhibits the phenomenon of dominant polarity ; the surface of the amœba is therefore physiologically more active than the interior. This gives rise to a physiological gradient running from the surface to the interior, which, as will be seen in the succeeding section, is the beginning of those excitation-transmission gradients out of which nervous systems evolve.

Embryonic protoplasm is characterized by intense metabolic activity. The embryo lives intensely, as may be seen from its rapid rate of growth. As the embryonic protoplasm differentiates progressively to form the protoplasm of bone, muscle, nerve, and connective tissue, it assumes a more rigid and stable organization. The derived tissues are better adapted structurally for the performance of particular functions. And of the derived tissues that constituting the nervous system dominates the rest.

Physiological Gradients.—When protoplasm is stimulated, the excitation aroused is transmitted through it, usually in diminishing degree from the point of application to points more remote. Such lines of diminishing intensity of vital reaction to stimulation are known as physiological gradients. A physiological gradient, therefore, represents a quantitative gradation in physiological condition in a definite direction. Associated with the physiological gradient are the correlative phenomena of dominance and subordination of parts, and of polarity and symmetry. The physiological gradient seems to be due to differences in the rates of metabolism. The parts exhibiting high metabolic rate exert a wider influence upon the surrounding protoplasm and become centres of dominance; those of low metabolic rate become subordinated.

In unicellular animals like the amœba the surface is physiologically dominant, the interior subordinate, so the physiological gradient is of the radiate or surface-interior kind. In plants the growing tip is physiologically dominant and the gradient is mainly of the apico-basal or antero-posterior kind. A third type occurs in bi-laterally symmetrical organisms such as man. While the main physiological gradient runs from the head downward, minor gradients running from the median to lateral and from back to front also appear.

A physiological gradient may be regarded as a primitive form of nervous system since it exhibits all the physiological characteristics of an excitation-transmission gradient and may be determined by any persistent local stimulus which changes the rate of metabolism. According to Child the excitation-transmission change in protoplasms exhibits the following characteristics: [1]

"First, all living protoplasms are to some extent irritable or excitable and capable of transmission. Second, excitation is a dynamic change involving increased energy-liberation in the protoplasmic system. Third, it is initiated by the impact from without of some form of energy upon the protoplasm excited, and the relation between the exciting factor and the process of excitation is non-specific; in other words, the same excitatory changes may be induced by different forms of external energy. Fourth, transmission results from the fact that an excited region is capable of inducing in some way excitation in adjoining regions within a certain distance. Fifth, in non-nervous transmission and in nervous transmission under certain conditions a decrement in intensity or energy, in short of physiological effectiveness, of the excitation very generally, if not always, occurs. In other words, the excitatory change loses in effectiveness in the course of its progress, so that finally at a greater or less distance from the point of origin it is no longer effective in exciting further points, and so transmission ceases. And finally, no specialized structure of any sort beyond that of a living protoplasm with limiting surface is necessary for the occurrence of excitation and transmission."

[1] Child, *Physiological Foundations of Behaviour*, p. 173.

As a matter of fact, the physiological gradients determine the position, structure, and function of the nervous system, for it is out of the physiological gradients that the nervous system evolves. In axiate animals the point of highest metabolism is generally the head. This becomes the centre of the nervous system and of the chief sense organs. Nerve tissue, with its higher rate of metabolism, dominates all other tissues with lower rates, such as cartilage, bone, muscle, connective and glandular tissues. If, however, a gland secretes an endocrine secretion which can effect reactions it may secure a temporary ascendancy over the nervous system. With respect to the apparatus of transmission and response, the sense organs are the highest points of the excitation-transmission gradients and dominate muscles which are immediately activated by them. Within the nervous system itself it is difficult to demonstrate any decrement in transmission, but it is impossible to believe that the radius of action of nerves is infinitely great. All gradients are diminished with advancing age, and vitality runs low. When the gradients disappear, death ensues.

The physiological gradients determine physiological polarity and symmetry. These in turn determine the rates of cell-division, growth, and differentiation. These again determine the behaviour patterns, so that finally behaviour can be traced to physiological gradients, which, as we have seen, are due to fundamental properties of protoplasm.

Many proofs can be cited to show that physiological gradients actually exist.

(1) Respiration. The oxygen consumed and the CO_2 given off at different levels of simple organisms can be measured. These measurements show graded variations in metabolic rates.

(2) Susceptibility to poisons, narcotics, heat, cold, and lack of oxygen. In general the susceptibility to poisons, etc., is greatest at the point of highest metabolic activity. If an earthworm is poisoned with potassium cyanide of appropriate concentration, the tissues at the head end of the body die first. When the head disintegration has involved several segments, disintegration of the tail begins. The middle of the body is affected last. This shows head dominance with a secondary centre of dominance in the tail, which fits all lines of evidence concerning regeneration of parts after severance, and with the behaviour of the animal under various forms of stimulation. In the same way a plant dies from the growing ends inwards since the growing tips of stem and root are the regions of highest gradient.

(3) Differences of electrical potential along the gradients. In

general, the heads of animals and the levels of more intense activity are electro-negative to lower levels.

(4) Oxidation-reduction reactions. There are graded differences in the reduction of potassium permanganate by protoplasms in different metabolic states as shown by the colour due to the deposition of manganese dioxide. The rate of reduction after penetration by stains such as methylene blue tells the same story.

(5) Structure and behaviour. Axial gradients are early visible in the protoplasmic structure of the developing embryonic area of eggs and early embryos. In axiate plants they occur in relation to the growing tips of both stem and root at all stages of growth. The dominance of certain parts with respect to behaviour is shown in all animals.

(6) The evidence from the rate of cell division, growth, and differentiation of parts confirms the conclusions drawn from all other lines of evidence.

If the foregoing arguments have been firmly grasped it will be seen that the behaviour of the higher organisms, including that of man himself, is simply an evolution of that which is found in lower animals. Given greater metabolic activity in any part of a developing organism, a physiological gradient will result. This physiological gradient determines the structure, growth of parts, and the subsequent behaviour of the organism.

Non-Variable and Variable Behaviour.—In studying the behaviour reactions of any organism a rough distinction can be made between the variable and non-variable forms. The avoiding reaction of the paramœcium may be taken as an example of the non-variable kind. If a paramœcium swimming in forward spirals by the lashing of its cilia encounters an obstacle, the following movements can be observed: First, that the paramœcium reverses its direction by spiralling backwards. Secondly, it turns through an angle by a side-paddling movement. Thirdly, it forges ahead on the new course. If it meets with a second obstacle the series is gone through again in the same order. This is a form of behaviour that is remarkably fixed and definite in character. But even this behaviour can be modified. If, for example, the paramœcium is placed in a length of water in a horizontal capillary tube just wide enough to permit of the forward movement, the paramœcium will swim to the end of the water by spiralling. The motion will then be reversed for some distance, but finding it impossible to side-paddle, the paramœcium will, by a series of rapid contractions, turn a somersault in the narrow tube and then spiral forward in the reverse direction.

In all lowly organized animals the regulatory movements

and adjustments are mostly of the non-variable kind. They are also concerned very directly with keeping the animal alive. In other words, every animal is organized to meet the usual variations found in its normal environment. Should these variations be too great—excessive heat, cold, etc.—the lowly organisms die, their behaviour patterns are so fixed that they cannot respond to the new demands. But even with the lowest types there is found some latitude of variability in behaviour. With organisms in the upper levels of the biological scale the non-variable behaviour, while present, plays a decreasingly important part. Thus in man, while the hand is retracted when pricked or burnt and while a tickling in the nose causes him to sneeze, the modifiability of his reactions is so great that the non-variable elements in a complex reaction are frequently hard to discover. If behaviour is represented on a scale running from non-variable, the lower the animal the more frequently its reactions are found at the non-variable end of the scale; and conversely, the higher the animal the more frequently its reactions are found at the variable end of the scale.

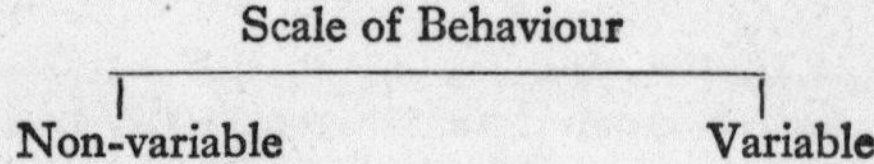

In man, while the non-variable physiological actions and reflexes necessary to keep him immediately alive are to be found, his chief forms of behaviour are preponderantly intelligent and variable. Fig. 12, although making no pretence to accurate quantitative expression, makes this plain.

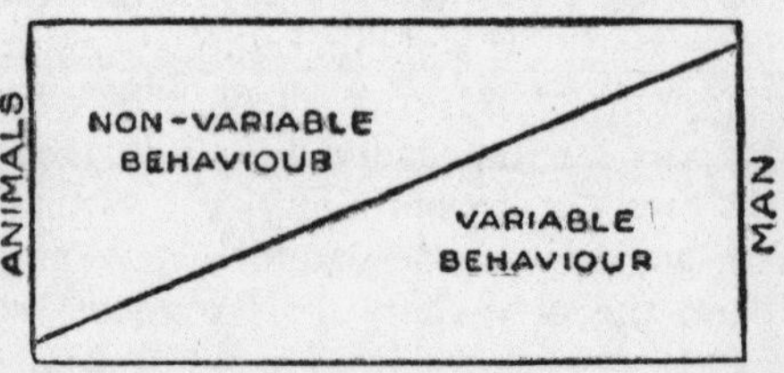

FIG. 12.—Diagram showing the relative proportions of non-variable and variable elements in the behaviour of man and animals.

Thus it is seen that the hereditary behaviour patterns are mostly of the non-variable kind, directly organized for preservation of the animal in its normal environment. In lowly animals practically the whole of their behaviour is of this type; their learning capacity is very meagre. With increasing complexity of structure the proportion of variable elements increases until, in man, the modifiable forms of behaviour completely swamp the non-modifiable. Man is eminently teachable. Nevertheless it should not be overlooked that even man needs to keep himself alive. So nature provides him with a series of unlearned, non-variable reactions which are conducive to this end.

References

In the preparation of this chapter the companion books by Herrick and Child, together with those by Sherrington and Verworn, have been freely drawn upon. To the writer these volumes, while distinctly difficult to read, seem to be fundamental to a proper understanding of the origins of behaviour.

Bernard, L. L. *Instinct: A Study in Social Psychology*. New York, Holt, 1924. Pp. ix+550.

Carr, H. A. *Psychology: A Study of Mental Activity*. New York, Longmans, 1925. Pp. v+432.

Child, C. M. *Physiological Foundations of Behaviour*. New York, Holt & Co., 1924. Pp. xii+330.

Dorsey, G. A. *Why we Behave Like Human Beings*. New York, Harper, 1925. Pp. xv+512.

Herrick, C. J. *Neurological Foundations of Animal Behaviour*. New York, Holt & Co., 1924. Pp. xii+334.

Sherrington, C. S. *The Integrative Action of the Nervous System*. New Haven, Yale University Press, 1923. Pp. xv+411.

Verworn, M. *Irritability: A Physiological Analysis of the General Effect of Stimuli in Living Substance*. New Haven, Yale University Press, 1913. Pp. xii+264.

Warren, H. C. *Human Psychology*. Boston, Houghton Mifflin, 1919. Pp. xx+460.

Watson, J. B. *Behavior: An Introduction to Comparative Psychology*. New York, Holt, 1914. Pp. xii+439.

Watson, J. B. *Psychology from the Standpoint of a Behaviorist*. Philadelphia, Lippincott, 1924. Pp. xvii+448.

Watson, J. B. *Behaviorism (Lectures-in-Print)*. New York, The People's Institute Publishing Co., 1925. Pp. 251.

Woodworth, R. S. *Psychology: A Study of Mental Life*. New York, Holt, 1921. Pp. x+580.

CHAPTER III

HOW THE HUMAN BODY WORKS

A. Organs of Response: Muscles and Glands

The Body as an Organic Machine.—The psychologist and physiologist both regard the human body as a highly complex organic machine in the workings of which they are interested. The psychologist is chiefly interested in what the machine does as a whole; the physiologist in the parts of the machine and the way they work. The psychologist could get along quite well without knowing anything at all about the intricacies of the machine, but such knowledge would not be very satisfying to a scientist intent on discovering the "whyfor" of things. So he learns as much as he can about the structure of the body and how it works.

The body is built up of tissues; the tissues are composed of cells which for any given tissue are, broadly speaking, of the same kind, having fairly definite characteristics and constant arrangements.

The tissues and cells can be classed into four groups:

(1) Epithelial tissue built up of epithelial cells.

(2) Connective tissue built up of connective tissue cells.

(3) Muscle tissue built up of muscle cells.

(4) Nerve tissues built up of nerve cells.

Epithelial tissue is a covering tissue. It covers the body as a whole (skin) and lines the tubes and tubular organs. The glands and sense organs are also composed of epithelial tissue.

Connective tissue is a supporting tissue. Bones, cartilage, ligaments, etc., which form the framework of the body and tie its parts together, are varieties of connective tissue.

Muscle tissue is a locomotor tissue, having to do with the locomotion of the body and the movement of its parts. There are three classes of muscles in the body:

(1) Striated (striped), skeletal or voluntary muscles.

(2) Plain (smooth or unstriated), visceral or involuntary muscles.

(3) Cardiac muscle (heart), which is imperfectly striated, and may be regarded as a special kind of striated muscle.

Nerve tissue is a connecting tissue. Composed of nerve cells with their processes it helps the body to respond quickly and in an orderly fashion by connecting the sense organs to the muscles and glands.

These four tissues give us a machine which is protectively covered; supple without being flabby; capable of locomotion and other movements; and able to respond quickly to changes in the environment. It is the most wonderful machine known, and millions of times more complex than any machine that man has succeeded in making.

When we consider the body as a behaving organism we can distinguish three principal parts:

(1) The reacting mechanisms or organs of response. Technically, they are termed *Effectors*, because they effect movements and secretions. The effectors, therefore, include the muscles that move and the glands that secrete.

(2) The receiving mechanisms. Other names for these are sense organs and *Receptors*. Their function is to receive the stimuli from the environmental world.

(3) The connecting mechanisms. These are the *Connectors* and comprise the whole of the nervous system. The function of connectors is to connect the sense organs with muscles and glands so as to expedite and co-ordinate the responses.

As psychology is interested in behaviour, a study of effectors, receptors, and connectors will now be made. We shall start with effectors, although logic would dictate beginning with receptors. However, the effectors are more obviously associated with behaviour, so the common-sense point of view will be adopted.

Classification of the Organs of Response.—An acceptable classification of effectors is given below:

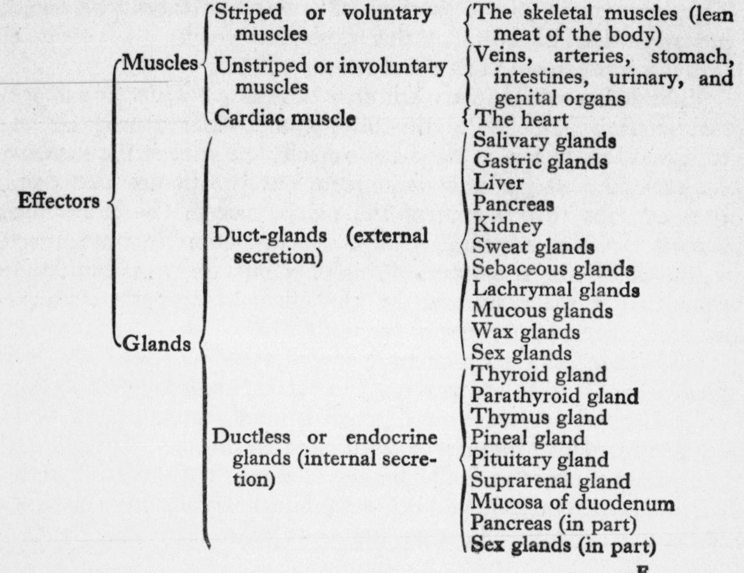

Effectors	Muscles	Striped or voluntary muscles	The skeletal muscles (lean meat of the body)
		Unstriped or involuntary muscles	Veins, arteries, stomach, intestines, urinary, and genital organs
		Cardiac muscle	The heart
	Glands	Duct-glands (external secretion)	Salivary glands Gastric glands Liver Pancreas Kidney Sweat glands Sebaceous glands Lachrymal glands Mucous glands Wax glands Sex glands
		Ductless or endocrine glands (internal secretion)	Thyroid gland Parathyroid gland Thymus gland Pineal gland Pituitary gland Suprarenal gland Mucosa of duodenum Pancreas (in part) Sex glands (in part)

Striped Muscles.—The striped muscles attached to bones constitute the principal mass (lean meat) of the body. The majority of the skeletal muscles cross a movable joint, being attached to the contiguous bones by tendons. Such an arrangement constitutes a lever, the muscle supplying the power and the joint acting as a fulcrum in each case. Levers are divided into three classes according to the positions occupied by the power, weight, and fulcrum respectively.

(1) Lever of 1st class	P F W (F: △)	(crowbar, pump-handle).
(2) Lever of 2nd class	P W F (F: △)	(wheelbarrow, nut-crackers).
(3) Lever of 3rd class	W P F (F: △)	(treadle, sugar-tongs).

All three classes of levers are to be found in the human body. Thus the head and trunk in their movements constitute levers of the first class; they are balanced like a pair of scales. The body raised on the toes by the muscles in the calf of the leg forms a lever of the second class. Such a lever always has a mechanical advantage, but power is gained at the sacrifice of speed. The bending of the arm at the elbow by the biceps muscle attached to the radial bone of the forearm constitutes a lever of the third class. Such levers always act at a mechanical disadvantage. They gain speed at the sacrifice of power. It should be noted, however, that in levers of this class the weight always moves through more space than the power.

The levers of the body are double acting. Thus in the arm the bending is done by the biceps, the straightening by the triceps. The biceps is the *flexor* muscle, the triceps the *extensor*. All skeletal muscles exist in antagonistic, flexor-extensor pairs. It is obvious that as one of the pair contracts the other must extend. A single stimulus produces excitation in one muscle and inhibition in the other. This phenomenon, which is due to peculiar nerve connections in the central nervous system, is known as *reciprocal innervation*.

The unit of a striped muscle is the striped muscle cell or fibre. Each cell is about 1/500 inch in diameter and may be an inch or more in length. Examined under a microscope, the surface is seen to be marked with alternate light and dark bands extending across the fibre (hence the name striped or striated), the bands being the outer manifestation of an exceedingly complex internal structure. To each fibre is attached, by means of a muscle plate, one or more fibres of a motor nerve cell. Fig. 13 shows a part of a striped muscle fibre and a motor nerve fibre ending in a muscle plate.

A muscle cell never wholly relaxes; it exhibits tonus. For example, when the arms are dropped to the sides of the body without any attention being paid to them, both the flexors and extensors are slightly contracted. If the nerve running to the muscles were severed, complete relaxation would take place. The subdued tone of the muscles is excellently shown in a one-sided paralysis of the face. The tonus of the muscles not involved in the paralysis causes a distortion of the mouth even though all the facial muscles are in so-called rest. The tonus of a muscle is also shown by the fact that if a resting muscle is cut across, the severed ends draw away from each other.

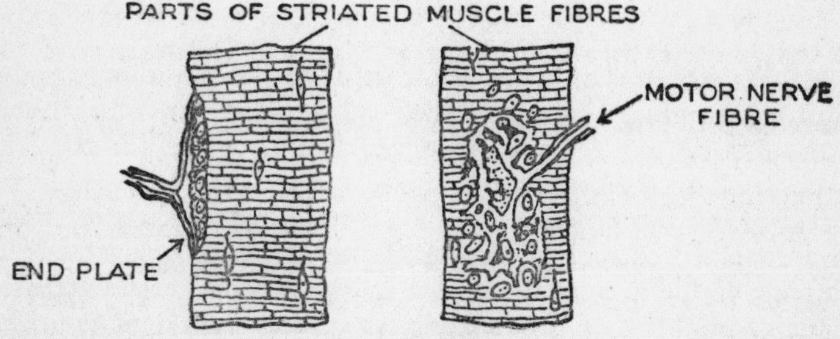

Fig 13.—Two views of a striped muscle fibre with the end plate of a motor nerve (after Kuhne).

This balanced tension in muscles makes for fine and smooth movements.

The tonicity of a muscle depends upon impulses brought from the spinal cord and also from the autonomic nervous system. The stimuli for the above impulses come from the sense organs in the muscle itself, so the whole may be regarded as a self-registering and self-maintaining mechanism. It is obviously important for the nervous system to know whether a muscle is tense or relaxed in order that movements may start directly from the position that the muscle actually occupies. For if there were no such self-registration of the muscles, we might, perchance, try to bend an arm that is already bent to its limits. The only possible movement for a fully bent arm is that of unbending.

Emotional states affect the tonus of muscles. Pleasurable states increase the tonus. The head is held a little higher, the shoulders are drawn back, and the step is firmer. Smiling comes easily to the man with well-toned muscles. Worry has the opposite effect: it causes the "down-in-the-mouth" look of the anxious person.

The chemical action of the muscle is also interesting. Like all protoplasm, a muscle cell is a machine for transforming energy. The blood carries blood sugar and other food materials which are transformed by the muscle cell into glycogen and other complex chemical compounds and there stored. The transformations of these food materials are at present imperfectly known. During muscle activity these food materials break down and oxygen is used up, thus producing the energy for movement. Heat is also liberated. The waste products of the action are CO_2, lactic acid, and acid potassium phosphate. Part of the lactic acid is further split up and oxidized, giving rise to more CO_2 and water. These waste products pass into the blood stream and are eliminated mainly through the lungs.

Muscle action, if prolonged, affects other parts of the body. To supply the extra nourishment and oxygen, and to remove the waste products that are formed, the circulation through the muscle is increased. The heart and lungs are stimulated. The fatigue products carried by the blood stream increase the resistances at the synapses of the central nervous system (see Chapter V) and cause general fatigue of the body. The heat engendered by muscle action raises the temperature of the body. This is regulated by an increased activity of the sweat glands. There is no doubt that muscular exercise is beneficial, especially to brain workers. "The razor-edge of the mind needs daily honing through physical exercise."[1] But the ultimate object of exercise is not the excessive development of skeletal muscles. The large-muscle cult has been overdone. Unless needed in daily life large muscles are parasitic, injuring the health and decreasing the span of life. As Woodworth says,[2] "Our ideal of a physical man should be Apollo rather than Hercules." But it is Kipling, in his *Just So Stories*, who gives the sanest advice about exercise when he recommends it as a cure for the hump:

"The cure for this ill is not to sit still,
Or frowst with a book by the fire;
But to take a large hoe and a shovel also,
And dig till you gently perspire."

Smooth Muscles.—Smooth or unstriped muscular tissue forms the chief muscular coat of the four great tracts or hollow organs of the body—the circulatory, the respiratory, the alimentary, and the urogenital tracts. It is also found in the iris

[1] Fisher and Fisk, *How to Live*.
[2] Woodworth, *The Care of the Body*, p. 1[illegible]
[3] Kipling, *Just So Stories*.

of the eye (for opening and closing the pupil), in the ciliary muscle of the eye (controlling the lens), in the skin muscles which cause goose-flesh, and in the walls of the ducts leading from glands. A smooth muscle, like a striated muscle, consists of long, thin, hair-like fibres, but differs from it in the following important particulars :

(1) It acts much more slowly than striped muscle, taking several seconds for a contraction in comparison with about one-tenth for striped.

(2) It acts more rhythmically than striped. The rhythmic movements of the stomach during the digestion of food and the peristaltic, wave-like contractions of the intestines are witness to this.

(3) Its tonus is higher and is maintained for a longer time than that of striped muscle. When the stomach and bladder are empty the cavities are virtually obliterated by the tonus of the gastric muscles and the smooth muscles of the bladder walls. As food is put into the stomach, the muscles relax and the wall stretches without any change of tension. In other words, the walls of the hollow organs accommodate themselves to the volume of their contents without any marked alteration in the internal pressure or in the tension of the wall.

(4) To a far greater extent than striped muscles, the smooth are concerned with the vegetative life of the organism. They are aroused by various organic stimuli. Their functioning is seen in hunger (aroused by the somewhat vigorous but rhythmical contractions of the stomach) ; in thirst (due to the dryness of the palate) ; in defæcation (initiated by the pressure of the fæces upon the muscular wall of the large intestine) ; in micturition (aroused by the pressure of urine upon the sphincters of the bladder) ; in the closing and opening of the pupil (aroused by light stimuli) ; in pain reflexes (such as those due to internal pressures, *e.g.* in the stomach) ; in vomiting ; in hiccoughing ; etc. The organic tone—state of health—is said to be good when the smooth muscles work in an orderly way.

(5) Striped muscles are connected directly with the spinal cord through the muscle plates and axons of motor neurons. Unstriped muscles, on the other hand, are only connected indirectly with the motor neurons of the cord through the intermediation of a sympathetic post-ganglionic neuron. Fig. 14 shows the connection in diagrammatic form.

(6) Unstriped muscle without a doubt is under a secretion control, especially the secretions of the endocrine or ductless glands, as well as a nervous control. Striped muscle, on the other hand, is solely under a nervous control.

The importance of unstriped muscles can hardly be overestimated. As they usually do not affect consciousness they were quite overlooked by the earlier psychologists. They are very difficult to observe and still more difficult to control; only two or three of them, of which the sphincters of the bladder and anal opening are the most important, can be said to be voluntarily controlled even by adults, while all of them act reflexly in infants. Reactions of smooth muscle often serve as stimuli to the major reactions of the whole body. If these latter take place without an obvious cause, it is wise to inquire either of the smooth muscles or glands. There is also a large amount of evidence to

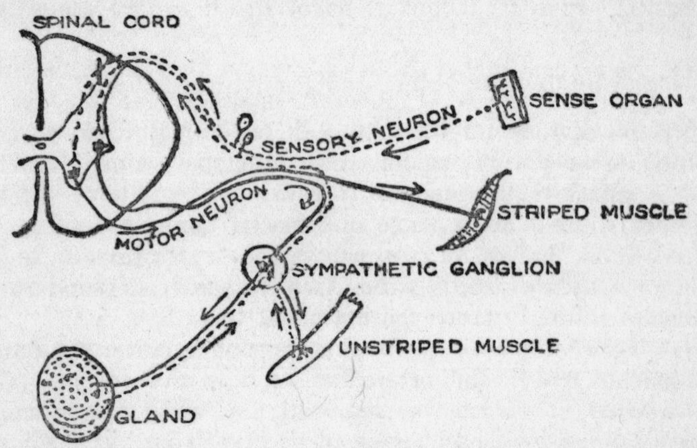

FIG. 14.—Diagram to show the connections of an unstriped muscle and a gland with the spinal cord. Note the interposal of the sympathetic ganglion.

show that movements of smooth muscles are closely connected with emotional states, and, therefore, with the personality as a whole. Their interest for the student of psychology is consequently justified.

Duct Glands.—Duct glands, or glands of external secretion, are so named because the secretions they make are poured down tubes or ducts into some bodily opening, or on to its surface. Although most of them seem to be concerned with digestion and elimination of waste products, they are nevertheless important organs of response. An onion, a cold wind, or a sad piece of news will each start a copious flow of tears. A Turkish bath causes every sweat gland in the body to react furiously. The smell of a savoury meal, when hungry, will cause the salivary and the gastric glands to secrete. The glands are undoubtedly important organs of reaction. As Watson [1] says:

[1] Watson, *Behaviorism*, p. 62.

"Will you take my word for it that our so-called higher forms of behaviour are terribly at the mercy of just these lowly secretions we have been talking about, especially when something goes wrong with one or more of them? Let the mouth glands begin to over-secrete or under-secrete as happens at times; or the small mucous glands begin to over-secrete as they do in the nose when we have a cold; let something go wrong with the digestive secretions, or let the throat become irritable and sensitive through lack of secretions; let the kidneys over-secrete and keep the bladder overly full, or the secretions from the sex organs become excessive—then our whole conduct may become modified. Even our social behaviour may become involved. We may insult or hurt the feelings of a friend, spoil a piece of fine work, even lose our jobs, and what is worse, if the faulty glands are deep down in the visceral cavity we may be able to give no verbal account of what has gone wrong. I shall speak again about this lack of ability to put anything in words about visceral and glandular behaviour."

Nor must it be forgotten that all the recent work on conditioned or transferred reactions, now bulking so large in psychological literature, began with Pavlow's conditioned reflex experiments on salivary secretions in the dog. A totally new field of work and of interpretation was thus opened up. As Pavlow's work will be described in the chapter on conditioned reactions nothing further need be said at this point.

Ductless Glands.—Far more important from the standpoint of behaviour and education are the ductless or *endocrine* glands of the body. They have no outlet, the substances they secrete being absorbed by the blood and carried to all parts of the body. For this reason they are often referred to as glands of internal secretion. The active materials of these secretions are powerful drug-like substances, which, because they affect other organs of the body situated at a distance from the gland, have been called chemical messengers (*hormones* or *autocoids*). The action may be excitatory or inhibitory, and frequently affects other endocrine glands.

The chief endocrine glands have been listed earlier in the chapter. From the standpoint of educational psychology, the thyroid, adrenal, pituitary, and the endocrine part of the sex glands are the most important. But all of them play interesting rôles, since their secretions have the power to produce effects similar to those of nervous discharges from the autonomic nervous system. In other words, they can affect smooth muscles and glandular tissue. Thus the endocrine secretions are stimuli from within the body which profoundly affect human conduct. To the psychologist they are of even greater interest than environmental stimuli. Further information about the more important glands will now be given.

(1) *The Thyroid Gland.*—The thyroid gland, purplish in colour, is situated on each side of larynx and windpipe. It consists of two wing-like lateral lobes which are connected by an isthmus across the front of the windpipe. If the head is thrown back and the act of swallowing performed, the mass of the thyroid gland can be seen with the aid of a mirror. Fig. 15 shows the thyroid gland and the four parathyroids which are closely connected with it. The parathyroids, however, have different functions from the thyroid.

If the thyroid gland is defective at birth, or later in life becomes atrophied, the following important effects upon development and behaviour can be discerned.

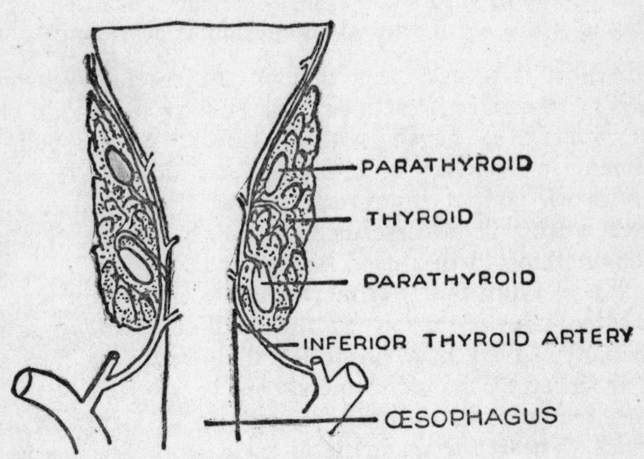

FIG. 15.—The thyroid gland and the four parathyroids. Only the two lateral lobes of the thyroid gland are shown; the medial lobe or isthmus is missing.

(*a*) In youth, *cretinism* appears. The growth of the body as a whole, and especially of the skeleton, is arrested; the development of the generative organs is delayed; the skin remains dry and the hair thin; the abdomen is swollen; the fontanelles of the cranium remain open; and the cells of the cerebral cortex remain undeveloped, causing feeble-mindedness of the imbecilic or idiotic type. A child born with a defective thyroid gland becomes a cretin—a mis-shapen dwarf of low intelligence who can be taught to do only the simplest of things.

(*b*) In adults, *myxœdema* appears. Myxœdema is characterized by a thickening and drying of the skin, falling out of the hair, low body temperatures, lethargy, diminished metabolism, diminution of sex function, and increased tolerance for sugar. The myxœdemic person, while retaining his stature, becomes very inactive, falling asleep without apparent cause.

Fortunately, however, relief from both these conditions can be secured by the administration of thyroid substance by the mouth. The substance most frequently used is obtained from the thyroid gland of a sheep. The cretin begins to grow and becomes much brighter, although he seldom becomes absolutely normal. The myxœdemic person also becomes normal again. To witness the administration of thyroid substance to a cretin and see him begin gradually to grow and develop into a normal human being is to see a miracle happen. Yet this miracle is happening in hundreds of cases every day. Thyroid substance, however, is not a cure; it must be given continuously throughout life.

The active drug in thyroid secretion is *thyroxin*, a chemical containing about 65 per cent. by weight of iodine. Thyroxin has been synthesized by Harington and can now be manufactured in the laboratory. Some places like the Appalachian region of the United States, the belt around the Great Lakes of North America, Derbyshire in England, and many Alpine valleys have no iodine in their soil and rocks, and consequently no iodine in the food plants grown in these localities. They lie on what is known as a goitre belt, since enlargement of the thyroid gland (goitre) is very prevalent among the inhabitants, especially the women, living in the area. Goitre of the exophthalmic variety leads to an excessive secretion of thyroxin. The body then works too quickly. All vital processes are speeded up. The heart-beat is much accelerated and there is great mental excitement and sleeplessness. The metabolism of the body is increased and the eyeballs become prominent.

Goitre is difficult to cure though easy to prevent. It can be prevented by supplying the body with iodine generally in the form of potassium iodide. The amount needed is quite small. Some communities dose the drinking water once or twice a year and the people are supplied with the necessary iodine without becoming aware of it. This practice is not to be commended, since one form of goitre is made worse by iodine. A better plan is to supply it individually in the form of iodized salt, iodized chocolates, or as a weak solution of potassium iodide. Especially is it necessary to supply growing girls between the ages of ten and sixteen with iodine compounds.

The thyroid gland, therefore, has a profound influence upon behaviour. It acts as a regulator of the whole body. It may be usefully compared with the draughts of a furnace. If no air enters, the fire languishes; if the draughts are opened wide, the fire burns fiercely. Upon its normal functioning depends normal mental and physical development, with all that these mean in the realm of behaviour.

(2) *The Adrenal or Suprarenal Capsules.*—The adrenal capsules are two small, yellowish, flat, somewhat triangular organs which surmount each kidney like a cocked hat. As long ago as 1855 Addison described the symptoms of a disease, now called Addison's disease, which was marked by a peculiar bronze-like pigmentation of the skin and always ended fatally. He associated it correctly with tuberculous degeneration of the adrenals.

The autocoid of the adrenal secretion is variously known as epinephrin, adrenin, or *adrenalin.* It is a powerful drug and has recently been synthesized in the chemical laboratory. Adrenalin is closely associated with the distribution of pigment within the body, with the growth of hair and other cutaneous phenomena. The "He-man" of the movies is of the adrenalin type. It is also associated with the expression of certain strong emotions, notably pain, fear, and anger. It has a direct effect upon the motor nerve endings of the sympathetic nerves. The smooth muscles which the sympathetic motor neurons contract, adrenalin contracts; those they inhibit, adrenalin inhibits. This is an excellent example of a phenomenon noted earlier, namely, that smooth muscles were under both a secretion and a nervous control.

Professor Cannon [1] has made a number of studies on the action of adrenalin. Under strong bodily emotions he showed that the amount of adrenalin in the blood was increased. Using a specially prepared segment of the intestines removed from a rabbit he showed that blood from a quiet animal had no effect on the contractions of the muscle, but blood drawn fron an animal in fear and rage always showed an inhibiting action. So delicate was the reaction that one part of adrenalin in 200,000,000 parts of the solvent produced an effect. Cannon also showed the inhibitory effect of adrenalin on the visceral movements of a living cat. If a cat is fed and the meal made visible to X rays through admixture with bismuth, the rhythmical movements of the stomach can be seen. If now the cat is angered and frightened by the introduction of a barking dog into the room, the digestive processes are inhibited and are not resumed for a considerable time (half an hour to an hour), even though the dog is immediately removed. Similar effects are produced by the injection of adrenalin. The detrimental effects of fear and anger on digestion in humans have long been known. Pleasant music and lively conversation during a meal are distinct aids to digestion.

Cannon, from his studies of the physiologic changes taking

[1] Cannon, *Bodily Changes in Pain, Hunger, Fear and Rage.*

place during emotions, formulated his "emergency theory" of adrenal activity. While some doubt has been cast by Stewart[1] on this theory, and even on some of his data, the following facts regarding the effect of adrenalin seem to be fairly well established: (1) Adrenalin has the power to split up glycogen stored in the liver and set it free in the blood in the form of blood-sugar. This blood sugar, as we have seen, is an easily available source of food supply and energy for striped muscles. (2) Muscular fatigue is reduced; in other words, the striped muscles can work more vigorously and for a longer time. (3) The action of the visceral muscles is inhibited; contraction of the blood vessels inside the abdomen makes more blood available for the supply of the voluntary muscles. (4) The coagulability of the blood increases, and the smaller blood vessels of the skin become constricted. (5) The heart-beat and lung action are both increased. (6) The action of the sweat glands is increased, so much so, that the individual often breaks out into a cold sweat. In brief, Cannon declares that adrenalin prepares a man either to fight or run away. The adrenal is, *par excellence*, the gland of the fighting man and the arrant coward. The adrenals, therefore, have played an important part biologically in the survival of man in a hostile environment.

(3) *The Pituitary Body.*—The pituitary body is a small organ about the size of a pea attached to the base of the brain by a hollow stalk, and lodging in a depression of the flooring of the cranial cavity. It consists of two distinct parts, the anterior and the posterior. Degeneracy of the anterior lobe in man leads to a fall in the body temperature, unsteadiness in gait, emaciation and diarrhœa. Over-secretion of the anterior lobe leads to *gigantism*. Many giants, when post-mortemed, are found to have abnormally large pituitary glands. If growth is complete before an excessive secretion is produced, then only those projecting parts like the nose (cf. Punch), hands, and feet are affected. The condition is known as *acromegaly*.

The posterior lobe is concerned with the tonus of visceral muscles and with the control of other glands, notably the kidneys and the mammary glands. A marked decrease in the activity of the posterior lobe increases the tolerance for sugar and the body becomes obese. Mental and sexual development are both retarded. Injection of the extract of the posterior part of pituitary has many results, among them being: (*a*) A great stimulation of the smooth muscles of the body, such as those of the blood vessels, alimentary canal, bladder, and uterus. Its

[1] Stewart, "Adrenalectomy and the Relation of the Adrenal Bodies to Metabolism," *Physiological Reviews*, 1924, IV, p. 163.

action on the uterus is so marked that it is now commonly used in hastening childbirth. The extract is also used to combat surgical shock owing to its power to increase the blood pressure. (*b*) The kidneys and mammary glands are stimulated. The amount of urine is markedly increased, but it is doubtful if the total production of milk is increased, the effect seemingly being to empty this gland more completely.

The pituitary body, like the thyroid, has a marked effect upon bodily behaviour. Normal development and behaviour are, in part, dependent upon its proper functioning.

(4) *The Sex Glands.*—The sex glands function both as duct and as ductless glands. With the onset of puberty the *interstitial cells* of the sex glands begin to secrete a hormone which causes the secondary sex characters to appear. In the male it leads to a growth of beard and a deepening of the voice. In the female it leads to the development of the hips and bust, and to the deposition of fat beneath the skin, thus giving rise to the roundedness of the feminine figure. The characteristic masculine or feminine behaviour is due to the hormones produced by these glands.

Of the other endocrine glands much that is interesting to educators has been learnt, but space forbids detailed mention. Suffice it to say that the four *Parathyroid Glands*, which are attached to the thyroid, secrete an autocoid which apparently prevents over-exertion and discharge of motor neurons. It also controls the growth of bones and the calcification of the teeth. The *Thymus Gland*, situated at the base of the neck (the neck sweetbread), is concerned with growth and development. It is antagonized by the hormones from the sex glands and atrophies after puberty. The *Pineal Gland*, a pinkish bud on the posterior surface of the brain under the cerebral hemisphere, is interesting because it is a changed form of a third (cyclopean) eye which still functions in a British snake (the slowworm) and a New Zealand lizard (the sphenodon). It probably secretes an inhibitory autocoid which controls the development of the generative organs. It gradually ceases to function after puberty is reached. The *mucous membrane of the duodenum* secretes a hormone called secretin which, on being absorbed, stimulates the pancreas to greater activity and possibly causes an increased flow of bile at the same time. The ductless part of the *Pancreas* (the islands of Langerhans) secretes insulin (isolated in the University of Toronto by Dr. Banting and his co-workers), which controls the sugar metabolism of the body. It is, therefore, useful in the relief of diabetes mellitus.

Endocrinology is a comparatively new science, but one in

which remarkable progress is being made. It has already shown us that the body, or rather the blood, has within it a delicate balance of potent drugs secreted by the ductless glands. If this balance is upset in any way, profound disturbances of development and behaviour inevitably result. It is probable that the difficulties of the unusual child, and even of the criminal, may be due to disturbances of the endocrine balance of the body.

References

Bainbridge, F. A. *The Physiology of Muscular Exercise.* London, Longmans, 1919. Pp. ix+215.

Cannon, W. B. *Bodily Changes in Pain, Hunger, Fear, and Rage.* New York, Appleton, 1915. Pp. 311.

Cannon, W. B. "New Light on Human Emotions," *Harper's Magazine* (July, 1922), pp. 234–240.

Fisher and Fisk. *How to Live.* New York, Funk and Wagnalls, 1915–26. Pp. xxviii+513.

Hoskins, R. G. "The Relation of the Adrenals to the Circulation," *Physiological Reviews*, 1922, II, 343.

Hutchinson, R. *Applied Physiology.* New York, Longmans, 1908.

Marine, D. "The Present Status of the Functions of the Thyroid Gland," *Physiological Reviews*, 1922, II, 521.

Marshall, F. H. A. "The Internal Secretions of the Reproductive Organs," *Physiological Reviews*, 1923, III, 335.

Myerhof, O. *Chemical Dynamics of Life Phenomena.* Philadelphia, Lippincott, 1924.

Schafer, E. S. "The Influence of the Internal Secretions on the Nervous System," *Journal of Mental Science*, vol. lxviii (1922), pp. 347–367.

Schafer, E. S. *The Endocrine Organs.* London, Longmans, 1916. Pp. 156.

Stewart, G. N. "Adrenalectomy and the Relation of the Adrenal Bodies to Metabolism," *Physiological Reviews*, 1924, IV, 163.

Vincent, S. *Internal Secretions and Ductless Glands.* London, Arnold, 1922. Pp. xx+464.

Watson, John B. *Behaviorism (Lectures-in-Print).* New York, The People's Institute Publishing Co., 1925. Pp. 251.

Watson, John B. *Psychology from the Standpoint of a Behaviorist.* Philadelphia, Lippincott, 1924. Pp. xvii+448.

Woodworth, R. S. *The Care of the Body.* New York, Macmillan, 1912. Pp. viii+359.

CHAPTER IV

HOW THE HUMAN BODY WORKS

B. Organs of Reception: Sense Organs

The Kinds of Sense Organs.—The world in which we live is full of energies or stimuli of various kinds. Light waves, sound waves, electrical waves, and heat waves are studied by the physicist. Chemical stimuli, both in the form of gases and solutions, are well known to the chemist. Movements of air and movements of parts of the body itself—hands, arms, fingers, legs, and larynx—register themselves continually. The environment is made up of energies pounding us and affecting us in a host of ways. To register these various energies, the body has evolved through the long course of ages many kinds of *receptors* or sense organs. Thus the eye is sensitive to ether waves ranging between the frequencies of red and violet, but insensitive to waves which are longer or shorter than these. The skin, however, has sense organs which are affected by the longer radiant heat waves. The ear registers sound waves from about 12–16 to about 25,000–30,000 vibrations per second. Sound waves as high as the squeak of a bat are inaudible to most humans, although they are responded to by dogs and other animals. Chemical substances in solution, such as sugar and salt, affect the sense organs of taste, while those in gaseous form, like ammonia, affect the receptors of smell. Gentle pressures as well as the painful prick of a pin are recorded by receptors in the skin. Movements of the body are also recorded, as are feelings of thirst, hunger, and nausea. From within and without the body, therefore, all kinds of energies, as it were, are endeavouring to stimulate us. Whether they do or not depends upon the presence or absence in the body of appropriate receiving apparatuses. At the moment of writing Hertzian waves of electricity (wireless) are passing through the room. But of these I am totally unaware. To make them evident, I must go downstairs and "tune in" the radio, that is, turn them into sound waves for which I have a receptor. Similarly, X-rays and ultra-violet rays were not discovered until their physical and chemical effects became visible to the eye. Things may be happening around us, but unless we have sense organs to make them evident, we remain in ignorance of them. We are not affected by magnetism and cannot turn unerringly to the north, but we can observe the direction of a suspended magnet. Some persons and many animals are affected by certain electrical conditions of the atmosphere, but how or by what mechanism is not yet known.

Milton coined the poetical phrase "The five gateways of knowledge" for the senses of touch, taste, smell, sight, and hearing. Modern science has increased this number very considerably, as the following list will show:

Sense.	Sense organs.	Stimulus.
Sight (visual sense).	Eye (retina).	Ether waves (400,000 billion to 800,000 billion vibrations per second).
Hearing (auditory sense).	Ear (cochlea).	Sound waves (12–16 to 25,000–30,000 vibrations per sec.).
Taste (gustatory sense).	Tongue (taste buds).	Sapid fluids (chemical energy in liquid form).
Smell (olfactory sense).	Nose (olfactory cells).	Soluble gaseous particles (chemical energy in gaseous form).
Pressure (pressure sense).	Skin (Pacinian, Meissner, and Krause corpuscles).	Contact with objects (mechanical energy).
Temperature (temperature sense).	Skin (end organs not definitely known).	Ether waves (Radiant Heat 3,000 billion to 800,000 billion vibrations per second). Also cold objects and warm objects.
Pain (pain sense).	Skin (free branched nerve).	Cutting, burning, pricking, intense chemical (acids) or electrical stimulation.
Movement or Strain (Kinæsthetic or muscle sense).	Muscles, Tendons, and Joints (end brushes in muscle and tendon spindles).	Mechanical energy from change in position of muscle, tendon, or joint.
Posture and Balance (equilibration sense).	Ear (semi-circular canals).	Mechanical energy from change of position of head.

In addition to the above, some scientists, like Sherrington and Herrick, would list a large number of visceral senses including those of hunger, thirst, nausea, suffocation, flushing and heart panics, sexual sensations, distension of cavities, visceral pain, and abdominal sensations associated with strong emotions.[1]

[1] Herrick, *Neurological Foundations of Animal Behaviour*, p. 27.

It is very probable that some of these senses are compounded of several simple ones. In general, it is better not to admit a sense unless its sense organ has been discovered.

Every sense organ has within its structure the peripheral ending of a sensory neuron. Every sense organ, with the exception of those for movement, contains epithelial cells. These epithelial cells are sensitive in a general way only to one form of stimulation, *e.g.* to ether waves or sound waves of a limited range of frequency. The rods and cones of the retina, the taste buds of the tongue, the hair cells of the cochlea, are examples of these modified epithelial cells. Sense organs, with the exception of that for pain, have accessory apparatuses which assist in bringing the stimulus to the sensory nerve ends. The eyeball for vision, the structures of the middle and internal ear for hearing, the tongue for taste, the body hairs for pressure, etc., are examples of accessory apparatuses.

Whenever a sense organ is stimulated by its appropriate form of energy, some kind of physical or chemical change takes place in the epithelial cell. This physico-chemical change sets up a neural impulse in the sensory nerve ending of the sense organ which is in contact with the epithelial cell. This impulse travels along the nerve fibre of a sensory neuron to the central nervous system (brain and spinal cord). Arriving there it stimulates other nerve cells to a similar form of activity and finally passes out by means of the fibres of a motor neuron to a muscle or gland. The muscle then moves or the gland secretes.

Receptors for Sight.—The receptors for vision are the rods and cones of the retina. The eye, which is mainly an accessory apparatus to the rods and cones, is an optical instrument so arranged that light rays, from objects which are looked at, are focussed on some part of the retina. Fig. 16, which is a diagram of a horizontal section of the eye, shows how this is accomplished.

In most particulars the eye resembles a camera. Instead of a rigid box the eye has a tough but flexible white coat, the *sclerotic*, which, at the bulging front of the eyeball, becomes the transparent *cornea*. The spherical shape of the eye is maintained by a clear jelly-like substance known as the *vitreous humour* which fills the interior of the eye; the bulge of the cornea is maintained by a more watery substance called the *aqueous humour*. The coloured *iris* of the eye corresponds to the shutter and the eyelids to the cap of the camera. The aperture of this instrument, known as the *pupil*, is made larger or smaller by the contractions and extensions of the muscles of the iris. The black coating of the eye, which prevents the reflection of light from blood vessels and other structures within the eyeball, is known as the *choroid* coat. The *crystalline lens* is the chief mechanism for focussing the light on the retina, although the cornea and the two humours also help. The *retina* corresponds to the film of the camera and occupies the rear

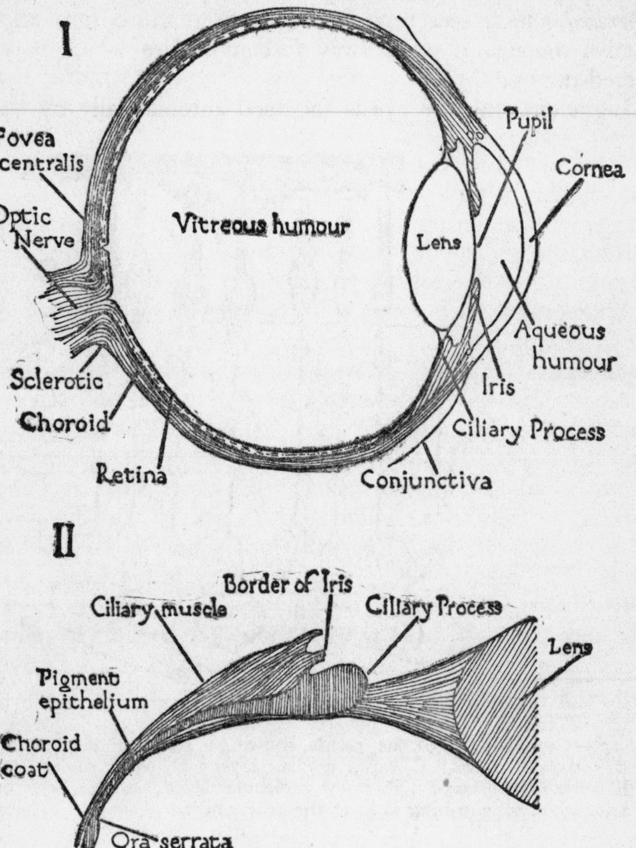

FIG. 16.—I. Horizontal section through the left eye (schematic after Gegenbaur). II. Meridional section to show the position of the ciliary muscle (Schultze).

two-thirds of the inner wall of the eyeball. The eye, however, is focussed in a different manner from the camera. Instead of being focussed by varying the distance between the lens and the film, the eye is focussed by making the lens thicker or thinner, according as the object is near or remote. This latter is accomplished by the *ciliary muscle*, which is attached to the *ciliary process* and to a sheath which encloses the crystalline lens. The line of sight is changed in direction by six muscles (four *recti*, two *oblique*) attached to the sclerotic coat and to the walls of the bony socket of the eye. The eyelashes and eyebrows are protective accessories and play no direct part in the act of seeing. They prevent foreign bodies from entering the eye. The *lachrymal glands* secrete tears which keep the cornea and conjunctiva moist and wash away foreign bodies which may have entered the eye.

Light entering the eye is focussed automatically by the lens

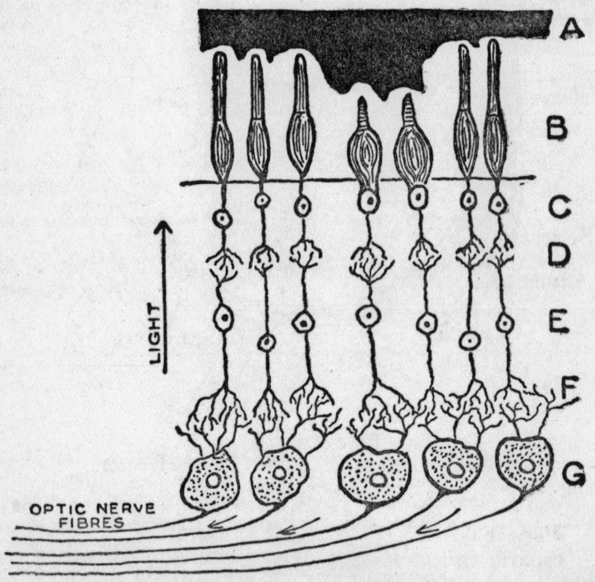

FIG. 17.—Cross-section of the retina, showing: A, layer of pigment cells; B, rods and cones; C, outer nuclear layer; D, outer molecular layer; E, inner nuclear layer; F, inner molecular layer; and G, layer of nerve cells with axons uniting to form the optic nerve.

and accessory organs upon the rods and cones of the retina. As Fig. 17 shows, the rods and cones lie at the back of the retina touching the choroid coat. The light can penetrate the translucent membranes of the retina but is blocked by the black choroid coat. Chemical action is set up in the rods and cones and an impulse is transmitted first to the bi-polar cells and from them to the optic nerve cells in the front of the retina. This arrangement of " amplifiers " is necessary because of the small amount of energy released by the action of light on the rods and cones. The axons of the optic nerve cells run along the inner surface of the retina and pass out of the eye as the optic nerve. The impulse is carried along a somewhat intricate path to the back part (occipital) of the cerebral cortex and results in seeing.

The rods are less highly developed than the cones, and function only in twilight. The cones give us daylight vision, when the rods are inactive through a kind of chronic fatigue. Immediately behind the centre of the pupil (Fig. 16) there is a slight depression in the retina, known as the *fovea* or *yellow-spot*. It contains about 40,000 cones but no rods, and is the most sensitive part of the retina. Where the axons of the optic nerve cells collect to form the optic nerve there are neither rods nor

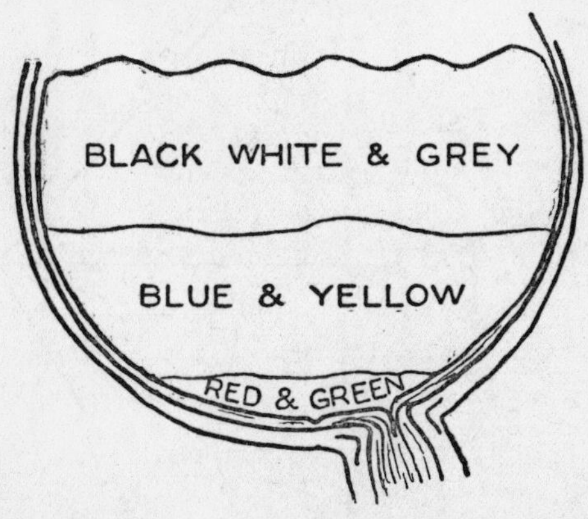

FIG. 18.—Colour distribution in the retina. The front portion is sensitive only to black, white, and grey; the back portion is sensitive to all colours—reds and greens, blues and yellows, as well as greys.

cones. This is the *blind-spot* of the retina. All other parts of the retina possess both rods and cones.

Different parts of the retina behave differently with respect to colours. The frontal and outer area of the retina is colour-blind for all persons. This constitutes an achromatic (non-coloured) area, blacks, whites, and greys only being distinguished (see Fig. 18). Behind this area is an irregular area which is sensitive to blues and yellows as well as to blacks, whites, and greys. At the back of the retina surrounding the yellow spot, is an area where reds and greens, as well as the yellows and blues, blacks, whites, and greys mentioned previously, can be seen. From this we deduce that all colours can be reduced to the four primaries, red and green, blue and yellow, with or without an admixture of grey. Since red and green, and blue and yellow, are complementary (a proper mixture of each pair giving grey) the colour octahedron shown in Fig. 19 may be conveniently used to illustrate the main facts of colour vision.

Total or partial colour-blindness of the red-green variety is present in about 4 per cent. of males and 0·4 per cent. of females. The preponderance of colour-blindness in the males, as we saw in Chapter I, is due to the fact that it is a sex-limited character, being transmitted through the female and inherited by the male.

The eyes of most civilized people are seriously over-worked.

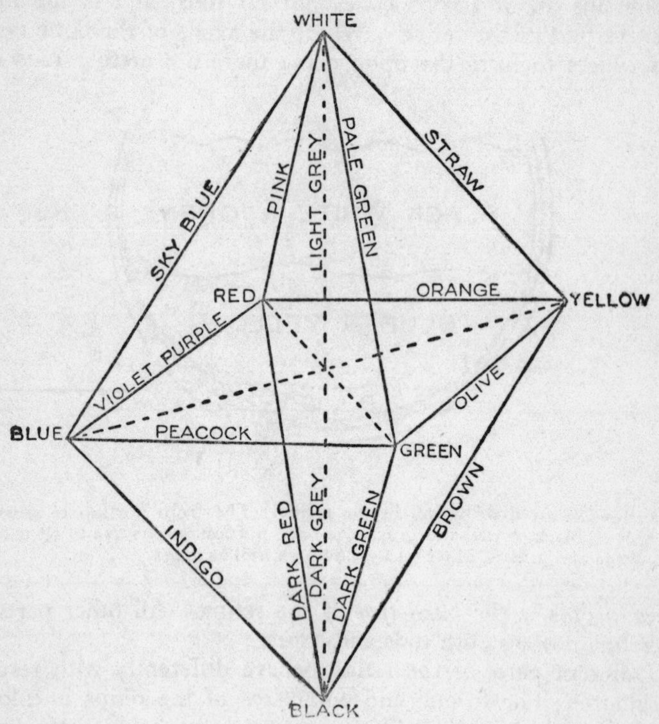

Fig. 19.—The colour octahedron.

Nature did not intend eyes to be focussed at short range upon printed books for six or more hours a day. Consequently *myopia*, or short sight, is very common among studious persons, being probably acquired in the majority of cases by the permanent set of the lens for near vision by the action of the ciliary muscle. Unlike colour-blindness it is a condition which can be remedied by the use of suitable spectacles.

Receptors for Sound.—The receptors for sound are the

auditory hair cells found in the cochlea, which forms a part of the inner ear. These cells are immersed in a fluid, which, when it vibrates, stimulates the hairs of the hair cells. The hair cells have attached to them the endings of auditory dendrons. When thus stimulated, they set up an action which results in the transmission of an impulse along the auditory nerve to the brain. Sound is then heard. Fig. 20 shows a section through one of the coils of the cochlea and an enlargement of the hair cells in the organ of *Corti*.

The stimulus for sound is a sound wave of the air—a longi-

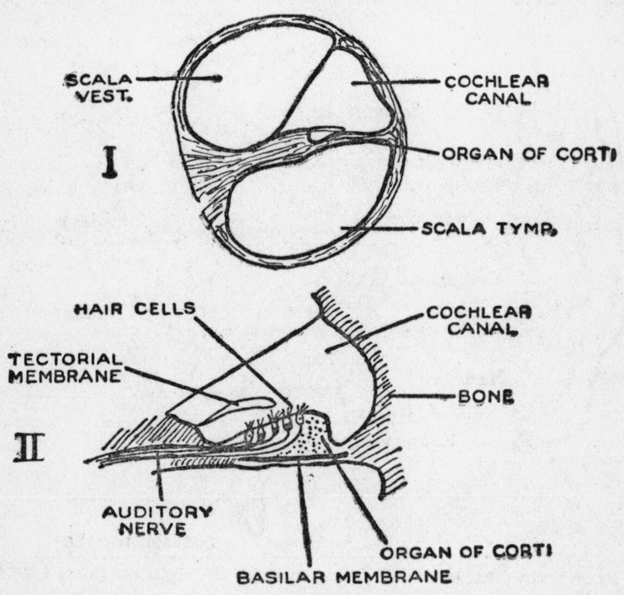

FIG. 20.—I. Cross-section of the cochlea. II. The hair cells of the Organ of Corti.

tudinal vibration of the air particles which travels at a uniform rate of about 1,100 feet per second, regardless of its frequency. The ear is an accessory sense-apparatus by means of which sound waves can be transmitted to the fluid in which the auditory hair cells are immersed. Just how this is accomplished is too complicated for discussion in an elementary text, but Fig. 21 gives some idea of the intricate nature of the mechanism. Suffice it to say that the sound waves of the air pass into the ear-hole (*meatus*) and set the ear-drum (*tympanum*), which closes its inner end, into vibration. These vibrations are carried across the hollow middle ear to the inner ear, containing the cochlea, by means of three minute bones (*ossicles*)—the hammer, anvil, and stirrup bones. The middle ear is connected to the pharynx by the *eustachian tube*, an arrangement which permits of the equalization of air pressure on both sides of the ear-drum. The foot of the stirrup bone is attached to a membrane (oval window) which closes a chamber containing a fluid. The vibrations of this fluid pass up one canal into which the cochlea is divided and down another to the round window, which lies in the wall of the middle ear but is closed by a thin membrane. During the transmission of these vibrations through the fluid of the cochlea from the oval to the round windows, the auditory hair

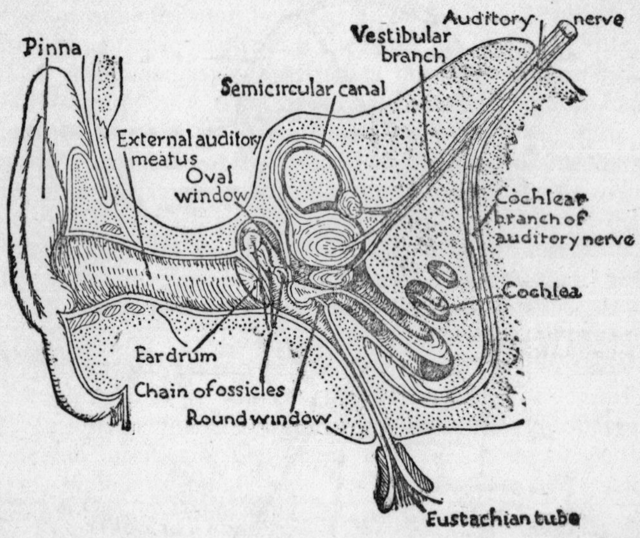

FIG. 21.—Semi-diagrammatic section through the right ear (after Czermak).

cells are stimulated and sound is heard. The whole mechanism is essentially an arrangement by means of which vibrations of the ear-drum are transmitted to the fluid of the cochlea in which the auditory hair cells are immersed.

Sound waves differ from one another in three ways—in frequency, which causes *pitch ;* in amplitude, or energy, which causes *loudness ;* and in the degree of mixture of different wave lengths, which gives colour or *timbre* to the tone.

The essential feature of a sound tone is its pitch. The lower limit of pitch is about 12 vibrations per second, but frequently 20–30 vibrations can be heard as pulsations rather than as a continuous tone. Indeed, electrical sparks below a frequency of 100 vibrations per second refuse to fuse into a tone. The upper limit of pitch lies probably between 25,000 to 30,000 vibrations per second, but the upper limit varies greatly among different persons. The upper limit decreases with age, being at 70 years about one-half of what it was at 16. Music uses the range of pitch lying between 32 and 4096 vibrations. The ability to discriminate pitch is a native physiological capacity, which is independent of intelligence and of training. Some people of perfectly normal hearing cannot distinguish differences in pitch amounting to a half-tone; others can distinguish pitch differences as small as 1/200 of a tone. Since pitch discrimination is fundamental in music only those pupils who can discriminate between pitches differing on the average by 1/30 of a tone or less should attempt a thorough musical education.

A pure tone without timbre is difficult to produce, and when produced sounds thin and colourless. Every sounding body—a piano string, violin string, organ pipe, the human voice—along with its fundamental wave gives off a series of shorter waves known as partials or *overtones*. This admixture of overtones gives the different timbres to the notes of the same pitch sounded by different instruments. Thus "C" on the piano sounds differently from "C" on a violin although both are stringed instruments. The richness of an orchestral piece largely depends on the timbre of tones produced by the different instruments of the orchestra.

A noise differs from a tone in the greater irregularity of its wave form. All noises have an element of tonality in them; and practically all tones contain an element of noise. The difference, therefore, between noises and tones is of degree not of kind. For example, in speaking, noise predominates; in singing, tone; but even in speaking some voices are more musical than others.

For a discussion of other complex features of sound, such as consonance and dissonance, beats and difference tones, time and rhythm, diatonic and chromatic scales, etc., the reader is referred to more advanced texts.[1]

Receptors for Equilibration.—The inner ear consists of the cochlea, the three *semicircular canals*, and a bulgy connection between the two called the *vestibule*. Only the cochlea is concerned with hearing; the vestibule and the semi-circular canals, especially at the enlargements of the canals known as *ampullæ*, contain hair cells immersed in a fluid which are insensitive to sound but sensitive to movements of the head,

[1] Seashore, *Psychology of Musical Talent*.
Myers, *Text-book of Experimental Psychology*.
Dunlap, *Elements of Scientific Psychology*.

either rotary or linear. These hair cells in the ampullæ and vestibule are, therefore, receptors for equilibration or balance. They are aided, of course, by tactile impressions from the skin, especially those from the soles of the feet, by visual impressions from the eye, and by kinæsthetic impressions from muscles and tendons, yet it can be confidently stated that the vestibular and ampullary hair cells are the chief receptors for the maintenance of bodily equilibrium. Movement of the head forces the fluid of the canals either towards or away from these receptors and the change in pressure arouses a nervous impulse, which, in part at least, is transmitted to the cerebellum, a part of the brain intimately associated with the control of muscles concerned with bodily posture.

Though the cochlea and the semicircular canals are independent organs, they have a common origin. In lowly aquatic animals both the cochlea and the canals are represented by a common sac which is sensitive either to water waves or to sound waves in water. At a later evolutionary stage, for example in the lamprey, the sac is found to be divided into two parts, one of which is concerned with hearing and the other with balance. The hearing part ultimately becomes the cochlea, while the part concerned with equilibration develops into the semicircular canals arranged in the three planes of space. The cochlea is stimulated by air movements (sound waves) outside the body; the semicircular canals by movements within the body. But unless the common origin of the two organs is realized, it is difficult to appreciate why the ear should perform two distinct functions—hearing and equilibration.

Receptors for Taste.—The receptors for taste are taste buds which are located in little pits opening upon the surface of the tongue. In the taste buds lie taste cells whose slender tips project into the pits of the tongue. Into the pits fall the solutions of food which stimulate chemically the hair-like projections of the taste cells. The impulse thus aroused is transmitted to the brain by the neurons of taste. Fig. 22 is a sketch of the sense organ of taste.

The stimulus for taste is a chemical in solution. Insoluble substances like glass or quartz are invariably tasteless. The receptors for taste are extremely sensitive. It is usually stated that 0·0005 gram of quinine dissolved in 100 c.c. of water can be detected on the root of the tongue, and sugar solution of a strength of 0·5 gram in 100 c.c. of water can be tasted on the tip of the tongue.

There are four elementary tastes—*sweet*, *sour*, *bitter*, and *salt*. Combined with these we have the cutaneous sensations of pressure, warmth, cold, and pain; the muscle sense which tells of the consistency of the food; and, above all, the odour of the food which stimulates the sense organ in the nose *via* the throat and the rear passage to the nose. These senses in combination give us the seemingly unlimited number of tastes. A simple experiment, however, will convince the reader that the only taste that coffee, tea, and quinine have is that of bitterness. If clear coffee, tea, and a solution of quinine are reduced to the same temperature and the same relative dilutions, and a subject, after being blindfolded and having his nostrils plugged with

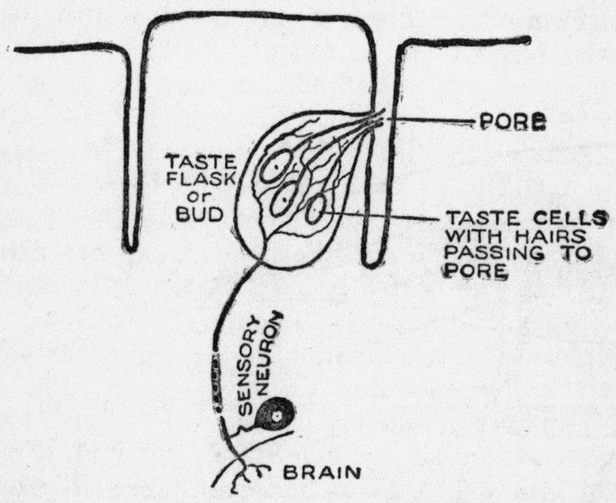

FIG. 22.—The sense organ of taste. A taste flask or bud lying in one of the circumvallate papillæ of the tongue is shown. The nerve endings twine around the taste cells whose hairs project into the crevice through the pore.

cotton wool, is given in succession a teaspoonful of each solution, he will be unable to name what he is drinking. Between experiments the mouth should be washed frequently with distilled water. They all taste alike—bitter, nothing but bitter, and the same kind of bitter. As coffee is usually taken, it is the temperature, the smoothness, and the odour that help to make up its characteristic taste. Similar experiments can be performed to show that sour wine and vinegar produce nothing but sour; that honey, syrup, glycerine, and molasses produce nothing but sweet; and that lemonade is a combination of sweet and sour. Further experiments of a like kind can be made to show that bitter is best tasted at the root of the tongue; sweet at the tip of the tongue; and salt and sour at intermediate areas.

The close connection between taste and smell becomes

evident when our noses are blocked by a cold. All foods then taste alike.

The biological function of taste is to act as a guardian to the digestive system. After foods have been judged by the eye and nose the tasting of them becomes the final court of appeal. Taste automatically controls the secretion of the salivary and, to some extent, of the gastric glands. Since eating is necessary to life, eating when hungry is a source of intense pleasure.

Receptors for Smell.—The receptors for smell are the olfactory cells imbedded in the lining of the mucous membrane in the upper and back part of the nasal cavity. Fig. 23 shows the general form of the organs of smell. Ordinarily the air we breathe passes below them, so to smell we make little eddies of

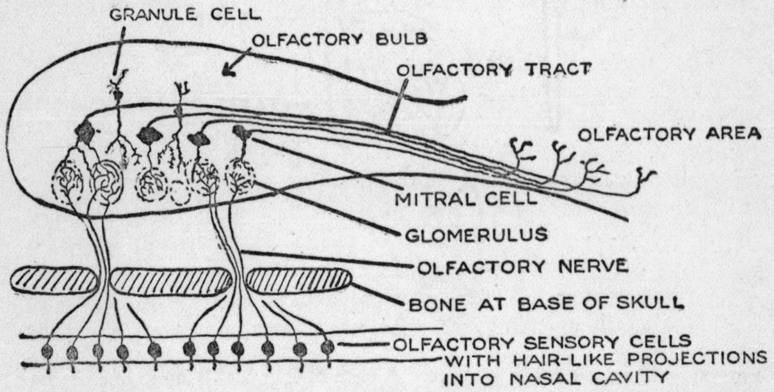

FIG. 23.—The sense organ of smell, showing the connections with the olfactory bulb and the olfactory area. Note that the cell body of the olfactory sensory cell is at the periphery.

air in the nose by sniffing. These air currents reach the olfactory cells and if laden with "smelly" substances in a gaseous form arouse a chemical action which is transmitted to the brain by the olfactory nerve, the shortest nerve of the body.

Henning [1] has attempted to determine the number of elementary odours by the method of fatigue. If, for example, ammonium sulphide, a substance with a very strong odour, be smelled for a minute or two, the receptors for that particular smell will become fatigued and the odour of the ammonium sulphide will be lost. If now a number of other odoriferous substances be tried on the fatigued nose, some, like oil of anise and oil of turpentine, can be recognized, while others, like

[1] Henning, *Der Geruch.* Leipsic, 1916.

sulphuretted hydrogen, bromine, and hydrochloric acid, cannot be smelled at all. The argument used is that one kind of receptor gives us the smells of ammonium sulphide, sulphuretted hydrogen, hydrochloric acid, and bromine. As a result of his experiments Henning concludes that there are six elementary odours, as follows :

1. Spicy—pepper, cloves, cinnamon, nutmeg.
2. Flowery—heliotrope, roses.
3. Fruity—apple, orange, vinegar.
4. Resinous—turpentine, pine needles.
5. Foul—decaying flesh, hydrogen sulphide.
6. Scorched—tarry substances, burnt foods.

However, much additional experimentation is required before Henning's classification can be finally accepted.

The sense of smell is extremely sensitive. Musk can be detected when present in the proportion of one part to 8,000,000 parts of air, and mercaptan if 1/460,000,000 of a milligram is present in 50 c.c. of air. The acuity of smell in dogs, rabbits, and other animals is beyond computation.

Like taste, the sense of smell has a biological value, helping in the selection and enjoyment of food. It creates an appetite and thus favours the flow of the digestive juices. To a considerable extent it informs us of substances that are injurious to eat. Generally speaking, decaying food has a bad odour and thus we are warned. However, odour is not an infallible guide as many cases of ptomaine poisoning prove. Many odoriferous gases are harmful when inhaled, but unfortunately carbon monoxide, a deadly poison, has no smell. One of the most fundamental biological functions of the sense of smell in animals is the attraction of sex.

The sense of smell has not much educational significance, except in such branches of study as chemistry and botany. Its æsthetic value, however, is very high, since it is associated with many emotional responses.

Receptors of the Skin.—Skin—the wonderful water-tight, air-tight, germ-tight, self-renewing covering of the body—contains a variety of receptors whose functions, unfortunately, are still imperfectly known. The following seem to be the accepted facts regarding them. First, careful sectioning of the skin and study under the microscope discloses not only a number of spring, spindle, and ball corpuscles (Pacini's, Meissner's, and Krause's) in which the sensory axons are carefully protected, but also free-branched nerve ends without any accessory apparatus, and sensory axons more or less free, which coil around the root of each hair. Fig. 24 shows their general form and arrangement. Second, if an area of skin is first shaved and then explored successively with a hair, a stiff bristle or fine needle, a blunt copper rod warmed to 45° C., and the same rod cooled to 5° C., points can be observed and marked which seem to indicate that there are four different kinds of receptors in the skin, namely, those for *pressure*, *pain*, *warmth*, and *cold*.

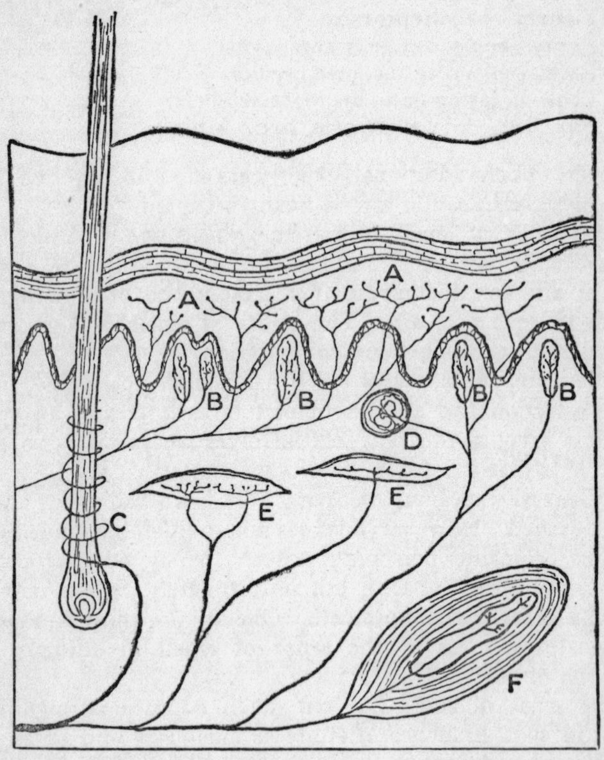

FIG. 24.—The cutaneous sense organs. A is a free nerve ending, the sense organ for pain. B is a Meissner corpuscle, the sense organ for light pressures. C is a nerve ending coiled around a hair, a sense organ for pressure aroused by movement of the hair. D is a Krause's corpuscle, probably a sense organ for cold. E is a Ruffini corpuscle, probably a sense organ for warmth. F is a Pacinian corpuscle, probably a sense organ for deep pressure or for warmth.

All other sense data from the skin, such as hard or soft, moist or dry, hot or cold, itching, tickling, pricking, stinging, and aching seem to be compound, being aroused by the stimulation of several kinds of receptors at the same time.

The receptors of the skin are distributed in irregular areas, perhaps in a punctiform fashion. Those for pressure are most numerous on the tip of the tongue, the tips of the fingers, the red part of the lips, and the tip of the nose ; least numerous in the middle of the back, the back of the neck, and along the breast bone. Receptors for pain are almost omnipresent in the body, being an ever-present warning against injuries of all kinds. Everywhere the receptor for pain is a free-nerve ending. The cornea of the eye is richly supplied with them. There is some dispute about the receptors for heat and cold, but the fact that the internal organs such as the stomach, intestines, and heart are devoid of thermal receptors as well as of those for pressure, seems to be well established.

Head and Rivers [1] seem to have definitely proven that the cutaneous nerves contain two systems of fibres giving rise to what they term *protopathic* and *epicritic* sensitivities. On severing the radial nerve, the area of the skin which it supplies became completely anæsthetic. Strong pressures and movements could still be felt, but only by means of receptors in the underlying muscles. As the nerve healed the sensitivity of the skin returned, but in two stages, first the protopathic, then the epicritic. The protopathic system functions for pressure, pain, and for widely separated degrees of temperature (above 45° C. and below 20° C.). Protopathic sensitivity is of a diffuse, low, and imperfectly localized kind. It is of vital importance to the life of the organism. The epicritic system of fibres, which regenerates more slowly than the protopathic, is sensitive to differences of moderate temperatures (between 26° C. and 37° C.) and of light pressures. Epicritic sensitivity is definitely and accurately localized. It probably evolved later than protopathic since it regenerates more slowly after the severance of a nerve. This contention is supported by the fact that the viscera and many other organs seem to be devoid of epicritic sensitivity. The confusion arising over the punctuate distribution of heat and cold spots in the skin seems to be due to a non-recognition of the two forms of thermal sensitivity—epicritic and protopathic. The recognition of these two systems does not mean that there are four kinds of receptors for temperature ; two suffice to explain all known phenomena. In other words, warmth and heat sensitivity always go hand in hand.

By means of certain drugs it is possible to abolish one or more skin sensitivities. Cocaine, for example, applied to the throat destroys pressure and pain, but not heat and cold

[1] Head and Rivers, "A Human Experiment in Nerve Division," *Brain*, 1908, XXXI, 323–460.
Myers, *Introduction to Experimental Psychology*, chap. i.

sensitivities. Certain injuries and diseases of peripheral nerves have been known to affect protopathic sensitivity alone or epicritic sensitivity alone. If the leg is made to " go to sleep " by pressing the nerve which supplies it, the sense of cold is almost altogether lost but that of heat remains. The cutaneous senses, therefore, are not quite so simple as they seem, and further experimentation is needed to elucidate some of the relationships existing among them.

Kinæsthetic Receptors.—The receptors which are stimulated by movements of parts of the body are found in tendons, muscles, and the joint capsules. They enable us to judge of the position of our limbs without the aid of our eyes. We " feel " when our arm is flexed or our fingers bent and we know to what extent our muscles are contracted. So accurate is this sense that we are able to lay our hands on objects in the dark, providing their position in space is known to us. Motor habits of all kinds involve the orderly working of a complex set of muscles, and this orderly working is dependent upon the proper functioning of the kinæsthetic receptors within the muscles concerned. For example, as I write the words of this chapter, a whole succession of kinæsthetic stimuli from the muscles of the hand makes for an orderliness of the successive movements. Without them the writing would be illegible and ill spelt. Practically everything connected with writing, as it were, has been turned over to the kinæsthetic system. The fact that we are but dimly conscious of the kinæsthetic sensations should not blind us to the fact of their importance.

Other Receptors.—The receptors of organic impulses are unknown and there is some doubt about the adequate stimuli for each. Being located internally, in the various organs and glands, they are difficult to study. But heart-beat, respiration, hunger, thirst, etc., are undoubtedly aroused by stimulation of organic receptors. A noted feature of the activities initiated by stimulation of organic receptors is their rhythmical character.

Development of Sensory Powers in Children.—Considering the importance of this problem in the field of educational psychology one finds that very little research has been done upon it. The problem is a difficult one since the functioning of the sense organ can only be inferred from the response of the muscle or gland which it stimulates. Consider, for example, the following problem : " What sensory powers in man are perfect at birth ? " To answer this question new-born babies must be observed carefully and as far as possible experimented upon. Observation shows that new-born babies can breathe, sneeze, cry, void urine, defæcate, turn their eyes towards a faint light, turn their heads, move arms and legs, feed from a nipple, grasp anything that touches the palm, etc. Experiment shows that a new-born baby does not react to a loud sound or to the cries of other babies in the nursery. Place a finger on the cheek near the mouth and the baby will attempt to work the finger into his mouth. Allow a baby to grasp a wooden rod with either hand and gradually raise the rod. Most babies under such circumstances can suspend themselves with either hand for a period of a minute. Wet the tongue of the new-born baby with glycerine or sugar solution and the mixture will be swallowed with evident enjoyment. Wet it with solutions of quinine, salt, or tartaric acid and movements of repulsion will appear. In water that is warm a baby rests content; in a bath too cool for him he cries. Turn a new-born baby towards a light and the pupils will be found to contract, and if the light is very bright the eyelids will close.

Shall we from these observations and experiments infer that the ear is imperfectly developed at birth or that the auditory nerve is non-functional? Nobody knows, although the best guess is that the middle ear is still filled with embryonic tissue which later disappears. The cutaneous senses seem to function well, for the baby reacts to light touches and to changes of temperature. The eyes are sensitive to light, although "seeing" in the adult sense of the term is clearly an impossibility. The sensory nerve endings in the sphincters of the bladder and anus must also be functional. The sense of taste is fairly well developed at birth and there are some who state that the sense of smell is sufficiently acute for the baby to distinguish between his mother's breast and that of the nurse. The latter, however, is doubtful.

As for the development of the sensory powers during infancy and early childhood we are at a similar loss for scientific evidence. When does a baby discriminate between colours? From the researches of Preyer, M. Baldwin, Myers, McDougall, Miss Tucker, and others we are led to the conclusion that brightness is perceived at about 5 or 6 months and that this is immediately followed by discrimination of reds and yellows from other colours. Baldwin and Stecher[1] devised two tests of colour discrimination for use with the children at the Iowa Child Welfare Research Station. One was the sorting of Holmgren worsteds and the other the sorting of cards. Neither test was wholly satisfactory, although children of two years made scores. The naming of colours is more difficult. In the Stanford-Binet

[1] Baldwin and Stecher, *Psychology of the Pre-School Child*, pp. 123–128.

test the naming of red, green, blue, and yellow is placed at the five-year-old level.

With regard to pitch discrimination Seashore [1] states:

> "The child may reach his finest use of the sense of pitch during the first year or two. Knowledge about pitch and ability to designate it of course comes later. The differences we find indicated for various ages in practical testing are fully accounted for by difference in knowledge of pitch and the power of attention in application to the task. There is no significant variation with sex, and perhaps no great variation with race."

The individual variations of sensory powers are great enough to prevent anything but general statements being made about them and their development. The fact that some children are born deaf, or blind, or without the sense of smell should make us cautious in the interpretation of results. Nor must it be forgotten that some deaf children have perfect ears, and some blind people perfect eyes. The trouble may not be with the sense organ, but with the brain or the connecting nerves.

References

BALDWIN and STECHER. *The Psychology of the Pre-School Child.* New York, Appleton, 1925. Pp. 305.

DARWIN, C. "Biographical Sketch of an Infant," *Mind*, vol. 2 (1877), pp. 285–294.

DEARBORN, G. VAN N. *Moto-Sensory Development.* Baltimore, Warwick & York, 1910. Pp. 215.

DUNLAP, K. *The Elements of Scientific Psychology.* St. Louis, Mosby, 1922. Pp. 368.

GESELL, A. *The Mental Growth of the Pre-School Child.* New York, Macmillan, 1925. Pp. x+447.

GRENFELL, W. T. *Yourself and Your Body.* New York, Scribners, 1924. Pp. xii+324.

HERRICK, C. J. *Neurological Foundations of Animal Behaviour.* New York, Holt, 1924. Pp. xii+334.

KIRKPATRICK, E. A. *Fundamentals of Child Study* (3rd ed.). New York, Macmillan, 1917. Pp. 403.

LADD, G. T., and WOODWORTH, R. S. *Elements of Physiological Psychology.* New York, Scribners, 1911. Pp. xix+704.

McDOUGALL, W. "An Investigation of the Colour Sense of Two Infants." *Brit. Jour. Psy.*, II, 1908, pp. 338 ff.

MYERS, C. S. *An Introduction to Experimental Psychology.* Cambridge University Press, 1911. Pp. vi+156.

MYERS, C. S. *A Text-book of Experimental Psychology* (2nd ed.), Part I. Cambridge University Press, 1911. Pp. xiv+344.

NORSWORTHY, N., and WHITLEY, M. T. *The Psychology of Childhood.* New York, Macmillan, 1918. Pp. xix+375.

[1] Seashore, *Introduction to Psychology*, p. 59.

PREYER, W. *Mental Development in the Child.* New York, Appleton, 1893. Pp. xxvi+170.

RIVERS, W. H. R., and HEAD, H. "A Human Experiment in Nerve Division," *Brain*, XXXI (1908), pp. 323–450.

SEASHORE, C. E. *Introduction to Psychology.* New York, Macmillan, 1923 Pp. xviii+427.

SHINN, M. W. *The Development of the Senses in the First Three Years of Life.* Univ. of California Publications in Education, Berkeley, Univ. of California, 1907. Pp. 258.

TERMAN, L. M. *The Measurement of Intelligence.* Boston, Houghton Mifflin, 1916. Pp. 362.

WADDLE, C. W. *An Introduction to Child Psychology.* Boston, Houghton Mifflin, 1918. Pp. xv+307.

WOODWORTH, R. S. *Psychology: A Study of Mental Life.* New York, Holt, 1921. Pp. x+580.

CHAPTER V

HOW THE HUMAN BODY WORKS

C. Organs of Connection: The Nervous System

Origin of the Nervous System.—In our study of organisms (Chapter II) we traced their behaviour to the protoplasmic substances of which they were composed. The protoplasms of even the simplest organisms were found to possess the fundamental properties of (1) *irritability* or *excitability*, the property of being stirred to activity by an external stimulus; (2) *conductivity*, the power of transmitting the excitation from one part of the organism to another; and (3) *integration*, the power of developing a unified control of bodily activities. In unicellular animals these three powers can only be exercised in the simplest degree. It is in multicellular animals, with man as the highest form, that we find these properties developed to the highest extent. And this development is intimately associated with the evolution of a specialized form of tissue—the nerve tissue of multicellular organisms. The main outlines of the evolution of the nervous system will now be briefly sketched.

The physiological gradient from the surface to the interior of the amœba was previously noted. Except for this difference of physiological potential, practically every part of the amœba is equal to every other part; no part is superior to any other, since all can digest, breathe, and perform other vital functions. There is nothing at all which resembles a nervous system. In some unicellular internal parasites we find what may be described as the beginnings of a nervous system. There is a separation of protoplasmic material into neuromotor and retractor strands, that is, into nervous and muscular elements. The next upward step in evolution is seen when colonies of unicellular animals collect together, as it were, for mutual protection. There is, however, no protoplasmic connection between them, each animal being as distinct as the separate fishes in a school of minnows. Somewhat higher in the scale are colonies of cells (Gonium and

Volvox are excellent examples) in which the colony behaves as a complex but unitary organism. The cells on the outside develop motor apparatuses (flagella) and specialized sensitivities to stimuli. By protoplasmic connection with each other, the colony behaves somewhat as a multicellular organism would do. The step between such a unitary colony and a true multicellular organism, in which there is true differentiation of parts and of function within one organism, is but a small one. In the cœlenterates, of which the hydra may be taken as the simplest representative, we find sensory cells, muscle cells, and nerve cells completely differentiated. All animals above the hydra show the same kind of differentiation but in more complex fashion. In the medusa or jelly fish (also a cœlenterate) the nerve material exists in the form of an elaborate network. Nervous impulses can pass around the net indiscriminately in either direction. A nerve net has its neurons fused together; it is non-synaptic. In the earthworm and other annelids we find the first synaptic or corded system. Each neuron is separated from its neighbour, the nervous impulse passing from one cell to another across a *synapse* (literally a clasping, but structurally a gap) and in one direction only. The earthworm and flatworms have two ventral cords with connections between the ganglia arranged somewhat in the form of a ladder. In the ladder type of nervous system, the head ganglia are larger than the others and dominate them. This dominance of the head is never lost, resulting ultimately in a true brain. The ladder type persists in all the arthropods — crustaceans, spiders, and insects (see Fig. 25).

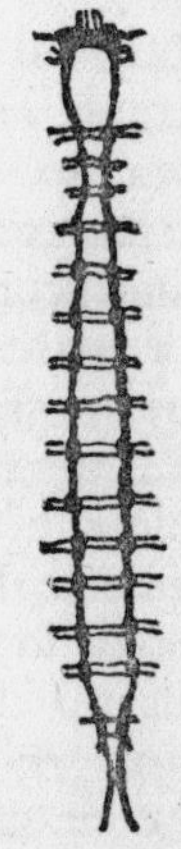

Fig. 25. — The ladder type of nervous system (after Hilton).

As the animal becomes more complex and multiplies its nerve cells, the two unprotected ventral cords become inadequate. In the vertebrates a single cord, protected first by a notochord and later by a backbone, is found. How the transition from a double ventral cord to a single dorsal cord is made, science cannot as yet say. It may be that the spinal cord grows out of the supra-œsophageal ganglion and that the ventral cords become atrophied and finally disappear altogether. This stage of evolution is reached in the vertebrates, which, in ascending order of complexity, are *fishes*, *amphibians*, *reptiles*, *birds*, and *mammals*. It is obviously impossible to follow all the details in the later evolution of the nervous system. Suffice it to say that there is exhibited an increased ascendancy of the brain over the rest of the nervous system. In the animals with skulls (craniata) the brain and the spinal cord are distinctly separated, although, in effect, the whole nervous system is still a hollow tube (spinal cord) with a balloon-like enlargement at the upper end (brain). Owing to the exigencies of space the brain has to be folded and neatly tucked away in order to accommodate itself to its bony case. Secondly, the cell-bodies of sensory cells, which in the cases of the hydra, worm, etc., are at the surface, retreat within the bony covering of the spinal cord, and are connected with the periphery by long fibres. Exceptions to this generalization are the olfactory nerve cells, which still retain their primitive form, with the cell-bodies lying at the surface. Thirdly, besides a large increase in the actual number of nerve cells, there is a still larger increase in the number of their potential connections. It is this feature which lies at the basis of the educability of the higher animals and especially of man himself. Fourthly, as the nervous system evolves, so, correspondingly, do the sensory receptors and the muscular and glandular effectors. The whole animal, as it were, becomes complex together. But there is reason to suppose that a contractile tissue not unlike the smooth muscles of man's visceral organs shows some priority in evolution. The next in order is the sensory cell, derived from the epithelium in the neighbourhood of an effector, whose function is to receive stimuli and to transmit them to the underlying muscle. This stage is reached in sea-anemones. Such a combination of nerve cell and muscle speeds up the reaction; the nerve cell behaves like a percussion cap which sets off the charge of powder in the muscle cells. The connecting cells of the nervous system, first found in such animals as the hydra and jelly-fish, evolve from sensory cells. This conduction system enables a stimulus to be transmitted from one part of the animal to muscle cells in other and distant parts. The whole system thus evolves as a co-ordinated whole

The function of the nervous system, even in man himself, must not be conceived as that of an intelligence bureau gathering information for a sovereign mind enthroned within a brain. The nervous system is nothing more nor less than an apparatus designed to receive stimulations from the various energies of the external world and to transmit them to muscles and glands which make such adjustments as are necessary for the maintenance of the fullest possible amount of life within the organism.

The Neuron.—The neuron or nerve cell is the structural unit of the nervous system. It is estimated that there are ten billions of them in man's nervous system. So small are they that a brain would have to be enlarged to the size of the world's biggest cathedral to make them visible to the naked eye, and it would take several life-times to trace the inter-connections among them.

Neurons vary in shape, size, and complexity, depending chiefly on the space relations of the parts they connect. The typical neuron has three parts—a central *cell-body* which contains the nucleus, and two fibre-like processes which grow out from the cell-body during development. The first of these processes is a relatively smooth, long, unbranched process called the *axon;* the second, termed a *dendron* or *dendrite*, is usually much shorter

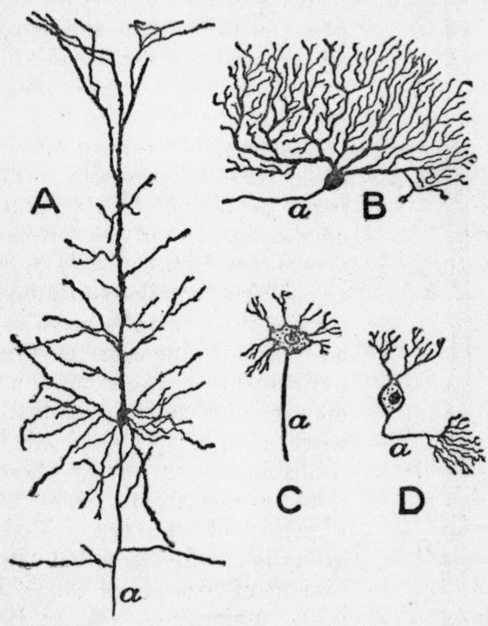

Fig. 26.—Typical forms of neurons. A is a pyramidal cell from the cortex. B is a neuron from the cerebellum. C is a motor neuron from the spinal cord. D is a connecting neuron. The axon in each case is marked "*a*."

and more branched than the axon, resembling the boughs and twigs of an oak tree. As a matter of fact each nerve cell has usually more than one dendron. There are frequently twenty of them, and some neurons are known to have hundreds. Fig. 26 shows a few typical neurons.

Every neuron has necessarily a cell-body and an axon, but not necessarily a dendron. The dendrons, as we have just noted, are very numerous. The axons and dendrons give the neuron a straggly appearance. Although its lack of compactness makes the neuron unique among the cells of the body, nevertheless it is a true genetic unit, since the cell-body and all the processes develop from a single embryonic cell. A neuron, therefore, is a nerve cell with all its processes.

The cell-body, which is the part of the neuron most closely resembling the other cells of the body, is bounded by a cell wall and contains a globular nucleus surrounded by cytoplasm. This cytoplasm contains flaky, stainable masses known as *Nissl granules*. Nissl granules are also found in the dendrons, but never in the axons. Running through the cytoplasm of the nucleus and extending along all the processes are hairlike fibres known as *neurofibrils*. There is reason for believing that the neurofibrils are the actual conductors of the nervous impulse. The axons are usually sheathed with two coverings—the *sheath of Schwann* (*neurilemma*) on the outside and the fatty *medullary* or *myelin sheath* immediately below. As the axons are bundled together to form nerves, these sheaths serve as insulators and help the neurons to preserve their individuality. The axons of a main nerve may thus be compared with the separate wires of a trunk telephone line. It is probable that the myelin sheath, in addition to insulation, assists also in the nutrition of the cell. Medullation of axons is closely associated with the functioning of neurons of which they form a part. Axons may, however, be connected with other axons by means of fine fibres known as *collaterals*. Collaterals are most numerous in the central nervous system and especially in the brain. At fairly regular intervals the myelin sheath of axons is restricted to form the *nodes of Ranvier*. Fig. 27 shows the nodes of Ranvier. Sectioning of an axon causes complete degeneration (Wallerian degeneration) of the fibre on the side remote from the cell-body, this degeneration extending towards the cell-body as far as the next node of Ranvier from where the sectioning took place. Partial degeneration of the part of the neuron containing the nucleus generally takes place. The Nissl bodies undergo solution (*chromatolysis*), the cell swells and its nucleus becomes displaced to the periphery,

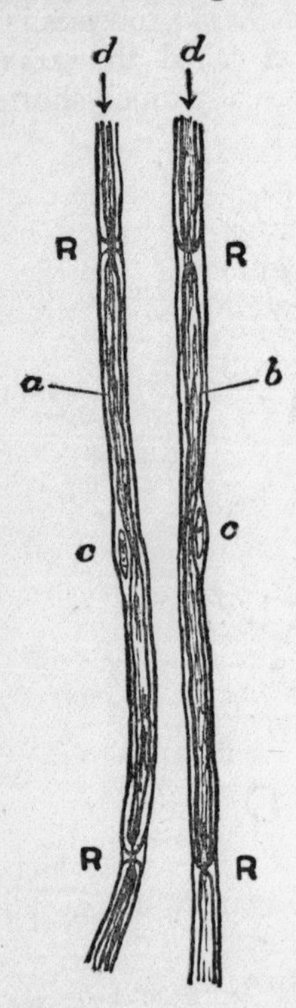

FIG. 27.—Portions of two nerve-fibres, showing nodes of Ranvier (R), nuclei (*c*), neurilemma (*a*), medullary sheath (*b*), and axis-cylinder (*d*).

and there are other changes. These changes are temporary, providing the injury has not been so profound as to cause the death of the whole neuron. In regeneration, which is very slow and may take more than a year, the renewed axon takes the path of the old one and ultimately ends in the same muscle fibre or sense organ as the original axon ended in.

A neuron exhibits a physiological gradient, that is, nerve impulses are received at one end of it and discharged at the other. The process conducting the impulse towards the cell-body is the dendron ; the process conducting away from the cell-body is the axon. In other words, dendrites are always receivers of impulses, axons dischargers of impulses. If this is borne in mind the confusion which has arisen through the use of the term "axon" for the longest process of the cell-body will be eliminated. Further, it should be noted that sensory neurons have only one dendron,

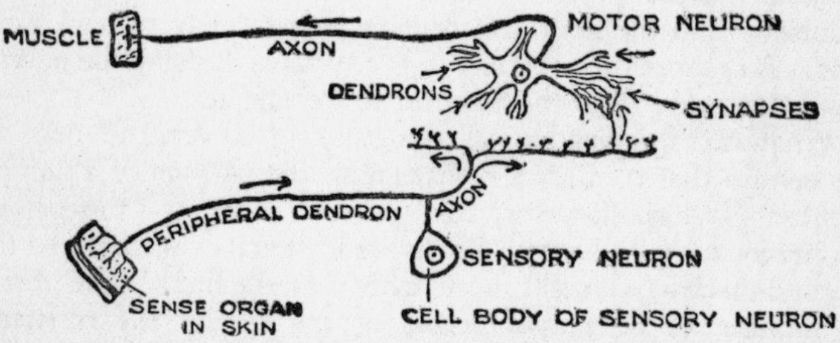

FIG. 28.—Path of conduction from a sense organ to a muscle. Arrows show the direction of conduction (after Ranson).

a peripheral one, which ends in a sense organ. Fig. 28, which shows the path of conduction from a sense organ to a muscle, should make the matter clear.

According to function, neurons may be classified as *sensory*, *motor*, or *connecting* neurons. Sensory neurons are connected with sense organs at the periphery and conduct the impulse towards the central nervous system. Their cell-bodies lie just outside the central nervous system, forming the dorsal root ganglia of the spinal nerves. Motor neurons are connected with muscles or glands and always conduct away from the central nervous system. Their cell-bodies lie within the central nervous system, those in the spinal cord forming the ventral horn of the grey matter. Connecting neurons lie wholly within the central nervous system. Their function is solely to connect one part of the nervous system with another and mainly to bridge gaps between sensory and motor neurons.

The Synapse.—In the lower animals a single nerve cell can transmit a stimulus to an underlying muscle. But in all animals with cords the transmission of a nerve impulse from a receptor to an effector requires at least two neurons, the impulse passing from one to the other along a neuron chain. The place where the two neurons come into functional relationship is called a *synapse*. At a synapse two neurons come into intimate contact, although it is very doubtful if there is a physical connection of neural matter between them. If a neuron dies, the degeneracy never crosses the synapse to affect its neighbour. A synapse, therefore, is not to be regarded as a thing, but a place where the end-brushes of axons and the ramifications of dendrons are in close proximity. There is, however, a membranous barrier between them. This membrane is probably permeable to ions dissociated during the excitation-conduction process. As the ions can pass in one direction only, the nervous discharge can pass in one direction only across a synapse (from the axon to the dendron), although the impulse within the neuron processes passes freely in both directions. A synapse thus acts as a one-way valve, causing the nervous impulse to move from the receptor to the effector.

Whatever the anatomical structure of a synapse may be, it is certain that it offers a resistance to the passage of a nervous impulse. It has, however, this peculiar property—the passage of a nervous impulse across a synapse lowers its resistance so that a second discharge crosses more easily than the first. The greater the number of discharges across it, the feebler the resistance becomes. A preferred path for the discharge is thus formed. This property of the synapse lies at the basis of habit formation and learning. If a connection between receptors and effectors is not established by the inner growth of the nervous system, it may be established, within limits, by education and training. The oftener a path is taken by the impulse, the firmer the habit is established, so that ultimately a learned habit may come to resemble an unlearned reflex. So far as neurology is concerned, learning is the establishment of preferred paths by the gradual breaking down of the resistances offered at synapses. If the path is not used over a period of time the resistance at the synapse is restored. In other words, what was once known becomes forgotten. An intelligent person, as we shall see later, is one whose individually acquired nervous patterns are both numerous and varied.

Certain drugs and the toxic products of fatigue change the resistances at synapses. Muscular fatigue invariably increases the resistance. Some drugs like ether, alcohol, chloroform, nicotine, and morphine also increase the synaptic resistances. This is the reason why a surgical operation performed while the patient is under the influence of an anæsthetic is never felt by him. Other drugs, such as strychnine and caffeine (the latter found in tea and coffee), decrease the resistance at synapses. The stimulating effect of a cup of tea is mainly due to the influence of caffeine on the synaptic resistances.

Laws of Neuron Action.[1]—From what has been said the following laws of neuron action should be almost self-explanatory:

1. *The Law of Expression.*—Every stimulus of a sensory neuron must have some result; it cannot come to nothing. This does not necessarily mean that the result is visible in some movement or glandular secretion. The result may be a hidden modification of the nervous system, or may be an inhibition of movement or secretion.

2. *The Law of Least Resistance.*—This may also be called the law of preferred paths. When any neuron is stimulated it will conduct along the line of least resistance, that is, along the line of strongest connection. Habitual use of a neuron tract so alters the synaptic connections along its course that it becomes the preferred path for the nervous impulse. It then becomes difficult to act in any but the habitual manner when the sensory ending of the tract is stimulated.

3. *The Law of Inborn Connections.*—Any neuron group discharges into the neuron group with which it is by the inner growth of the nervous system most closely connected. As we have seen, sense organs for the most part are naturally connected, *viâ* the central nervous system, with muscles or glands in the same general neighbourhood. Thus we move the hand when it is pricked or tickled in preference to the other parts of the body. If, however, the stimulus is an intense one, it may spread to other parts of the body, to the legs and the larynx, for example, because these are in secondary connection with the sense organs of the hand.

4. *The Law of Acquired Connections.*—When any neuron group is stimulated the nervous impulse will be transmitted to the neuron group with which it has been most nearly connected; which has been aroused by it most recently, most frequently, most energetically, for the longest time, and with the most satisfaction to the individual. This is the law of associative learning. Later we shall see how this law may again be subdivided into the various laws of learning.

The Reflex Arc.—If the neuron be regarded as the structural unit, the *reflex-arc* or *sensori-motor arc* may be said to constitute

[1] Thorndike called them Laws of Brain Action.

the functional unit of the nervous system. The transmission of a nerve impulse from a receptor to an effector requires a chain of at least two neurons, the impulse passing from one neuron to another across a synapse. The simplest functional unit that can be imagined is the arc consisting of a sensory and a motor neuron. Although such short reflex arcs are not unknown in the body, far more frequently a central connecting neuron (or a chain consisting of several of them) is interposed between the sensory and motor neurons, being connected with each through synapses.

In order to make the matter definite we shall try to see how a prick of the hand causes a reflex contraction of it. Fig. 29 will be of assistance. The prick stimulates a receptor or sense organ of pain situated in the skin. This receptor is the modified peri-

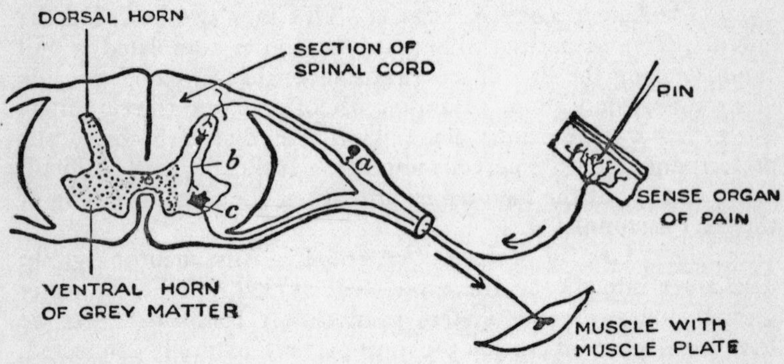

FIG. 29.—Simple reflex arc of three neurons—sensory neuron (*a*), connecting neuron (*b*), motor neuron (*c*). The stimulus from the prick of the pin passes through the spinal cord and causes the muscle to react.

pheral end of the dendron of a sensory cell. The impulse so generated passes along the peripheral branch of the sensory neuron, past (or through) the cell-body of the sensory neuron which lies just outside the spinal cord, and enters the spinal cord to reach the grey matter of the dorsal horn. Here the end brush of the sensory axon comes into close contact with the branching dendron of a connecting neuron. The impulse jumps the synapse, passes through the cell-body and passes out by the axon. The end brush of this axon in turn is in contact with a dendron of a motor neuron. Once more the synaptic gap is jumped. The impulse passes along the dendron, through the cell-body of the motor neuron, and out by a long axon which emerges from the spinal cord at the ventral surface. This axon forms part of the same nerve as the incoming peripheral dendron. The impulse passes down the axon until it reaches the muscle cell with which the axon is connected by means of a muscle plate. The muscle is stimulated and a movement of the arm is made. The whole operation is completed even before a cry of pain can be made. It is therefore called a *spinal reflex*, comparison being made in the name to the quickness of the reflection of light.

There are hundreds of thousands of these comparatively short reflexes in the body. The sense organs of the skin are connected with the spinal cord and muscles in short reflex arcs. The eye-blink, iris movements, movements for balancing the body, swallowing, knee jerk, fanning of the toes, sneezing, and a host of other responses to stimuli, mostly to those of a dangerous character, are made through the instrumentality of short arcs.

Actually, however, our description has over-simplified the matter. For example, the branchings of the sensory axon at the end brush in the spinal cord are in contact with a host of connecting neurons, and these in turn with hundreds of motor neurons. It is by reason of these connections that a deep pin-prick can cause a jumping movement of the legs and a cry of " ouch ! " from the throat. Further, in the retraction of the hand the biceps muscle contracted, the triceps stretched. The muscles of the shoulder are similarly affected, one of each pair contracting, the other extending. There must, therefore, be somewhat elaborate connections in the neurons of the spinal cord to make even this simple movement possible. In technical terms we have produced a co-ordinated movement of muscles from a simple stimulus. Such co-ordination is possible only through the action of a *central* nervous system.

The basis of all reactions is the sensori-motor arc. The elaborations are due to extensions of the simple reflex arcs in the form of a series of additional loops. In theory, every sensory ending can be connected with every muscle cell or gland cell through additional loops of the central nervous system, just as every subscriber to a telephone system can be connected with every other subscriber through the additional loops at the central telephone exchange.

Arcs of the central nervous system are thus seen to be of varying degrees of complexity. The simplest never reach beyond the spinal cord level. They are known as arcs of the *first*, or *spinal*, or *reflex level.* They are mostly concerned with the making of quick responses to dangerous stimuli. They may be compared with local telephone calls. Other arcs are longer and more involved. Those reaching the part of the brain lying between the upper part of the spinal cord (medulla) and the cortex (grey matter of the brain) are called arcs of the *secondary* or *sensory level.* The contraction of the pupil to the stimulation of light thrown into the eye is an example. They may be likened to fairly near long-distance telephone calls. Arcs completed in the cortex of the brain, those involved in thinking and judging—the so-called higher thought processes—are known as arcs of the *third level.* They may be compared with the distant long-distance telephone calls.

The pathway for a nervous impulse resulting in a reflex movement is more or less fixed. Most of them can become conditioned, as, for example, when the sphincter reflex of the bladder in childhood has its pathway extended to the cortex in early childhood; but a few of them, like the knee-jerk (patellar reflex) and the iris reflex (pupillary), remain unchanged throughout life. The synaptic connections of reflexes, and, of course, of physiological actions, are formed before birth, follow an hereditary pattern, and are practically the same for everybody. Primitive man and his animal forebears had the same reflexes as we have to-day. These pathways or tracts in the nervous system are perfect in their action at birth. Other pathways, like those for crawling, standing, and walking, are perfected a little later. But it is very probable that in certain parts of the nervous mechanism new connections can always be established by suitable training. Men in later middle life frequently learn to play a good game of golf. The adult reader who meets the facts of this section for the first time has to make a large number of synaptic connections, chiefly between the neurons concerned with vision and the motor neurons which stimulate the action of the muscles of the larynx, the tongue, and perhaps the lips.

The Nature of Nervous Impulse.—The ancients thought the nerves were hollow tubes filled with animal spirits which flowed through the nerves and conducted the impulse. Whatever the nature of conduction it is certainly not due to the movement of any fluid or juice. Whether the conduction is due to chemical action or to electrical action or to a combination of the two, is not definitely known. The weight of evidence shows it to be due to a series of rapid chemical decompositions essentially electrical in nature (a wave of negativity), since conduction is invariably accompanied by chemical action and electrical phenomena.

That it is not solely an electrical conduction is shown by the velocity of the nervous impulse. Whereas electrical conduction travels at the speed of light, 186,000 miles per second, the speed of conduction in the larger nerves of man is about 120 metres per second. Further, oxygen is necessary for conduction, since the nerve fails to conduct if the oxygen supply be cut off. If a nerve is ligatured with a moist thread it fails to conduct; this treatment, however, does not hinder an electric current.

Nerves are difficult to fatigue. Either they are non-fatiguable or they have the power of very rapid recovery. It is probable that the latter statement represents the facts more correctly.

Subdivisions of the Nervous System.—Having studied the microscopic units of the nervous system and the ways in which they are connected, it now remains to name the various parts of the nervous system as they present themselves to the naked eye. Many classifications of parts could be made, but the following table is perhaps as logical as any:

1. *The Central Nervous System.*

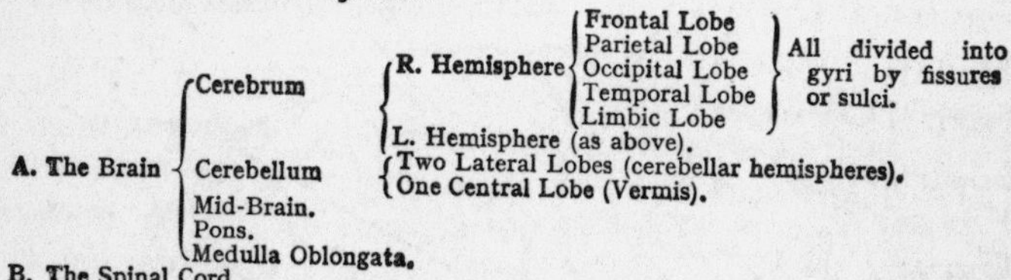

- A. The Brain
  - Cerebrum
    - R. Hemisphere
      - Frontal Lobe
      - Parietal Lobe
      - Occipital Lobe
      - Temporal Lobe
      - Limbic Lobe
      - (All divided into gyri by fissures or sulci.)
    - L. Hemisphere (as above).
  - Cerebellum
    - Two Lateral Lobes (cerebellar hemispheres).
    - One Central Lobe (Vermis).
  - Mid-Brain.
  - Pons.
  - Medulla Oblongata.
- B. The Spinal Cord.

2. *The Peripheral Nervous System.*

- A. Cerebrospinal nerves
  - 12 Cranial Nerves.
  - 31 Spinal Nerves.
- B. The Autonomic Nervous System
  - Two Gangliated cords or trunks.
  - Plexuses.
  - Nerves.

The *brain* consists of those parts of the central nervous system (the *cerebrum*, *cerebellum*, *mid-brain*, *pons*, and *medulla oblongata*) which are contained within the bony cavity of the skull. Continuous with it, and protected by the vertebræ of the spinal column, is the spinal cord. Both brain and cord are surrounded by three membranes. These are the delicate *pia mater* immediately surrounding them; the *arachnoid membrane* which has the tenuity of a spider's web; and the thick fibrous *dura mater* which lines the bony cavity. Between the arachnoid membrane and the pia mater is a space filled with cerebro-spinal fluid. The dura mater remains attached to the skull when the brain is removed from it.

The most conspicuous parts of the brain are the *cerebrum* and *cerebellum*. The former is divided into two hemispheres (right and left) by a deep median fissure. Since all fibres conducting impulses to and from the lower parts of the nervous system cross, mostly at the upper part of the spinal cord, it follows that the left hemisphere controls the right side of the body and *vice versâ*. Each hemisphere is convoluted, the various convolutions being separated by *fissures*. The major divisions of the hemispheres are *lobes*, the minor ones *gyri* (see Fig. 30). The fissures and convolutions, though varying slightly in different brains, are sufficiently constant to be named and classified. The most noted fissures are the *central fissure* (fissure of Rolando), which separates the frontal from the parietal lobe, and the fissure of *Sylvius*, which separates the *temporal* lobe from the frontal and the parietal lobes. The gyri, into which each lobe is divided, are named according to the positions they occupy.

A section of the cerebrum down the centre shows that the right and left hemispheres are united latitudinally by a thick

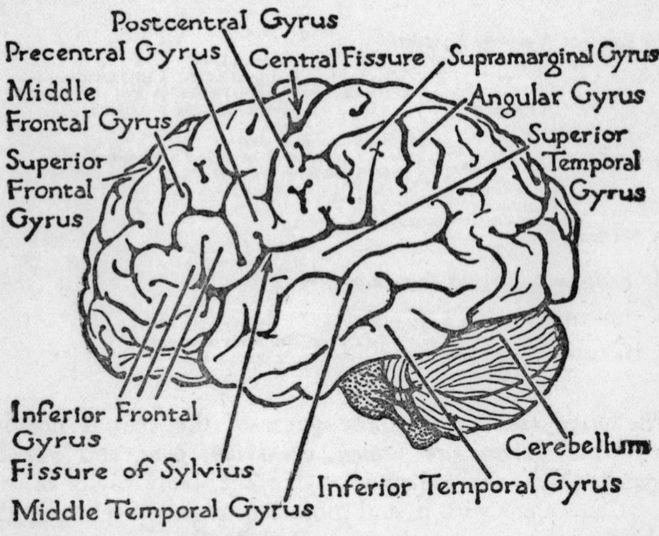

FIG. 30.—View of left side of brain showing cerebrum and cerebellum.

band of fibres called the *corpus callosum*. Thus the right side of the brain, as it were, knows what the left side is doing. A section through a cerebral hemisphere shows that it is composed of two layers—an outer grey layer from $\frac{1}{8}$ to $\frac{1}{4}$ inch thick, known as the *cortex*, and an inner white mass composed of medullated nerve fibres. The cortex, as we have seen, is concerned with the highest forms of man's behaviour. The fibres of the cerebrum are grouped mainly into three systems: (1) the *Projection System*, which connects the cortex to the lower parts of the nervous system, and especially to the spinal cord; (2) the *Association System*, which connects the various lobes and gyri, both near and remote, one with another; and (3) the *Commissural System*, which connects the right and left hemispheres through the corpus callosum. Fig. 31 shows two of the fibre systems.

The *cerebellum* lies behind and beneath the cerebrum. Its chief function is to maintain the equilibrium of the body, and probably also to maintain the steadiness and general efficiency of muscular contractions. The *mid-brain* contains fibre tracts connecting the cerebrum with lower parts of the nervous system and also has groups of nerve cells (nuclei) important from the point of view of eye-movements and of the tone of voluntary muscle throughout the body. Of the *pons* nothing need be said

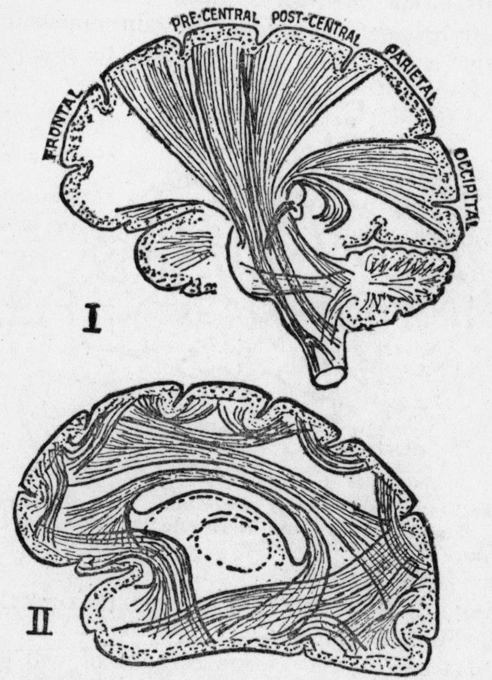

FIG. 31.—The fibre systems of the brain. I. The projection system of fibres. II. The association system of fibres (after Starr).

except that it forms an important part of the conduction path which unites the cerebrum to the cerebellum. The *medulla oblongata*, which structurally is the upper part of the spinal cord, contains nerve cells and fibre tracts associated with certain of the cranial nerves. These include the central mechanisms which control the reflex activities of the tongue, pharynx, larynx, and, in part, those of the thoracic and abdominal viscera also. All nerve tracts uniting the spinal cord with the higher nerve centres pass through the medulla.

The *spinal cord*, which occupies the canal running through

the centre of the vertebrae, like the cerebrum, is made up of grey and white tissue. Unlike the cerebrum, where the grey matter is found outside, the spinal cord has its grey matter inside, roughly shaped in section like the letter H. The grey matter is largely composed of the cell-bodies of central and motor neurons ; the white matter consists of fibre-tracts connecting upper and lower parts of the cord to each other and to the brain above. Branching from each side of the spinal cord are 31 spinal nerves, running to every part of the periphery. Each nerve has both sensory and motor fibres, the former bringing in impulses from the receptors, the latter taking out impulses to muscles. Func-

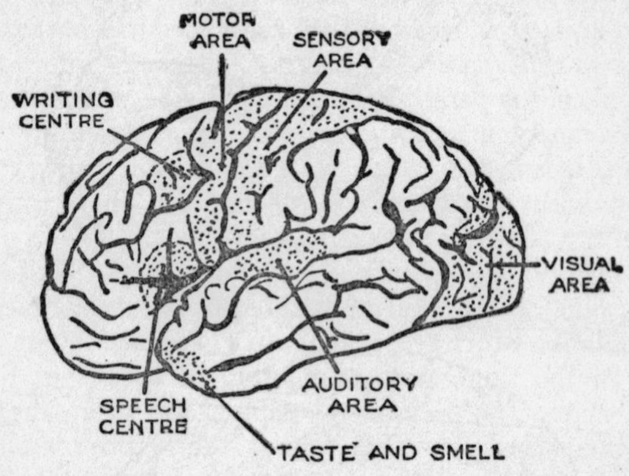

FIG. 32.—Localization areas of the cerebrum. View of left cerebral hemisphere. The unshaded parts constitute the so-called association or silent areas.

tionally, the cord, as we have seen, serves as the central connecting link in reflex muscular movements.

The *autonomic nervous system* consists of two ganglionated cords or trunks which parallel the spinal cord on either side. It is connected on the one hand to the spinal cord, and on the other to the glands and smooth muscles (viscera) of the body. The autonomic system, through its control of the blood supply to the various parts of the body and its connections with the vital organs, is closely concerned with the expression of the emotions (Chapter VII).

Localization of Functions.—From what has been said regarding the finer and gross structure of the nervous system, the reader will not be surprised to learn that the central nervous system does not function as a whole, but by parts. Especially is this true of the cortex of the brain. Part of it is specialized to control movements of muscles, part of it is concerned with seeing, another part with motor speech, another with hearing, another with reception of stimuli from the periphery, and so forth. These so-called areas have been mapped out from evidence obtained from injuries, from extirpation of parts, from electrical stimulation of the cortex, from experimentation with anthropoid apes, from comparative anatomy, and from actually tracing the fibre tracts.

The first area to be mapped was the *motor area* (see Fig. 32) which lies in the pre-central gyrus, that is, alongside and in front of the central fissure. The upper parts of this area control, through the lower motor centre of the spinal cord, the muscles of the lower limbs. As we descend the gyrus, the muscles of the trunk, arm, neck, and head are controlled in what may roughly be described as an ascending order. Disease or injury of the left motor area causes paralysis of the right side of the body. It is the possession of a motor area, with loops extending from the spinal cord below, which enables us to control reflexes like those connected with excretion, and to perform the various skilled actions of the adult.

The *sensory area* parallels the motor area. It lies on the opposite side of the central fissure in the post-central gyrus. Any stimulation which reaches this area is referred to its peripheral origin. In the same way stimulation of a sensory fibre some distance above its peripheral ending, as when the so-called "funny-bone" is jarred, is felt at the sensory ending. The same kind of thing causes a person with an amputated arm or leg to feel the hand or foot that is not there. Since any stimulation coming along that particular tract was previously referred to the hand or foot, the sensory area still refers it to that region.

The *visual area* lies in the hindmost part of the occipital lobe, particularly in its median aspect. Injury to the visual area causes cortical blindness—an inability to see although the eyes are perfect.

The *auditory area* is located in the middle third of the superior surface of the superior (upper) temporal gyrus.

Besides the visual and auditory areas mentioned above, two other areas—the *motor speech* and the *writing areas*—are concerned with language. The interconnections among them are shown in Fig. 33. The speech and writing centres are excellent examples of what have been called super-motor centres. It is probable that the motor areas extend beyond the boundaries of the pre-central gyrus, the outlying parts being solely concerned with such delicate muscular adjustments as are necessary in speech, writing, and skilled movements. It is possible to lose the adjustments for speech and writing, etc., without losing the cruder adjustments for walking and for moving the arms.

Conclusion.—A great deal of ground has been covered in this chapter. All in all, any description of the most astounding mechanism in the universe must necessarily be complicated. Years of study are required to learn all the details of the central

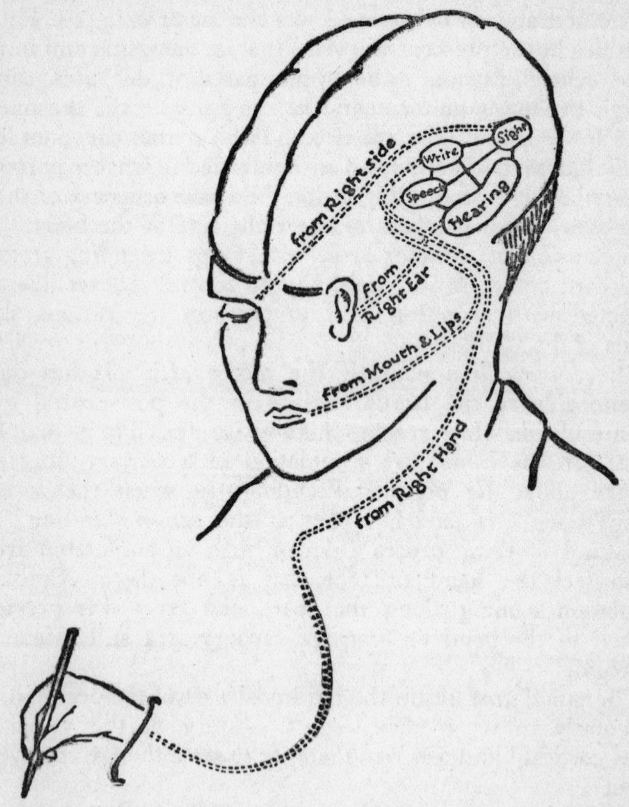

FIG. 33.—Diagram to show the relative positions of the four centres concerned with the reception, the production, and the storing-up of memories of speech, reading, and writing. Note the association fibres joining up the four centres, each with the other three.

nervous system, but if the student has grasped the main fact that the function of the central nervous system is to connect receptors and effectors so that reactions can both be co-ordinated and speeded up, he will have gained a knowledge that is of fundamental importance. If, further, he has grasped the fact that the connections of the nervous system necessary for survival are born with us, and that to these we add thousands of others through the process of learning, he will have gained a working knowledge of the part the central nervous system plays in education. So far as crude living is concerned the lower arcs of the central nervous system are all that are necessary. Compared with these fundamental arcs those formed by education within the walls of the schoolroom seem of little consequence. But with man's evolving nature the lower arcs become inadequate. The brain with its thousands of upper arcs grows, develops, and becomes functional. The "learning brain" contrasted with "living spinal cord" thus puts us in intimate relationship with the great world of knowledge we call civilization. Man's abundance of connectible neurons, therefore, makes him human. It is training and education that lead to the higher and more complex neuron connections, and place man far above the level of the beast.

References

Head, H. *Aphasia and Kindred Disorders of Speech* (2 vols.). Cambridge University Press, 1926. Pp. 401 and 407.

Herrick, C. J. *Neurological Foundations of Animal Behaviour*. New York, Holt, 1924. Pp. xii+334.

Ladd and Woodworth. *Elements of Physiological Psychology*. New York, Scribners, 1911. Pp. 704.

Ranson, S. W. *The Anatomy of the Nervous System*. Philadelphia, Saunders, 1923. Pp. 421.

Sherrington, C. S. *The Integrative Action of the Nervous System*. New Haven, Yale University Press, 1923. Pp. xvi+411.

Thorndike, E. L. *The Elements of Psychology*. New York, Seiler, 1907 Pp. xix+351.

Watson, J. B. *Behaviorism* (*Lectures-in-Print*). New York, People's Institute Publishing Co., 1925. Pp. 251.

Zoethout, W. D. *A Textbook of Physiology*. St. Louis, Mosby, 1925. Pp. 616.

CHAPTER VI

NON-VARIABLE BEHAVIOUR: REFLEXES AND INSTINCTS

Evolution of Behaviour.—From previous chapters the reader will have learned that the evolution of behaviour exactly parallels the evolution of structure in animals. As the animal structure becomes complex, so does its behaviour. So true is this that an animal's behaviour may be said to be absolutely conditioned by the number and kind of sense organs, muscles and glands, and nerve cells that it possesses. Further, although animals evolve or become complex as a whole, no better index of their stage of development can be found than that of their nervous systems. The elaboration of the nervous system in animal evolution exhibits the following well-defined phases:

1. From the inorganic to the organic.
2. From unicellular to multicellular bodies.
3. From generalized structure to specially differentiated tissues.
4. From ordinary protoplasmic to nervous apparatus of excitation and conduction.
5. From non-synaptic to synaptic type of nervous system.
6. From relatively diffuse ganglionic to the dorsal tubular pattern of central nervous system with cephalization and bilateral symmetry (vertebrate type).
7. From aquatic to terrestrial mode of life with increase in complexity of sensori-motor equipment and extensive evagination of cerebral hemispheres from the primitive neural tube.
8. Differentiation of superficial cortex in the cerebral hemispheres and rise of intelligence.
9. Elaboration of cortical association centres with powers of symbolic thinking, ideation, and conscious personal and social control.[1]

Owing to the close similarity existing between individual and racial development (cf. the biogenetic law or law of recapitulation), the above outline also represents fairly accurately what happens to man's individual nervous system in the course of its develop-

[1] Herrick, *Neurological Foundations of Animal Behaviour*, pp. 296–297.

ment. Man starts as an undifferentiated unicellular organism without any nervous system. In the course of his development he rapidly becomes a multicellular organism whose nervous system, however, is extremely primitive. The nervous system elaborates and even at birth has assumed many of its final forms. Development proceeds, and in the adult stage the connections are extraordinarily numerous, consonant with the rôle man plays as a language and tool-using animal.

Paralleling this bodily development we find a corresponding development in behaviour. At birth man is largely restricted to inherited forms of behaviour of a non-variable kind. As he grows and develops the proportion of non-variable elements rapidly diminishes until at the adult stage only those non-variable forms

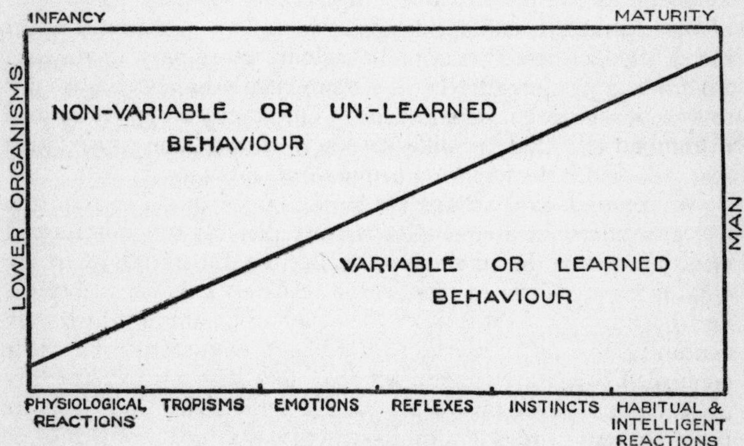

FIG. 34.—Diagrammatic representation of the development from non-variable to variable behaviour.

that are directly life-conserving seem to remain. Adult behaviour is mainly of the variable kind, giving a character and personality to human beings that is largely denied to all sub-human species. The transition from non-variable to variable behaviour is shown diagrammatically in Fig. 34. Too much stress must not be placed on the relative proportions of variable and non-variable behaviour at each stage of development. All that we wish the diagram to indicate is that the lower animals make stereotyped responses to environmental stimuli. This is quite true of all animals below insects. The lower animals mostly live in the relatively unchanging environment of water, the higher animals in the constantly changing environment of air. The apparent exceptions to this rule—the insects—return to water or the ground for their metamorphoses. With regard to human behaviour all that need be read into the diagram is that with increasing age an increasing proportion of variable elements enter into behaviour.

The Forms of Non-Variable Behaviour.—Non-variable behaviour is best defined as those stimulus-response processes or action-patterns which are inherited in the sense that they are determined by inherited organizations of structures. There is one sense in which all behaviour, learned as well as unlearned, is determined by inherited mechanisms; but we shall take the common-sense viewpoint and limit non-variable behaviour to that in which environmental learning plays the least possible part. Obviously, then, the most non-variable forms of behaviour are those *physiological actions* which most directly keep us alive by taking care of the intake and digestion of food, the elimination of waste products, and the oxygenation and the circulation of the blood. Even these forms of behaviour are slightly modifiable. An Eskimo perspires freely in a room that is barely comfortable to a person inured to tropical life. The stomach may be trained to respond effectively to different kinds of diets, and constipation may be alleviated by regular habits of evacuation.

All physiological actions are perfect at birth. The requisite neural connections are completely patterned and the muscles and glands necessary for their performance are functional when the child is born. Thus as soon as the relatively cold air strikes the new-born baby's chest it starts the action of breathing which then continues as long as life lasts. Although education is but little concerned over physiological actions, since they are so refractory under training, yet the reader should understand that they are based on neural arcs identical in structure and function with those which are concerned with other forms of behaviour.

Secondly, in lowly animals in particular, there are simple responses to light, temperature, and chemical stimulation which have been termed *tropisms*. Loeb considered that instincts were merely elaborations of tropic responses. In explanation of the way in which tropisms operate Loeb states: "If a moth be struck by the light on one side, those muscles which turn the head towards the light become more active than those of the opposite side, and correspondingly the head of the animal is turned towards the source of light. As soon as the head of the animal has this orientation and the median plane (or plane of symmetry) comes into the direction of the rays of light, the symmetrical points of the surface of the body are struck by the rays of light at the same angle. The intensity of light is the same on both sides, and there is no more reason why the animal should turn to the right or left than away from the direction of the rays of light. Thus it is led to the source of the light. Hence the 'instinct' that drives the animal into the light is nothing more than the chemical—and indirectly the mechanical—effect of light, an effect similar to that which forces the stem of the plant at the window to bend toward the source of light." In the same way Loeb maintained that "the tendency of many animals to creep into cracks and crevices has nothing to do with self-concealment, but only with the necessity of bringing the body on every side in contact with solid bodies." Crucial experiments, in which the action was reversed, were performed with a number of marine animals which normally go away from light. They were forced "to go to the light in two ways: first by lowering the temperature, and second by increasing the concentration of the sea-water (whereby the cells of the animals lose water)."[1] Tropisms, however, must be dependent upon an hereditary behaviour pattern, which gives the effective reaction directly. This pattern is remarkably stable and non-variable, comparable to the pattern of a physiological action. As, however, tropisms play but a very small part in human behaviour, we need not consider them further.

Thirdly, those very simple responses which involve relatively few arcs and muscles are called *reflexes*. The patterns are inherited and are perfect at birth. Reflexes are difficult to modify; they constitute one of the less variable forms of behaviour. Although the reflex arc is a convenient fiction of both psychology and physiology, the concept is a convenient one. Just what actions are to be regarded as reflex is merely a matter of convenience in classification. So long as they are relatively simple, frequent, and rapid, and relatively perfect at birth, they may be classed as reflexes. As the only scientific way of classifying reflexes is that based on inner structure and organization, any list that is attempted, owing to our present lack of knowledge, is bound to be partial and probably incorrect. With this caution in mind the following list of reflexes, compiled by Warren,[2] is given:

A. *Purest—least subject to central modification in adults.*

"Pupillary" or iris reflex.
Ear twitching (controlled in some individuals).
Hand withdrawal (to heat and pain).
Mesenteric reflexes (operation of stomach and intestinal muscles in digestion).
Snoring.
Shuddering.

[1] See Loeb, J., *Forced Movements, Tropisms and Animal Conduct.*
[2] Warren, *Human Psychology*, p. 101.

Starting (to sudden noise).
Trembling.
Shivering.
Rhythmic contractions (in epilepsy, paralysis agitans, etc.).

B. Largely pure—subject to inhibition or reinforcement.

Winking.
Accommodation, ciliary reflex.
Eye-fixation and convergence.
Hiccoughing.
Sneezing.
Patellar reflex (knee-jerk).
Dizziness reflexes.
Yawning.
Vomiting.
Facial reflexes (to bitter taste, etc.).
Salivation.
Tickle reflexes.
Hand twitching (to dermal pain).
Plantar reflex (to stimulus on sole of foot).
Great toe reflex.
Vasomotor changes (blushing, paling).
Breathing changes (to specific stimuli and to onset of sleep).
Sudorific reflexes.
Groaning.
Laughing.
Cramp movements.
Squirming.

C. Occasionally pure, more often centrally modified.

Coughing.
Swallowing and gulping.
Visceral discharge (etc.).
Functioning of sex organs.
Reflexes to odours.
Gasping.
Weeping.
Sobbing.
Smiling.
Wincing (etc.).
Scowling.
Stretching.
Convulsive contractions (to deep pressure and heat, to pricking and other dermal pains, and to visceral pain).

D. Pure in infancy, centrally modified in adult.

Sucking.
Biting and grinding.
Spitting.

Hunger and thirst reflexes.
Lip and tongue reflexes.
Vocal reflexes.
Turning the head.
Tossing.
Grasping (finger reflexes).
Tugging (wrist reflexes).
Clasping (elbow reflexes).
Reaching (shoulder reflexes).
Kicking (knee reflexes).
Jumping (ankle reflexes).
Sitting up.
Bending forward.
Rising.

E. Posture reflexes.

Holding head erect.
Sitting.
Standing.
Equilibration.

The reflex response usually involves the operation of a number of arcs acting simultaneously. They may be regarded as simple or compound according as they involve few (in some cases a single arc) or many arcs ; or higher or lower according to the place of co-ordination in the nervous system. The simple arcs are usually lower arcs, but this is not invariably the case. The patellar reflex (knee-jerk) is a typical simple and lower (spinal) reflex. Sucking is a typical compound and higher reflex. The reflex response is usually on the same side of the body as the stimulus. Reflexes are exceedingly prompt and definite. They are quicker than the reaction-time of any learned response. The eye-wink takes about 1/20 of a second ; the knee-jerk about 3/100 of a second. The reflex, therefore, through its neural connections made by the inner growth of the nervous system, is always ready for action and plays an important part in the conservation of life.

Fourthly, there are the *instincts* around which have centred so many verbal wars. It is very probable that Psychology will have to give up instincts, for no two persons can agree as to their number or names. Watson [1] has given up instincts and substitutes for them the *activity stream.* The human action systems begin as unlearned reactions, but most of them become conditioned before the age of five years is reached. Because the learned elements are so numerous, Watson refuses to call them instincts

[1] Watson, *Behaviorism* (*Lectures-in-Print*), chaps. v and vi.

He admits that some of them are not modified, existing in the activity stream throughout life without increasing in complexity. Bernard [1] has presented in a most complete fashion the evidence which shows the present disagreement over the term, but even he has failed to confine instinct within the limits of a technical term.

It is a pity that instinct is an unusable term. From our point of view it merely represents one step further in the progress towards the variable end of our diagram (Fig. 34). Feeding is undoubtedly more elaborate, say, than swallowing. Feeding has an inherited basis, for each animal must eat or die. Why not regard feeding as a complex of reflexes unfolding serially under appropriate stimulation? For this is what feeding really is. And if swallowing, the simpler and constituent element of the feeding response, is called a reflex, why not call feeding an instinct? But there are lions in the way. Bernard would say that the term "feeding" is only one name for this particular activity. Different writers have variously described it as food-getting, hunger, hunting, seeking the breast, etc. Watson would say that feeding responses have an unlearned beginning, but within a month have become so conditioned that the original responses are swamped with the later habits. Why, then, call it an instinct when it is mostly a habit? Nevertheless, it is obvious that the inherited basis is more clearly traceable in actions like feeding than in those like factoring in algebra. We shall, therefore, retain the term for those action-patterns that are more elaborate than reflexes, that are probably compounded of a series of reflexes, and that have undoubtedly an inherited basis. This does not exclude the element of learning. For as every careful observer knows, instinctive responses in man are quickly modified by his social contacts.

Fifthly, we must classify among the forms of non-variable behaviour those reactions, like fear and anger, which everybody agrees in calling *emotions*. As we shall speak of emotions in the next chapter we can dispense with further discussion at this stage.

All other forms of behaviour are mostly learned, that is, are habitual or intelligent, in which the non-variable or unlearned element is reduced to a minimum. But, as stated previously, every form of behaviour, from one point of view, has a non-variable, unlearned element in it. Piano-playing is as learned or as habitual a form of behaviour as can possibly be imagined. Yet piano-playing is dependent upon certain muscular mechanisms, certain movements of fingers which are indubitably innate. It

[1] Bernard, *Instinct: A Study in Social Psychology*, 1924.

would be impossible to teach a horse to play the piano, simply because he is not built that way.

Criteria of Non-Variable Behaviour.—Assuming, as we have every right to assume, that non-variable behaviour is due to an inherited structure and organization, what criteria can be applied to discover which of the numerous responses of an organism are truly innate?

Several of the criteria of innateness that have been used are open to criticism. Take, for example, universality which is commonly assumed to be a valid criterion. Sometimes a common social contact, such as religion affords for Arabs and Thibetans, is sufficient to account for a universality of behaviour. Applying this criterion, a visitor from Mars might rightfully assume that newspaper reading was innate among Britishers and Americans. If the criterion be guarded by certain restrictive clauses its validity is increased. Thus Gates says: "When a trait is found universally among members of the same species, whatever their environment and training, the assumption is that it is native unless evidence to the contrary is produced."[1] But even in this form it must still be used with caution.

Biological utility, appearance at a definite period of development, full-fledged at their first appearance, similarity within the species, inevitability, can become abnormally exaggerated without any general mental abnormality, not amenable to control, and many others of a similar kind are all fallacious criteria. Since, however, the non-variable elements of behaviour tend to appear early in life, earliness of appearance is a valuable criterion, though by no means an infallible one. Similarly, the more non-variable a form of behaviour is, the more frequently it tends to occur, hence frequency of occurrence might possibly become a useful criterion. We breathe more often than we wink, wink more often than we swallow, swallow more often than we eat, etc. However, we have no scientific records of the frequency of occurrence of the various responses, so, for the present, it must be regarded as unusable. The comparison of responses in fraternal and identical twins would provide a useful criterion of innateness, but the studies so far made cannot be regarded as adequate.

What criteria, then, are valid? The following three criteria appear to be above suspicion:

(1) If there is a true biological inheritance which expresses itself in the Mendelian ratio irrespective of environment, the trait may be regarded as truly innate. This transmission from

[1] Gates, *Psychology for Students of Education*, p. 120.

generation to generation, when the factor of environmental inheritance (social heredity) is excluded, is a characterictic of all non-variable behaviour.

(2) When a trait can be assigned to a structural characteristic of the organism it is indubitably innate. This is probably the best criterion that can be applied.

(3) If a response appears when all possible opportunities of learning have been excluded, it is innate. This is a valid criterion providing we are sure that opportunities of learning have been excluded. Birds apparently inherit their songs ; in reality they learn them through the action of social contacts on a modifiable structure. Conradi reared young English sparrows with canaries and they learned, somewhat imperfectly it is true, the canary song.[1]

Instincts and Education.—Most educational psychologists devote a considerable proportion of their treatises to the discussion of instincts. They first endeavour to isolate the instincts, then proceed to discuss their attributes (transitoriness, waxing and waning ; indefiniteness and variability ; transferability ; need of a stimulus ; chain-reaction tendencies ; all-or-noneness ; etc.), and finally show how they may be controlled for educational ends. The reasons for this are not far to seek.

(1) If the task of isolating instincts could be performed successfully, it would provide educators with a knowledge of the universal characteristics of man. Armed with this knowledge teachers could arrange a course of study and apply methods of teaching which would be universally applicable, because they would be built on the secure foundation of human nature. As we have shown, this task has never been accomplished, so the practical applications designed for the schoolroom have been as diverse and mutually contradictory as the lists of isolated instincts.

(2) By tracing the order of the appearance of instincts a knowledge of normal mental development would be secured. This in itself would be very valuable, since it would at least prevent teachers from trying to feed a mental pabulum to babes and sucklings that was suited only to adults. Thus if it could be proved that an instinctive interest in the functions of the body never developed before adolescence, then all attempts to teach physiology to young pupils would be abandoned as futile.

(3) What behaviour was "natural" to man would become known, and juster judgments regarding such behaviour could be formed.

(4) Possessing a knowledge of what was "natural" behaviour,

[1] Conradi, E., "Song and Call-notes of English Sparrows when reared by Canaries," *American Journal of Psychology*, vol. xvi, p. 190.

the teacher or parent could anticipate it in children and initiate measures for its control. If, for example, it was found that stealing was a "natural" form of behaviour for five-year-old children, then as five years was approached (*a*) opportunities for stealing could be withheld from the child; (*b*) stealing, when first attempted, could be conditioned by a severe punishment; or (*c*) some form of redirection or sublimation of the instinct might be attempted.

(5) Since instincts are powerful motivating factors, education would have a constant and dependable supply of them with which to motivate learning.

(6) Habits are based on instinctive activities. If the instinctive bases were known, then habit formation could be undertaken in a more intelligent and economical way.

Unfortunately for education, what is inherited is not a series of full-fledged instincts—curiosity, protection, flight, climbing, acquisitiveness, pugnacity, gregariousness, construction, and the like—but a series of potential arcs connecting receptors and effectors. Some of these arcs are connected up by the inner growth of the nervous system. They enable an act to be performed with a minimum of practice. Others, starting always from arcs that are already functional, are developed solely through environmental learning. The actual form they take is dependent on the environmental contacts (chiefly social in character) that the organism makes. As so frequently emphasized in this volume, both factors are essential—the hereditary equipment and environmental stimulation. The result as exhibited in any organism is a continuous series of responses running from the most non-variable (unlearned) to the most variable (learned). Few, if any, of the responses can be classed as wholly unlearned; few, if any, as wholly learned. The instinctive responses, while possessing native elements common to the whole of the species, develop in a variety of ways, dependent upon the particular environment in which the organism lives. Most children crawl, but a few do not; most children climb, but a few do not; most children play, but the form the play takes is dependent upon the environment in which the children are reared. Most of the so-called instincts are chiefly habits. The isolation of the innumerable inherited elements has not been successfully accomplished, nor have the variations due to a variable environment been traced. The problem has still to be solved. That it is an incredibly difficult one no psychologist doubts.

Instincts and the Nursery.—Much of the work done on instincts will have to be discarded and a new start made. The most hopeful place for starting would seem to be the nursery.

Watson and Mrs. M. G. Blanton have carefully studied the birth equipment of the human young. So far no one has yet traced the transition of the unconditioned responses to the conditioned state. The following is a summary of Watson's list of true unlearned responses :

(1) Sneezing. Full-fledged from birth.
(2) Hiccoughing. Not present at birth, but observable from seven days of age on with great ease.
(3) Crying. Present at birth and soon conditioned because it leads to the control of nurse, parents, and attendants.
(4) Erection of penis. This can occur at birth and from that time on throughout life.
(5) Voiding of urine. This occurs from birth. The unconditioned stimulus is unquestionably intra-organic, due to the pressure of the fluid in the bladder. Conditioning of the act of urination can begin as early as the second week. Usually, however, conditioning at this age requires almost infinite patience. Anywhere from the third month on, the infant can be conditioned easily by a little care.
(6) Defæcation. This mechanism seems to be perfect from birth ; it can be conditioned from a very early age.
(7) Early eye movements. Infants from birth will slowly turn their eyes towards a faint light, but the movement is not so well co-ordinated for some time.
(8) Smiling. Appears as early as the fourth day, most often after a full feeding. It can be conditioned by the thirtieth day.
(9) Turning the head. From birth.
(10) Holding up head when the infant is held in upright position. Some new-born infants can support their heads for a few seconds. The head can be held up in most infants from the sixth month on.
(11) Hand movements. Such movements as closing and opening the hand, stretching and spreading the fingers can be observed at birth.
(12) Grasping. With few exceptions infants at birth can support their full weight with either right or left hands. It begins to disappear around the 120th day.
(13) Arm movements. Arm, wrist, hand, and shoulder responses can be aroused from birth by stimulating the skin slightly anywhere, but the most pronounced reactions are brought about by holding the nose of the infant.
(14) Leg and foot movements. Kicking is one of the most pronounced movements to be seen at birth. It can be brought out by touching the soles of the feet, by stimulating with hot and cold air, but best of all by pinching the knee.
(15) Trunk, leg, foot, and toe movements. When an infant is suspending itself with either right or left hand, marked climbing movements in the trunk and hips are noticeable

Tickling the foot produces marked movements in the foot and toes. Stroking the sole with a match stick produces the Babinski reflex (extension of big toe, flexion of others, but toes may simply be fanned). Many infants almost from birth can turn over from face to back when placed naked, face downward, on an unyielding surface.

(16) Feeding responses. Touching the face of a hungry baby causes movement of the mouth towards source of stimulation. Sucking and swallowing can be demonstrated within an hour of birth.

(17) Crawling. This is an indeterminate response. Mostly a habit, since many babies never crawl at all.

(18) Standing and walking. These, though of slow development, are probably innate and develop from the extensor thrust of the legs. A great deal of the act of walking, balancing, and the like is learned. It may be positively conditioned by coaching and negatively conditioned by injuries from falling.

(19) Vocal behaviour. Begins with crying and babbling. These native cries become conditioned and organized into word habits.

(20) Blinking when the eye is touched is unconditioned at birth; the blink when a shadow crosses the eye is learned between 40 and 80 days.[1]

In addition Watson found that swimming and handedness were not innate. Children are born neither right- nor left-handed; handedness is socially conditioned.

If the reader will compare the above list of responses with the list of reflexes given previously in the chapter, he will discover that most of them are of the relatively simple reflex type. These discoveries of the nursery should be followed up into childhood to find out what part they play in later learning. Many of them, we feel sure, would be discovered to be the foundations on which the later habits are built. Some of them, like sneezing, would be found in a "pure," that is, unmodified, form throughout the whole of life. New unlearned responses would probably be found as the body developed. In these cases it would be difficult to decide what was due to mere development, and what could be rightfully regarded as a true "instinctive" response.

References

BALDWIN and STECHER. *The Psychology of the Pre-School Child.* New York, Appleton, 1925. Pp. 305.

BERNARD, L. L. *Instinct: A Study in Social Psychology.* New York, Holt, 1924. Pp. ix+550.

[1] Watson, *Behaviorism* (*Lectures-in-Print*), chap. vi.

Carr, H. A. *Psychology: A Study of Mental Activity.* New York, Longmans, Green, 1925. Pp. 432.

Child, C. M. *Physiological Foundations of Behaviour.* New York, Holt, 1924. Pp. xii+330.

Gates, A. I. *Psychology for Students of Education.* New York, Macmillan, 1924. Pp. xvi+489.

Gesell, A. *The Mental Growth of the Pre-School Child.* New York, Macmillan, 1925. Pp. x+447.

Herrick, C. J. *Neurological Foundations of Animal Behaviour.* New York, Holt, 1924. Pp. xii+334.

McDougall, W. *Outline of Psychology.* New York, Scribners, 1923. Pp. xvi+456.

Norsworthy and Whitley. *The Psychology of Childhood.* New York, Macmillan, 1924. Pp. xix+375.

Thorndike, E. L. *Educational Psychology.* Vol. i. *The Original Nature of Man.* New York, Teachers College, 1921. Pp. xii+327.

Waddle, C. W. *An Introduction to Child Psychology.* Boston, Houghton Mifflin, 1918. Pp. xvi+317.

Warren, H. C. *Human Psychology.* Boston, Houghton Mifflin, 1919. Pp. xx+460.

Washburn, M. F. *The Animal Mind.* New York, Macmillan, 1926. Pp. xiii+431.

Watson, J. B. *Behaviorism (Lectures-in-Print).* New York, People's Institute Publishing Co., 1925. Pp. 251.

Watson, J. B. *Psychology from the Standpoint of a Behaviorist.* Philadelphia, Lippincott, 1924. Pp. xvii+448.

CHAPTER VII

NON-VARIABLE BEHAVIOUR: EMOTIONS

The Nature of Emotions.—The non-variable (unlearned or innate) element in emotion, like that in reflexes and instincts, constitutes a considerable part of the whole. In its first expression the emotion of fear is as truly unlearned and non-variable as the reflex grasp of the baby. Yet emotions differ from reflexes and instincts in several important particulars. In the first place an emotion involves the whole body; when angry or fearful we are angry and fearful all over; while an instinct or reflex involves only a part, sometimes, indeed, especially in the case of reflexes, a very limited part of the body. Secondly, to a very much greater extent than a reflex or instinct, an emotion involves the glandular and visceral systems of the body. The autonomic nervous system which controls smooth muscles and glands, plays a major part in emotions, just as the spinal cord and brain play the major rôle in reflexes and instincts. Recent research has shown that the ductless glands are intimately associated with emotional expression. The hormones of endocrine secretions are known to produce important changes within the body and to have the power, similar to that of the autonomic nervous system, of stimulating the viscera and glands into action. It may be that the solution of the still unsolved riddle of the emotions lies within the ductless glands. Thirdly, emotions are chaotic and of an incoherent nature. In contrast with reflexes and instincts which run smoothly and for which we seem to be ready, emotions overwhelm us every time, because we never seem able to prepare for them. Fourthly, they are sudden and are accompanied by arrested movements, organic modifications of circulation, respiration, and metabolism, which are intimately related to the preservation of the individual or the species. In other words emotions are innate responses (hereditary pattern-reactions) essentially chaotic in their nature, involving the whole body in their expression, but particularly the glandular and visceral systems and their nervous connections, and having intimate relationship with the preservation of the individual or the species.

The Study of Emotions.—In comparatively recent times the elucidation of the problem of the emotions has been attempted from many angles. Charles Darwin, in characteristic fashion, attacked the problem from the strictly objective viewpoint. His treatise entitled *On the Expression of Emotions in Man and Animals* (1872) was the successor of numerous previous studies [1] on physiognomy and emotions, but it differed from all earlier work in that the emotional expressions of man and animals were linked together on an evolutionary scale. According to Darwin three principles accounted for most of the expressions and gestures both of men and of animals. (1) The principle of serviceable associated habits, by which he meant that some expressions of emotion are frequently remnants of habits that were previously of value to the animal but had no longer any direct use. Clenching the fist in anger and unfleshing the eye-teeth are examples of serviceable associated habits. (2) The principle of antithesis, by which he meant those emotional expressions which were in direct contrast to those normally present in the animal. Friendliness on the part of a dog is shown by signs directly opposite in character to the more normally expected signs of hostility or anger. (3) The principle of actions due to the constitution of the nervous system, independently from the first of the Will, and independently to a certain extent of habit. Perspiring during pain, trembling during terror, and the jumping up and down of the child in sheer *joie de vivre* are illustrations of this third principle. It is from the first principle, which states that human emotion is expressed in ways that were once needed to meet a crisis, that most light has been thrown upon the subject. Since Darwin's time the biological usefulness of emotion has never been lost to view. But his example of scientific objectivity has never been completely recaptured except, perhaps, by behaviourists.

A *second* line of inquiry was opened up by the theories of emotion propounded independently by W. James and C. Lange in 1884 and 1885 respectively. These theories were so similar that they are usually compounded into one—the James-Lange theory of emotion. This theory (and the modifications introduced by Sergi) consists essentially of the claim that the stimulus which is the exciting cause of the emotion acts first on the nervous centre ruling the viscera and their reactions then generate visceral

[1] Lavater, G., *Essay on Physiognomy destined to make Man known and loved* (1772).
Bell, C., *Anatomy and Philosophy of Expression* (1806).
Burgess, *The Physiology or Mechanism of Blushing* (1839).
Duchenne, *Mécanisme de la Physionomie Humaine* (1862).
Spencer, H., "Physiology of Laughter," in *Essays, Scientific, Political, and Speculative*, Second Series (1863).

sensations which, in turn, induce the psychical state known as the emotion. The matter will become clearer if we introduce a few excerpts from the explanation given by James.[1]

"Our natural way of thinking about these coarser emotions is that the mental perception of some fact excites the mental affection called the emotion, and that this latter state of mind gives rise to the bodily expression. My theory, on the contrary, is that *the bodily changes follow directly the perception of the exciting fact, and that our feeling of the same changes as they occur* IS *the emotion.* Common-sense says, we lose our fortune, are sorry and weep; we meet a bear, are frightened and run; we are insulted by a rival, are angry and strike. The hypothesis here to be defended says that this order of sequence is incorrect, that the one mental state is not immediately induced by the other, that the bodily manifestations must first be interposed between, and that the more rational statement is that we feel sorry because we cry, angry because we strike, afraid because we tremble, and not that we cry, strike, or tremble, because we are sorry, angry, or fearful, as the case may be." "*Every one of the bodily changes, whatsoever it be, is* FELT, *acutely or obscurely, the moment it occurs.* If the reader has never paid attention to this matter, he will be both interested and astonished to learn how many different local bodily feelings he can detect in himself as characteristic of his various emotional moods." "*If we fancy some strong emotion, and then try to abstract from our consciousness of it all the feelings of its bodily symptoms, we find we have nothing left behind*, no 'mind-stuff' out of which the emotion can be constituted, and that a cold and neutral state of intellectual perception is all that remains." "If I were to become corporeally anæsthetic I should be excluded from the life of the affections, harsh and tender alike, and drag out an existence of merely cognitive or intellectual form."

These views of James, Lange, and Sergi, that the psychical process of emotion is secondary to a discharge of nervous impulses into the vascular and visceral organs of the body suddenly excited by certain peculiar stimuli and that it depends upon the reaction of those organs, have met with opposition from the neurologists and from the experimental physiologists. Sherrington [2] made combined spinal and vago-sympathetic nerve sections in dogs in such a manner as to remove completely and immediately the sensation of the viscera and all the skin and muscles behind the shoulder. At the same time the procedure cuts from connection with the organs of consciousness the whole of the circulatory apparatus of the body. Reporting the case of a bitch of markedly emotional temperament he states:

"The reduction of the field of sensation in this animal by the

[1] James, W., *Principles of Psychology*, vol. ii, pp. 449 ff.
[2] Sherrington, C. S., *The Integrative Action of the Nervous System*, pp. 259–261.

procedure above mentioned produced no obvious diminution of her emotional character. Her anger, her joy, her disgust, and when provocation arose, her fear, remained as evident as ever. Her joy at the approach or notice of the attendant, her rage at the intrusion of a cat with which she was unfriendly remained as active and thorough. But among the signs expressive of rage the bristling of the coat along the back no longer occurred."

While the experiment is not a crucial one it does seem to point to the fact " that the visceral expression of the emotion is *secondary* to the cerebral action occurring with the psychical state."

" We may with James accept visceral and organic sensations and the memories and associations of them as contributory to primitive emotions, but we must regard them as reinforcing rather than initiating the psychosis. Organic and vascular reaction, though not the actual excitant of emotion, strengthen it. This is the kernel of the old contention about the actuality of emotion in the art of the artist. Hamlet's description of the actor as really moved by his expression may be accepted as an answer."

From the above we may gather that the James-Lange theory is somewhat discredited. Its fatal weakness is that it regards emotions as a complex of bodily sensations. Emotion, as we have seen, is always the expression of feeling ; it is never the reception of impressions, but is always the response to them. And this response consists in the alteration of respiration, secretion, and circulation on the one hand, and the bracing or relaxation of various voluntary muscles on the other.

The *third* line of investigation of the emotions is from the side of endocrinology. In Chapter III we reviewed Cannon's work on adrenalin and its connection with the emotions of fear and anger, so we need not go into it again. The endocrinologists tell us that our bodies contain a delicate balance of hormones, some of which incite muscles and glands to action while others inhibit them. If this endocrine balance of the body is destroyed then normal intellectual and especially normal emotional life is also destroyed. What these hormones of endocrine secretions really are, is at present unknown. They are drug-like substances, but their potency is beyond that of ordinary drugs. Their action in the body is somewhat similar to that of vitamines, incredibly small doses producing marked effects. Catalysts in the chemical world are the nearest approach to them, and it may be that their effects are those of enzymes acting catalytically.

Certain drugs upset the emotional balance of the body. The effects of alcohol and caffeine are fairly well known, while there are well-authenticated instances of marked sexual disturbances resulting from the use of certain anæsthetics in dentistry.

A *fourth* type of work on emotions centres round psycho-analysis and psycho-therapy. Prior to the War Freud, Krafft-Ebing, Jung, Janet, Sidis, Prince, Jones, and others had shown that emotional disturbances were not so hopelessly irrational as they seemed and that with proper methods and infinite patience the problems they presented could be unravelled. Some of these investigators undoubtedly over-emphasized the part that sex played in the creation of the symptoms. The War redressed the balance, for it showed conclusively that fear could be extremely potent in the creation of psycho-neuroses. Thousands of mental breakdowns were treated according to the accepted methods of psycho-analysis and many permanent cures were reported.

The *fifth* and most promising method of study is that which has been developed by Watson and his co-workers. It is a combination of the genetic and experimental approach.[1] Watson by observation of infants, especially during the first months of life, could only discover three emotional reactions which indubitably were innate. These were fear, rage, and love (using love in approximately the same sense that Freud uses sex). Fear was aroused by removal of support, by loud sounds, and occasionally, when the infant was just falling asleep or was just ready to waken, by a sudden push or slight shake, or by suddenly pulling the blanket upon which the baby was lying. Rage was evoked by hampering the child's movements in any way whatsoever. Love responses were stimulated by stroking, or manipulation of some erogenous zone, tickling, shaking, gentle rocking, patting, and turning upon the stomach across the attendant's knee. All other experiments—with rabbits, darkness, cats, dogs, animals at the zoo—failed to elicit emotional responses. This method of study is in its infancy, but the results so far achieved are most promising.

[1] Watson, J. B., " Experimental Studies of the Growth of the Emotions." Powell Lecture in Psychological Theory at Clark University, Jan. 17, 1925. *Pedagogical Seminary*, June, 1925, vol. 32, No. 2, pp. 328–348.

Rayner, Rosalie, and Watson, J. B., " Studies in Infant Psychology," *Scientific Monthly*, December, 1921, pp. 493–515.

Watson, J. B., *Psychology from the Standpoint of a Behaviorist* (1924), chap. vi.

Watson, J. B., and Morgan, J. J. B., " Emotional Reactions and Psychological Experimentation," *American Journal of Psychology*, vol. 28 (1917), pp. 163–174.

Watson, J. B., and Rayner, R., " Conditioned Emotional Reactions," *Jour. Exper. Psy.*, vol. 3 (1920), pp. 1–14.

Watson, J. B., " A Schematic Outline of the Emotions," *Psy. Rev.*, vol. 26 (May, 1919), pp. 165–177.

Watson, J. B., " Recent Experiments on How we Lose and Change our Emotional Equipment," *Ped. Sem.*, vol. 32, No. 2 (June, 1925), pp. 349–371.

The experimental method known as conditioning has provided some interesting results. These will be discussed in the chapter devoted to Conditioned Reactions.

The *sixth* method of study, a variety of experimental method, is that which attempts to measure objectively the emotional equipment of the individual. The method is not quite clear cut, being associated with the measurement of moral qualities and character traits. Nor are the tests so far evolved as reliable as the corresponding intelligence and educational tests, but the work of Woodworth, Downey, Pressey, Voelker, and the Columbia research workers bids fair to overcome the difficulties inherent in the task. When completed, we shall have a measure of a person's emotional equipment that is as reliable as an intelligent quotient or an educational quotient.

Characteristics of Emotions.—The main characteristics of an emotion would seem to be the following:

(*a*) *A Characteristic Bodily Expression.*—We *see* when a man is angry, sorrowful, or full of fear. We become red with anger, bent with grief, and rigid with fear. The success of the moving picture is a testimony to this feature of the emotions. Illiterate and half-savage peoples can interpret correctly the characteristic bodily signs of emotion as depicted by the movie actor or actress. Darwin's book, mentioned earlier in this chapter, runs almost to 400 pages, yet it is mostly devoted to descriptions of the bodily expressions of the various emotions. His technique is illustrated by the following abridgment of his account of *rage* or intense anger.

"Rage exhibits itself in the most diversified manner. The heart and circulation are always affected; the face reddens or becomes purple, with the veins on the forehead and neck distended. . . . With one of my infants, under four months old, I repeatedly observed that the first symptom of an approaching passion was the rushing of the blood into his bare scalp. On the other hand, the action of the heart is sometimes so much impeded by great rage, that the countenance becomes pallid or livid, and not a few with heart-disease have dropped down dead under this powerful emotion.

"The respiration is likewise affected; the chest heaves and the dilated nostrils quiver. . . .

"The excited brain gives strength to the muscles, and at the same time energy to the will. The body is commonly held erect for instant action, but sometimes it is bent towards the offending person, with the limbs more or less rigid. The mouth is generally closed with firmness, showing fixed determination, and the teeth are clenched or ground together. Such gestures as the raising of the arms, with the fists clenched, as if to strike the offender are common. Few men in a great passion, and telling some one to be gone, can resist acting as if they intended to strike or push the man violently away. The desire, indeed, to strike often becomes so intolerably strong, that inanimate objects are struck or dashed to the ground ; but the gestures frequently become altogether purposeless or frantic. Young children, when in a violent rage, roll on the ground on their backs or bellies, screaming, kicking, scratching, biting everything within reach. . . .

" But the muscular system is often affected in a wholly different way ; for trembling is a frequent consequence of extreme rage. The paralysed lips then refuse to obey the will, ' and the voice sticks in the throat ' ; or it is rendered loud, harsh, and discordant. If there be much and rapid speaking, the mouth froths. The hair sometimes bristles. . . . There is in most cases a strongly marked frown on the forehead, for this follows from the sense of anything displeasing or difficult, together with concentration of mind. But sometimes the brow, instead of being much contracted and lowered, remains smooth, with the glaring eyes kept widely open. The eyes are always bright or may, as Homer expresses it, glisten with fire. They are sometimes bloodshot, and are said to protrude from their sockets—the result, no doubt, of the head being gorged with blood, as shown by the veins being distended. . . .

" The lips are sometimes protruded. . . . The lips, however, are much more commonly retracted, the grinning or clenched teeth being thus exposed. . . .

" Under moderate anger the action of the heart is a little increased, the colour heightened and the eyes become bright. The respiration is likewise a little hurried ; and as all the muscles serving for this function act in association, the wings of the nostrils are somewhat raised to allow of a free indraught of air."

This excellent description of Darwin's bears a close resemblance to Cannon's account of the action of adrenalin which was given in Chapter III.

The emotion of rage may be taken as typical of the coarser emotions in general. What should be noted is that the most characteristic expressions of emotions are connected (1) with changes in the circulation of the blood ; (2) with changes in respiration ; (3) with disturbances of secretions ; (4) with movements of involuntary muscles ; and (5) with marked variations in the muscular strength of the body. Of course, the movements of involuntary muscles are hidden from direct observation unless X-rays are used, goose-fleshing and raising of the hair being exceptions. The striped muscles frequently receive great accessions of strength. The blow given when fighting mad is always stronger than an ordinary one. And there is recorded the instance of a boy who, on being chased by a bull, jumped a fence which he could not clear again in a non-emotional state until he was several years older.

(*b*) *Appearance at all Ages.*—Fear and anger responses appear very early in life and persist until death. A baby can be made angry by restraining his movements and fearful by subjecting him to a sudden noise. A grown man, hemmed in by a crowd, pushes vigorously and tends to become angry. He can also be made afraid. An octogenarian can be made both fearful and angry, though by this time the emotional life, it must be confessed, is neither so rich nor so varied as it was earlier, say in adolescence.

(*c*) *Wide Range and Easy Arousal.*—Fear, as we have seen, is normally aroused in a young infant by sudden loud sounds and by insecurity of posture (falling). This emotion, however, is so easily conditioned that practically anything may excite fear in a child. There is not just one thing that makes him afraid, but several; and the ease of arousal from various sources is often a sore trial to the adult. These conditioned fears—of the dark and the like—may be experienced at every stage of development. A child of three months may be afraid of falling, while a man of forty may be afraid of losing his job or his loved ones. If fear of want and dependency could suddenly be cast out of the lives of the majority of civilized mankind, the world would be a happier place than it now appears to be.

(*d*) *Persistency.*—Another characteristic is their persistence when once aroused. An angry man is usually angry for a long time; he refuses to cool down and vents his anger right and left on both the innocent and the guilty. A child sobs on his mother's breast long after he has discovered that the fearful ogre is only his brother disguised with a mask. Even when the emotion has passed, it is generally followed by a mood which we designate by the same name as the emotion.

(*e*) *Interference with Judgment.*—Mark Twain in the aphorisms of "Pudd'nhead Wilson" humorously wrote, "When angry count four; when very angry, swear." The first part of his dictum is certainly good advice, although very difficult to put into practice. As for the second, there are obvious drawbacks to it, although a great many people undoubtedly use swearing as an emotional outlet. Emotions master us; they refuse to be used either for intellectual or practical ends. We do and say things under the influence of emotion, which sober reflection declares to have been stupid and unwise. "Sleep on it" before making important decisions, is wise advice, since sleep will tend to dissipate any emotion that interferes with judgment.

(*f*) *Easily Conditioned.*—Pavlow and the Russian school demonstrated the ease with which reflexes could be conditioned (transferred). The behaviourists have shown that emotions are conditioned with equal ease. As a result it is rare for a "pure" emotion to be experienced by an adult or even by an older child. Since conditioning is dealt with in a chapter under the learning process, nothing further need be said at this point.

Number of Emotions.—The number of emotional responses is undoubtedly very large. The coarser ones—fear, anger, and love—are basic, but owing to conditioning and to the ease with which they fuse and compound together, it is impossible to give a list which commands universal acceptance. In addition to the above, the following are the ones generally recognized: joy, amusement, grief, lust, tenderness, coyness, hatred, envy, pride, jealousy, wonder, disgust, timidity, shame, pity, awe, regret, affection, cordiality, revenge, suspicion, scorn, distress, detestation, and gratitude. Most of these words undoubtedly enrich our language, but the list has little scientific value since the majority are due to introspections instead of scientific investigation.

The Autonomic System and the Emotions.—The autonomic system, that part of the nervous system through which those semi-independent organs—the viscera, glands, heart, and blood vessels, as well as smooth muscle in other situations—receive their innervation, is divided, like Gaul, into three parts. These are the *cranial autonomic system*, whose pre-ganglionic fibres make their exit by way of the third, seventh, ninth, tenth, and eleventh cranial nerves; the *thoracico-lumbar autonomic system*, generally termed the *sympathetic system*, whose pre-ganglionic fibres make their exit by way of the thoracic and upper lumbar spinal nerves; and the *sacral autonomic system*, whose pre-ganglionic fibres run in the visceral rami of the second, third, and fourth sacral nerves. The cranial and sacral divisions have anatomical connections that are different from those of the sympathetic division, by reason of which they work in opposition to it. Thus the upper or cranial division favours digestion by promoting the flow of gastric juice and the movements of the stomach and intestines. The lower or sacral division controls the bladder, rectum, and sex organs. The middle or sympathetic system checks digestion, visceral movements, and sexual excitement. The activity of the upper and lower divisions is shunted out of action by the middle division, and *vice versâ*. Since emotional reactions are intimately connected with glandular and visceral action, opposing emotional effects are obtained by the activity of the cranial-sacral and the sympathetic divisions respectively. Pleasurable bodily reactions, digestion, and sex are associated with the cranial and sacral systems; unpleasant reactions, fear, and anger, with the sympathetic system. And it is impossible to have the opposing emotional reactions taking place simultaneously; it is impossible to be angry and in love at one and the same time.

Emotions and Instincts.—Following the false lead of James and Lange, McDougall elaborated a theory of connection between instincts and emotions which yearly becomes more explicit. Apparently there is, according to McDougall, an emotion which is aroused by or corresponds to each of the instincts. This would necessitate that the number of emotions and of instincts should exactly equal each other, which is probably not the case. While there is undoubtedly a close connection between fear and flight, and pugnacity and anger, McDougall's latest list,[1] reproduced below, contains a number of " instincts " and " emotions " which have such preponderant elements of learning in them that their classification as instinctive or emotional is very dubious, to say the least.

Names of Instincts (Synonyms in Parentheses).	Names of Emotional Qualities accompanying the Instinctive Activities.
1. Instinct of escape (of self-preservation, of avoidance, danger instinct).	Fear (terror, fright, alarm, trepidation).
2. Instinct of combat (aggression, pugnacity).	Anger (rage, fury, annoyance, irritation, displeasure).
3. Repulsion (repugnance).	Disgust (nausea, loathing, repugnance).
4. Parental (protective).	Tender emotion (love, tenderness, tender feeling).
5. Appeal.	Distress (feeling of helplessness).
6. Pairing (mating, reproduction, sexual).	Lust (sexual emotion or excitement, sometimes called love—an unfortunate and confusing usage).
7. Curiosity (inquiry, discovery, investigation).	Curiosity (feeling of mystery, of strangeness, of the unknown, wonder).
8. Submission (self-abasement).	Feeling of subjection (of inferiority, of devotion, of humility, of attachment, of submission, negative self-feeling).
9. Assertion (self-display).	Elation (feeling of superiority, of masterfulness, of pride, of domination, positive self-feeling).
10. Social or gregarious instinct.	Feeling of loneliness, of isolation, nostalgia.
11. Food-seeking (hunting).	Appetite or craving in the narrower sense (gusto).
12. Acquisition (hoarding instinct).	Feeling of ownership, of possession (protective feeling).
13. Construction.	Feeling of creativeness, of making, of productivity.
14. Laughter.	Amusement (jollity, carelessness, relaxation).

To remove such a list as the above from the realm of the speculative, a great amount of careful experimentation will be

[1] McDougall, *Outline of Psychology*, p. 324.

necessary. Fortunately a beginning has been made by those who have used "conditioning" as their method of experiment.

Emotional Mood.—Emotions are often followed by moods. Conversely, a mood may "flare up" into a true emotional response. The mood is probably correctly described an organic or physiological state. Common experience shows that a hungry person, or one who is thoroughly fatigued, is more "touchy," more liable to exhibit anger, than one who has just eaten or had a good night's rest. "Feed the brute," as every wife should know, is no mere figure of speech. The tired child is notoriously difficult to manage; his nerves are on edge. Similarly, the receipt of good or bad news affects our emotional outlook. Passing a difficult examination, or even the receipt of an unexpected cheque, puts us in a good humour (mood) for the rest of the day. Experiences which under other circumstances would rouse in us "the terrible temper of Mr. Bangs," then pass us harmlessly by.

Emotional Levels or Attitudes and Outlets.—But in addition to these more or less temporary, evanescent moods, we recognize the more permanent emotional levels or attitudes of individuals. We speak of persons being high-strung, or stolid. The former seem to be highly emotional, in the sense that their emotions are easily aroused. Persons of artistic temperament seem to live on a higher emotional plane than ordinary mortals. In the young, also, tears and laughter seem ever to lie just beneath the surface. Those people, whom we describe as full of energy, likewise seem to live at a higher emotional level than others. The stolid, on the other hand, are unemotional and placid. Between these extremes we recognize the normal—those who can be roused, but whose emotional responses are under good control. These emotional attitudes, these permanent emotional sets of individuals, are probably dependent upon the endocrine balances of the body, but little is known about them that has scientific validity.

Society does not permit an indiscriminate expression of the emotions. Young children are allowed a certain amount of quarrelling and fighting, but if a grown man allows his pugnacity free play, he soon finds himself behind prison bars. But this does not mean that the emotion is never present in adults, or if present, finds no outlet. We condition our emotions in a host of ways. If a man is made angry by his employer, his wife and children may be made to suffer. The coffin containing a loved one may be smothered with flowers to assuage the grief. Swearing may be an emotional outlet for an angry man. Outlets for emotions seem to be necessary. Certainly those in whom emotions are too tightly bottled tend to become psychopathic.

School and society should provide socially desirable outlets for emotions. In school the fields of art, music, and literature are desirable outlets. But strong emotions should be discouraged, for their results are entirely harmful. Crile [1] has produced proof that, biologically, all strong feeling, or emotion, entails a stupendous expenditure of energy; that the physiological effects of emotions are identical with those of the expenditure of energy in muscular activity.

"The development of civilization has removed the need for these muscular expressions of fear, flight, fighting, etc., in a large measure, yet they persist. Moreover, when the brain, the thyroid, the adrenals, and the liver are activated by the distance stimulus which gives rise to the emotion, and then the action is inhibited, the presence of these impulses and secretions in the relatively inactive system is practically certain to prove injurious. In other words, the activation provided for does not take place adequately for the relieving of the created tensions. . . .

"The fact then that emotions are great spenders of energy, that they throw the organism into strains that must be released through some kind of action, and that the release and the return to equilibrium are the satisfying elements in all such behaviour, would tend to put it beyond doubt that the strong annoyances are off-equilibrium conditions and that strong satisfactions are toward-and-on conditions." [2]

While the topic "emotions, their arousal and control," is one of the least known in the psychological field, genetic psychology and mental hygiene are making great strides in its scientific elucidation. These studies in course of time will undoubtedly change many current methods of child management, not only in the home, but in the school as well.

References

ANGELL, J. R. "A Reconsideration of James's Theory of Emotions in the Light of Recent Criticisms," *Psychological Review*, vol. 23 (July, 1916), pp. 259–261.

BREESE, B. B. *Psychology*. New York, Scribner, 1921. Pp. x+483.

BROWN, W. *Psychology and Psychotherapy*. London, Arnold, 1922. Pp. xi+196.

BURNHAM, W. H. *The Normal Mind*. New York, Appleton, 1924. Pp. x+702.

BURTON-OPITZ, R. *Textbook of General Physiology*. Philadelphia, Saunders, 1920. Pp. v+1185.

CANNON, W. B. *Bodily Changes in Pain, Hunger, Fear, and Rage*. New York, Appleton, 1914. Pp. 311.

CRILE, G. W. *Man, an Adaptive Mechanism*. New York, Macmillan, 1916. Pp. xvi+387.

---

[1] Crile, G. W., *Man, an Adaptive Mechanism*.
[2] Raup, R. B., *Complacency: The Foundation of Human Behavior*, pp. 85, 86.

CRILE, G. W. *The Origin and Nature of the Emotions*. Philadelphia, Saunders, 1915. Pp. vii+240.

DARWIN, C. *The Expression of the Emotions in Man and Animals*. London, Murray, 1872. Pp. vi+374.

DEARBORN, N. H. *An Introduction to Teaching*. New York, Appleton, 1925. Pp. xv+337.

FRINK, H. W. *Morbid Fears and Compulsions*. New York, Moffatt, Yard & Co., 1918. Pp. xviii+568.

GATES, A. I. *Psychology for Students of Education*. New York, Macmillan, 1924. Pp. xvi+489.

HOLT, E. B. *The Freudian Wish and its Place in Ethics*. New York, Holt, 1915. Pp. vii+212.

JAMES, W. *Principles of Psychology*, vol. 2. New York, Holt, 1908 (1st ed. 1890). Pp. vi+704.

JUDD, C. H. *Psychology*. Boston, Ginn, 1917. Pp. xix+358.

MCDOUGALL, W. *An Introduction to Social Psychology*. London, Methuen, 1922 (17th ed.). Pp. xxiv+459.

MCDOUGALL, W. *Outline of Psychology*. New York, Scribners, 1923. Pp. xvi+456.

MORGAN, J. J. B. *The Psychology of the Unadjusted School Child*. New York, Macmillan, 1924. Pp. xi+300.

NEUMANN, H. "The Child's Moral Equipment and Development," in *The Child: His Nature and His Needs*. Valparaiso, The Children's Foundation, 1924. Pp. 88–91.

NORSWORTHY and WHITLEY. *Psychology of Childhood*. New York, Macmillan, 1918. Pp. xix+375.

RAUP, R. B. *Complacency: The Foundation of Human Behavior*. New York, Macmillan, 1925. Pp. xii+197.

SEASHORE, C. E. *Introduction to Psychology*. New York, Macmillan, 1923. Pp. xviii+427.

SHERRINGTON, C. S. *The Integrative Action of the Nervous System*. Newhaven, Yale University Press, 1923. Pp. xvi+411.

SKINNER, GAST, SKINNER. *Readings in Educational Psychology*. New York, Appleton, 1926. Pp. xxvii+833.

STRATTON, G. M. *Anger: its Religious and Moral Significance*. London, Allen & Unwin, 1924. Pp. x+277.

THOM, D. A. *Child Management*. Washington, U.S. Dept. of Labour, Children's Bureau Publication, No. 143, 1924. Pp. 24.

WARD, J. *Psychological Principles*. Cambridge, University Press, 1918. Pp. xiv+478.

WATSON, J. B. "A Schematic Outline of the Emotions," *Psychological Review*, vol. 26 (May, 1919), pp. 165–177.

WATSON, J. B. *Behaviorism: Lectures-in-Print*. New York, People's Institute Publishing Co., 1924. Pp. 251.

WATSON, J. B. "Recent Experiments on how we Lose and Change our Emotional Equipment," *Pedagogical Seminary*, vol. 32, 2 (June, 1925), pp. 349–371.

WATSON, J. B. "Experimental Studies of the Growth of the Emotions," *Pedagogical Seminary*, vol. 32, 2 (June, 1925), pp. 328–348.

WOODWORTH, R. S. *Psychology: A Study of Mental Life*. New York, Holt, 1921. Pp. x+580.

CHAPTER VIII

INTELLIGENCE: ITS NATURE AND MEASUREMENT

Native Intelligence.—By placing the topic " Intelligence " in this section of the book we register our conviction that it is innate. That some people are born stupid, some clever, no serious student of education now doubts. That men in general are more intelligent than chimpanzees, chimpanzees than dogs, dogs than guinea-pigs, guinea-pigs than frogs, and frogs than fishes is also universally conceded. That some men are literally born idiots, and nothing that we can do in the way of education and training will raise them to normal mentality, is no longer open to question. That others are born geniuses and that these, given half a chance, will inevitably reach higher mental levels than their fellows is generally recognized. Even the fact that some animals, such as chimpanzees and dogs, are born cleverer than others of the same species is common knowledge. But what has confused the issue and has resulted in such spirited controversies as that between Bagley and Lippmann on the one hand, and Terman and Whipple on the other, is the fact that intelligence must be manifested in behaviour before it can be judged.[1] Environment and training must first play upon native talents in order that they may be recognized. Hence the paradox that *achievement is the test of potentiality*; that the capacity to learn is judged, and can only be judged, by the amount that one has actually learned. Intelligence is undoubtedly inherited, but it needs a proper environment to bring it to fruition. That this common-sense view is the right one will become increasingly evident in the course of this chapter, especially in those parts which deal with the contributions of Spearman and the London school.

The Nature of Intelligence.—The word " intelligence " is used by educators and by laymen in two ways—for brightness and for mental age—and an unfortunate confusion has thereby arisen. These two usages are clearly seen in the following statement: " That boy of five is an intelligent little chap; he has the intelligence of an eight-year-old." The adjective " intelligent "

[1] See especially Bagley, W. C., *Determinism in Education*, Baltimore, Warwick and York, 1925, and the articles in *School and Society* on April 8, June 3, and August 5, 1922 (vol. xvi).

obviously refers to his brightness, that is, to his intelligence in comparison with other children of the same age. Intelligence here is a relative or comparative affair, which, as will be seen later, is measured by the intelligence quotient (I.Q.). The second use of intelligence refers to the boy's mental age. It is an absolute affair. His brightness, presumably, will remain constant, but his mental age will increase with time.

Intelligence has been defined in scores of ways. The commonest features of the various definitions are (1) the ability to adapt oneself to novel situations; (2) the ability to carry on the higher processes of thought, especially abstract thinking; and (3) the ability to learn. It is probably best defined as a function of the central nervous system. If a person has a nervous system which integrates easily and tenaciously, he is likely to be bright or intelligent. If, on the other hand, his nervous system forms neuron paths with difficulty, if associations are hard to form and are soon lost, he is certain to be dull and stupid. Specific training, of course, is needed to form the connections, but the learning is easy if there is good nerve material to work upon. This definition, it will be observed, reconciles the views of Spearman and Thorndike. The general factor is the inherited state of the nervous system; but the relatively independent traits need specific training. Thus, so far as education is concerned, intelligence and capacity to learn are practically synonymous terms.

The Concept of "g" and "s."—As far back as 1904, a year before Binet published his first scale for the measurement of intelligence, Spearman [1] printed a paper in which he stated that "all branches of intellectual activity have in common one fundamental function (or group of functions), whereas the remaining or specific elements seem in every case to be wholly different from that in all the others." This is the first statement of the now famous "two factor" theory of intelligence developed by Spearman and his co-workers. These factors are now labelled "g" and "s." The factor "g" represents general ability or general intelligence, the thing which intelligence tests measure with some degree of success. It is constant for the same individual, but varies greatly from individual to individual. But it is the common element which makes the measures of an individual in a number of traits exhibit positive correlation. The second factor "s" represents the specific factor inherent in the act or performance under consideration. It may represent musical capacity in musical performance and mathematical capacity in mathematical performance, and these two "s's" may be markedly different in

[1] Spearman, C., "General Intelligence, Objectively Determined and Measured," *American Journal of Psychology*, vol. xv (1904), pp. 201–293.

amount in the same individual. It is the variation of these independent " s " factors which occasions the variety of performance in different tasks when undertaken by the same individual. But a person's success in any form of response or performance is the joint products of his " g " and " s," his ability in general, and his specific ability for the task in question.

Since the theory was first promulgated it has met with considerable opposition. His first proof of it was shown to be insecure by Thomson, but Spearman in twenty years of research claims to have proved it correct in every detail, and flawless both from the experimental and the mathematical side.[1] It would be out of place to give even a summary of the evidence in a work of this description. Suffice it to say that the basis of it lies in the *tetrad equation :*

$$r_{ap} \times r_{bq} - r_{aq} \times r_{bp} = 0$$

The value on the left-hand side constitutes the *tetrad difference.*

" An illustration may be afforded by the following imaginary correlations between mental tests (actually observed correlations will be given later on) :

	Opposites.	Completion.	Memory.	Discrimination.	Cancellation.
Opposites . . 1	—	0·80	0·60	0·30	0·30
Completion . . 2	0·80	—	0·48	0·24	0·24
Memory . . 3	0·60	0·48	—	0·18	0·18
Discrimination . 4	0·30	0·24	0·18	—	0·09
Cancellation . . 5	0·30	0·24	0·18	0·09	—

For instance, let us try the effect of making—

a denote opposites
b ,, discrimination
p ,, completion
q ,, cancellation

From the table of correlations above, we see that r_{ap} will mean the correlation between opposites and completion, which is 0·80. Obtaining in a similar fashion the other three correlations needed, the whole tetrad equation becomes

$$0{\cdot}80 \times 0{\cdot}09 - 0{\cdot}30 \times 0{\cdot}24 = 0$$

which is obviously correct. And so will be found any other application whatever of the tetrad equation to this table.

" So far, the business is confined to matters of observation ; we simply try out the tetrad equation on any table of actually observed

[1] Spearman, C., *The Abilities of Man : their Nature and Measurement.* London, Macmillan, 1927. The mathematical argument and proof is given in a valuable appendix running to 33 pages.

correlations and examine whether it fits. . . . Whenever the tetrad equation holds throughout any table of correlations, and *only* when it does so, then every individual measurement of every ability (or of any other variable that enters into the table) can be divided into two independent parts which possess the following momentous properties. The one part has been called the 'general factor' and denoted by the letter 'g'; it is so named because, although varying freely from individual to individual, it remains the same for any one individual in respect of all the correlated abilities. The second part has been called the 'specific factor' and denoted by the letter 's.' It not only varies from individual to individual, but even for any one individual from each ability to another. The proof of this all-important mathematical theorem has gradually evolved through successive stages of completeness, and may now be regarded as complete." [1]

What is the character of "g"? Psychologically, it may be interpreted as intelligence or mental energy. Physiologically, it may be explained by energy, plasticity of the nervous system, the condition of the blood, endocrine balance, oxygenation, and by many other factors. It may be due to chance, providing the "g's" are equal in every individual. Spearman leans to the view that "g" is analogous to energy, "that is to say, it is some force capable of being transferred from one mental operation to another different one. Even on the physiological side, there are some grounds for hoping that some such energy will sooner or later be discovered in the nervous system, especially the cerebral cortex." But an energy needs an engine in which to operate. This engine is supplied by the nervous system.

The experimental evidence adduced by Spearman shows that "g" is "involved invariably and exclusively in all operations of eductive nature." A corollary of this is that any test which involves the perception and use of relations is the best type to apply in the measurement of intelligence. The factor "g" has also intimate relationships with clearness and speed, with intensity and extensity of span, but is surprisingly independent of retentivity or memory.

In opposition to Spearman's two-factor theory we have that of Thorndike's, which maintains that a person's total intelligence is made up of a large number of specific abilities, not bound together by a common factor. These abilities usually show a high degree of correlation, but on the other hand they may not. Whenever correlations are found between abilities it is due to elements that are common to many of them.

For the very practical task of measuring intelligence it does not matter very much which view we adopt—Spearman's, which says that high correlations are due to the central factor "g," or

[1] Spearman, *The Abilities of Man*, pp. 73–75.

Thorndike's, which maintains that it is due to common elements. In practice we have to measure intelligence by its products, and the best measures are those which measure those products in the fairest way.

Basic Problems in Intelligence Measurement.—Although we do not know what the ultimate nature of intelligence will prove to be, we are certain that in its observable forms it is always expressed through behaviour. It is difficult to conceive of any act which has absolutely no intelligence behind it, so we may posit intelligence as an ingredient of every response. The actions of the lowest idiot, we all agree, are not very intelligent, while the highest forms of behaviour exhibited by a genius we regard as extremely intelligent. There are, however, just as many forms of intelligence as there are forms of behaviour. Therefore, if we are to measure intelligence it will be necessary to get as wide a sampling of a person's behaviour as possible. If a special manifestation of intelligence is to be measured, such, for example, as *abstract* intelligence which manifests itself in the management of abstract symbols, or *social* intelligence which is exhibited in various forms of social behaviour, or *concrete* intelligence such as that which is concerned with mechanical and concrete things, then a fair sampling within the group under consideration may fulfil all requirements. All measurements of intelligence will be unreliable in so far as all samplings are unfair and unrepresentative. And it is extremely unlikely that any single test will yield a measure of intelligence that is valid for every situation. Intelligence testers are therefore justified in using tests which include measures of attention, of thinking ability, of abstraction, of judgment, and of breadth of knowledge in their batteries. If Spearman's claims are justified, it will be possible in future to test the tests and to discard those which do not fufil their purpose.

In the construction and scoring of tests three principles are widely applied. The first is that the harder the task a person can perform, the greater is his intelligence. This is the principle of *difficulty or level*. It employs the touchstone of rarity; the rarer a thing is the more valuable it must be. Fewer people can use the calculus than the multiplication table, therefore the intelligence needed for the calculus is higher than that needed for the multiplication table. We employ this principle when we say that the acts of an Aristotle are more intelligent than those of an unskilled workman. The range of level of intelligence is from that of the lowest idiot to that of an Aristotle, a Shakespeare, or a Newton.

The second principle is that of *range or width*. The person who can do more tasks of a given degree of difficulty than another, the greater is his intelligence. Here it would seem that time enters freely into the question. Given sufficient time, it would seem that a person of low intelligence can master all the tasks which fall below his vertical level. But, in practice, it is found that there is a very close relationship between level and width. The higher the level the greater the width.

The third principle is *speed* of performance. He who can respond more quickly than another is regarded as the more intelligent. Certainly in commerce and industry the principle is widely applied. The workers who can do more than others in a given time are paid more, and are rightfully regarded as more intelligent.[1]

The discovery of a true zero and a scale of equal units are basic problems in intelligence measurement. In the Binet scale there is a true zero, but it is very unlikely that a scale of mental ages is a scale of equal units. In scales which use variability in their determination both the zero and equal unit desiderata are approximated, but not secured. Thorndike's work on the CAVD gives the nearest approximations to a true zero and equal units that have so far been determined. The task of securing them was intricate and arduous, but the description of the method merits the careful attention of all who are concerned with measurements of intelligence.

The Growth of Intelligence.—Intelligence tests confirm the common-sense conclusion that intelligence goes on growing from birth to maturity. Yet psychologists are still uncertain of the rates of growth at different stages and of the normal age of maturity of intelligence. The difficulty lies in the fact that there is no absolute scale for the measurement of mental growth. To plot mental age against chronological age, as Baldwin and Stecher[2] have done, is futile, since the only possible result which can be got with unselected subjects in such cases is a straight, I.Q. line. From our knowledge of physical growth and from a consideration of the scores obtained in group tests, the best prediction that can be made at present is represented by the curves of Fig. 35. These curves show that there is a gradual slowing up of intellectual growth during childhood and that, for normal persons at least, it ceases around sixteen. Brighter children grow in intelligence more quickly and for a longer time than normal children, and normal children than subnormal ones. What happens after maturity is reached we do not know. Probably the level of intelligence remains fairly constant during the adult period, falling off gradually as senile decay sets in. But the curves should

[1] For a fuller discussion of these principles see Thorndike *et al.*, *The Measurement of Intelligence*, chap. i.

[2] Baldwin and Stecher, *Mental Growth Curve of Normal and Superior Children*, Univ. of Iowa Studies 2, No. 1.

not be interpreted to mean that a man of forty knows no more than a boy of sixteen. All that they show is that in performances such as current tests of intelligence measure, a boy of sixteen does just as well as an adult.

The age of maturity of intelligence is still unknown. Binet, from his results, considered that intelligence reached its maturity at fifteen. Terman fixed it at sixteen. Ballard, by means of an extended Binet absurdities test, determined it to be sixteen. Otis and Monroe both regard eighteen as the age of maturity of intelligence. Thorndike found that mental growth with High School pupils continued practically undiminished to the end of the High School period. Doll collected evidence which seemed

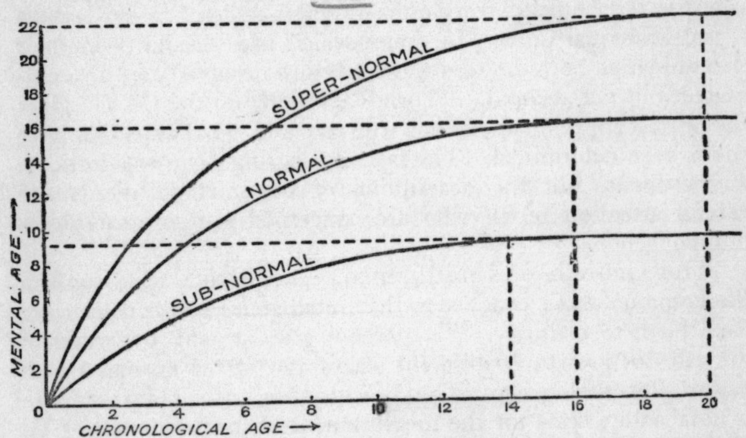

FIG. 35.—Curves showing the growth of intelligence from birth to maturity. Note that the subnormal reach maturity in mental growth at an earlier age than the others.

to indicate that it should be reduced to thirteen years. This latter figure agrees fairly closely with the results of mental testing in the United States Army, where it was found that the average recruit made a score equal to that of a mental age of 13·08 on the Stanford Binet. We can say with some degree of confidence that with most of the present instruments of measurement the final level reached is somewhere between fourteen and sixteen. With more delicate instruments it may be discovered that even for normal people a slight but definite growth up to twenty-three or twenty-four takes place.

The curves in Fig. 35 are drawn smoothly, but we have no indisputable evidence that intelligence grows in any such regular fashion. For the average of a group, the picture drawn is the correct one, since any deviations, *plus* and *minus*, tend to cancel each other. But for the individual, the growth may be in spurts and starts, or interrupted by illness, as we know physical growth to be. Some evidence of regularity of growth is found in the relative constancy of the I.Q. in successive and repeated measurements. Numerous studies have been made on the constancy of the I.Q.[1] and all agree in showing that it remains fairly constant from the time of one test to the next, whether the subjects be bright, normal or dull, or whether the interval between measurements be long or short. In most investigations, as the list given below shows, the coefficient of correlation between earlier and later results has exceeded 0·80, with the average around 0·87

Stenquist . . .	0·72	(274 cases)
Rugg and Colloton .	0·84	(137 cases)
Terman	0·93	(435 cases)
Baldwin	0·72–0·93	(various groups)
Jordan	0·84	(44 cases)
Bobertag	0·95	
Rosenow	0·82	
Cuneo and Terman .	0·85	(31 cases)
	0·94	(21 cases)
	0·95	(25 cases)
Garrison	0·88	(298 cases, 1 year's interval)
	0·91	(127 cases, 2 years' interval)
	0·83	(42 cases, 3 years' interval)
Mean .	0·87	

In Terman's investigations the following were the salient facts discovered:

(1) The central tendency of change is represented by an increase of 1·7 in I.Q.

(2) The middle 50 per cent. of changes lies between the limit of 3·3 decrease and 5·7 increase.

(3) The probable error of a prediction based on the first test is 4·5 in terms of I.Q.[2]

From all of which, considering the unreliability of the measuring instruments, the personal equations of the examiners, and the variability of the individuals due to illness or fatigue, we may conclude that the growth of intelligence proceeds fairly steadily from year to year without any marked fluctuations.

Vertical and Horizontal Growth in Intelligence.—But the sceptical reader will immediately remark that surely a person of forty is cleverer, more intelligent, than he was at sixteen. The answer is that, so far as intelligence tests show, he

[1] Dickson, V. E., *Mental Tests and the Classroom Teacher.* Yonkers-on-Hudson, World Book Co., 1923, pp. 65–71, gives a summary of the evidence to 1923.

[2] Terman, L. M., *The Intelligence of School Children.* Boston, Houghton Mifflin, 1919, p. 142.

is not. The concept of vertical and horizontal growth is helpful here. In the preceding section we presented a diagram which showed that a mental age of sixteen was the level of an average mature intellect. Fig. 36 presents another aspect of the situation. The vertical line indicates levels of intelligence measured in terms of mental age. For convenience, we assume that a mental age scale is one of equal units. The average performance of an adult is at the sixteen-year-old level, that is, he can do tasks which a normal sixteen-year-old can do. A genius usually works at a

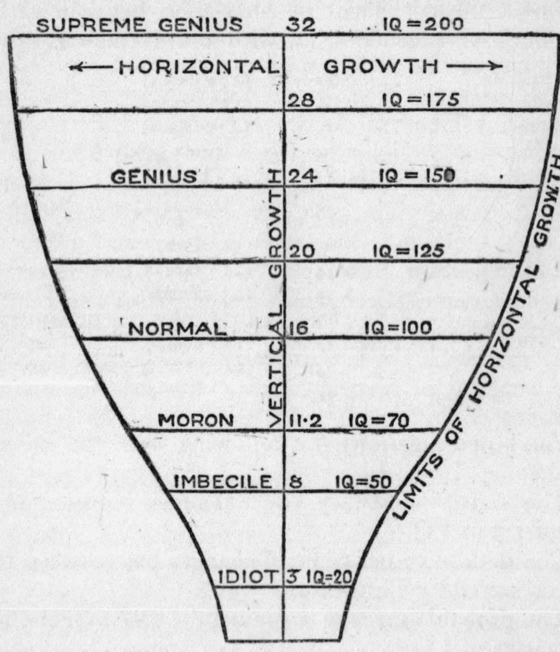

FIG. 36.—Diagram to show horizontal and vertical growth in intelligence. For morons, imbeciles, and idiots the highest levels achievable are shown.

higher level—an Aristotle, conceivably, at a thirty-year or even higher level. Subnormal people work at a lower level than sixteen. For an idiot the average limit in vertical growth is 3 years; for an imbecile the limit is 7 or 8; for a moron, 11 or 12 Nature fixes the level, so the vertical growth may be regarded as representing the contribution of heredity. No matter how long or how zealously a person studies, his average performance remains around this fixed and predetermined level. Education, therefore, cannot alter the level, but it can, and does, determine the extent of horizontal development at any level. The horizontal lines of Fig. 36 represent the environmental factor in learning.

Theoretically, horizontal growth is unlimited; in practice it exhibits fairly well-defined limits which seem to bear a direct relationship to its level on the vertical scale. In other words, a genius can actually learn more things than a subnormal. These limitations at various levels are indicated by the curved lines. Nobody knows the exact relationship of height and width, but that it is a positive one there is no possible shadow of doubt. The product of the vertical and horizontal distances—a sort of area—gives an acceptable measure of intellect.

An illustration may make the matter plainer. The writer is, or thinks he is, a fair historian, but has no special gifts for history. Let us suppose his level for history is sixteen. Suppose also that he could live to be as old as Methuselah and spend the rest of his life in acquiring historical facts. He would, conceivably, learn more facts on the sixteen-year level than John Richard Green, or any other eminent historian, ever knew. But he would not be a better historian. The great historians work at a higher level than ordinary mortals. Historians in this sense are born, not made. Through their greater native capacity they have a power of relating cause and effect which is denied to lesser intellects. The facts of history may lie along the horizontal plane, but their proper interpretation, which, after all, is the only true history, is wholly a matter of vertical height. Further, the assumption that the writer could actually learn more facts than John Richard Green is entirely unwarranted.

In the future the tasks which can be efficiently performed at various levels will be determined. But at present we know little about them. Hoeing turnips can probably be done efficiently by adults with a mental age of four years; simple cooking by one with a mental level of eight years; but it needs a level, perhaps, of twenty years to comprehend Einstein's theory of relativity, and a still higher level to apply the theory effectively in practice. The task of determining the minimum age-levels of various occupations present an opportunity for experimentation along very interesting lines. From the empirical experience of teachers working with subnormal children we know conclusively that there are literally hundreds of jobs of a routine and mechanical nature which feeble-minded children can do quite well. In fact, one of the major discoveries of intelligence testing is that no person above the level of a low-grade imbecile need lack for jobs in which he can find both profit and satisfaction.

History of Intelligence Testing.—Early attempts to measure intelligence missed the mark either because they depended on physical traits, or because the mental traits they used as a measuring stick were too simple to discriminate between the clever and the stupid.[1] Lavater, in his *Essay on Physiognomy Destined to make Man known and loved* (1772), tried to determine a man's disposition and abilities from the features and expression of his face. This we now know to be a feat impossible of execution. No teacher can arrange his pupils in the order of intelligence from their looks alone, or from a careful study of their photographs. Gall's attempt (1810) to determine character and intelligence from an examination of cranial protuberances proved equally futile. Similarly, all attempts to use such things as head measurements, anatomical anomalies, or even simple psychological tests like reaction times and tests of sensory capacities, have proved singularly disappointing as measures of intelligence. The mental defective does not differ from the normal person so much in his sensory capacities (he can usually see and hear quite well) as in his powers of thinking, reasoning, relating, and judging.

England, France, and Germany were the sources of the stream which has resulted in the flood of intelligence testing that has almost overwhelmed the North American continent. While it is somewhat invidious to select from the vast array of workers those who appear to have contributed most to the solution of the problem of intelligence measurement, the following seem to be the most significant:

England.

Galton (Individual Differences).
Burt (Tests of Higher Thought Processes, and London Revision of Binet Tests).
Spearman (Concept of "g" and "s," and Contributions to Mathematical Theory).
Pearson (Basic Mathematical formulæ).
Thomson (Work on Validity of "g").
Porteus (Australian, Maze Test).

France.

Seguin (First Form Board).
Binet (The first usable Intelligence Test, 1905).

Germany.

Wundt (First Psychological Laboratory, 1879).
Stern and Bobertag (I.Q.).
Ebbinghaus (Completion Tests).
Bobertag (German Revision of Binet Tests).

America.

Cattell (First Battery of Psychological Tests, first American Psy. Lab., and Individual Differences).
Thorndike (Statistical Methods, Tests for College Students, and C.A.V.D.).
Goddard (First American version of Binet Tests).
Terman (Stanford revision of Binet Tests).
Knox (Tests for Immigrants).
Yerkes (Point Scale, and Report on Army Tests).
Otis (First workable Group Test).
Pintner (Non-language and Performance Tests).
Engels (First Group Test for Young Children).
Kelley (Statistical Methods).
McCall (Scaling Tests).
Haines (Scales for Blind)

[1] Report of the Consultative Committee, English Board of Education, on *Psychological Tests of Educable Capacity and their Possible Use in the Public System of Education*. London, H.M. Stationery Office, 1924.

Binet provided the world with the first workable series of intelligence tests. Binet succeeded where others failed because he incorporated in his tests the following important features:

(1) He used a variety of test problems designed to measure intelligence along whatever lines it was exhibited. The test problems were of such a nature that the answers to them were dictated by a general training in a common environment, and not by any special training which might be given to some and not to others. His final average result may be compared with the grading of a car of grain by taking samples from different parts of the car, or, better still, with the valuation of a mine from the average of its sample borings. Previous to his time, psychologists had been employing a single test, or, at most, only a few. Binet was the first to see that intelligence was a highly complex thing, exhibited in many directions, and therefore, to sample it thoroughly, an extensive and diverse series of tests must be employed in its diagnosis.

(2) He standardized the methods of administering and scoring the tests so that they would give strictly comparable results when employed by other workers.

(3) He used the concept of mental age for the expression of his intelligence ratings. Thus a child of five has a mental age of five provided he can do the tasks which, on the average, a large and unselected group of five-year-olds can do. In other words, any person's intelligence is rated directly against that of persons of the same age. If he can perform them better than his equals in age he is of superior intelligence; if he cannot do them as well, then he is of inferior intelligence. The Binet tests, then, are standardized on an age scale. The validity of the standardization depends upon the selection, or rather non-selection, of subjects in sufficient numbers to give a constant average to the performance.

The placing of a test in a given age group has been a matter of considerable controversy. Binet's plan was never consistent. He thought a test too easy for a given age if 90 per cent. of children at that age succeeded with it, but if as few as 65 per cent. passed he considered it to be correctly assigned. The custom on the North American continent, following the quartile divisions of a normal distribution, has been to adopt 75 per cent. as the standard of assignment. The correct procedure, as Burt [1] has shown, is to assign a test to a given year when it is passed by 50 per cent. of the children who are normally of the year below. Thus a test is a five-year test when it is passed by 50 per cent. of four-year-olds.

[1] Burt, C., *Mental and Scholastic Tests*. London, P. S. King, 1922, p. 140.

A mental age is a score in a test, and the accuracy of the score depends upon the accuracy of the standardization. As a rating of intelligence which is easily understood by laymen, mental age surpasses all others. Even in the shape of a derived form known as the intelligence quotient (I.Q.), the ratio of the mental to the chronological age, it is understood and used intelligently by millions of people. But as a scientific measure it has serious drawbacks. Owing to the fact that intelligence normally matures around the age of sixteen, it naturally follows that all normal adults have the same mental age, namely, sixteen. The term is only really significant for children. Consequently other methods of expressing intelligence ratings have been evolved, chief of which are median mental ages, percentile ratings and age-variability measures.

Individual tests, such as the Binet and all its revisions, consume a great amount of time in their administration. It is no unusual thing for a bright boy of ten to take an hour or more with the Stanford Binet before the examiner can be certain that he has done all that he is capable of doing. Attempts to reduce the time element resulted in the discovery of the group test—one that could be given to many pupils at a time. The first really successful group test was evolved by American psychologists during the Great War for the determination of the mentality of drafted recruits. To Otis, more than to any single worker, must be given credit for the discovery of the basic principles used in this test. A group test usually consists of a number of tests called a battery, five to ten in number, printed in the form of a booklet. Each test of the battery consists of a number of short questions or problems printed on a single page, and requiring a minimum amount of writing on the part of the pupil. It is not unusual to have as many as two hundred questions which are to be answered by the pupil in half an hour. One booklet is distributed to each candidate, who writes or marks his answers on the pages according to precise instructions. The questions are such that the answers are either right or wrong, thus obviating the necessity of giving partial credits. The group test, owing to the ease and economy of its administration, may now be regarded as the normal type of intelligence test.

Both tests so far described involve a knowledge of the mother tongue—in this case English. They are obviously unsuited to foreign children, to the deaf, who cannot hear instructions, and to very young pupils who have not learned to read and write. It was, therefore, a natural step forward to attempt the construction of tests which would be suitable for these important groups. For foreign children and the deaf, performance tests of various kinds have been evolved. The Pintner and Paterson " Scale of Performance Tests " uses a variety of form boards ; the Porteus " Maze Tests " require the pupil to draw lines which show the correct paths through various kinds of mazes. Group tests for kindergarten pupils and primary grade children have also been invented. These require of the pupil nothing but the marking of pictures with a pencil according to instructions given by the examiner.

We thus see that, in a period of less than two decades from the construction of Binet's first scale, the major problems connected with intelligence testing have been solved. Literally hundreds of quite good tests have been prepared. Practically all of them fall within the four main classes listed below, where samples of each are listed by name :

I. *Individual Tests involving Language.*—Binet Tests in all Revisions.

II. *Group Tests involving Language.*—The National Intelligence Test ; Terman Group Test of Mental Ability ; Haggerty Delta II ; Otis Group Intelligence Scale, Advanced Examination ; Army Alpha ; and Thorndike Intelligence Examination for High School Graduates.

III. *Individual Tests not involving Language.*—Pintner and Paterson Scale of Performance Tests ; and Porteus Maze Tests.

IV. *Group Tests not involving Language.*—Detroit First-Grade Intelligence Test ; Pintner-Cunningham Primary Mental Tests.

What is now needed is a really good test for the pre-school child. Gesell[1] has done some important pioneering work in this direction, but his tests so far are too cumbersome to use, owing to the peculiar method he adopted for scaling them. Finally, much more work needs to be done on the standardization of tests—their validity and reliability. Spearman's criteria, for example, should be thoroughly tested out, likewise partial and multiple correlation methods. The work will be long and arduous but, in the long run, it will be worth the effort.

The Discovery of Intelligence Tests.—The discovery of a reliable intelligence test is largely an empirical, hit-and-miss kind of affair. If we choose for the purposes of a test such things as quality of handwriting, or spelling, or even simple computations in arithmetic, and arrange the members of a class in order of merit according to any of these criteria, we find that the order is

[1] Gesell, A., *The Mental Growth of the Pre-School Child.* New York, Macmillan, 1925.

very dissimilar from that in which any competent person who knows them well, the teacher for example, arranges them for intelligence. In technical terms, the coefficients of correlation between handwriting, spelling, or computation and intelligence are quite low. This is due to the fact that the brightest pupil may write very badly while the dullest may write a copper-plate hand. Common experience shows that quite intelligent people often write illegibly or have great difficulty with spelling and computation. Writing, spelling, and computation, therefore, cannot be used profitably as measures of intelligence. Similarly, reaction times, tests of sensory discrimination, and physical measures such as size of head are ruled out of order because of low correlation with intelligence. If, by good luck, we discover a test which agrees very closely with the order of merit that the teacher or other competent person assigns every time it is given, we begin to have confidence in it. So much so, that if it fails to agree with a single teacher's rating after it has agreed rather closely with thirty or forty others, we are justified in thinking that it is the teacher's judgment which is at fault, not the test. Such a procedure looks like arguing in a circle. First we find a test which agrees with the judgments of competent persons, and then we say that if the judgments do not agree with the test the persons are incompetent. Fortunately, it is not a vicious circle, for the combined judgment of a large number of teachers is obviously more reliable than any single judgment. Anyway, it is a principle used in law, in politics, and in every walk of life when matters of opinion are in dispute; in such cases we bow to the judgment of the majority.

In just such a manner as the above, the tests known as Analogies, Best Answer, Proverbs, Classification, Information, Extent of Vocabulary, Sentence Completion, Reasoning, Digit-symbol Substitution, Dissected Sentence, Number Series Completion, and scores of others have been discovered. While any single test may not be too reliable, a selection of a number to be used in conjunction usually works well. The principle used in the selection of a battery of tests is to choose each one so that it correlates highly with the criterion for intelligence used, but poorly with all the rest of the battery. This ensures a widespread sampling of intelligence.

Standardization of Tests.—After suitable tests have been discovered and the directions for administering and scoring them have been drawn up, they are still unready for use. They need to be standardized, that is, the median or average scores for various ages, grades, or other groups, must be determined. To do this the tests are given to unselected pupils within the group for which standardization is required. If a standard for ages is required, then a large number of pupils, selected at random for each age, must be tested and the mean or median scores determined. This is not so simple as it sounds. The pupils selected for each year of age must contain a normal proportion of rich and poor, retarded and accelerated, children from good schools and children from poor schools, children of manual workers and children of professional workers, and so forth. Suppose that 500 ten-year-old pupils have been selected at random and the median score calculated. How can we be sure that the selection was truly representative of the millions of ten-year-olds to whom it may possibly be given? There are two crucial tests which may be applied. The first is to test an additional number of pupils, say 200, and recalculate the median for the new total, 700. If the median remains the same the test may be regarded as standardized; if it changes then more pupils must be tested until the median becomes constant. The second is to make a graph of the medians determined for each age. If the graph is either a straight line or a smooth curve without sudden jogs in it, the norms are probably reliable.

In addition to standard scores, expressed in various kinds of units, most tests add a table which enables any given score to be converted into a mental age from which the I.Q. may be calculated. The I.Q. gets rid of the age factor and enables the examiner to judge if the brightness of a pupil is up to normal, or not.

Testing the Test.—An intelligence test, like any other form of examination, is judged by its validity, reliability, objectivity, ease of administration and scoring, and by the satisfactoriness of its norms.

By *validity* is meant the degree to which a test measures that which it claims to measure. An intelligence test claims to measure intelligence, and therefore it should measure this factor. In the making of the test the items are selected because they measure something which competent people call intelligence. To this degree they are valid. If, further, the measurements by the test forecast the subsequent progress of pupils in school, or their later success in life, or their achievements in any way, we should regard their validity highly, because the factor of intelligence is singly the most important factor in all these things. Table VII [1] gives a summary of the recent findings from the standpoint of prognosis. The correlations are those for the intelligence test and pooled subjects in the stated grades for High Schools.

[1] Ruch and Stoddard, *Tests and Measurements in High School Instruction.* Yonkers-on-Hudson, World Book Company, 1927, p. 221.

Name of test.	r.	Number of cases.	Grade range.	Source.
Haggerty, Delta 2 . . .	0·56	55	IX	Haggerty
Army Alpha . . .	0·34	494	IX–XII	Proctor
Army Alpha . . .	0·41	480	IX–XII	Proctor
Miller	0·56	55	IX	Miller
Haggerty, Delta 2 . . .	0·50	55	IX	Miller
Terman A	0·59	55	IX	Miller
Army Alpha (8) . . .	0·56	55	IX	Miller
Stanford-Binet (I.Q.) . .	0·45	111	IX–XII	Terman

TABLE VII.—Prediction of school marks in pooled High School subjects.

The correlations of Table VII are admittedly low. But progress in school depends upon other factors besides intelligence —health, zeal, morality—and these affect the correlations adversely. Low as these correlations are, they indicate that good intelligence tests are more truly prognostic of progress than teachers' opinions or marks obtained in achievement examinations, since correlations from the latter usually run lower than 0·50.

By *reliability* is meant the accuracy with which the test measures whatever it does measure. It is, therefore, synonymous with accuracy in measurement. Reliability is measured by finding the coefficient of correlation of the measures obtained by repeating the same test, or, better still, by correlating two sets of scores from two different forms of the same test applied to the same group of pupils. If the coefficient of reliability falls below 0·90 the test is open to suspicion. Table VIII is a record of some reliabilities which have been published.

Name of test.	r.	No. of cases.	Age range.	Grade range.	Source.
Haggerty, Delta 2 .	0·88	40	15–6 to 16–5	H.S.	Haggerty
Miller	0·91	109	Median C.A. 16–3	Sophomores	Miller
Otis Self-Administering	0·92	128	—	IX–XII	Otis
Stanford-Binet (I.Q.)	0·93	428	3 to 15	—	Terman
Stanford-Binet . .	0·95	114	Adults	—	Rugg

TABLE VIII.—Reliability of intelligence tests.

The coefficient of reliability shows the accuracy of the measurement, but it does not tell us if what is measured is really intelligence. Some idea as to whether or not intelligence is really measured by intelligence tests, that is, if all the tests measure the same things, is obtained from the inter-correlations of various tests. Some facts bearing on the problem are given in Tables IXA and IXB.

Name of Tests.	Correlations.
Binet Mental Ages with—	
Otis Group Test	0·66 ± 0·047
Army Alpha	0·69 ± 0·044
Miller Group Test	0·53 ± 0·060
Terman Group Test	0·68 ± 0·045
Composite of Alpha, Otis, Miller, and Terman with—	
Otis Group Test	0·93 ± 0·012
Army Alpha	0·91 ± 0·015
Miller Group Test	0·90 ± 0·016
Terman Group Test	0·91 ± 0·015
Teachers' estimates of intelligence with—	
Otis Group Test	0·73 ± 0·039
Army Alpha	0·61 ± 0·052
Miller Group Test	0·68 ± 0·045
Terman Group Test	0·66 ± 0·047

TABLE IXA.—Correlations of five intelligence tests for 64 pupils of High School age (from Jordan, A. M., "The Validation of Intelligence Tests," *J.E.P.*, XIV (1922), pp. 348–366, 414–428).

Test.	Average Correlation.
Terman Group Test	0·75
National A	0·74
Haggerty	0·73
Illinois	0·72
Otis	0·71
Mentimeter	0·66
Pressey Survey	0·65
National B	0·62
Thorndike Reading	0·59
Dearborn—1	0·58
Pressey Cross-Outs	0·56
Dearborn—2	0·55
Wylie opposites	0·53
Myers	0·46

TABLE IXB.—Average correlations of fourteen group intelligence tests with each of the other thirteen tests (from Franzen, R., "Attempts at Test Validation," *J.E.R.*, VI (1922), pp. 145–158).

Sometime, as we have previously suggested, the validity and reliability of tests will be established by means of the elaborate technique outlined by Spearman in his *Abilities of Man*, or by the use of partial and multiple correlations.

By *objectivity* is meant the extent to which the test is freed from the personal judgment of the examiner in the marking of the answers. It is in this regard that intelligence tests, by the mechanics of their construction, have achieved their best results. The instructions for scoring are so precise and the arrangements of the items so excellent, that few tests to-day, if marked by different examiners, yield different scores.

The terms *ease of administration and scoring* explain themselves. Intelligence tests usually rank highly in both these features

The *satisfactoriness of the norms* depends upon their form and accuracy. The norm, as we have seen, may be a mean, a median, a measure of variability, a percentile, etc., calculated for any special group. If a central tendency is used, the probable error, calculated from the standard formula, provides a good index of accuracy. But, as we remarked in the section dealing with standardization, all norms must be secured from a fair sampling of the population under consideration.

The Distribution of Intelligence.—Since intelligence is a native trait we should expect it to be distributed, like all other natural variants, according to the curve of chance. There is a vast accumulation of evidence to show that this is the form of distribution actually followed. Terman [1] reported the distribution of I.Q.'s of 1,000 unselected American children to be the following:

I.Q.	Percentage falling with group.
56–65	0·33
66–75	2·3
76–85	8·6
86–95	20·1
96–105	33·9
106–115	23·1
116–125	9·0
126–135	2·3
136–145	0·55
Total . .	100·18

The distribution closely follows the curve of chance. The various grades of intelligence are symmetrically grouped about the central tendency and decrease gradually without abrupt changes towards the two extremes. Any division of intelligence into groups such as genius, normal, feeble-minded, etc., is an arbitrary proceeding since no sharp lines of demarcation can be drawn at any point. Nevertheless the divisions drawn in Table X have been found useful in practice, although they have undoubtedly encouraged the belief among the unthinking that they represented a sharply defined and immutable classification.

[1] Terman, *Measurement of Intelligence*, p. 66.

Classification.	I.Q.	Percentage of all children included.
"Near" genius or genius	above 140	0·25
Very superior	120–140	6·75
Superior	110–120	13·00
Normal, or average	90–110	60·00
Dull, rarely feeble-minded	80–90	13·00
Borderline, sometimes dull, often feeble-minded	70–80	6·00
Feeble-minded	below 70	1·00
Total	—	100·00
Subdivisions of Feeble-minded—		
(*a*) Moron	50–70	0·75
(*b*) Imbecile	20 or 25 to 50	0·19
(*c*) Idiot	below 20	0·06
Total	—	1·00

TABLE X.—Distribution of I.Q.'s in a normal population.

Fig. 37 presents the facts of Table X. in graphical form, the curve being smoothed to show its close approximation to the curve of chance.

The raw scores from group tests, while approximating the distribution shown by the probability curve, are generally skewed. If, however, they are subjected to the technique employed by Thorndike and described below, very close approximations to the curve of chance are obtained. The problem Thorndike [1] set himself was that of testing the validity of the assumption that the distribution of intellect followed the Gaussian curve. He analysed the results obtained from a large number of group tests given to sixth, ninth, and twelfth grade pupils, and to college freshmen. The technique employed was: (1) plotting the percentage distributions, using the mean as central tendency, for each test in units of 1/10 S.D. of each distribution; (2) combining them into a composite distribution for each grade; (3) plotting the resulting curve; and (4) testing it by Pearson's Goodness of Fit Method (P). His results are given below:

Grade.	P (Goodness of Fit).
Sixth	0·999999
Ninth	1·000000
Twelfth	0·999911
College Freshmen	0·999988

[1] Thorndike, *The Measurement of Intelligence*, Appendix III.

M

Since a perfect fit is represented by unity these results present an impressive verification of the normal distribution of intelligence. So much so, that if results are obtained which show deviations from the normal distribution, we are justified in believing that they are due either to the limitations of the test or to the selective nature of the sampling.

Uses of Intelligence Tests.—Intelligence tests find their greatest use in classifying and grading pupils. In Ontario the pupils in "auxiliary" classes are selected by means of intelligence

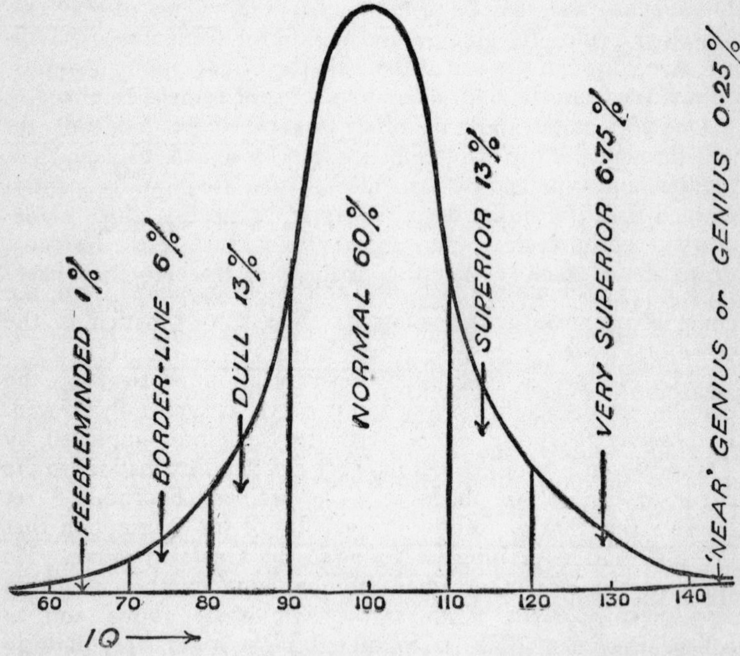

FIG. 37.—Diagram showing the distribution of I.Q.'s in a normal population.

tests, and this course is universally followed wherever the segregation of the feeble-minded is desired. In many cities, for example in Detroit, the children are tentatively graded by means of intelligence tests as soon as they begin their schooling. Three grades (X, Y, and Z) are employed. There is a bright section composed of the highest 20 per cent., a medium section composed of the middle 60 per cent., and a dull section comprising the lowest 20 per cent. These groups are given respectively an enriched course of study, the regular course, and a simplified course. Although the classifications are considered provisional only, and shifting pupils from one group to another is permitted, very little shifting in practice has been found necessary.

As a device for regrading pupils in a school so that more homogeneous groups may be obtained, intelligence tests have proved of the greatest value. Pupils of approximately the same mental age are placed in the same grade.[1] Since by this procedure the young bright pupils and the dull older pupils, whose rates of progress and social maturity differ, are thrown together, the further step of grading these pupils (of the same mental age) according to I.Q.'s, or what amounts to the same thing, by chronological age, may be profitably adopted. This may be expressed as a rule—for grading use M.A.; for sectioning use I.Q. or C.A. Through the use of this rule the bright, younger pupils are divided from the dull, older pupils of the same mental age.

One curious but quite definitely established fact has come to light through the use of intelligence tests in school, namely, that brighter pupils, judged by their mental ages, are more frequently retarded than the duller ones. They are generally above grade for their chronological ages, so why should anybody be concerned about them? Yet this attitude of teachers may have serious results. By allowing the brighter pupils consistently to work below their mental levels, teachers induce habits of slothfulness. What to do with the talented pupil has not been satisfactorily solved. The consensus of opinion at present is that it is inadvisable to accelerate their rate of progress through the grades unduly, but to give them more work to do in each grade by the enrichment of the curriculum. In other words, it is better not to place the bright boy of ten, who has a mental age of fourteen, with first-year high school pupils, but to let him read more good books, and take extra subjects while he is still in the elementary grades.

[1] According to Terman (*Intelligence Tests and School Reorganization*, Yonkers-on-Hudson, World Book Co., 1923, pp. 13–14) the following may be regarded as the mental age standards for the different grades of the United States:

Grade.	No. of cases.	Actual median mental age.	Proposed standard mental age.	Standard mental age at mid-grade.
I	341	6–10	6–6 to 7–5	7 years
II	189	7–11	7–6 to 8–5	8 ”
III	181	9–0	8–6 to 9–5	9 ”
IV	253	9–11	9–6 to 10–5	10 ”
V	226	11–0	10–6 to 11–5	11 ”
VI	236	12–1	11–6 to 12–5	12 ”
VII	193	13–1	12–6 to 13–5	13 ”
VIII	180	14–2	13–6 to 14–5	14 ”
IX	137	15–4	14–6 to 15–5	15 ”

In colleges and universities of the United States, intelligence tests are widely used as a partial basis determining admission, and of grading afterwards. The work at Columbia College, so ably described by Wood,[1] and that at Brown University described by Macphail,[2] was the beginning of a movement that has already reached considerable proportions.

The second important application of intelligence tests is found in the diagnosis of feeble-mindedness, superior intelligence, special abilities and disabilities of children, and mal-adjustments of an educational or social nature wherever found. For diagnostic purposes, individual tests must be employed, since a close contact with the individual is necessary in such cases.

The third main use is in prognosis, in forecasting the intellectual or vocational future of young persons. It should be remembered, however, that intelligence is only one of the factors, albeit an important one, determining success. Intelligence tests will not tell us which pupils will succeed in school, but only which pupils will succeed providing they work hard, and remain reasonably free from disease, and from mental and moral degeneration. Consequently the forecasts from intelligence tests may be quite wide of the mark. But so may forecasts made on any other basis. It is customary in some quarters to belittle the prognostic powers of intelligence tests, yet, all in all, they give us the most reliable estimate of what a pupil will subsequently accomplish. Anyhow, from what we have already gleaned from them, we know that it is unwise to encourage a person of low intelligence to attempt a professional career; he is practically certain to be disappointed.

Vocational tests, a special form of intelligence test, are still in their infancy. Their accomplishments, so far, have been singularly disappointing, chiefly because the makers of the tests have not sufficiently taken into account the specialized nature of the problem confronting them.

The Results of Intelligence Testing.—In order to give merely a synopsis of the results of intelligence testing up to 1923, Pintner had to employ more than 200 pages of his book.[3] Any attempt to summarize the results of intelligence testing would require a treatise rather than a paragraph. We must, therefore, be content with saying that the incidence of feeble-mindedness among delinquents has been found to be higher than among the general population—from 15 to 30 per cent. in

[1] Wood, B. D., *Measurement in Higher Education*, 1923.
[2] Macphail, A. H., *The Intelligence of College Students*, 1924.
[3] Pintner, R., *Intelligence Testing: Methods and Results*. New York, Holt, 1923.

contrast with 1 per cent. Any group in the population suffering from a serious sensory defect, such as blindness or deafness, is found to contain a greater percentage of dull children than the rest of the community. Certain racial groups, like the Negro, have invariably tested below others; while certain national groups, such as Britishers and English-speaking Canadians, have invariably tested highly. These findings about racial groups, immigrant groups, groups with sensory defects, etc., must be interpreted cautiously, since we do not know the proportionate parts played by heredity and environment in determining the scores made in a test. With regard to sex differences disclosed by the tests, the best evidence seems to indicate that they are negligible; the central tendencies of scores by boys and girls seem to coincide. Finally, the results from vocational groups show that occupational status correlates positively with intelligence; professional people test high, unskilled labourers test low. Further, whenever the children of these people in different occupations have been tested, those from professional homes have invariably tested higher than those from homes of manual labourers. In other words, intelligence sufficiently great to achieve success in a profession tends to be passed on to the next generation.

References

Bagley, W. C. *Determinism in Education.* Baltimore, Warwick and York, 1925. Pp. 194.

Ballard, P. B. *Group Tests of Intelligence.* London, Hodder and Stoughton, 1922. Pp. x+252.

Ballard, P. B. *Mental Tests.* London, Hodder and Stoughton, 1923. Pp. ix+235.

Book, W. F. *The Intelligence of High School Seniors.* New York, Macmillan, 1922. Pp. 371.

Brigham, C. C. *A Study of American Intelligence.* Princeton, University Press, 1923. Pp. 210.

Burt, C. *The Distribution and Relations of Educational Abilities.* London, P. S. King & Son, 1917. Pp. xiii+93.

Burt, C. *Mental and Scholastic Tests.* London, P. S. King & Sons, 1922. Pp. xv+432.

Dickson, V. E. *Mental Tests and the Classroom Teacher.* Yonkers-on-Hudson, World Book Co., 1923. Pp. xi+231.

Freeman, F. N. *Mental Tests; their History, Principles and Application.* Boston, Houghton Mifflin, 1926. Pp. ix+503.

Gaw, F. *Performance Tests of Intelligence.* Industrial Fatigue Research Board, Report No. 31. London, His Majesty's Stationery Office, 1925. Pp. iv+45.

Hart and Spearman. " General Ability, its Existence and Nature. *Br. J. Psy.*, vol. v (1912–13), pp. 51–84.

MACPHAIL, A. H. *The Intelligence of College Students.* Baltimore, Warwick and York, 1924. Pp. 176.

NATIONAL SOCIETY FOR THE STUDY OF EDUCATION. *Twenty-first Yearbook,* Parts I and II, "Intelligence Tests." Pp. 270.

PETERSON, J. *Early Conceptions and Tests of Intelligence.* Yonkers-on-Hudson, World Book Co., 1925. Pp. xiv+309.

PINTNER, R. *Intelligence Testing: Methods and Results.* New York, Holt, 1923. Pp. vii+406.

PROCTOR, WM. "Psychological Tests and Guidance of High School Pupils," *J.E.R. Monograph,* No. 1 (October 1923). Pp. 125.

Psychological Tests of Educable Capacity. Report of Eng. Board of Education Consultative Committee. London, H.M. Stationery Office, 1924. Pp. xi+248.

RUCH and STODDARD. *Tests and Measurements in High School Instruction.* Yonkers-on-Hudson, World Book Co., 1927. Pp. xix+375.

SPEARMAN, C. "General Intelligence, Objectively Determined and Measured," *Am. J. Psy.,* vol. xv (1904), pp. 201–293.

SPEARMAN, C. "The Theory of Two Factors," *Psy. Rev.,* vol. xxi (1914), pp. 101–115.

SPEARMAN, C. *The Nature of "Intelligence" and Principles of Cognition.* London, Macmillan, 1923. Pp. viii+358.

SPEARMAN, C. *The Abilities of Man: their Nature and Measurement.* London, Macmillan, 1927. Pp. viii+415+Appendix, pp. xxxiii.

TERMAN, L. M. *The Measurement of Intelligence.* Boston, Houghton Mifflin, 1916. Pp. xviii+362.

TERMAN, L. M. *The Intelligence of School Children.* Boston, Houghton Mifflin, 1919. Pp. xxii+317.

TERMAN *et al. Intelligence Tests and School Reorganization.* Yonkers-on-Hudson, World Book Co., 1923. Pp. vi+111.

TERMAN *et al. Genetic Studies of Genius.* Stanford University Press, 1925. Pp. xv+648.

THOMSON, G. H. "General versus Group Factors in Mental Activities," *Psy. Rev.,* vol. xxvii (1920), pp. 173-190.

THOMSON, G. H. *Instinct, Intelligence and Character.* New York, Longmans, 1925. Pp. 282.

THORNDIKE *et al. The Measurement of Intelligence.* New York, Teachers College, Bureau of Publications, 1927. Pp. xxvi+616.

THURSTONE, L. L. *The Nature of Intelligence.* New York, Harcourt Brace, 1924.

WEBB, E. "Character and Intelligence," *Brit. J. Psy. Monog.,* No. 3, 1913.

WOOD, B. D. *Measurement in Higher Education.* Yonkers-on-Hudson, World Book Co., 1923. Pp. 337.

WOODROW, H. *Brightness and Dulness in Children.* Philadelphia, Lippincott, 1919. Pp. 322.

YERKES, R. M. "Psychological Examining in the U.S. Army," *Academy of Science Memoirs,* vol. xv (1921). Pp. 890.

PART II

THE LEARNING PROCESS

CHAPTER IX

CONDITIONED STIMULI AND CONDITIONED REACTIONS

Association Psychology.—From the earliest times the problem of how two things become associated together in experience has challenged the attention of psychologists. A very young child associates the name " Mamma " with the sight of his mother, so that when his mother appears she is called by name. It is easy to say that the sight of the mother (S) has been so frequently associated with the response Mamma (R), that S—>R is the natural connection, but it does not explain how the original association first took place. There is obviously no natural or inevitable connection between the sight of the mother and the name Mamma, as there is, for example, between the stimulus " pricking the skin " and the response of " retraction of the part of the body pricked." Aristotle more than 2000 years ago formulated four laws of association : (1) contiguity in space ; (2) contiguity in time ; (3) similarity ; and (4) contrast. It was soon seen that association by contiguity in space was only a special form of association by contiguity in time or in experience ; and that association by contrast was a special form of association by similarity, hence the four laws were reduced to two—association by contiguity in experience and association by similarity. Still later, the law of association by similarity was found to be merely a special case of association by contiguity, so all association was found to be due to contiguity in experience. However, this observed fact about learning—that in order to become associated two things must be experienced together, which happens to hold true in every case—does not show the mechanism of the association, nor explain why contiguous experiences sometimes fail to produce associations. The problem is not yet solved by any means, but much light has been thrown on it by the work of Pavlow and his associates in Russia and by Watson and his co-workers in America.

The Pavlow Experiment.—If a dog is given a piece of meat to eat, one of the natural responses is an increased flow of saliva from the salivary glands. This flow is due to natural connections, *viâ* the medulla, between the smell and taste receptors and the salivary gland effectors. If now a bell is rung every time the dog is fed, the ringing of the bell will eventually become an adequate stimulus for salivation, so that the sound of the bell in the absence of meat will induce a flow of saliva. This connection between the receptor for sound and the effectors for salivation is not a natural one—it is a learned reaction, which may be represented by the following outline:

S_1 (meat) ————————→ R_1 (salivation, an original tendency).
S_2 (sound of bell) ————————→ R_2 (responses to sound, an original tendency).
S_1+S_2 (presented simultaneously) → R_1 (salivary response). Several trials.
S_2 (bell) ————————→ R_1 (salivation).

The sound of the bell leads to salivation; the salivary reflex is said to have become *conditioned*.

At this point it is necessary to define the term *conditioned*. When the response, for example to food, is the natural one (salivation) the reflex is said to be a natural or unconditioned one. When, however, it functions in response to an arbitrary stimulus, in the above case to the sound of a bell, then it is said to be artificial or conditioned. The unconditioned responses are the more natural, permanent, regular, and racial forms of response due to the natural growth of inherited tendencies of the nervous system. The conditioned responses are the more temporary, individual, and learned forms of behaviour due to connections of the nervous system acquired during an individual's lifetime.

In the above classical experiment salivation is the *unconditioned response* to food and the *conditioned response* to the sound of a bell. The sound of a bell is the *unconditioned stimulus* of the normal responses to sound and the *conditioned stimulus* for the salivary response. In conditioning, then, it is the whole bond, S—>R, nay the whole organism, which has become conditioned. Instead of the word "conditioned" we could use the word "substituted" or "associated" or "transferred," for a conditioned response is simply one caused by the association of an indifferent stimulus with, or the substitution of an indifferent stimulus for, one that is biologically adequate to produce the response; or, there has been a transference of the response from the stimulus naturally associated with it to another not naturally associated with it. Pavlow used the term *conditioned* in order to denote their very large dependence upon the conditions of their establishment.

Pavlow varied his experiment in many ways. Instead of using a bell to produce the conditioned response in the dog, he scratched the dog gently in the neighbourhood of the ribs. After several repetitions the scratching alone was sufficient to induce the flow of saliva. Similarly, applications of ice to the body while the animal was eating became the conditioned stimulus for the salivary response. In general, it may be shown that the stimulation of any receptor occurring simultaneously with the reaction of an effector leads to the formation of a new S⟶R bond. Learning has taken place. But it should be noted that learning is always built, as it were, upon the foundation of an existing natural response.

Conditioning of Emotional Responses.—The original experiment on the conditioning of emotions was made by Rosalie Rayner and John B. Watson [1] and was reported by them in the *Scientific Monthly*, December, 1921. Accounts of the same experiment are to be found in Watson's *Psychology from the Standpoint of a Behaviorist* and in *Psychologies of 1925*. The following abstracts are taken from the latter volume (pp. 51–54):

"We chose as our first subject Albert B, an infant weighing twenty-one pounds, at eleven months of age. Albert was the son of one of the wet nurses in the Harriet Lane Hospital. He had lived his whole life in the hospital. He was a wonderfully 'good' baby. In all the months we worked with him we never saw him cry until after our experiments were made! . . .

"Our first experiment with Albert had for its object the conditioning of a fear response to a white rat. We first showed by repeated tests that nothing but loud sounds and removal of support would bring out fear response in this child. Everything coming within twelve inches of him was reached for and manipulated. His reaction, however, to a loud sound was characteristic of what occurs with most children. A steel bar about one inch in diameter and three feet long, when struck with a carpenter's hammer produced the most marked kind of reaction.

"Our laboratory notes showing the progress in establishing a conditioned emotional response are given here in full:

"*Eleven months, three days old.*—(1) White rat which he played with for weeks was suddenly taken from the basket (the usual routine) and presented to Albert. He began to reach for the rat with left hand.

[1] Rayner, R., and Watson, J. B., "Studies in Infant Psychology," *Scientific Monthly*, December, 1921, pp. 493–515.

Just as his hand touched the animal the bar was struck immediately behind his head. The infant jumped violently and fell forward burying his face in the mattress. He did not cry, however.

"(2) Just as his right hand touched the rat the bar was again struck. Again the infant jumped violently, fell forward and began to whimper.

"On account of his disturbed condition no further tests were made for one week.

"*Eleven months, ten days old.*—(1) Rat presented suddenly without sound. There was steady fixation but no tendency at first to reach for it. The rat was then placed nearer, whereupon tentative reaching movements began with the right hand. When the rat nosed the infant's left hand, the hand was immediately withdrawn. He started to reach for the head of the animal with the forefinger of his left hand, but withdrew it suddenly before contact. It is thus seen that the two joint stimulations given last week were not without effect. He was tested with his blocks immediately afterwards to see if they shared in the process of conditioning. He began immediately to pick them up, dropping them and pounding them, etc. In the remainder of the test the blocks were given frequently to quiet him and to test his general emotional state. They were always removed from sight when the process of conditioning was under way.

"(2) Combined stimulation with rat and sound. Started, then fell over immediately to right side. No crying.

"(3) Combined stimulation. Fell to right side and rested on hands with head turned from rat. No crying.

"(4) Combined stimulation. Same reaction.

"(5) Rat suddenly presented alone. Puckered face, whimpered, and withdrew body sharply to left.

"(6) Combined stimulation. Fell over immediately to right side and began to whimper.

"(7) Combined stimulation. Started violently and cried, but did not fall over.

"(8) Rat alone. The instant the rat was shown the baby began to cry. Almost immediately he turned sharply to the left, fell over, raised himself on all fours and began to crawl away so rapidly that he was caught with difficulty before he reached the edge of the mattress.

"Surely this proof of the conditioned origin of a fear response puts us on a natural science ground in our study of emotional behaviour."

As before, let us pattern it out in a formula. It would be somewhat like the following:

S_1 (sharp, loud noise) ——→ R_1 (crying, original response).
S_2 (sight of white rat) ——→ R_2 (manipulation, original response).
S_1+S_2 (simultaneously) ——→ R_1 (this was repeated seven times).
S_2 ————————————→ R_1 (original tendency conditioned).

Sight of white rat leads to crying.

Transfer of Conditioned Emotional Responses.—That Albert was not only conditioned to the white rat but also to other objects of a furry kind is clearly shown by the following evidence:

"Before the above experiment on the rat was made, Albert had been playing for weeks with rabbits, pigeons, fur muffs, the hair of the attendants and false faces. What effect will conditioning him upon the rat have upon his response to these animals and other objects when next he sees them? To test this we made no further experiments upon him for five days. That is, during this five-day period he was not allowed to see any of these objects. At the end of the sixth day we again tested him first with the rat to see if the conditioned fear response to it had carried over. Our notes are as follows:

"*Eleven months, fifteen days old.*—(1) Tested first with blocks. He reached readily for them, playing with them as usual. This shows that there has been no general transfer to the room, table, blocks, etc.

"(2) Rat alone. Whimpered immediately, withdrew right hand and turned head and trunk away.

"(3) Blocks again offered. Played readily with them, smiling and gurgling.

"(4) Rat alone. Leaned over to the left side as far away from the rat as possible, then fell over, getting up on all fours and scurrying away as rapidly as possible.

"(5) Blocks again offered. Reached immediately for them, smiling and laughing as before.

"This shows that the conditioned response was carried over for a five-day period. Next we presented in order a rabbit, a dog, a sealskin coat, cotton wool, human hair, and false face.

"(6) Rabbit alone. A rabbit was suddenly placed on the mattress in front of him. The reaction was pronounced. Negative responses began at once. He leaned as far away from the animal as possible, whimpered, then burst into tears. When the rabbit was placed in contact with him he buried his face in the mattress, then got up on all fours and crawled away, crying as he went. This was a most convincing test.

"(7) The blocks were next given to him, after an interval. He played with them as before. It was observed by four people that he played far more energetically with them than ever before. The blocks were raised high over his head and slammed down with a great deal of force.

"(8) Dog alone. The dog did not produce as violent a reaction as the rabbit. The moment fixation of the eyes occurred the child shrank back and as the animal came nearer he attempted to get on all fours, but did not cry at first. As soon as the dog passed out of his range of vision he became quiet. The dog was then made to approach the infant's head (he was lying down at the moment).

Albert straightened up immediately, fell over to the opposite side, and turned his head away. He then began to cry.

"(9) Blocks were again presented. He began immediately to play with them.

"(10) Fur coat (seal). Withdrew immediately to the left side and began to fret. Coat put close to him on the left side, he turned immediately, began to cry, and tried to crawl away on all fours.

"(11) Cotton wool. The wool was presented in a paper package. At the ends the cotton was not covered by the paper. It was placed first on his feet. He kicked it away but did not touch it with his hands. When his hand was laid on the wool he immediately withdrew it, but did not show the shock that the animals or fur coat produced in him. He then began to play with the paper, avoiding contact with the wool itself. Before the hour was up, however, he had lost some of his negativism of the wool.

"(12) Just in play W., who had made the experiments, put his head down to see if Albert would play with his hair. Albert was completely negative. The other two observers did the same thing. He began immediately to play with their hair. A Santa Claus mask was then brought and presented to Albert. He was again pronouncedly negative, although on all previous occasions he had played with it.

"Our notes thus give a convincing proof of spread or transfer."

And so we leave Albert. He was conditioned for fear in the case of furry things at the end of the experiment and probably will be for the rest of his life unless some one unconditions him.

Unconditioning of Emotional Responses.—Peter was a boy of approximately three years of age. Like Albert he feared furry things, but these were "home grown," not produced experimentally as were Albert's. His reactions were positive towards toys, strongly negative towards a fur rug, fur coat, cotton, a hat with feathers, but neither positive nor negative to a white toy rabbit or a wooden doll. He was partially unconditioned when he took scarlet fever and was sent away to a hospital. As he was returning, a large barking dog attacked Peter and his nurse as they were getting into a taxi-cab. In Peter's case all his fear reactions to animals and furry things returned in an exaggerated form. The method used to uncondition him was as follows: [1]

"We seated him at a small table in a high chair. The lunch was served in a room about forty feet long. Just as he began to eat his lunch, the rabbit was displayed in a wire cage of wide mesh. We displayed it on the first day *just far enough away not to disturb his eating*. This point was then marked. The next day the rabbit was brought closer and closer until disturbance was first barely noticed. This place was marked. The third and succeeding days the same

[1] Murchison, C. (Ed.), *Psychologies of 1925*, pp. 64–65.

routine was maintained. Finally the rabbit could be placed upon the table—then in Peter's lap. Next tolerance changed to positive reaction. Finally he would eat with one hand and play with the rabbit with the other, a proof that his *viscera were retrained along with his hands.*"

Later, Peter was tested with a rat, fur rug, fur coat, cotton, feathers, etc. Fear responses to cotton, the fur coat, fur rug, and feathers had entirely disappeared, and he was sufficiently tolerant of the rat to carry it around the room in a tin box. Schematically, the unconditioning of Peter may be represented by:

S_2 (animals and furry objects) ⟶ R_1 (conditioned and transferred fear).
S_3 (food) ⟶ R_3 (eating, normal response).
S_3+S_2 (gradually but simultaneously) ⟶ R_3 (eating) to which was added later R_2 (manipulation, the unconditioned response to S_2).
Finally S_2 (furry things alone) ⟶ R_2 (manipulation, the normal response).

Peter has been unconditioned to fear of animals.

In general, unconditioning is securing the return of the normal response. Peter could probably have been unconditioned by allowing him to play with his toys and gradually introducing the furry things, but there is no doubt that eating food that is liked proved a very potent factor in the process. In the above case our diagram would be:

S_2 (animals and furry objects) ⟶ R_1 (conditioned and transferred fear).
S_3 (toys) ⟶ R_3 (manipulation).
S_3+S_2 (gradually brought together) ⟶ R_3 (manipulation).
S_2 (furry things) ⟶ R_3 (manipulation).

It should be noted that R_3 is the same as R_2, the normal response to S_2.

Types of Conditioned Responses.—So far we have dealt only with one type of conditioning, namely, that in which the conditioned and unconditioned stimuli for a reaction were presented practically *simultaneously*.[1] The response evoked is called the *simultaneous conditioned response*. It is the easiest and most quickly formed of all learned reactions, sometimes, indeed, after one experience, and is the one normally thought of when conditioning is mentioned.

What happens when the two stimuli are separated by an

[1] By simultaneity Pavlow appears to mean that the bell is rung first and then the dog is fed while the bell is still being rung. Hence his term "signal reflexes" for them. His simultaneous reflex is really a short-time, delayed reflex, with a few seconds between the conditioned stimulus and the unconditioned one, in contrast with a long-time, delayed reflex, with an interval of a minute or more between the stimuli.

interval of time? Pavlow found that if the dog was fed *before* the bell was rung *no conditioned reflex was formed*. This is confirmed by other workers and is the result that common sense would lead us to expect. Why should the dog take notice of the bell when he was enjoying the food quite independently of it? Thus the rule, which has important educational implications—*If the unconditioned stimulus precedes the conditioned stimulus no new reflex is formed.*

S_1 (meat) ——→ R_1 (salivation).
S_2 (bell) ——→ R_2 (response to bell).
S_1 *before* S_2 —→ R_1 (salivation).

But S_2 alone will not lead to R_1.
No conditioning takes place.

But if the bell is rung continuously and the feeding of the dog *delayed* for some time after the commencement of the ringing of the bell, a conditioned response is established but of a peculiar kind. Suppose the dog is fed 2 mins. after the bell is first rung, then the conditioned salivation will start exactly 2 mins. after the commencement of the ringing of the bell (without food being present). The latent period of the conditioned reflex is equal to the time interval between the two stimuli. Such a conditioned reflex is known as *delayed conditioned reflex*.

S_1 (meat) ——————→ R_1 (salivation).
S_2 (bell) ——————→ R_2 (response to bell).
S_1 *after* S_2 (rung continuously) → R_1 (salivation).
S_2 (bell) ——————→ R_1 (after some delay).

A delayed conditioned reflex has been formed.

Suppose that the bell is rung and then, *after a pause*, the dog is fed. This leads to a conditioned response. The trace or memory of the sound of the bell is sufficient to cause the conditioned response, hence such responses are known as *conditioned trace or memory reflexes*. As in the case of the delayed conditioned reflex, the latent period of response in a conditioned trace or memory reflex is the same as the interval between the two stimuli.

The formula for conditioned memory reflex will be:

S_1 (meat) ——————→ R_1 (salivation).
S_2 (bell) ——————→ R_2 (response to bell).
S_1 *after* S_2 (rung and discontinued) → R_1 (salivation).
S_2 (bell) ——————→ R_1 (salivation, after some delay).

A conditioned memory or trace reflex has been formed.

Other Experiments in Conditioning.—There is now a considerable literature on conditioned responses, and the variations of Pavlow's basic method have been both numerous and original. We have already mentioned Watson's adaptations of the method to the field of emotion. A few of the other more significant advances will now be mentioned.

1. *Lashley's Adaptation to Human Salivary Reflexes.*—To obtain a count of the drops of saliva secreted by a dog the cheek has to be opened. The method is therefore inapplicable to human beings. Lashley, however, devised a cup which could be attached by suction to the inside of the human cheek, over the outlet of the parotid gland duct. From the cup the saliva ran down a tube which passed through the corner of the mouth. The measure of secretion was the number of drops of saliva which fell in a given time. For example, Lashley, after determining the normal flow of saliva in a subject, presented him with a bar of chocolate, which he held at arm's length, smelled, and brought to his lips. The following results were obtained :

Normal rate : about one drop per minute.	
Chocolate placed in subject's hand—	
1st minute	4 drops
2nd minute	3 drops
3rd minute	4 drops
Subject smelled chocolate	5 drops
Brought chocolate to lips but kept mouth closed	9 drops

Most of us are conditioned to chocolate, but few would believe that by holding chocolate at arm's length we increase our flow of saliva.

2. *Bechterew's Method for Conditioning Muscular Responses.*—The subject's foot was placed on a metal electrode and stimulated by an electric shock. The foot moved. If now a bell is rung, or a light is flashed, or some coloured object is presented simultaneously with the shock, the subject becomes conditioned ; the foot will move when the bell is rung (or light flashed or object presented) without the intervention of the electric shock. The method has its drawbacks for young people since they are loath to subject themselves voluntarily to pain.

Watson used Bechterew's method but substituted the movement of the fingers for those of the foot and toe. He used the method to determine experimentally the spectral range and found that one subject reacted from $760\mu\mu$ (red) to $397\mu\mu$ (violet), but not beyond these ranges. This conditioned reflex method is more refined than the verbal report method and is applicable to senses other than sight.

Using this method Watson determined the differential sensitivities of subjects to two sounds of unequal pitch. With one subject he obtained perfect differentiation when the sounds were 6 double vibrations apart; with another when the difference was 3 d.v.[1]

3. *Krasnogorski's Adaptation of Pavlow's Method.*—Instead of measuring the drops of saliva, Krasnogorski recorded the number of swallowing movements that infants made by means of a Marey tambour placed over the thyroid cartilage or the hyoid bone, and connected by a rubber tubing with a recording arm which traced each movement upon a kymograph. In order to get rid of conditioning due to sight, the subjects were blindfolded.

4. *Miss Mateer's Modification of Krasnogorski's Technique.*—In some preliminary experiments Miss Mateer found that bandaging the eyes frequently causes emotional disturbances. She then hit upon the plan of using the bandage itself as the conditioning stimulus.[2]

"The bandage was applied by gently sliding it down over the child's eyes from above, with a slight but firm pressure of one finger over each eye, thus inducing the most certain exclusion of light and then the bandage was kept in place twenty seconds. In the eleventh second the child was fed a bit of sweet chocolate and the bandage was removed at the end of the twentieth second." This established a conditioned salivary reflex to the bandaging of the eyes. Later, a brown sugar solution was used instead of the chocolate. This procedure was used for the study of such forms of behaviour as (1) the learning ability of the child expressed in the number of trials necessary to form a conditioned response to the bandage; (2) memorial functioning of the association learned after an interval of 24 hours, measured by the number of trials necessary to obtain its refunctioning, fewer trials meaning better memory; (3) the number of trials necessary to effect unlearning of the associative act learned when the conditioning stimulus is absent; and (4) the number of trials necessary to correct the unlearning developed and to restore the refunctioning of the first association. These experimental results were then correlated with those from a number of intelligence and other psychological tests, and with those from a number of anthropometric measurements.

Some of the results obtained by Miss Mateer with 67 children are given below:

1. The learning of a conditioned reflex requires from 3 to 9 trials in normal children.

[1] Watson, J. B., *Psychology from the Standpoint of a Behaviorist*, pp. 36–38.

[2] Mateer, Florence, *Child Behaviour: A Critical and Experimental Study of Young Children by the Method of Conditioned Reflexes.* Boston, Badger, 1918. Pp. 97.

2. With children of the same age those who learn more rapidly are also brighter as measured by the results obtained through the use of the Binet and Yerkes scales.

3. In general there is a slight tendency for the children who are more rapid in learning the association to be more rapid in the performance of the Seguin Form Board, although when we study the order of merit for Form Board ability we find the most rapid learners on the Krasnogorski method are medium in their ability there.

4. The number of trials needed for learning decreases as the grip ability increases.

5. The rate of learning increases as the spirometer ability increases.

6. The number of trials needed for relearning varies only from 2 to 7, being less than the learning range.

7. This variability in retention appears independent of the age of the child.

8. There is a moderate relation between learning ability and retention.

9. The range of trials required for relearning is less among the girls than among the boys.

10. The mechanism of inhibition or unlearning of the association was developed in 41 of the unselected group.

11. The number of trials needed for developing the inhibition or unlearning ranged from 3 to 12, the range being greater for the boys than for the girls.

12. In general the number of trials needed for unlearning the conditioned reflex decreases as age increases.

13. The number of trials needed for unlearning tends to decrease as the number of trials needed for learning increases.

14. The learning process in mental defectives is such that they require anywhere from 3 to 18 trials to develop a conditioned reflex.

15. With defectives the average number of trials needed to develop a reaction after 24 hours is greater than with normal children.

16. Among mental defectives the number of trials required for inhibition or unlearning varies from 8 to 21.

General Properties of Conditioned Responses.—(1) A conditioned response, like any other learned response or habit, and unlike a natural or unconditioned response, is more or less temporary and unstable. They obey the law of forgetting or disuse, that is, if not exercised over a period of time their strength is impaired. Therefore, in order to maintain the strength of a conditioned response it must be regularly and repeatedly reinforced by the unconditioned stimulus. However, a lapsed response can be reawakened with fewer trials than were needed to establish it originally. Relearning is easier than learning.

(2) A conditioned response, like any other learned reaction, is highly specific, that is, it cannot be called out by any stimulus except the one to which it is conditioned. If a response is

conditioned to sound, then tactile or visual stimulation fails to evoke it. However, similar sounds of a pitch in the neighbourhood of the one to which the reaction is established will sometimes produce the response. This specificity of the reaction has an important bearing on the question of transfer of training.

(3) A conditioned response obeys the *law of summation.* If the same conditioned response has been established separately, say, to sound and to cutaneous stimulation, then a simultaneous application of both conditioned stimuli results in a more powerful response.

(4) Conditioned responses can be extinguished. They fade, as we have seen, through disuse. But they may be extinguished experimentally by applying the conditioned stimulus several times in rapid succession without the accompaniment of the unconditioned stimulus.

An experimental extinction of a conditioned reflex is reported below:

The conditioned stimulus was given without being followed by the unconditioned.

Intervals between successive applications of conditioned stimuli.		Time necessary for extinction.
2 minutes	. . . .	15 minutes
4 ,,	. . . .	20 ,,
8 ,,	. . . .	54 ,,
16 ,,	not extinguished in	120 ,,

In other words, you can't fool the dog all the time. It will respond to the first bell, but if it is not fed, then frequent successive ringings will destroy the salivary response. Educationally, a similar result is obtained by "nagging." The "don't touch" and "sit up" of the nagging parent soon lose their efficacy. Some people become "sermon-proof" by a somewhat similar process. It should be noted, however, that a conditioned response, experimentally extinguished, regenerates spontaneously after a time. It is also easier to extinguish delayed and memory reflexes by this means than the corresponding simultaneous reflexes.

(5) If a number of conditioned reflexes have been established then the extinguishing of one of them does not lead to the extinction of any of the others. In this respect the strength of the stimulus plays only a minor part. A strong stimulus may be extinguished, while a weak one still remains potent, calling out the response in full force.

(6) If during or shortly before the occurrence of a conditioned reflex an additional (and distracting) stimulus is presented, the conditioned reflex becomes weaker. The stronger

this additional or extra stimulus, the greater its inhibitory effect. This inhibition is only temporary. On repetition of the extra stimulus its inhibitory effect becomes smaller. Consider the following results where a dog had become conditioned to a visual stimulus and the extra stimulus was a gramophone record played for a few seconds :

Strength of visual conditioned reflex		=100	per cent.
Effect of gramophone,	1st application	= 10	”
” ” ”	2nd ”	= 50	”
” ” ”	3rd ”	= 65	”
” ” ”	4th ”	= 85	”
” ” ”	5th ”	= 90	”
” ” ”	6th ”	= 94	”
” ” ”	7th ”	=100	”

Thus :

S_2 (light stimulus) ⟶ R_1 (salivation).
S_3 (sound of gramophone) ⟶ R_3 (responses to sound).
S_2+S_3 (together) ⟶ R_3 (mainly, but some R_1).
S_3 partially inhibits ⟶ R_1.

Gramophone, however, loses its potency in time, and the conditioned salivation returns to its original strength.

(7) Inhibitions may be inhibited. The same extra stimulus when applied together with, say, a sound stimulus which has been rendered ineffective by discrimination from an effective sound stimulus, results in a response.

(8) Conditioned reflexes may be more rapidly established in young people than in old people.

Applications to Human Learning.—Most of the data so far reported have been derived from experiments with animals. Is conditioning an explanation of learning in humans as well as in animals ? Will it explain, for example, why " the burnt child dreads the fire " ? Let us try to sketch it out in accordance with our formula :

S_1 (touching very hot things) ⟶ R_1 (retraction of hand to pain, a native response).
S_2 (sight of stove) ⟶ R_2 (manipulation, touching, a native response).
S_1+S_2 ⟶ R_1 (retraction of hand).

Generally after one experience :

S_2 (sight of stove) ⟶ R_1 (retraction ; avoidance of stove, a conditioned response).

The burnt child has learned to dread the fire.

In the above case the experience " being burnt " is ordinarily such a painful one that the conditioned reaction is learnt immediately without the necessity of repetition ; one experience is sufficient to establish the new bond. Further, there may be a transfer, such as we found in Albert's emotional reactions, to a wide number of similar situations—in fact, to all kinds of hot things where the identical element (heat) is involved. From which we may conclude the strength or vigour, as well as the radiation, of the conditioned response (retraction) is due to the intensity of its unconditioned stimulus (hot things). If hot things were not so exceedingly painful, then learning not to touch them would not be such a permanent affair.

How do children learn the names of things, for example, a ball? Will it fit the formula?

S_1 (mother says "ball") → R_1 (child says "ball," an imitative response).
S_2 (sight of ball) → R_2 (manipulation).
S_1+S_2 → R_1 (word "ball" pronounced, repeated many times)
S_2 (sight of ball) → R_1 (saying word "ball," a conditioned response).

The sight of the ball becomes associated with its name.

Or take Rivers's classical case of the medical officer who, during the war, much preferred dodging shells above ground to the security of a dug-out. He suffered from a severe attack of claustrophobia (fear of confined spaces). Bit by bit Rivers discovered the origin of the fear. As a boy of five the medical officer took some old bottles for sale to a rag-and-bone man in Edinburgh who lived in one of the "closes." As he was coming out, a dog, accidentally imprisoned in the close by the shutting of the gate, barked furiously. So we have the setting—a barking dog and a little boy in a confined space. Let us plot it out:

S_1 (barking dog) → R_1 (fear, a normal response).
S_2 (confined space) → R_2 (feeling of security).
S_1+S_2 → R_1 (fear).
S_2 → R_1 (a conditioned emotional response, fear).

Claustrophobic fear had been developed.

Similarly, all forms of learning may be brought within our formula.

The process of conditioning illustrates several of the better known laws of learning. For example, conditioning usually requires several repetitions before the new bond is learned. This is the well-known law of exercise (use) of Thorndike. If a conditioned response is not exercised for a considerable period of time its strength is impaired. This is the law of disuse or forgetting. And so for several other laws.

But the chief value of the experimental work on conditioning lies in the fact that it has made the educators of children analyse out the elements of the situation and response (S→R) which led to their association, and also made them much more sensitive to the extreme delicacy of the mechanisms used in the learning processes. We now know that very soon after birth the unconditioned bonds of children become conditioned in hundreds of ways. These new bonds we call conditioned responses and, later, habits or learning. The education of the child is largely a process of acquiring in the first place conditioned reflexes, and then the more permanent associations and systems of conditioned reflexes that we call habits. Individual differences with respect to intellectual ability and emotional stability are largely due to the ease with which conditioned responses are formed and broken. In the well-endowed children these associations are easily made and remade; in the feeble-minded, as Miss Mateer has shown, they are both difficult to form and to re-form. Feeble-minded children learn and unlearn with great difficulty, while the normal, and especially the super-normal, children retain a plastic condition of the nervous system for the greater part of their lives. Finally, children (and adults as well) are usually unaware of the stimuli to which they become conditioned. Most of the conditioned responses we learn can never be introspected, and had it not been for the objective studies of Pavlow and Watson we should have remained in ignorance of them to this day. The conditioned response, therefore, is a triumph for experimental psychology. It is remaking the whole field of learning and emotion.

References

ANREP, G. V. "Pitch Discrimination in Dogs," *Journal of Physiology*, XXXIII (1919–20), pp. 367–385.

BECHTEREW, V. M. VON. *La psychologie objective*. Trans. from Russian by N. Kostyleff. Paris, Alcan, 1913. Pp. 478.

BURNHAM, W. H. *The Normal Mind*. New York, Appleton, 1924. Pp. xx +702.

BURNHAM, W. H. "Mental Hygiene and the Conditioned Reflex," *Ped. Sem.*, XXIV (1917), pp. 449–488.

BURNHAM, W. H. "The Significance of the Conditioned Reflex in Mental Hygiene," *Mental Hygiene*, V (1921), pp. 673–706.

EVANS, C. A. L. *Recent Advances in Physiology*. London, Macmillan, 1926. Pp. xiii+370.

LASHLEY, K. S. "The Human Salivary Reflex and its Use in Psychology," *Psy. Rev.*, XXIII (1916), pp. 446–464.

LASHLEY, K. S. "Reflex Secretion of the Human Parotid Gland," *Jour. Exp. Psy.*, I (1916), pp. 461–493.

MATEER, FLORENCE. *Child Behaviour : A Critical and Experimental Study of Young Children by the Method of Conditioned Reflexes*. Boston, Badger. 1918. Pp. 239.

MORGULIS, S. "The Auditory Reactions of the Dog studied by the Pavlow Method," *Journal Animal Behavior*, IV (1914), pp. 142–145.

MORGULIS, S. "Pavlow's Theory of a Function of the Central Nervous System and a Digest of some of the more recent Contributions to the Subject from Pavlow's Laboratory," *Jour. Animal Behavior*, IV (1914), pp. 362–379.

MURCHISON, C. (Ed.). *Psychologies of 1925*. Worcester, Clark University Press, 1927. Pp. 412.

PAVLOW, I. P. "The Scientific Investigations of the Psychical Faculties o Processes in the Higher Animals," *Science*, XXIV (1906), pp. 613–619.

PAVLOW, I. P. *Twenty Years' Objective Study of the Higher Centres of Nervous Activity (Behaviour) of Animals*. Petrograd and Moscow, State Publication, 1923. (Mostly in Russian. Translated into German in 1926 and published by Bergmann, München.)

PAVLOW, I. P. "L'Excitation psychique des glandes salivaires," *Jour. de Psychologie*, VII (1910), pp. 107–114.

PAVLOW, I. P. "L'inhibition des reflexes conditionnels," *Jour. de Psychologie*, X (1913), pp. 1–15.

PAVLOW, I. P. "Sur le secretion psychique des glands Salivaires," *Archiv. Internationale de Physiologie*, I (1904), pp. 119–135.

PAVLOW, I. P. *Conditioned Reflexes*. Oxford, University Press, 1927. Pp. xv+430.

SYMONDS, P. M. "Laws of Learning," *J.E.P.*, XVIII, 6 (Sept. 1927), pp. 405–413.

WATSON, J. B. *Behaviorism, Lectures-in-Print*. New York, People's Institute Publishing Co., 1925. Pp. 251.

WATSON, J. B. *Psychology from the Standpoint of a Behaviorist*. Philadelphia, Lippincott, 1924. Pp. xvii+448.

WATSON, J. B. "The Place of the Conditioned Reflex in Psychology," *Psy. Rev.*, XXIII (1916), pp. 89–116.

WATSON and RAYNER. "Conditioned Emotional Reactions," *Jour. Exper. Psy.*, III (1920), pp. 1–14.

WATSON and RAYNER. "Studies in Infant Psychology," *Scientific Monthly* (Dec. 1921), pp. 493–515.

CHAPTER X

THE LAWS OF LEARNING

Learning in Animals.—Compared with experimentation on human beings, that on animals is relatively easy. Not only is animal behaviour less varied, less complex than that of humans, but, what is still more important, it also lends itself more easily to experimental control. So we need not be surprised to learn that psychology is indebted to animals for the formulation of its "laws of learning" and for the enunciation of "conditioning" as a basic principle of learning. Thorndike's "laws of learning" were a natural outgrowth of his experiments with fishes, chickens, cats, dogs, and monkeys, and, as we saw in the preceding chapter, Pavlow discovered the "conditioning" of the salivary reflex from his experiments on dogs. These formulations have been found to be applicable to human learning, a convincing argument that man belongs to the animal biological group. Moreover, some of the methods employed in the study of animal learning have, with certain necessary modifications, been adapted to the experimental study of human learning. No apology, therefore, is needed for introducing descriptions of a few typical animal studies such as the following:

(*a*) *Fishes.*—Möbius, in 1873, trained a pike to desist from snapping at minnows by causing it to live in a tank separated from the minnows by a glass plate. Owing to the fact that the pike stubbed his nose against the glass plate whenever he tried to catch the minnows, his original nature was reversed, so that he even refrained from catching them when the glass partition was removed.

Triplett[1] repeated the experiment in 1901 using two perch, male and female, instead of the pike. Prior to the experiment the perch had been fed with minnows. After the glass partition had been inserted, their food was changed to angle-worms. The

[1] Triplett, N., "The Educability of Perch," *Amer. Jour. Psy.*, XII, pp. 354–360.

minnows, instead of being allowed to remain continuously on one side of the partition, as in Möbius's experiment, were put in for thirty minutes only, after which the perch were fed with worms. The perch in the earlier stages of the experiment butted the glass partition very vigorously, especially when the minnows presented themselves head on, the normal position for being "struck" by a predatory foe. In course of time the efforts of the perch to catch the minnows became less violent and less continuous, though fluctuating somewhat according to their state of hunger. Being fed only on Mondays, Wednesdays, and Fridays, Monday's efforts were noticeably more determined than the other days'. After a month the perch were first fed with worms and the partition separating them from a single minnow then removed. The minnow joined the perch and swam beside them. The male was completely indifferent to the minnow, and the female, although stalking it and making truncated attempts at grabbing, always turned aside at the last moment, thus inhibiting her grabbing impulse in the face of repeated opportunity.

In later experiments, which were performed in the manner of Möbius, the inhibitions continued except in the face of excessive hunger, or when the minnows moved with too great a speed. Rapidity of movement, apparently, was the prime incentive for striking. But the perch could always be retrained; so much so, that when the partition was removed they swam to the place where it had been and then turned alongside as if it were still there. Only in a very dubious and hesitating manner did they finally cross the imaginary division. The experiment leaves little doubt that perch, like the pike, can be trained by punishment not to grab.

Thorndike [1] (1899) showed that the fundulus, a sea minnow whose forebrain lacks a cortex, could be trained to thread a simple maze. His method was as follows:

"The fishes were kept in an aquarium (4′×2′×9″) represented by Fig. 38. The space at one end, as represented by lines in the figure, was shaded from the sun by a cover, and all food was dropped in at this end. Along each side of the aquarium were fastened simple pairs of cleats, allowing the experimenter to put across it partitions of wood, glass, or wire screening. One of these in position is shown in the figure by the dotted line. These partitions were made each with an opening as shown in the figure. If now we cause the fish to leave his shady corner and swim up to the sunny end by putting a slide (without any opening) in behind him at D and moving it gently from D to A and then place, say, slide 1 across the aquarium at I, we shall have a chance to observe the animal's behaviour to good purpose.

[1] Thorndike, E. L., "A Note on the Psychology of Fishes," *Amer. Nat.* 33, pp. 923–926. Reprinted in *Animal Intelligence*, 1911, pp. 169–171.

"This fish dislikes the sunlight and tries to get back to D. He reacts to the situation in which he finds himself by swimming against the screen, bumping against it here and there along the bottom. He may stop and remain still for a while. He will occasionally rise up toward the top of the water, especially while swimming up and down the length of the screen. When he happens to rise up to the top at the right-hand end, he has a clear path in front of him and swims to D and feels more comfortable.

"If, after he has enjoyed the shade fifteen minutes or more, you again confine him in A, and keep on doing so six or eight times for a day or so, you will find that he swims against the screen less and less, swims up and down along it fewer and fewer times, stays still less and less, until finally his only act is to go to the right-hand side, rise up and swim out. In correspondence with this change in behaviour you will find a very marked decrease in the time he takes to escape. This fish has clearly profited by his experience and modified his conduct to suit a situation for which his innate nervous equipment did not definitely provide. He has, in common language, *learned* to get out."

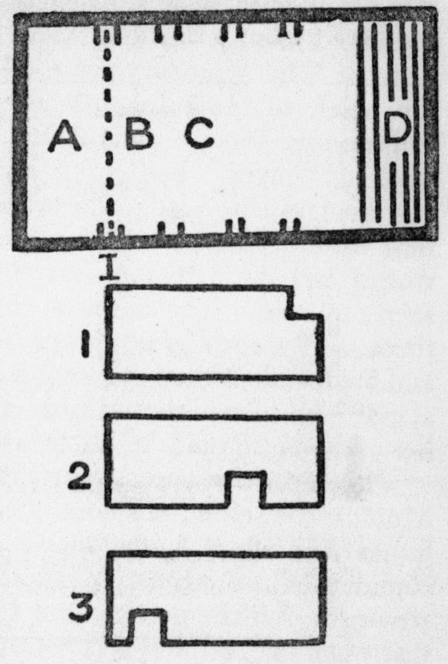

FIG. 38.—Apparatus used by Thorndike in experiment with fundulus.

In other experiments all three slides were used and the fish was required to find his way from A to B, B to C, and C to D. The motive used in all experiments was the fish's desire to be in the shade, and, perhaps, to be in the place where it was habitually fed. The wrong reactions, that is, those which did not lead to the above satisfactions, were gradually eliminated; the right ones were gradually stamped in. In other words, associative or conditioned bonds had been formed in the nervous system which permitted escape reactions to be made.

(*b*) *Turtle*.—Yerkes [1] kept a spotted turtle in a box (3′×2′×10″), in one corner of which was a nest of damp grass where the turtle liked to hide himself. Using this love of hiding

[1] Yerkes, R. M., "The Formation of Habits in the Turtle," *Pop. Sci. Mo.* 58 (1901), p. 519.

as a motive, Yerkes taught the turtle to find his way home through a simple maze. The arrangement is shown in Fig. 39. Partitions in which holes (2″×4″) had been cut were placed across the box. The turtle was placed at A and records of his wandering and the time he took to reach the nest were made. Some of the results are shown in Table XI.

Trial.	Time taken.	Remarks.
1st.	2,100 seconds.	Much wandering, many stoppings.
2nd.	900 "	Wanderings and stoppings.
3rd.	300 "	
4th.	210 "	
5th.	420 "	Some meandering.
10th.	185 "	Two mistakes in turning.
20th.	45 "	
30th.	40 "	Direct path taken.
50th.	35 "	Direct path taken.

TABLE XI.—Turtle learning to run the maze shown in Fig. 39.

As with the fish, the turtle gradually reduced the time and eliminated the unnecessary wanderings and stoppings.

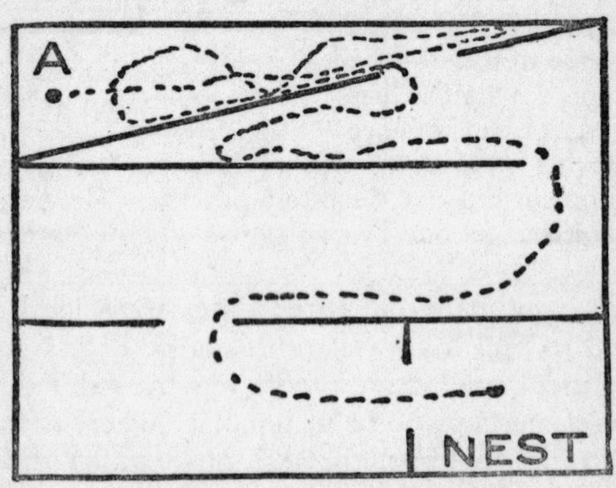

FIG. 39.—Simple maze used with turtle. The dotted line shows the path taken in the fifth trial (Yerkes).

(*c*) *Canada Porcupine.*—Sackett [1] studied the learning processes of the porcupine. Experiments were conducted on 12 animals. Porcupines are fearless animals, easily tamed, nocturnal and perennial, showing little or no tendency to hiberna-

[1] Sackett, L. W., "The Canada Porcupine: A Study of the Learning Process," *Behavior Monographs*, vol. 2, No. 2, 1913. Pp. 84.

tion. As a subject in experimental study, the porcupine is steady, industrious, cleanly, and harmless. Apparently the only drawback from the viewpoint of experimentation is that they will not breed in captivity.

In his preliminary observations Sackett notes that both young and old would usually eat from the experimenter's hand one day after capture and were regularly at work within a week. Porcupines do not throw their quills. This erroneous impression has probably arisen from the fact that against all enemies except their own species (whom they face and fight with adpressed quills) the porcupine is quick in making his powerful strokes of the tail and upward lunges of the body and that the quills, being barbed, stick on very slight contact.

Sackett showed that porcupines normally take food which is offered to them with their mouths, but that the habit may be modified so that the animals seize and carry food to the mouth with the hands. Animal No. 3 was trained to become right-handed (it was previously ambidextrous) in nine days. The experiment was then modified so that the animal was forced to take it from the experimenter's right hand with its left. In five series of twenty offerings each the following results were obtained:

Series.	No. correct.	Per cent. correct.
1st twenty.	7	35
2nd „	14	70
3rd „	14	70
4th „	16	80
5th „	19	95
Total 100	70	70

The learning was quickly acquired. In 2,024 tests No. 3 made 54 errors, 30 of which were made in the first hundred as shown above.

This same animal was then trained to reach for cabbage with the right hand and carrot with the left. The result of the entire practice was that after about 350 changes of food and hands involving nearly 5,000 tests and 160 errors, No. 3 reached for cabbage with his right hand, whenever, wherever, and by whomsoever it was offered. Thirty days later, with no practice with his hands in the meantime, he showed little or no loss of ability to make the discrimination.

Experiments with a puzzle-box were next inaugurated. The box was fitted with the following locks and combinations :

(1) A simple push-down lever.
(2) A plug which, when pulled, released the door.
(3) A horizontal thumb button adjusted to turn upward.
(4) A hook of the ordinary screen-door variety.

Partial records of Porcupine No. 11 with the puzzle-box are given in Table XII.

Trial.	Lever.	Plug.	Button.	Hook.	Lever and plug.	Combination.
1	80	315	147	67	241	315
2	30	17	206	1	39	39
3	64	15	171	14	87	283
4	24	4	157	8	230	185
5	19	6	73	15	16	140
6	12	23	145	13	97	310
7	10	26	25	10	46	120
8	10	15	17	7	10	60
9	20	13	30	7	98	21
10	5	3	14	10	43	15
11	9	1	17	9	21	67
12	3	1	12	12	7	122
13	3	1	30	10	40	80
14	3	1	15	5	10	50
15	5	1	27	5	6	414
16	1	1	10	5	32	48
17	3	1	10	7	4	222
18	1	1	23	6	5	130
19	1	1	8	6	5	29
20	3	1	12	6	8	42

TABLE XII.—Time records in seconds of Porcupine No. 11 with the puzzle-box.

A mere glance at the figures shows the tendency towards a speedier solution of the problem with successive trials. This reduction in time is never regular and may, indeed, with a difficult combination of locks, be quite irregular.

Sackett also showed (*a*) that porcupines learned to discriminate the circle presented pair-wise with other forms which were constructed to appeal to their denning proclivities ; (*b*) that their brightness discrimination was about 10 shades in Nendel's series of grey papers ; (*c*) that they cannot react intelligently to coloured papers and cannot probably discriminate between them ; (*d*) they learned very rapidly to thread a maze of the Hampton Court pattern which, once learned, could be followed in the dark ; (*e*) rotating the maze through 90 degrees, or even shifting the runways made by the feet of the animals, proved very confusing to them ; and (*f*) a maze once learned could be threaded without error after a lapse of 100 days. All in all, therefore, the animals proved to be possessed of more intelligence, as expressed by a capacity to learn, than they are usually credited with.

(*d*) *Rats*.—The white rat is the most satisfactory of all animals for laboratory experiments in learning. Easily bred, handled, and kept in good physical condition, with a consuming curiosity which makes him teachable, his qualities have caused him to be used in literally thousands of experimental investigations. Some

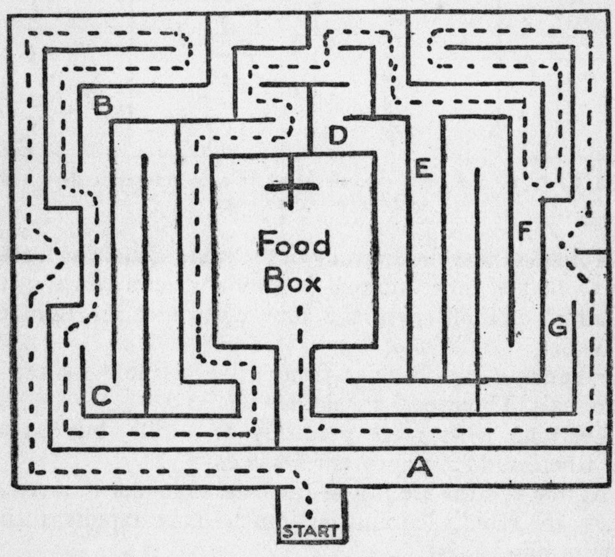

FIG. 40.—The Hampton Court maze (slightly modified). The blind alleys are shown at A, B, C, D, E, F, and G. The correct path is shown by the dotted line.

of these have been very ingenious, but the commonest experiment is one that investigates the learning of some variety of maze. Of the mazes, the form known as the Hampton Court maze has been more frequently used than any other. Fig. 40 shows the plan of this maze and its solution. Food provides the stimulus for the rat. If the *cul-de-sacs* are painted white and the correct path black, or *vice versâ*, both the time and error records are found to be superior. The same holds true if entry into a *cul-de-sac* is followed by punishment in the form of an electric shock. Some records from Miss Vincent's study [1] are given in Table XIII.

[1] Vincent, Stella B., " The White Rat and the Maze Problem : the Introduction of a Visual Control," *Jour. Animal Behavior*, vol. v, 1 (1915), pp. 1–24.

The figures are the averages from a group of five animals. Leaving the true path, entering a *cul-de-sac*, was counted as one error.

	Time in seconds.		Errors.	
	Normal maze.	Black-white maze.	Normal maze.	Black-white maze.
1.	1,804	1,342	14·9	7·5
2.	966	413	11·9	4·3
3.	542	254	10·4	3·0
4.	847	211	7·4	3·0
5.	233	98	4·1	1·6
6.	193	72	3·5	1·0
7.	63	37	1·6	0·5
8.	49	48	1·4	0·2
9.	37	54	1·5	0·5
10.	33	39	1·1	0·4

TABLE XIII.—Time and error records of white rats, first ten trials, on normal and black-white mazes.

It is obvious that the learning of the rat in general is markedly similar to that of other animals in similar circumstances; there is a gradual diminution of the time taken and the number of errors made.

Summarizing the findings from maze learning by rats and other animals, Thomson [1] states that:

1. Learning takes place gradually as a rule, but cases are quoted where sudden improvements occur.

2. At first returns are just as frequent as forward movements, but they are rapidly eliminated, much more rapidly than the entering of blind alleys.

3. Blind alleys near the food box are eliminated more quickly than those near the entrance.

4. Returns also persist longer near the entrance.

5. The distance penetrated into blind alleys decreases before the alley is eliminated.

6. Short blind alleys are more rapidly eliminated than are long.

To this summary Woodworth's [2] acute and illuminating analysis of the rat's *method of learning* should be added.

"The rat, placed in a maze, explores. He sniffs about, goes back and forth, enters every passage, and actually covers every square inch of the maze at least once; and in the course of these explorations hits upon the food box. Replaced at the starting-point, he proceeds as

[1] Thomson, G. H., *Instinct, Intelligence, and Character*, p. 63.
[2] Woodworth, R. S., *Psychology: A Study of Mental Life*, p. 305.

before, though with more speed and less dallying in the blind alleys. On successive trials he goes less and less deeply into a blind alley, till he finally passes the entrance to it without even turning his head. Thus eliminating the blind alleys one after another, he comes at length to run by a fixed route from start to finish.

"At first thought, the elimination of the useless moves seems to tell the whole story of the rat's learning process; but careful study of his behaviour reveals another factor. When the rat approaches a turning-point in the maze, his course bends so as to prepare for the turn; he does not simply advance to the turning-point and then make the turn, but several steps before he reaches that point are organized or co-ordinated into a sort of unit.

"The combination of steps into larger units is shown also by certain variations of the experiment. It is known that the rat makes little use of the sense of sight in learning, guiding himself mostly by the muscle sense. Now if the maze, after being well learned, is altered by shortening one of the straight passages, the rat runs full tilt against the new end of the passage, showing clearly that he was proceeding not step by step, but by *runs* of some length. Another variation of the experiment is to place a rat that has learned a maze down in the midst of it, instead of at the usual starting-point. At first he is lost, and begins exploring, but, hitting on a section of the right path, he gets his cue from the 'feel' of it, and races off at full speed to the food box. Now his cue cannot have been any single step or turn, for these would all be too much alike; his cue must have been a familiar *sequence* of movements, and that sequence functions as a unit in calling out the rest of the habitual movement.

Fig. 41.—Puzzle-box used in experiment with cats (Thorndike).

"In short, the rat learns the path by *elimination* of false reactions and by *combinations* of single steps and turns into larger reaction units."

(*e*) *Cats.*—For his experiments with cats Thorndike[1] used boxes (20″×15″×12″) of the general shape shown in Fig. 41. Various forms of catches or fastenings were used. In the one to which the following results relate, a string was attached to the bolt which held the door and ran up over a pulley on the front edge of the box. The string was tied to a wire loop ($2\frac{1}{2}$ inches in diameter) hanging above the floor in the front centre of the box.

[1] Thorndike, *Animal Intelligence*, pp. 29–42.

Clawing or biting it, or rubbing against it even, if in a certain way, opened the door.

The cat was made hungry by withholding food for 24 hours. This was necessary, as a well-fed cat would not react, but curled up and went to sleep when placed in the box. Food (fish) was placed outside the box at such a distance that the cat could not push a paw through the bars and claw it in. When the hungry cat was introduced, through the twin stimuli of confinement and hunger, reactions became numerous. The head was pushed between the bars, the paw was thrust through to rake in the fish, and various random clawings were made. All of these, of course,

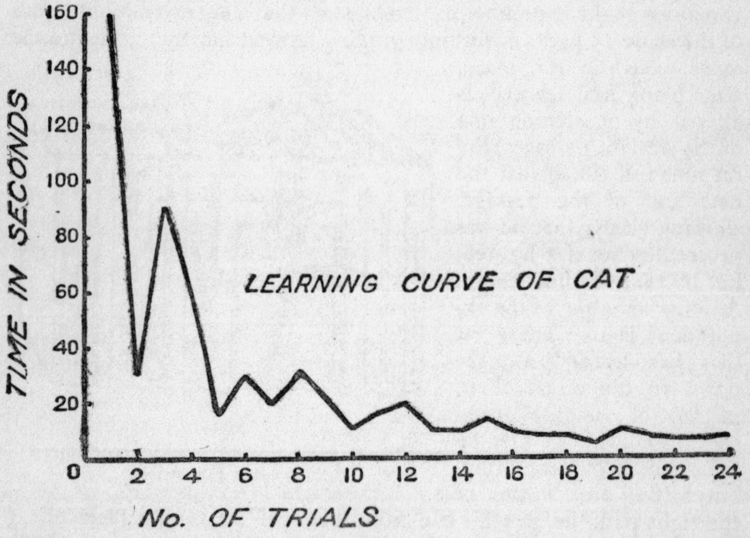

Fig. 42.—Learning curve of cat. "Time" is the time taken to escape from a puzzle-box.

were unsuccessful except the one that accidentally pulled the string and released the catch. Release from confinement and securing food were pleasant and gave satisfaction. In successive trials the random movements gradually disappeared and the cat, in a shorter time, pulled the string, escaped, and ate the fish. Cat number 12, a young one, took the following times in seconds to perform the act: 160, 30, 90, 60, 15, 28, 20, 30, 22, 11, 15, 20, 12, 10, 14, 10, 8, 8, 5, 10, 8, 6, 6, 7. These results are graphed in Fig. 42.

The most noticeable feature about the time curve is that it gradually descends, albeit in a somewhat irregular fashion. The fall of the curve is a fair measure of the rate of formation of associative bonds ; the right actions are gradually stamped in by success, the wrong ones are gradually eliminated by failure.

(*f*) *Chimpanzees and Gorillas.*—Koehler's studies of learning in chimpanzees carried out during the war years on the Island of Teneriffe, Canary Islands, is different from the usual run of experimentation with animals.[1] The chimpanzees (12 in number) were given a great deal of freedom in their compound. They were not confined in the sense that Thorndike's cats and monkeys were confined and forced to learn tricks before they could escape. Rather, poles, sticks, ropes, boxes, etc., were provided which they could use, if they thought fit, to help them in securing bananas. In this way they learned to utilize a five-yard pole to reach a banana fastened to the canvas ceiling of their compound. Their method was to place the pole upright on the ground, swarm up it quickly and snatch the banana before the pole fell to the ground. This seems very wonderful ; no human being could do such a thing, but humans are not built for climbing poles, and chimpanzees are. On the other hand, the chimpanzees could never learn to pile boxes in an orderly way to aid them in reaching a banana fastened beyond their reach. This task apparently was beyond them ; they piled big boxes on little ones in a most haphazard way. The general method of piling was to take a box, big or little just as it happened to come, place it on the ground, stand on it and then take a second box and try to place it on the first—the one on which they were standing. As often as not they failed to pile the second one, especially when it happened to be bigger than the first. Sometimes, however, they were successful in getting a wobbly pile of boxes to remain steady long enough to enable them to reach up and hurriedly grasp the banana before the boxes came tumbling down. Koehler maintains that in all of the experiments the chimpanzees learned by *insight*. They could not see how to do a trick for some time, then they saw through it, and ever afterwards did it perfectly. This may have been true of the simpler tasks, but, after seeing the moving pictures of chimpanzees piling the boxes, the writer is convinced that insight is not the whole explanation. But of this later.

Yerkes[2] made a six-weeks' study of a female gorilla, aged five years, named Congo. With out-of-doors as a laboratory, and by observation under natural and experimental conditions, a survey of the gorilla's mental traits was made. Contrary to expectation, Congo initially exhibited neither ability nor tendency

[1] Koehler, W., *The Mentality of Apes*, 1925.

[2] Yerkes, R. M., "The Mind of a Gorilla," *Genetic Psychology Monographs*, II Nos. 1 and 2, 1927, p. 193.

to use such objects as sticks, wires, or boxes as appliances or aids in adaptation. She was seldom randomly active or curious and practically never destructive. In contrast with chimpanzees, Congo was strangely calm, placid, even-tempered, and self-dependent. "Neither spontaneously nor imitatively did she, in this investigation, use or learn to manipulate skilfully such devices as hooks, snaps, hasps, and locks. By means of sticks, ropes, chains, bottles, boxes, a mirror, and other simple appliances, more than a score of novel problems were set for Congo. Most of them she solved eventually, some by what appeared like random action and the selection of profitable acts, others by observation of essential features or relations in the situation and immediate adaptation. Evidences of psycho-physiological processes in the gorilla are abundant and varied. Clearly 'trial and error' as a description of adaptive procedure is incomplete and frequently inapplicable. Often there appear evidences of 'critical points' in adaptive endeavour at which the nature of activity suddenly changes. Many of the objective characteristics in these suddenly achieved adaptations are observed in human ideational behaviour. It therefore seems probable that the animal experiences insight. Various experiments prove that 'out of sight' is not necessarily 'out of mind.'"[1]

"Insight" and "Trial-and-Error" Learning.—A careful study of learning curves of animals, such, for example, as may be drawn from data given in the tables of this chapter, show that learning is a gradual affair. The wrong responses are gradually eliminated and the right ones organized into new wholes which become more and more efficient until a practical limit is reached. This type of learning is usually mis-called "trial-and-error" learning. It should be called "learning by selection of the successful variant," for it is by the selection of the right way rather than by the elimination of the wrong one that learning takes place. The wrong one is usually eliminated because it cannot exist in the presence of the right one. This form of learning is by no means confined to animals; it is very prevalent in human learning also. Learning to play golf, to ride a bicycle, use a typewriter, drive a car, to skate, swim, plane wood, write with a pen, play a musical instrument, model with clay, paddle a canoe, spell, compute, and thousands of other human accomplishments have "trial-and-error" learning as an essential element. If we

[1] Bertrand Russell in his latest work (*Philosophy*, Norton & Co., 1927) humorously remarks that animals which have been observed have "all displayed the national characteristics of the observer. Animals studied by Americans rush about frantically, with an incredible display of hustle and pep, and at last achieve the desired result by chance. Animals observed by Germans, sit still and think, and at last evolve the solution out of their inner consciousness."

could imagine a child of ten years confined in a puzzle box the early attempts of escape would be largely of the trial-and-error type. His time of escape, after he had once solved the trick of getting out, would, however, be very short. His curve of learning would resemble the " insight " curves of Koehler's chimpanzees. If, however, instead of a simple fastening to undo, the child were given a two-piece, complicated wire puzzle to solve, the random movements characteristic of animal learning would appear, and the curve of learning, as Ruger has shown, would be similar to that of animals. There may be " insight " in the sense that a person solving a puzzle tends to follow " hunches," but the simpler " trial-and-error " learning tends to dominate.

Nor is trial-and-error learning confined to motor acts. We solve deductions in geometry largely by trial-and-error methods, never by any chance in the logical way we set them down on paper. And thinking is largely of the same trial-and-error kind.

" Insight " in Koehler's sense is only a case of rapid learning, and is generally confined to the simpler problems. Nor is the curve, where no improvement is shown, really a curve where no learning takes place. It simply means that the scale we use to measure it with is too crude to show whatever improvement has been made. Take the case of measuring improvement in swimming by " yards swum " or in juggling balls by " number of tosses made." In the former case no improvement would be shown until after, perhaps, ten hours of practice. But it would be nonsensical to say that the swimmer after nine hours of practice is no better than he was in the first hour, although the scale of accomplishment in both cases would register zero. Improvement has taken place, but it is hidden as inner co-ordinations of the nervous system. And the same thing applies to tossing balls. The chimpanzee which cannot do a thing and then suddenly does it may have been learning by inner co-ordinations, but these do not show on any curve of learning. A man thinking out a problem suddenly says, " I've got it," but " insight " in this case is the end-point of a lot of trial-and-error thinking. Insight, therefore, is an un-analysed form of learning ; and one in which trial and error may still play a hidden though important part.

The thing which really sets apart man from animals in learning capacity is his ability to utilize implicit and explicit language habits. Where non-language habits are concerned man is not greatly the superior of some of the lower animals, but if language can be employed, a short-circuiting takes place which places him at an immeasurable advantage. But it should be remembered that habits which are possible to the idiot and imbecile are remarkably animal-like in the hit-and-miss way they are acquired.

Thorndike's Laws of Learning.—As previously stated, Thorndike's laws of learning, the first comprehensive formulation of the rules which learning obey, grew out of his experiments on learning in animals. They have proved of great value to the teacher and, indeed, have almost created a revolution in teaching methods. We shall, therefore, spend some time in discussing them.

1. *The Law of Effect.*—This law is sometimes called the "law of satisfaction and annoyance." In Thorndike's[1] words the law runs: "When a modifiable connection between a situation and a response is made and is accompanied or followed by a satisfying state of affairs, that connection's strength is increased; when made and accompanied or followed by an annoying state of affairs, its strength is decreased." In other words, *a modifiable bond is strengthened or weakened according as satisfaction or annoyance attends its exercise.*

By modifiable bonds we mean those that can be changed by learning. Some bonds we have seen, like those concerned with physiological actions (breathing and digestion), and some reflexes (the pupillary reflex, snoring, and shivering) are practically beyond our control. They belong to the non-variable forms of behaviour. Others (sneezing, yawning, vomiting) are modified with extreme difficulty. Others again are modified with comparative ease. It is with this last group that the law of effect is concerned.

By a satisfying state of affairs Thorndike means "one which the animal does nothing to avoid, often doing things which maintain or renew it. By an annoying state of affairs is meant one which the animal does nothing to preserve, often doing things which put an end to it." This is a purely objective definition and one from which introspections have been eliminated.

Nobody in his senses doubts the reality of original satisfiers and annoyers. To eat when hungry is satisfying; to eat when satiated is usually annoying. "To be with other human beings rather than alone, to be with familiar human beings rather than strange ones, to move when refreshed, to rest when tired, to be not altogether unenclosed when resting at night" are samples of original satisfiers. We can add to these almost indefinitely. We like cats better than snakes, sweet foods rather than bitter, moderate temperatures and humidity rather than extreme temperatures and humidity, soft beds to sleep on better than hard floors, sunlight better than darkness, praise and approval rather than blame and disapproval, and sweet odours of flowers and

[1] Thorndike, E. L., *Educational Psychology*, vol. ii, Introduction.

fruit better than the smell of putrefying flesh and excrement. On the other hand, being checked in locomotion by an obstacle, being hungry, being scorned, being thwarted after an original behaviour series has been started, are all original annoyers.

Why are some actions satisfying, some annoying? The secret seems to lie in evolution. What was painful in the first instance was harmful; what was pleasant or satisfying was conducive to survival. These are the first of the original satisfiers and annoyers. No animal could survive if extremes of heat and cold were not annoying in the sense that the animal avoids them. The animals that felt no discomfort in sudden changes to icy surroundings or extremes of heat have vanished from the earth; those that did, and adjusted themselves accordingly, have survived. The polar bear through long evolution is now so well adjusted to cold that he can survive in frigid temperatures, but even he hibernates in his icy cave during the long arctic winter. The whole gamut of satisfiers and annoyers from sex to starvation can be explained in this way. The apparent exceptions of intemperance in drugs and inactivity during freezing can be satisfactorily explained. Most drugs (nicotine is an excellent example) are annoying when first taken, and if it were not for the physiological craving they create, would never lead to habitual indulgence. The onset of freezing is annoying and leads to active exercise; only when the sweets of rest after great bodily fatigue from exercise override the annoyance or fear of freezing do we sink into bodily torpor. In the past, the pleasant satisfiers led to survival and perpetuation of the species, original annoyers led to extinction, and a study of original satisfiers and annoyers shows that these factors have lost little of their potency as civilization has developed.

Yet Watson, as a behaviourist, denies that the law of effect plays any part. Frequency and recency explain the learning. The successful action in maze learning must occur in every series; no other need so occur; therefore, the successful action is learned mainly through frequency. This is an interesting contention and Thomson [1] has counteracted it very ingeniously. He states:

"Let us try an artificial experiment in which we throw a coin at each choice of paths and imagine we turn to the right hand for heads, left hand for tails. Here is one such trial, made by actually throwing a coin (the letters show the path according to the letters of the diagram).

P.

N or V? The coin gives a tail, so we take N. Go to N, discover it is a blind alley, come out again, and then ask:

P or V? The coin gives tail, so take V.

[1] Thomson, *Instinct, Intelligence, and Character*, pp. 58–64.

Z or L ? The coin gives head, so take L. On coming out of L we ask :

V or Z ? Coin says V. We reach P and ask :

P or N ? Coin says N.

P or V ? Coin says V.

And so on, the path finally being found to be (including the above moves) as follows :

PNVLVNVLVPVLVNPNVZFZVPNVLVPVZFZLZKEQBOBQBO TATOTCYSJSUSJH

" This path, if traced out on the diagram, looks quite like a real maze-run ; but really a rat would not keep on taking blind alleys repeatedly, for dissatisfaction at coming to a dead wall would make them less likely to be re-entered. However, assume that, on this first occasion, chance alone has led the rat, as chance alone led our choice of a path with the aid of a tossed penny.

" Now suppose the rat is started on a second run of the maze, and let us see what would happen if only the law of use acted. More-

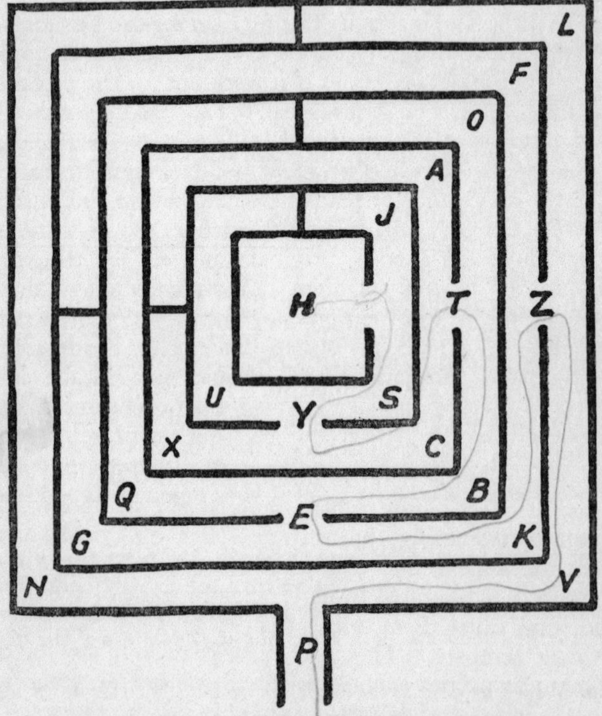

FIG. 43.—Thomson's maze (learning by chance).

(From Thomson's " Instinct, Intelligence, and Character." George Allen and Unwin, Ltd.)

over, suppose that it acts infallibly. On entry at P, will the rat take N or V ? If we examine the record we find that on its previous entries it took N three times and V only twice. It will, therefore, take N, and the law of use alone will never enable it to get rid of entering N. In the same way we can find the whole route which the rat would take on this its second trial. It would be PNVLVPNVLVPNVLVP and so on *ad infinitum*. By the law of use it would never reach the food box."

In the same way Thomson has shown that if *recency* entirely overrides *frequency* we get PVZKEQBOTCYSJH. The blind alleys Q, O, J, in this run would never be eliminated by recency or frequency if they alone acted. And recency if applied during the first run would effectually prevent any rat which once took a return path from ever getting to the centre, which is not true to the facts. Thomson also demonstrated the necessity for the law of effect in human as well as in animal learning.

The law of effect is undoubtedly universal in both animal and human learning. In the case of animals we found that food was an original satisfier for all of them ; shade was a satisfier for the fundulus ; blows received from bumping the glass partition was annoying to the pike and perch ; and confinement coupled with hunger was sufficiently annoying to the cat to cause it to try to get out.

In the home and school original satisfiers and annoyers are constantly used. Praise is satisfying, blame is annoying, hence their universal use in the teaching process. Some activities, as it were, provide their own repertory of annoyers and satisfiers. In playing the piano dissonance is annoying, consonance pleasurable. In typewriting the wrongly struck letters cause annoyance, the rightly struck ones pleasure. To get one's head under water is originally annoying, consequently the strokes which keep us afloat in swimming are stamped in. In skating and cycling the bumps and falls are gradually eliminated and we learn to progress on an even keel because such progression is satisfying.

But wrong bonds may be formed as easily as the right ones if the law of effect is not rightly understood. A spoiled child is the result of rewarding the attitude " if I only make myself a sufficient nuisance I shall get what I want." Being the centre of attention is pleasurable to children, and some of them, finding that tantrums cause them to be attended to, form habits of flying into violent tempers. The teacher who uses school tasks as a punishment associates school work with punishment and annoyance. If teachers and parents would only ask themselves, " What am I encouraging, what bond am I strengthening or weakening by this particular line of conduct ? " there would be far more happy children in the world than there are to-day. The thing to do in this connection is to think out the psychological bearings of a line of conduct and, if it proves a desirable course, to stick to it at all costs.

2. *The Law of Exercise or Frequency.*—This law has two parts—*Use and Disuse.* The *law of use* is—when a modifiable connection is made between a situation and a response, that connection's strength is, other things being equal, increased. The *law of disuse* is—when a modifiable connection is *not* made between a situation and a response over a length of time, that connection's strength is decreased. The phrase " other things being equal " refers mostly to the satisfyingness or annoyingness of the situation. " Practice makes perfect," but not if the resultant is painful. Nobody ever became perfect in sitting on a bent pin or in poking the fire with the finger.

Closely associated with the law of exercise are the factors of *intensity* and *recency*. A bright light, a loud sound, or concentrated effort leads to fairly permanent bonds with but few repetitions. Thunder and lightning make profound impressions on children ; interest in a task makes it easier. Recency is the law of disuse turned the other way round, as it were. The bond recently formed can be recalled more easily than the one formed a long time ago. Disuse has not had time to play its part.

In terms of the nervous system the law of exercise refers to the strengthening or weakening of the synaptic connections. The repeated passage of a nervous impulse across a synapse breaks down the resistance. Use cements the bonds of the nervous system ; disuse weakens them.

The law of exercise and effect work hand in hand. We normally practise the things we are successful at ; these things are satisfying. In similar fashion the association of the two laws is seen in the proverbs " Distance lends enchantment to the view " and " Every nation has its golden age." The satisfying things are remembered, the annoying things are forgotten, simply because we dwell more frequently upon the pleasant than the unpleasant. It isn't that " school days are one's happiest days," but that we recall the pleasant things that happened in school more frequently than we recall the unpleasant. To do so is normal for human beings.

3. *The Law of Readiness.*—The law of readiness is : " When any conduction unit is in readiness to conduct, for it to do so is satisfying. When any conduction unit is not in readiness to conduct, for it to conduct is annoying. When any conduction unit is in readiness to conduct, for it not to do so is annoying." More briefly the law may be stated : *When a bond is ready to*

act, to act gives satisfaction and not to act gives annoyance. When a bond which is not ready to act is made to act, annoyance is caused.

A moment's reflection shows that readiness is intimately associated with the condition of the neurons of the nervous system. Sometimes these are ready to act, sometimes not. If they are ready to act, then acting gives satisfaction, and not acting gives annoyance; but if the neurons are forced to act when they are not ready to do so, annoyance results. To be made to do things when fatigued is most annoying, yet even vigorous action after a good rest is distinctly satisfying. Examples of this law as it works out in school are innumerable. The boy who is bursting to show his knowledge is pleased if allowed to do so, and annoyed if the teacher ignores him.

Minor Laws of Learning.—In addition to the three major laws enumerated above, Thorndike gives *five* secondary laws. These are:

(*a*) *Multiple Response to the same External Situation.*—Failure on the part of the cat to get out of the cage by one kind of action results in an inner change, and a different action results. This law seems to run contrary to the universal law of cause and effect. But it is not really so. Our different reactions to a groaning dinner table are due to physiological differences in ourselves—whether we are hungry or not.

In an earlier chapter we stated that a paramœcium, a single-celled animal which moves spirally through the water by movement of ciliary hairs, on encountering an obstacle when swimming first back paddles, then side paddles until it has rotated through an angle of 30° to 45°, and then forges ahead again. If a second obstacle is encountered, the series of responses is repeated. This is a multiple response, but of so definite a character that learning new things is practically precluded.

Contrast this with the varied responses of a child to a box of bricks. The responses are not only more numerous but more varied. The situation—toys and child—may set off a series of reactions which last for an hour or more. Similarly, a chance word or observation may set off a train of thoughts which runs for a long time. Some external stimulus seems always to be necessary, but once a train of reactions is started, it provides its own stimulus for continuance. One thing leads to another. At bottom, these multiple reactions to a single situation lie at the basis of all learning. Through the laws of effect and exercise, the desirable ones may be selected and practised. The higher the animal in the evolutionary scale, the greater the number and variety of its responses, and the greater its educability. Further, the higher the stage of learning the less the stimulus necessary to set off significant responses. A perched block may tell a geologist the glacial history of a country. From a few bones a palæontologist can reconstruct the extinct dinosaur. A slight stimulus in each case has led to a very complex series of responses.

(*b*) *Attitude, Set, or Disposition*—determines the particular response that is made, and also whether it will be satisfying or annoying. A well-fed cat goes to sleep in the cage ; a hungry one tries to get out.

(*c*) *Law of Partial Activity.*—" A part, or element or aspect of a situation may be prepotent in causing response, and may have responses bound more or less exclusively to it regardless of some or all of its accompaniments." Thorndike states that a cat which has learned to get out of a dozen boxes is more attentive to small objects on the side of a new box than an inexperienced cat. A pupil who has solved a number of puzzles or done a great number of intelligence tests " gets on to the thing " more quickly than one who has not had similar experiences. Similarly, to a trained mechanic a machine is not a blur of whirring wheels ; he sees the connection of part to part and their relationship to the whole far more easily than one who is not so trained. Schooling in this sense is helping the pupil to notice and to react to the significant elements in a situation.

(*d*) *Law of Assimilation or Analogy.*—Situations having no original or acquired responses give rise to responses made previously to similar situations. The small girl of two years who triumphantly scooped up the water in a finger-bowl with a spoon was responding by analogy. The polite use of finger-bowls was unknown to her, but bowls with porridge in them were, so she responded to the water in a bowl as she had previously responded to porridge. In school, the most usual responses by analogy are found in the so-called " howlers." The boy who wrote " craven image " as part of the second commandment was responding by analogy.

(*e*) *Law of Associative Shifting.*—This is the conditioned response. A response may be shifted from one situation to another which is presented at the same time. There are numberless examples to be found in schooling. In learning to read, the situation is gradually transferred from element to element until the " ghostly outline " of words is sufficient to arouse the reading response. Conditioning is so universal that it may truly be said that the teacher can get any response of which a pupil is capable associated with any situation to which he is sensitive.

Symonds's Laws of Learning based on Conditioned Reactions.—Taking Chapter XIV, " Conditioned Reflexes," in C. Lovatt Evans's *Recent Advances in Physiology*, as a basis,

Symonds [1] has recently presented twenty-three laws of learning couched in the language of the conditioned reaction. Although many of them have been discussed in the preceding chapter, the whole of the laws are reproduced below because of their intrinsic interest and permanent value :

1. Stimulation of any receptor organ occurring simultaneously with a reaction of an effector organ leads to the formation of a new stimulus-response bond. (Thorndike's Law of Associative Shifting.)

2. Repetition is necessary before the conditioned reaction is formed. (Thorndike's Law of Use or Frequency.)

3. If the unconditioned stimulus precedes the conditioned stimulus, there is no new reflex formed.

4. If the conditioned stimulus precedes the unconditioned stimulus, a new reflex is formed.

5. Simultaneous conditioned reflexes are formed more quickly than others.

6. The latent period of response (time interval between stimulus and response) in a conditioned response is the same as the interval between the two stimuli.

7. The rate at which the conditioned reflex becomes established is correlated with the strength of the conditioned stimulus.

7*a*. A very strong conditioned stimulus delays the function of the reflex. (Calls out emotional responses.)

8. The vigour or strength of the conditioned response is proportional to the strength of the unconditioned stimulus.

9. Discontinuous conditioned stimuli lead to more rapid learning than continuous conditioned stimuli (basis of the practice of spaced learning).

10. The reflex resulting from two simultaneous conditioned stimuli is more powerful than when one is used. (Law of Summation.)

11. A conditioned reflex established to any given stimulus does not lead to formation of other conditioned reflexes. (Law of Specificity.)

12. If a conditioned response is not exercised for a considerable period of time, its strength is impaired. (Thorndike's Law of Disuse or Forgetting.)

12*a*. Though weakened through disuse, conditioned reflexes will be found present after a lapse of time and can be brought to original strength in a much shorter time than is required for the development of new reflexes (relearning).

13. If a conditioned stimulus is applied several times in succession without the accompaniment of the unconditioned stimulus, the reflex undergoes rapid diminution in strength, and can in this way quickly be extinguished. (Law of Fatigue.)

13*a*. The shorter the interval between the isolated applications of the conditioned stimulus, the quicker will be the extinction.

[1] Symonds, P. M., "Laws of Learning," *J.E.P.*, XVIII, 6 (Sept. 1927), pp. 405–413.

13*b*. Delayed and trace reflexes undergo a much more rapid process of extinction than the corresponding simultaneous reflexes.

14. A conditioned reflex which has undergone such extinction, regenerates spontaneously after an interval of a few hours. (Effect of rest.)

15. Repeated extinction has a much more profound effect and the spontaneous regeneration is slower and less complete. When this has happened it may take a longer time to re-establish the response than even for the formation of a new response.

16. Extinction of a conditioned reaction for a particular stimulus has no effect upon the strength of other conditioned reflexes.

17. If during or shortly before the occurrence of a conditioned reflex an additional stimulus is presented, the conditioned reflex becomes weaker.

17*a*. The stronger this additional or extra stimulus, the greater its inhibitory effect.

17*b*. This inhibition is only temporary.

17*c*. On repetition of the extra stimulus its inhibitory effect becomes smaller.

18. Inactivity which results from the repetition of the conditioned stimulus without the unconditioned stimulus and inactivity in delayed trace reactions are in themselves conditioned reactions—a state of acquired inactivity. The different internal inhibitions undergo summation, they may be experimentally extinguished, the stimuli causing internal inhibitions may be discriminated from each other and they can be made to reappear by the application of an extra stimulus.

19. If a stimulus has been positively conditioned to a certain reaction and another stimulus has been conditioned to the absence of that reaction, an application of the latter stimulus reduces the strength of the former stimulus.

19*a*. The shorter the time interval between the two the greater the effect.

20. Conditioned stimuli may serve as unconditioned stimuli in subsequent reactions to neutral stimuli.

21. The process of establishment of inhibitions, particularly the establishment of very fine discriminations, leads to a disturbing effect on other reactions and inhibitions, and if extreme will result in a general excitability and neurotic state.

22. Internal organic states, as well as glandular secretion, influence the strength of conditioned reflexes and the rate at which they may be learned.

23. Conditioned reflexes may be more rapidly established in young people than in old people.

Conclusion.—We have now enumerated the laws of learning derived from animal learning and from experiments in conditioning. Thorndike's laws centre around "learning as the modification of native reactions" and Symonds's around "learning as conditioning." Since these are two views of the same process, we find that Symonds's laws confirm and supplement Thorndike's in a most remarkable way. Only in one thing is there a serious discrepancy. The laws derived from conditioning apparently find no place for the law of effect, thus supporting Watson's position that it is an unnecessary one.[1] But we have shown that it is essential in learning. Can a reconciliation be made? Not at present. The law of effect is probably based on a different bodily mechanism than the other laws. Symonds hazards the guess that "the law of effect seems to describe the influence of one reaction on another, particularly the influence of reactions to peripheral stimuli on reactions to organic and visceral stimuli. Just as its name implies, this law represents the *effect* of one set of reactions on another set of reactions. Utilization of the law of effect in the control and guidance of learning is not so much a matter of understanding the way in which learning takes place as by the keen and skilful analysis of desires, motives, and drives, and the means by which they may be satisfied by skills and habits."

Whatever the solution of the difficulty that the law of effect presents, one thing stands out clearly as a conclusion to be drawn from the material in this chapter, namely, that a better control of educational processes will come from, first, a careful analysis of the elements into which the processes can be divided and, second, an arrangement of conditions so that the findings expressed by the laws of learning can be put into effective operation.

References

HAGGERTY, M. E. "Imitation in Monkeys," *Jour. Comp. Neur. and Psy.*, XIX, 4 (July, 1909), pp. 337–455.

HICKS, VINNIE C. "The Relative Values of the Different Curves of Learning," *Jour. Animal Behaviour*, I, 2 (March–April, 1911), pp. 138–156.

KOEHLER, W. *The Mentality of Apes*. Trans. by E. Winter. New York, Harcourt Brace, 1925. Pp. viii+342.

SACKETT, L. W. "The Canada Porcupine: A Study of the Learning Process," *Behavior Monographs*, II, 2 (1913), No. 7. Pp. 84.

SANDIFORD, P. "Thorndike's Contributions to the Laws of Learning," *T.C. Record*, XXVII, 6 (Feb. 1926), pp. 523–531.

SYMONDS, P. M. "Laws of Learning," *J.E.P.*, XVIII, 6 (Sept. 1927), pp. 405–413.

THOMSON, G. H. *Instinct, Intelligence, and Character: An Educational Psychology*. George Allen & Unwin; Pub. Jan. 1925. Pp. 282.

THORNDIKE, E. L. *Educational Psychology*. Vol. II. *The Psychology of Learning*. New York, Teachers College, Columbia University, 1913. Pp. xi+452.

[1] Some unpublished results communicated to me by Humphrey since the above was written show that conditioning obeys the law of effect. There is, therefore, no need to consider the law of effect as in any way different from the other laws of learning.

THORNDIKE, E. L. *Animal Intelligence: Experimental Studies.* New York, Macmillan, 1911. Pp. viii+297.

TRIPLETT, N. "The Educability of the Perch," *Amer. Jour. Psy.*, XII, 3 (April, 1901). Pp. 534–360.

WASHBURN, MARGARET F. *The Animal Mind: A Text-Book of Comparative Psychology.* New York, Macmillan, 1926. Pp. xiii+431. (Chief value lies in its comprehensive bibliography of 1135 titles.)

WATSON, J. B. *Behavior: An Introduction to Comparative Psychology.* New York, Holt, 1914. Pp. xii+439.

WATSON, J. B. *Psychology from the Standpoint of a Behaviorist.* Philadelphia, Lippincott, 1919 and 1924. Pp. xvii+448.

WOODWORTH, R. S. *Psychology: A Study of Mental Life.* New York, Holt, 1921. Pp. x+580.

YERKES, R. M. "The Formation of Habits in the Turtle," *Pop. Sci. Mo.*, 58 (1901), pp. 519 ff.

YERKES, R. M. "The Mind of a Gorilla," *Genetic Psychology Monographs*, II, Nos. 1 and 2, 1927. Pp. 193.

CHAPTER XI

IMPROVEMENT IN LEARNING

The Problem of Improvement.—Having discussed the *ways* in which learning or improvement takes place, we proceed now to study those problems which centre around the *amount of improvement* which can be made. Are all children able to learn the same absolute amounts providing that suitable training is given to them ? Are there any limits to the amount of knowledge that can be learned or the degree of skill that can be acquired by individuals ? In the same individual, is the rate of learning during practice constant at all times or do fluctuations occur ? What factors or conditions govern the rate of learning ? Do they apply with equal force to the acquirement of both knowledge and skill ? Are some methods of learning more economical than others ? If so, can they be described so that teachers and pupils may benefit from them ? These are some of the questions that immediately present themselves, but the list could be greatly extended.

A casual inspection of the above problems shows that most of them are concerned with variability of performance. Without any detailed experimentation, teachers have long known that improvement in learning is extremely irregular, varying not only from individual to individual but also in the same individual from time to time. Sometimes the improvement is fast, sometimes slow. Never by any chance is the rate so steady that we can say the amount learned in 100 hours of practice will be 100 times the amount learned in one hour. Interest, attention, the quality of teaching, the amount of learning previously acquired, the spacing of the practice periods, the age and the hereditary equipment of the learner, fatigue, and a host of other factors enter into the problem and make the rate of improvement variable. Obviously some of these factors are extremely elusive and difficult to control, yet it is the one part of the field of education about which the classroom teacher urgently needs reliable information. Unfortunately for education most of the experimental work on learning has been performed with animals as the subjects, or on such remote branches as telegraphy, tapping, and typewriting, where the improvement can be measured fairly objectively. What the practical teacher would most like to know is how progress is made in thinking, in acquirement of foreign languages, and in appreciation of art, but about such things very few attested data are available at present.

Improvement in Typewriting.—In order to make the discussion as definite as possible we shall present some figures from one of our Toronto studies.[1] Table XIV presents an adaptation of material given by Edward in his report of an experimental study of typewriting.

Pupil.	Hours of Practice.															
	50	60	70	80	90	100	110	120	130	140	150	160	170	180	190	200
D. A.	73	99	116	148	171	111	176	186	171	206	201	208	200	221	220	229
V. B.	75	87	103	136	152	132	166	169	189	195	169	178	199	209	210	211
V. D.	73	99	114	120	152	120	156	164	153	185	193	197	200	216	208	217
C. H.	51	75	102	124	140	120	187	208	214	223	211	224	229	239	247	239
M. M.	38	57	75	92	120	83	133	125	146	135	159	162	163	170	170	181
P. N.	82	116	135	170	188	131	166	197	199	212	219	222	238	246	250	245
J. P.	91	109	138	149	157	141	147	179	196	199	220	212	227	230	222	233
M. R.	40	106	147	149	154	118	165	167	199	191	194	205	224	211	223	247
I. S.	71	111	141	173	206	118	157	200	202	202	226	223	214	222	242	246
E.T.	94	117	127	151	160	131	186	177	203	228	230	220	223	233	237	240
Average	69	98	120	141	162	120	164	177	187	198	202	205	212	220	223	229

Pupil.	Hours of Practice.														
	210	220	230	250	260	270	280	290	300	310	320	330	340	350	360
D. A.	235	236	230	180	230	219	216	253	270	253	261	256	290	304	334
V. B.	224	247	254	237	297	239	230	251	309	277	267	267	287	326	329
V. D.	233	240	233	239	318	298	236	265	254	248	252	283	286	312	329
C. H.	251	263	282	250	278	241	244	251	260	254	241	256	269	291	317
M. M.	169	181	170	139	189	208	213	229	236	241	249	244	251	283	275
P. N.	260	272	273	256	325	317	279	299	303	308	299	285	303	318	350
J. P.	231	241	239	200	236	264	254	246	270	260	258	261	272	277	310
M. R.	263	277	269	199	220	241	221	237	252	249	253	250	260	276	290
I. S.	224	242	233	220	243	278	270	292	273	271	265	284	310	313	337
E. T.	236	232	245	238	293	252	245	222	214	270	268	272	288	290	311
Average	233	243	243	216	261	256	241	254	261	263	261	266	282	299	319

Table XIV, showing number of words correctly typed in 5 minutes' test by each of ten students after the number of hours' practice indicated at the head of the table. The table reads that student D. A. typed 73 words in 5 minutes after 50 hours of practice and 334 after 360 hours of practice. Between the records of 90 and 100 hours and between those of 230 and 250 hours long summer holidays intervened.

[1] Edward, W. G., *Improvement Curves in the Learning of Typewriting*, 1923.

The subjects used in the experiment were upwards of 1000 pupils in the High School of Commerce, Toronto. Care was taken to make the experiment as natural as possible, all the records being taken from regular class work. The pupils practised on a carefully planned series of budgets, which were the same for all. In order to make sure that the whole learning curve was being studied, and not merely the initial portion of it, records extending over 360 hours (three school years) were made. Once a week—that is, at the end of every five hours of practice—each pupil was given a five-minute speed and accuracy test, where a penalty of one word off for each error made was exacted. The figures in Table XIV are, therefore, the net number of words typed in these weekly tests after deducting one word for each error made. The table is condensed to show the results obtained between 50 hours and 360 hours of practice, that is, between half a year and three years of training in typewriting.

Casual inspection of the table shows great individual differences among the pupils. The pupil P. N. is obviously superior to M. M. at all stages of practice, ending with 350 words (70 per min.) against 275 words (55 per min.) at the conclusion of the three-year course. Differences in zeal and concentration may explain these figures, but it is very probable that they represent actual differences in the hereditary equipment of the two individuals; M. M., as we say, was not born to be a typist. Secondly, the progress is irregular for every pupil. Successive tests at the end of ten-hour periods do not invariably show that improvement has been made during the interval; that is, ten hours of practice may be insufficient to ensure a better record than the previous one. Thirdly, the long summer vacation coming between 90 and 100 hours, and between 230 and 250, causes great losses in ability, which, however, are always made up more rapidly than they were gained in the first instance. Relearning is easier than learning, showing that there is considerable permanence in typewriting habits. Fourthly, the rate of increase in improvement is greater at the beginning than at the end. The average number of words typed by ten pupils at the end of the first year (90 hours) was 162; at the end of the third year (360 hours) it was 319, less than twice the amount. This is an illustration of the law of diminishing returns; greater effort is required to effect improvement of the skilled than the unskilled. Fifthly, the records show that each pupil had periods when little or no improvement was shown over as much as thirty or forty hours of practice. These periods, as we shall see later, have been called *plateaus*. Since plateaus do not occur in the same place for each pupil, averaging results tends to get rid of them. Averaging results, however, discloses rather extended plateaus which are probably genuine tendencies for touch typewriting.

The Practice Curve.—Although it is probably safer to draw conclusions from an analysis of the original numerical results, yet the method is difficult as well as tedious. (Those readers who faithfully followed the arguments in the previous section by referring constantly to the figures of Table XIV need no further proof of the tediousness and the inconvenience of the operation.) Consequently, students of psychology resort to graphical methods to aid them in their interpretations. The graphical representation of measured results of learning extending over a considerable period of time is called a *practice curve* or *curve of learning.* In its commonest form it shows periods of practice plotted on the X axis and improvement, measured in as constant a unit as can be found, on the Y axis. In Fig. 44 the practice curves of P. N. and J. P. and the average of ten pupils are shown. The unit used for measuring improvement is one word typed. Since words vary in length and difficulty the unit is far from being a perfect one, but it is convenient and probably averages out evenly. A better unit would be the number of strokes made, but even this is a variable unit, since some strokes are harder to make than others.

The change in slope of the upward curve to the right is the index of improvement. Many curves of skills such as typewriting and telegraphy, in addition to daily irregularities, show (1) initial periods of rapid progress followed by (2) periods of little or no progress (plateaus) followed again by (3) periods of rapid progress, (4) plateaus, and so on. This " regular irregularity " in learning curves has been compared with a series of " perchings and flyings."

Theoretically a smoothed curve showing improvement in the acquirement of a skill may be: (1) a straight line where the rate of improvement is constant; (2) a convex curve of the logarithmic type where the initial rate of progress gradually diminishes and the curve becomes a straight line on a final plateau; (3) a concave curve where the initial rate gradually increases; (4) various combinations of the concave and convex, especially the form where the concave is followed by a convex curve, creating, of necessity, a plateau between them.

In practice, however, the straight line (type 1) is seldom found, and only in restricted experiments. The straight line form probably represents a short section of a longer curve. The convex type (2) is the one most commonly found. The concave curve (3) is seldom found in measurements of skills.

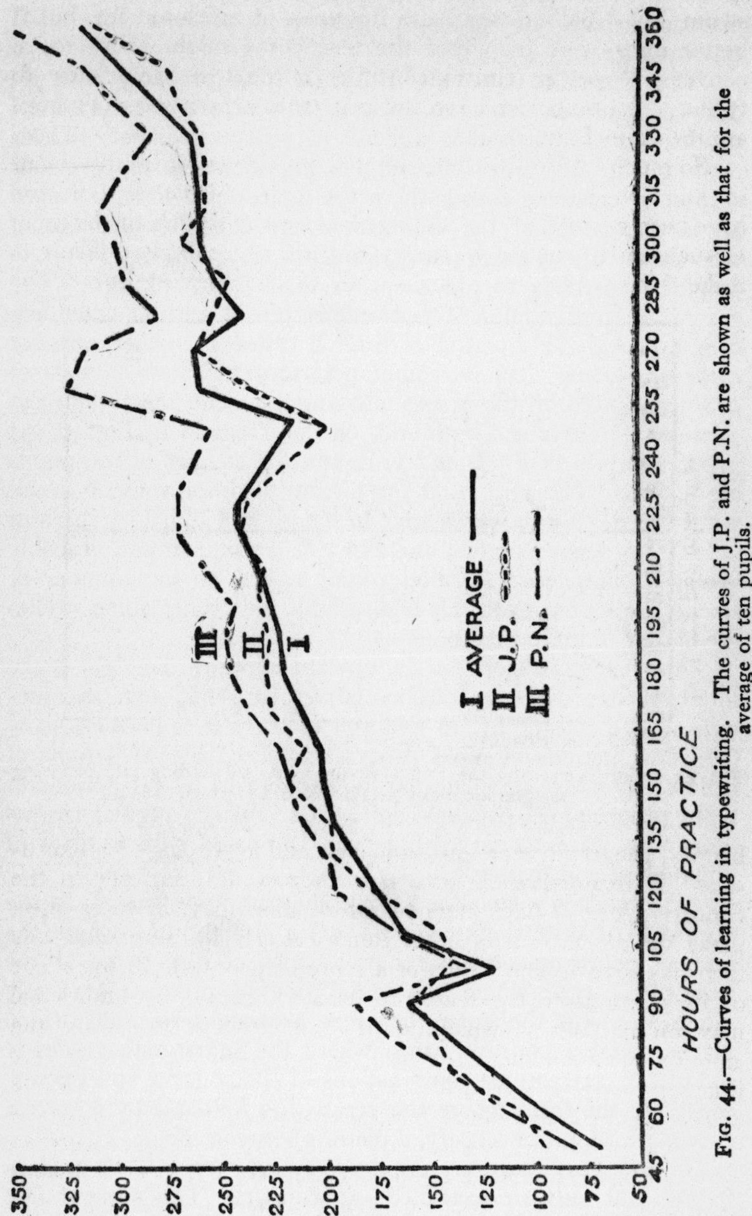

FIG. 44.—Curves of learning in typewriting. The curves of J.P. and P.N. are shown as well as that for the average of ten pupils.

It is represented in swimming and tossing balls when "yards swum" or "balls tossed" are the units of measurement, but if better units were employed the true curve might prove to be convex. Type 4 (convex-concave) is next in frequency to type 2. A number of curves drawn from experimental findings are shown in Figs. 45–48.

So much for skill curves; what about curves for improvement in knowledge? Unfortunately very few reliable experiments have been conducted; verbal responses complicating the learning to such an extent that measurements are exceedingly difficult to make What would be the shapes of the learning curves for

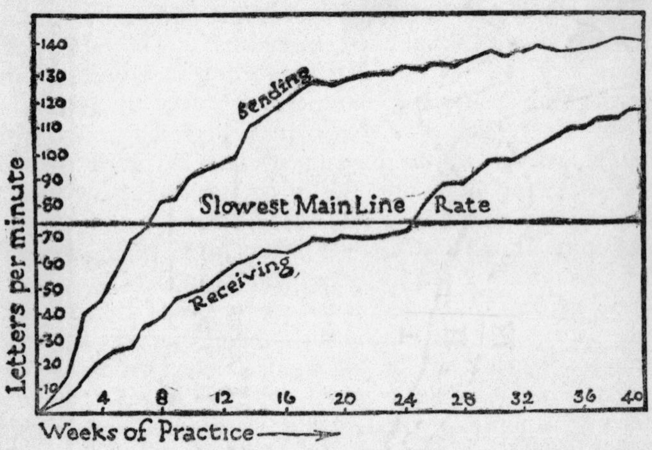

Fig. 45.—Curves showing the improvement made in sending and receiving telegraphic messages (Bryan and Harter).

history, geography, foreign languages, and psychology? Thorndike[1] is inclined to believe that they would conform to the concave type. "Each item of information may, in such cases, make the acquisition of other items easier; learning some one fact may involve knowledge of a score of new facts in the shape of its relations to the facts previously learned. So knowledge may roll up like a snowball, its sum being, say, as the cube of the amount of time spent. What we may call the 'knowledge functions' do, as a rule, show, to say the least, very much less of the diminishing returns from increasing practice than do the functions of skill in some single line of work which figure so often in the experimental studies of practice." But it is obvious that if the curve remained concave the speed of learning would ultimately become infinitely fast, which is not the case. The

[1] Thorndike, E. L., *Educational Psychology*, II, p. 257.

curve probably changes its form, but to which type we cannot say at present.

If, instead of using "words typed" as a measure of improvement, the records had shown the time taken to type 100 words, the practice curve would have run downwards from left to right. Increasing efficiency would be indicated by the downward slope of the line to the right.

Care must be taken in the interpretation of practice curves. In every case one should ask, are the units of practice used true units, that is, equal to each other on all parts of the scale? "Time spent" is a better unit than "number of repetitions" as a measure of the amount of exercise. Secondly, the zero point of the practice should be kept in mind. Thorndike defines zero efficiency as "just not any production in a unit of time," and warns against lumping the interpretation of the form of the curve for ninety hours at typewriting, beginning only with a general knowledge of the instrument and keyboard, with the form of curve for ninety minutes of adding, beginning with the arithmetical equipment of an educated adult.

Plateaus in Learning.—Plateaus in learning were first discovered and discussed by Bryan and Harter.[1] The research, now classical, was conducted at the University of Indiana and in the schools of telegraphy of the surrounding states. Telegraphy is a subject which must be practised for many months before even a moderate skill is acquired, while years of practice are necessary to attain expertness. More than three-fourths of the candidates who begin to learn, fail to reach the main-line rate of 72 letters per minute. Fig. 45 shows a student's progress over a period of forty weeks. Later, the receiving curve of all candidates mounts higher than the sending curve.

In telegraphy the Morse code of dots and dashes is used. After a subject has learned the code he can begin to send messages and his rate of progress is fairly rapid. Not so with receiving. Even when a subject is fairly expert in sending, messages coming over at the main-line rate cannot be received. In order, therefore, to secure the results in the receiving curve of Fig. 45, Harter empirically determined a rate of sending which corresponded to the learner's capacity. If the learner failed to interpret, a slower rate was tried; if he succeeded too easily, a faster rate was used. Both in sending and receiving the averages of several two-minute periods were employed.

These workers also showed that the curve for letters progressed more slowly than that for individual words, and this, in

[1] Bryan and Harter, "Studies in the Physiology and Psychology of the Telegraphic Language," *Psy. Rev.*, IV, 27–53; and VI, 345–375.

turn, more slowly than that for words forming a connected discourse. The curves are shown in Fig. 46.

If now the various curves are examined it will be found that each exhibits one or more plateaus. They are more clearly defined in telegraphy than in typewriting, but Bryan and Harter believed the phenomenon to be universal in learning. What is the explanation of a plateau? Bryan and Harter gave the following: Telegraphy is not a simple habit, but a *hierarchy of habits*, the later and more complex habits being built upon the earlier and simpler ones. The basic habit in telegraphy is the

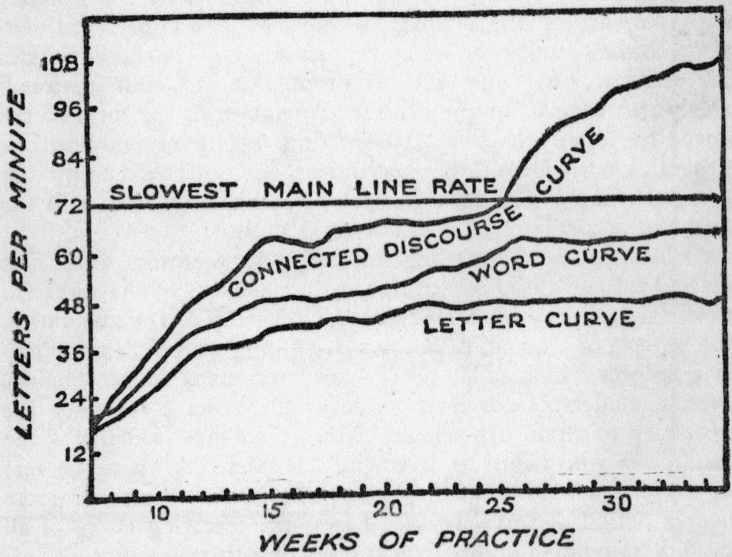

FIG. 46.—Curves showing the learning of letters, words, and connected discourse in telegraphy (after Bryan and Harter).

"letter habit." As learning proceeds the "word habit" appears. The "word habit" is dependent upon, in fact, is built upon, the "letter habit." Similarly, phrases depend upon words, the whole forming a hierarchy in which the higher habit is always based upon a lower one. When a plateau appears some higher form of habit is being attempted before the lower ones, on which it is based, are perfected. As soon, however, as these lower ones are perfected another upward flight of progress is made. A plateau, therefore, is nothing more nor less than a period in learning when lower habits of the hierarchy, as yet imperfectly learned, are made automatic. The freedom so obtained eventually permits of progress to a higher plane.

Other explanations of plateaus have been offered. Book[1] suggested that they are due to *boredom*. The first flush of interest in the new subject has disappeared and the task has become irksome. As soon as interest reappears the curve mounts upwards once more. Probably both factors, perfecting of lower habits and flagging of interest, enter in. But whatever the true explanation of the plateaus, whenever they appear effort is needed to rise from them. In fact, at all parts of the practice curve it is the intense effort that educates.

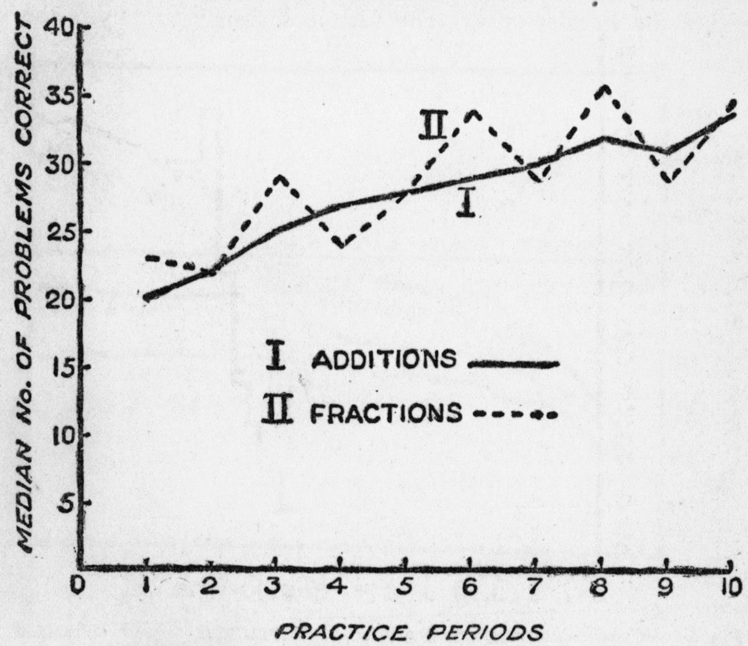

FIG. 47.—Practice curve, additions and fractions (Seaton).

Experimental evidence has not supported the contention of Bryan and Harter that plateaus must inevitably appear in all forms of learning. In some of them, except for minor daily fluctuations, progress has been shown to be fairly regular over a long period of time. But their other contention, namely, that habits were essentially hierarchical in their nature, has met with general acceptance. It fits in with what we know about the connections of the nervous system—the elaboration of reflexes into more complex units of behaviour. In some activities the

[1] Book, W. F., *The Psychology of Skill: With Special Reference to its Acquisition in Typewriting*. University of Montana Publications in Psychology: Bulletin No. 53, Psychological Series No. 1.

hierarchical nature is self-evident. Take the ordinary variety of skating as an example. The basic habit is striking out, moving forward, and preserving one's balance. Such a habit, of course, is built up of a multitude of co-ordinated reflexes. But long before the basic habit is perfected the skater becomes ambitious to try a new trick. He tries, let us say, to turn a corner more quickly by "cutting," that is, by crossing one leg over the other at the turn. While the new accomplishment is being learned, the earlier and more basic habit is still being perfected From

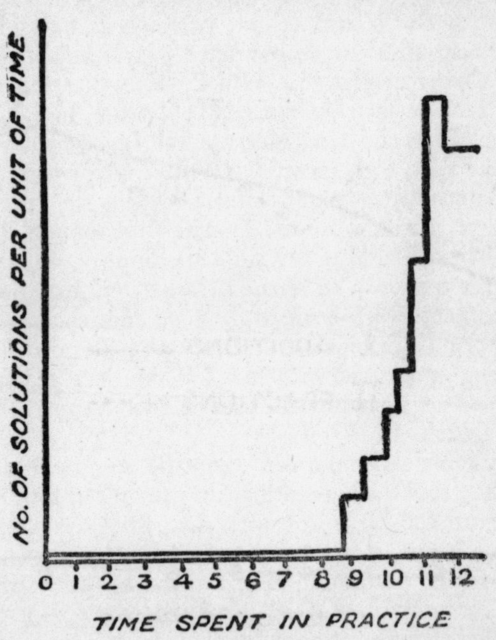

FIG. 48.—Curve to show the progress in solving puzzles. After Ruger ('10), as reconstructed by Thorndike ('14), II, p. 342.

this stage he may progress to the Dutch roll, to skating backwards, and to other accomplishments, the final "skating" being a composite of these several habits. Each stage of learning represents a curious mixture of old and new habits, of those more firmly established, and those that are less so.

Our writing habits, habits of computation, and language habits are all complex and to a very large extent are hierarchical in their nature. The basic habits of arithmetic are connected with the addition combinations and the multiplication tables. These are woven into very complex habit patterns, but patient analysis leads to the discovery of the fundamental bonds.

The practice curves for swimming, solving puzzles, and juggling with balls may be regarded as starting on a plateau. Koehler's animals before they got "insight" were also on a plateau. This does not mean, as we have previously indicated, that no progress is made during the early practices, but that the unit of measurement, "yards swum" or "balls juggled," is inadequate to measure the improvement that is made.

The Limit of Improvement.—The student P. N. in Table XIV made a record of 70 words a minute after 360 hours of typewriting practice. This is a high degree of skill, but compared with the record (about 200 words per minute in a ten-minute test after 10 words have been deducted for each error) it is almost negligible Will P. N. ever reach 200 words per minute? The chances are heavily against him, for few are born with nervous and muscular mechanisms which will enable them to make such high records. Will P. N. by sound methods of practice and concentrated effort be able to reach records higher than 70 words a minute? The probabilities are that he will, but it is impossible to say what the limit of his achievement will be. This can only be learned from actual experience. But just as some people are born to be good musicians, some to be relatively poor ones, so some are born with high potential abilities in typewriting and some with low. There is a *physiological* or *theoretical limit* set by nature for every skill and capacity possessed by any individual.

The physiological limits can easily be comprehended in the case of skills. It is easily seen that no person can type 300 words a minute or run 100 yards in 6 seconds. But physiological limits in knowledge seem to belong to a different category. Persons who freely admit the limitation of possibilities in regard to skill, deny it vigorously in regard to knowledge. But there are theoretical limitations to knowledge as well as to skill. This aspect of the subject was fully discussed under "Vertical and Horizontal Growth of Intelligence," and needs no further elaboration. It was shown that vertical growth was definitely limited, and that horizontal growth seemed to correlate closely with vertical growth. The chief argument in favour of a theoretical limit is the one which says: if there are no limits to learning, then, given the opportunity, anybody can learn anything. But all known facts are against this doctrine. As a matter of fact only about one-third of the pupils now in school could, under the most favourable of circumstances, acquire sufficient knowledge to pass the B.A. examinations of an average North American University. Yet no one would claim that this standard of knowledge is unduly high.

Several factors confuse the issue. The first is that the physiological limit may be approached but never reached. Learning may be compared with the summation of the series $\frac{1}{2}+\frac{1}{4}+\frac{1}{8}$, etc., which approaches but never reaches unity. Any given function may be improved by zealous practice, but perfection can never be achieved. This *practical limit* of learning may approach the *physiological limit*, yet the two never coincide. But the person who can type 200 words a minute, run 100 yards in 9·6 seconds, average bogey for a season's golf, break 99 clay pigeons out of 100 shot at, score 3000 runs in a season's cricket,

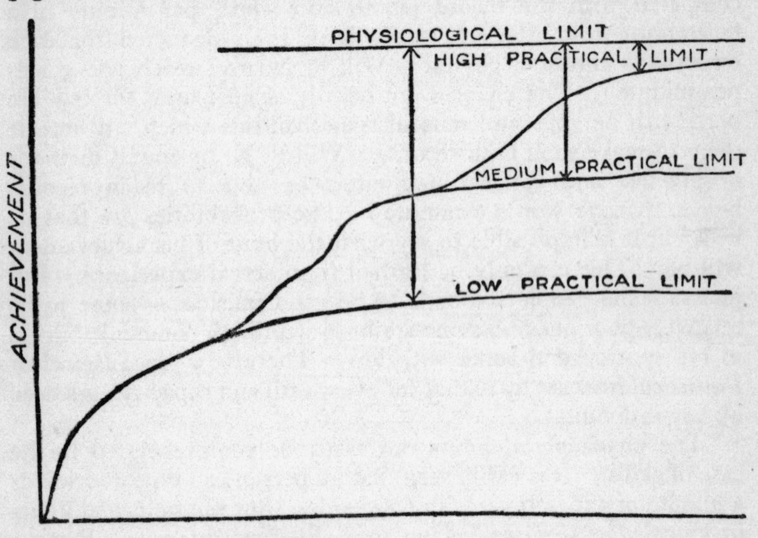

Fig. 49.—Diagram showing the relationship between the practical and the physiological limits. A function practised to three different practical limits is shown.

make 60 home runs in a summer, play the piano like a Paderewski, the violin like a Kreisler, or sing like a Galli Curci, has reached a practical limit in each of these activities which closely approximates the theoretical. Ordinarily, however, as may be seen from Fig. 49, the distance between the two limits is considerable; most functions can easily be improved by practice. The writer's present skill in adding numbers is mediocre. After a spell of work on statistics it noticeably improves, while there is no doubt that if he had to gain a living as a bank clerk or chartered accountant it would reach a still higher limit.

An illustration may be added from another Toronto study.[1]

[1] Seaton, E. T., *Practice in Arithmetic*. University of Toronto Press, 1924.

The subjects were the teachers in training at the Hamilton Normal School and the functions practised were additions and simple exercises with fractions. Although these mature students had practised the functions for eight years or more, the rapidity of improvement in ten practices of five minutes each (see Table XV) was most marked. In other words, the practical limits reached by the students were far removed from the physiological limits they were theoretically capable of reaching.

Function practised.		1	2	3	4	5	6	7	8	9	10
Addition of Numbers :											
No. attempted	1. 75 per centile .	25	30	32	35	38	39	40	42	41	44
	2. Median . .	22	25	27	30	31	32	33	34	33	35
	3. 25 per centile .	18	21	23	23	24	26	27	27	27	29
No. correct	1. 75 per centile .	24	29	31	33	36	36	39	41	39	42
	2. Median . .	20	22	25	27	28	29	30	32	31	34
	3. 25 per centile .	16	19	21	22	23	24	25	25	25	26
Computations with Fractions :											
No. attempted	1. 75 per centile .	30	28	33	33	36	42	37	41	39	43
	2. Median . .	25	24	31	27	31	36	32	37	32	37
	3. 25 per centile .	20	21	27	24	27	30	26	32	27	32
No. correct	1. 75 per centile .	27	25	33	30	34	40	35	40	37	41
	2. Median . .	23	22	29	24	28	34	29	36	29	35
	3. 25 per centile .	18	19	25	22	25	28	24	31	25	29

TABLE XV.—Table showing the improvement in 10 five-minute practices of 195 Normal School students in addition of numbers and computations with fractions (adapted from Seaton).

Most of our powers are exercised on a comparatively low plane. The reasons for this are obvious. We are each endowed with so many hereditary powers that we cannot find time to develop more than the merest fraction of them. The very multitude of possible connections among our billions of neurons precludes us from reaching the hereditary limits in anything more complex than the simplest of functions. The majority of us have never studied Chinese, but we could learn it if we had to. Intensive practice of simple functions causes the practical limit to approach the physiological one, but in more complex ones the theoretical limit is approached with greater difficulty.

A second factor, which disturbs the issue, is the confusion between amount of a function and its rarity. We ordinarily think of Shakespeare being several thousand times better than the average hack writer. But when the amounts can be accurately measured the rates are found to be much smaller. An average typist can type about one-third as well as an expert one; and he is a poor golfer indeed who takes twice as many strokes for a round as the national champion. Expertness is rare and we value it highly, but in terms of measured amount it is not greatly superior to mediocrity. We may be quite willing to pay the president of a bank very highly for his services, but he is probably not much more expert in banking than the average of his clerks.

Thirdly, the law of diminishing returns applies to so many of our habits. The upper limits of learning are reached only at the cost of much time and effort. In other words, the practice curve in its upper reaches tends towards a zero slope. Moreover, the higher the skill, the sooner is it lost through disuse; the upper slopes of the practice curve are very slippery. Hence the penalty for success is more effort. The famous preacher cannot afford to preach a sermon from a barrel, and the virtuoso musician is forced to practise his eight hours a day in order to maintain his high reputation with the musical public.

Lastly, because of the tendency for a nervous discharge to take the path that it has taken before, we find our hereditary and habitual patterns standing in the way of new learning. Uneconomical ways of doing things become stamped in our natures, and it is only by careful and assiduous practice that these may be overcome. For these reasons, the practical limits of learning lie much below the theoretical, but this should never be interpreted to mean that the theoretical ones have no existence.

Length and Distribution of Practice Periods.—Suppose that a teacher had 120 hours to spend on a subject, what length and distribution of practice periods would give the best returns, that is, lead to the greatest efficiency for the least amount of time spent in practice? He might select one of the following lengths for each practice:

1	of	120	hours	each
2	„	60	„	„
10	„	12	„	„
60	„	2	„	„
120	„	1	„	„
240	„	$\frac{1}{2}$	„	„
360	„	$\frac{1}{3}$	„	„

Without any experimentation whatsoever we feel sure that the first three choices would be unwise and uneconomical, but any of the last four might prove to be appropriate. Again, we must regret the lack of experimental findings on such subjects as History, Geography, and Modern Languages. A few researches in arithmetic and substitution in typewriting, etc., have been made, and the findings of these will be given for what they may be worth.

Hahn and Thorndike [1] state: "One hundred and ninety-two pupils—42 in the 7th grade, 54 in the 6th, 43 in the 4th—took part in this experiment, which consisted in adding columns, each of ten one-place numbers, as rapidly as was consistent with accuracy. Each child was led to compete with his own past record—was told repeatedly 'to beat himself.' Seven different sheets, each sheet containing 48 columns of equal difficulty, were used.

"With the exception of certain groups used as controls and called 'the control group,' each pupil took an initial test of 15 minutes, 90 minutes of practice divided into periods of 5, 7½, 10, 11¼, 15, 20, or 22½ minutes, and a final test of 15 minutes.

"The 'control groups' consisted of pupils who took the initial and final tests, without having any of the intervening practice."

The results arranged to show the influence of long and short practice periods are given in Tables XVI and XVII.

Grade.	Length of period.	Average initial score.	Average final score.	Gain.	Advantage of the A Group.
7A }	22½	25·9	51·6	25·7	8·2
7B }	11¼	26·0	43·5	17·5	
6A }	20	16·3	27·0	10·7	0·0
6B }	10	17·4	28·1	10·7	
5A }	15	13·5	24·9	11·4	1·4
5B }	7½	14·8	24·8	10·0	
4A }	10	7·5	21·1	13·6	9·8
4B }	5	7·5	11·3	3·8	

TABLE XVI.—Long-period and short-period groups of equal initial ability compared, a wrong answer counting zero.

Grade.	Length of period.	Average initial score.	Average final score.	Gain.	Advantage of the A Group.
7A }	22½	32·2	56·0	23·8	6·2
7B }	11¼	33·1	50·7	17·6	
6A }	20	22·0	33·3	11·3	−3·4
6B }	10	22·2	36·9	14·7	
5A }	15	17·2	32·5	15·3	−2·3
5B }	7½	19·5	37·1	17·6	
4A }	10	11·1	26·6	15·6	7
4B }	5	11·6	20·1	8·5	

TABLE XVII.—Long-period and short-period groups of equal initial ability compared, a wrong answer counting 0·5.

[1] Hahn and Thorndike, "Some Results of Practice in Addition under School Conditions," *J.E.P.*, V, 2 (Feb. 1914), pp. 65–84.

Scored in either of the above two ways, these results, while indeterminate, somewhat favour the longer periods.

In a similar investigation Kirby,[1] using addition and division with 1300 pupils in the third and fourth grades, found the gains from practice in addition, in 22½-, 15-, 6-, and 2-minute periods were in the relation of 100, 121, 101, and 146½ respectively. In division the gains from practice in 20-, 10-, and 2-minute periods were in the relation of 100, 110½, and 177 respectively. The short period of two minutes was by far the most effective, although the superiority is probably exaggerated by the nature of the experiment.

In a substitution experiment Pyle [2] first trained a group of students for sixteen days, using the same length of practice period and the same distribution of practices. The students then used different lengths of practice periods, and their learning curves were compared with those made when all used the same method of procedure. Fifteen-, thirty-, forty-five-, and sixty-minute periods were compared. Four methods of comparison were used: (1) on the basis of average speed; (2) on the basis of final speed; (3) on the basis of average speed, same amount of time; and (4) on the basis of final speed, same amount of time. The comparative figures are given in Table XVIII.

Method of comparison.	Improvement measured in terms of check experiment (100).			
	A (15 minutes).	B (30 minutes).	C (45 minutes).	D (60 minutes).
1	95·2	130·3	120·6	122·9
2	87·3	93·9	103·3	94·3
3	122·3	136·1	125·0	114·8
4	95·1	118·1	94·6	54·5
Average . .	100·0	119·6	110·9	96·6

TABLE XVIII.—Different lengths of learning periods compared by four methods of measuring the improvement which was made.

Pyle's results are indubitably in favour of the thirty-minute period.

Starch,[3] experimenting with forty-two students in a substitution experiment (numbers for letters on the typewriter) and using periods of 10, 20, 40, and 120 minutes respectively, obtained

[1] Kirby, T. J., *The Results of Practice under School Conditions.* Columbia Contributions to Education, 1913.

[2] Pyle, W. H., *The Psychology of Learning*, 1921, p. 40.

[3] Starch, D., "Periods of Work in Learning," *J.E.P.*, 3 (1912), pp. 209–213.

the results graphed in Fig. 50. The shorter periods of work are more economical.

The conclusions which can be drawn from a consideration of these experiments and also from those carried out by Ebbinghaus, Jost, Miss Perkins, Dearborn, and others point to the following advice as being the soundest which can be given to teachers at the present time in respect of *length* of practice periods for children; short periods not exceeding thirty minutes

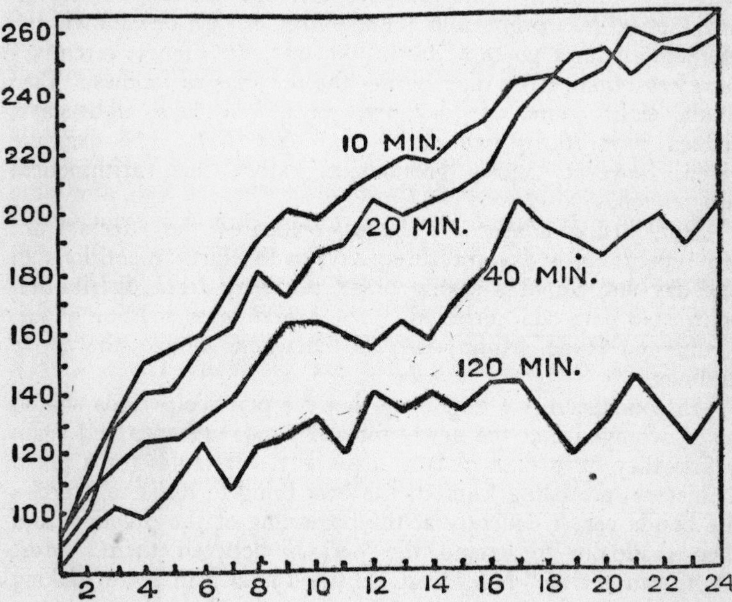

FIG. 50.—Graphs of improvement in a substitution experiment with four different practice periods (Starch).

should be used generally, but the age of the children and the nature of the subject practised should receive consideration.

The proper *distribution* of practice periods presents greater difficulties than the determination of their length. Dearborn,[1] using a substitution test (numbers for letters in typewriting), divided his subjects into two groups, one practising daily and the other twice daily. The periods were ten-minute periods for both groups. The once-a-day group completed the tests in 15 days of practice; the twice-a-day group in 18 days. The daily intervals were productive of the higher rate of progress.

[1] Dearborn, W. F., "Experiments in Learning," *J.E.P.*, I, 7 (Sept. 1910), pp. 373–388.

Lyon, D. O.,[1] used memorization of nonsense syllables and poetry; and of digits and prose. The material was either learned at one sitting or by the once-per-day method. For poetry and prose the two methods took about equal times; for digits and nonsense syllables there is a considerable saving of time by the once-per-day method, that is, by distributing instead of crowding the practice. Lyon is of opinion "that the most economical method is to distribute the readings over a rather lengthy period, the intervals between the readings being in arithmetical (*sic*) proportion. For example, with one individual, in memorizing a poem of twenty stanzas, the highest retentiveness was obtained by distributing the readings as follows: Two hours, eight hours, one day, two days, four days, eight days, sixteen days, thirty-two days, etc." (p. 161). The example given, however, shows geometrical rather than arithmetical progression.

Jost,[2] using nonsense syllables, compared the effects from ten repetitions a day for three days with thirty repetitions in one day and found a saving of 15 per cent. from distribution contrasted with concentration. The experiments of Ebbinghaus, Leuba and Hyde, Munn, etc., on the whole confirm the above findings.

In conclusion, we might say that the practice periods should be so arranged that the newly formed bonds are exercised again before they have time to fade materially. If tables (or a poem or history) are being learned, the best thing to do is to exercise the bonds very frequently at the beginning of the practices and then gradually to extend the periods between them. Most adults can recite "Mary had a little Lamb" in spite of long periods of disuse, because the bonds in the first place were so firmly established, and, secondly, because the poem has been re-perfected at varying intervals. Other poems they learned in youth are partially forgotten although many of them could be kept in mind by practising them, say, once a year. The bonds of chemistry, physics, modern languages, history, and other subjects are so numerous that none, except a very few, get sufficient exercise to make them permanent, consequently they fade away in a most distressing way. On the other hand, we practise the alphabet so frequently that we cannot forget the A B C's if we would. The same may be said of the simpler bonds in arithmetic, 2+1, 2+2, and the like, whereas the

[1] Lyon, D. O., "The Relation of the Length of Material to the Time taken for Learning, and the Optimum Distribution of Time," *J.E.P.*, V, 1, 2, 3 (Jan., Feb., Mar.), 1914.

[2] Jost, A., "Die Assoziationsfestigkeit in ihrer Abhängigkeit von der Verteilung der Wiederholungen," *Zeit. f. Psy.*, XIV (1897), pp. 436–472.

harder ones, 9+8, 7+8, etc., are insufficiently exercised as a rule. Striking the bar in typewriting, in comparison with the other movements, is over-learned. So also are the strokes in swimming and skating. Some bonds, therefore, are over-learned, over-exercised; while others are under-exercised and fade out from lack of practice. What the teacher should strive to do is to distribute the practice so as to keep all useful bonds at a reasonably high level. But what these conditions of practice are for history, geography, and modern language nobody knows; only careful experimentation will lead to a correct answer. It is very probable, however, that each subject has optimal lengths and distributions of practice periods for pupils of varying capacities, as measured by their mental ages.

Whole and Part Learning.—If one had to memorize a long poem, say, of 40 stanzas, would it be better to learn it one stanza at a time, or to read the whole poem again and again until it was mastered in its entirety? Experiments show that the second, the "whole" method, is more economical than "learning by parts," although part learning is the method more commonly employed in school.

Pyle and Snyder[1] tested out the whole and part learning methods on different portions of the same poem (Longfellow's translation of Dante's *Divine Comedy*) up to a total of 240 lines. In the longest portions about 35 minutes per day were required. The "whole" method consisted of three readings per day till it could be recited; the "part" method in memorizing 30 lines per day and reviewing the whole until it could be recited. The results are given in Table XIX.

Number of lines.	Part method time in learning.	Whole method time in learning.	Percentage of time saved by whole method.
20	16 mins.	14 mins.	12
30	27 "	24 "	13
40	39 "	35 "	9
50	49 "	44 "	12
60	81 "	64 "	22
120	169 "	140 "	17
240	431 "	348 "	19

TABLE XIX.—Whole *versus* Part Method of learning poetry (adapted from Pyle and Snyder).

The authors conclude: "Experiments occupying some six months, though mainly restricted to a single observer, show that whether five lines or two hundred and forty lines (approximately

[1] Pyle and Snyder, "The Most Economical Unit for Committing to Memory," *J.E.P.*, II, 3 (Mar. 1911), pp. 133–142.

six pages) of poetry are memorized, learning by wholes is, without any exception, more economical than learning by parts, and that the relative saving is much greater in the case of long selections that require more than a single sitting (to memorize them). Corroborative results were obtained from tests on school children."

In Meumann's [1] laboratory at Zurich the whole method also proved to be superior to the part method when children were employed as subjects. Meumann states :

" When significant material is learned, the whole procedure proves to be almost as advantageous for children as for adults, as is shown by the following data : Employing the part procedure an eight-year-old boy learned a verse of Goethe's *Erlkönig* in seventeen repetitions; in eleven repetitions when he employed the whole procedure. He learned another verse of the same poem in fifteen repetitions when it was divided into two sections, and immediately afterwards he learned the next verse as one section in ten repetitions. Approximately the same state of affairs was found with all school children. Subsequent relearning was easier when the stanzas had originally been learned by the whole procedure. This is true also for larger amounts of material so long as they do not fatigue the child. . . .

" But what is to be said of the learning of material which does not constitute a coherent whole, such as names, dates, the words of a foreign language, etc.? Experiments which have been conducted in my laboratory show that with this sort of material also it is more advantageous to employ the whole procedure than to learn it in parts."

So much for whole and part learning when the habits are verbal ones. Are the conclusions valid when the learning is concerned with motor acts? Pechstein, from his experiments on maze learning, came to the opposite conclusion, namely, that part learning was the more economical. The experiment was to trace a " pencil maze " (pencil running in the grooves of the maze) hidden by a screen from the subject. Groups A and B learned the maze by wholes ; groups C and D by parts. Groups A and C had two trials per day ; B learned it at a sitting, while D learned one part a day for four days and on the fifth day learned to put the parts together. The results are given below :

Part and Whole Learning, Spaced and Unspaced, in a Pencil Maze (Pechstein).

	Spaced trials.	Unspaced trials.
Whole Learning . . .	A 641 seconds	B 1250 seconds
Part Learning . . .	C 1220 "	D 538 "

[1] Meumann, E., *The Psychology of Learning*. Appleton, 1913. Pp. 284-285.

The whole method of learning is only better when the trials were spaced; when trials were grouped part learning proved to be the superior. Pechstein also found that the part method was superior in the learning of nonsense syllables. These findings contradict those from spaced practice given earlier in the chapter and also those from whole learning involving language habits. Further experimentation is needed to determine the validity of the results.

Why should learning poetry by wholes, for example, be more economical than learning by parts? The main reason no doubt is due to the fact that no wasteful associations are formed by the whole method; the bonds are learned in the order in which they will be needed; whereas, in the part method the end word of a stanza is connected with the first word of the same stanza, instead of with the first word of the next. In learning "Mary had a little Lamb" by the part method the word "go" at the end of the first stanza is associated with "Mary" instead of with "He," the first word of the second stanza. This often leads to the need for prompting at the beginning of each new stanza, a weakness which is non-existent in the whole method of learning. Secondly, learning by wholes enables the subject to gather the broad outline of meaning, to see the relationships between part and part in their proper sequence. This firmer grasp of meaning undoubtedly helps the memorization. Thirdly, the attention must be concentrated more in learning by wholes. This facilitates learning with adults, although it may discourage the young who find it hard to concentrate on anything longer than a few lines. Whatever the reason, things which are to be learned in serial order are best learned as wholes, provided, of course, that the wholes are not unreasonably great. And when learned by wholes they are remembered for a longer time than if they had been learned by parts. It would be interesting to investigate the memorization of pieces of music to see if memorization of the whole was more economical than memorization of part by part. Some musicians adopt one plan, some the other, but which is the better is not known. In learning golf, cricket, baseball, and other motor acts, the part method must necessarily be followed, although the grasp of a meaningful whole may help the learning of each part.

Perhaps too much space has been devoted to the topic of learning by wholes and by parts, but if it has shown the reader the necessity for cautious interpretation of experimental results, and, above all, has indicated a field wherein investigations could be profitably pursued, the effort will not have been made in vain.

Other Factors involved in the Economy of Learning.—In this and previous chapters such factors as use and disuse, satisfaction and annoyance, length and distribution of practice periods, which influence the improvement of learning, have been discussed. There are a few additional ones to which attention should be drawn.

(A) *Age.*—Youth has always been regarded as the golden period for learning, age as a time when habits are permanently fixed. We say that "you can't teach an old dog new tricks," by which we mean that people cannot learn after middle age has been reached. This, of course, is only very partially true. Many persons learn to play golf after reaching forty years of age, but such late learners seldom win championships. The preferential paths of the nervous system formed in plastic childhood are so well established by the time middle age is reached that they seriously interfere with any new form of learning. But bonds can be formed at any age, only later in life more time and effort must be devoted to their establishment.

Thorndike [1] in an extensive study of adult learning, in which the learning of Esperanto was the chief exercise, found that the loss of learning ability due to age was much less than had previously been supposed. Briefly, he found that the learning capacity increased on the average to about twenty years of age, then remained constant for a decade, and then decreased fairly steadily to middle age with a loss of about 1 per cent. in ability for each additional year of age. Thus persons in the early forties still possessed about 85 per cent. of the learning capacity they had when at the height of their powers.

The factor of age in improvement in learning should be compared with the factor of age in improvement in intelligence test scores. The latter, it will be remembered, ceased to improve as a rule somewhere between 14 to 16 years. In the same way reasoning tests and detection of absurdities behave in the same way as the stock forms of intelligence tests. Burt's average scores for reasoning and Ballard's averages for absurdities are given below:

Age.	7.	8.	9.	10.	11.	12.	13.	14.	15.	16.	17.
Burt (Reasoning)	5·0	11·0	17·2	23·2	30·0	34·1	39·1	44·7			
Ballard (Absurdities)					13·1	14·4	15·1	17·4	18·5	18·9	18·9

[1] Communicated personally. At the time of going to press, Thorndike's study had not been published.

The difference between the maturity of learning capacity as found by Thorndike and by intelligence testers is due to the measurement of different things. Intelligence testers chiefly measure vertical growth in the learning capacity; Thorndike measured a function in which the width of knowledge received ample recognition in the tests.

Thorndike's conclusions seem to be supported by the work of adult students in the W.E.A. classes of England and elsewhere. These students, most of them middle-aged, frequently write essays comparable in quality with those written by honour students in the University of Oxford, although at the start of the classes their style is invariably cramped and infantile.

(B) *Attentiveness, Concentration, Zeal.*—Some form of attention is a *sine quâ non* of learning, and learning is invariably facilitated by concentrated attention. Bryan and Harter concluded that "it is the intense effort which educates," and few would quarrel with their conclusion. In some mental functions such as multiplying mentally any four-figure number by any other, the concentration needed is so great that only a few can achieve it, and of these only a handful have ever voluntarily undertaken the task. Attention cannot be measured accurately, but a shrewd judgment of its degree can be obtained from a study of its bodily and physiological accompaniments. The attentive learner is tense; he shuts out all distractions.

It is well known that we can become adapted to distractions—to sounds, pressure of clothing, and spectacles—quite easily, but less easily to persons. But what is not so well known is that distractions, providing they are not sufficiently great to produce an emotional disturbance, may actually aid learning. Pyle [1] reports: "In Geissler's important attention experiments it was found that the best adding records were made under conditions of distraction. This seems paradoxical, but is really in harmony with the principles laid down above. The subjects in Geissler's experiments had distraction series and no-distraction series. In a no-distraction series, the subject said, 'Oh, this is easy, I can take my time.' He would consequently relax and leisurely perform the adding, making only a moderately fast record. But if it was a distraction series, the subject took a different attitude. He said, 'Now, this is difficult; this will take all there is of me.' He became rigid, tense, used every known device to give the adding processes the right-of-way and keep the distracting stimuli out. As a rule, he was successful. The distracters did not really distract; they were not able to

[1] Pyle, W. H., *The Psychology of Learning*, p. 57.

become focal; they beat in vain at the gates of central neural activity."

Further, those intelligence tests which demand a severe concentration of attention on the part of the testee have proved themselves to be the most discriminative in their action.

(C) *Physiological Conditions.*—Hunger, thirst, fatigue, vitiated air, sickness, etc., probably affect the rate of learning adversely, but our knowledge about them is distinctly limited. Certain experiments with drugs have been made, but the results need to be interpreted cautiously, owing to the possible introduction of an emotional factor of unknown potency into the situation. Some drugs, like morphine, nicotine, and alcohol, seem to be detrimental to learning; some, like caffeine and strychnine, to facilitate it, but the results of different experiments are not always in agreement.

Alcohol.—Kraepelin and his pupils found that a half to a whole litre of beer was sufficient to lower intellectual power, to impair memory, and to retard simple mental processes, such as the addition of simple figures. Habitual association of ideas and free association of ideas were also interfered with.

Rivers found that small doses of alcohol, varying from 5 to 20 c.c. of absolute alcohol, had no effect on the amount or nature of the work performed with the ergograph, either immediately or within several hours of their administration, the results previously obtained by other workers being almost certainly due to defects of the experimental method.

Dodge and Benedict [1] discovered that language habits were less disturbed than motor habits. Complex functions, such as memory and thinking, show less effect under the influence of alcohol than do the simple reflexes, but any effect shown is a lowering of power.

These results, in total, show that, while small doses of alcohol may not decrease the ability to learn, larger ones always do. Other effects of alcohol are such as to cause it to receive a condemnatory verdict from members of the medical profession and from life insurance companies.

Caffeine.—Rivers found that caffeine (the active principle of tea and coffee) increased the capacity for both physical and mental work, without leading to depressive after effects. Hollingworth found similar results to Rivers's when small doses (2 to 5 grains) were administered, but larger doses decreased the efficiency of motor co-ordinations, such, for example, as are needed in typewriting.

[1] Dodge and Benedict, *The Psychological Effects of Alcohol.* Carnegie Institute of Washington, 1915, No. 232.

Tobacco.—In view of the rapidly increasing consumption of tobacco in Great Britain and on the North American continent, the effects of nicotine should be carefully determined. Bush [1] studied the effects of smoking on associations, memory, imagery, etc. He found as a result of his fifteen tests :

1. A 10·5 per cent. decrease in mental efficiency.
2. The greatest actual loss was in the field of imagery, 22 per cent.
3. The three greatest losses were in the fields of imagery, perception, and association.
4. The greatest loss, in these experiments, occurred with cigarettes.

Pack [2] studied university students in six educational institutions, especially in regard to the frequency with which they competed for places on the football teams. He discovered :

1. Only half as many smokers as non-smokers are successful in the " try-outs " for football squads.
2. In the case of able-bodied men smoking is associated with loss of lung capacity amounting to practically 10 per cent.
3. Smoking is invariably associated with low scholarship.

On the other hand, Rivers [3] found that although nicotine reduced the efficiency (ergograph), the decrease in efficiency was very small.

All in all, as O'Shea [4] has shown in his conservative compilation, the general trend of the data upon tobacco is unfavourable to its use.

Strychnine.—Jones, working in Rivers's laboratory, found that the effect of both large (4·2 mgrms.) and small (1·8 mgrms.) doses of strychnine led to an increase of efficiency as measured by the ergograph. The rise of efficiency for large doses was more rapid than for small doses. But in both cases the rise was followed by a fall, although the decline took place more slowly in the case of the small doses. In both cases, also, the total output of work was less.

On the other hand, Poffenberger found no effect from doses ranging from $\frac{1}{50}$ to $\frac{1}{20}$ grain upon steadiness and accuracy in speed of movement.

(D) *Life Bents and Dispositions.*—This is of the same nature as readiness or set, previously described, but is more protracted.

[1] Bush, A. D., " Tobacco Smoking and Mental Efficiency," *New York Medical Journal*, XCIX, 11 (Mar. 1914), pp. 519–527.

[2] Pack, F. J., " Smoking and Football Men," *Popular Science Monthly*, LXXXI (Oct. 1912), p. 336.

[3] Rivers, W. H. R., *Influence of Tobacco and other Drugs on Fatigue*. London, Arnold, 1908, p. 113.

[4] O'Shea, M. V., *Tobacco and Mental Efficiency*. New York, Macmillan, 1923.

A good start in a school subject by a skilful and enthusiastic teacher often disposes the child to like it for the rest of his life. Contrariwise, an unsympathetic teacher with warped views of child life often creates a distaste for his subjects, or for schooling as a whole, which lasts throughout childhood and frequently for life.

(E) *Knowledge of Success and Failure.*—Acting on the principle of the law of effect, the teacher should, wherever possible, give the learner definite knowledge of his success or failure. Only when this is done can right bonds be formed and wrong ones eliminated. This principle holds true not only for the daily exercises of the pupil, but also for the formal examinations set to determine what progress the pupil has made over a considerable period of time. Fortunately, the newer objective tests enable the information to be given with a high degree of confidence.

Knowledge of success stimulates the relevant, promising bonds. In the game of hunt the thimble the cry of " warmer " obviously stimulates the subject to increased efforts. Success also favours repetition. Everybody likes to be successful and, therefore, we practise the things we do well. In those branches, such as typewriting, spelling, addition in arithmetic, etc., where knowledge of success or failure can be learned without dubiety, progress is made more rapidly than in subjects like handwriting, literary style, and drawing, where success and failure is more a matter of opinion (frequently that of the teacher).

(F) *Significance of Task.*—If the task is significant for the pupil, if it has some bearing on a subject he desires information about, or on some problem he wishes to solve, learning is facilitated. That is why the project and problem methods, which create desirable attitudes in the pupils, are so helpful to progress.

(G) *Absence of Worry and Irrelevant Emotional Excitement.*—Worry and emotional excitement both decrease the rate of learning. Worry is always bad—bad in its physiological as well as in its educational effects. However, a slightly heightened emotional state, relevant to the situation, such as comes from a knowledge of increasing mastery, probably enhances the learning rate. This is also the explanation of the end spurt in learning, wherever this is found, since the knowledge that the task is nearly ended creates a pleasurable feeling which is conducive to effort.

How to Study.—Many of the findings presented in this chapter may be practically applied by the individual student. Obviously, in studying, the pupil should control his attention, should adopt a proper attitude towards his work, should put himself in proper physical and bodily attitude towards his work, should remove environmental distractions as far as possible, should adopt a problem-solving attitude, should recall at frequent intervals the essential ideas of what has been studied, should, in committing to memory, learn by wholes rather than by parts, etc.

Whipple [1] has drawn up a list of thirty-eight rules, which, if obeyed by the student, will certainly lead to increased improvement in learning. They are as follows :

1. Keep yourself in good physical condition.
2. Attend to, remove, or treat physical defects that often handicap mental activity, such as defective eyesight, defective hearing, defective teeth, adenoids, obstructed nasal breathing.
3. See that external conditions of work (light, temperature, humidity, clothing, chair, desk, etc.) are favourable to study.
4. Form a place-study habit.
5. Form a time-study habit.
6. When possible, prepare the advance assignment in a given subject directly after the day's recitation in it.
7. Begin work promptly.
8. Take on the attitude of attention.
9. Work intensely while you work : concentrate.
10. But don't let intense application become fluster or worry.
11. Do your work with the intent to learn and to remember.
12. Seek a motive, or, better, several motives.
13. Get rid of the idea that you are working for the teacher.
14. Don't apply for help until you have to.
15. Have a clear notion of the aim.
16. Before beginning the advance work, review rapidly the previous lesson.
17. Make a rapid preliminary survey of the assigned material.
18. Find out by trial whether you succeed better by beginning with the hardest or with the easiest task when you are confronted with several tasks of unequal difficulty.
19. In general, use in your studying the form of activity that will later be demanded when the material is used.
20. Give more time and attention to the weak points in your knowledge or technique.
21. Carry the learning of all important items beyond the point necessary for immediate recall.
22. You must daily pass judgment as to the degree of importance of items that are brought before you, and lay special stress on the permanent fixing of those items that are vital and fundamental.
23. When a given bit of information is clearly of subordinate importance and useful only for the time being, you are warranted in giving to it only sufficient attention to hold it over the time in question.

[1] Whipple, G. M., *How to Study Effectively*, 1916.

24. Make the duration of your periods of study long enough to utilize "warming-up," but not so long as to suffer weariness or fatigue.

25. When drill or repetition is necessary, distribute over more than one period the time given to a specified learning.

26. When you interrupt work, not only stop at a natural break, but also leave a cue for its quick resumption.

27. After intensive application, especially to new material, pause for a time and let your mind be fallow before taking up anything else.

28. Use various devices to compel yourself to think over your work.

29. Form the habit of working out your own concrete examples of all general rules and principles.

30. Form the habit of mentally reviewing every paragraph as soon as you have read it.

31. Don't hesitate to mark up your own books to make the essential ideas stand out visibly.

32. Whenever your desire is to master material that is at all extensive and complex, make an outline of it. If you also wish to retain this material, commit your outline to memory.

33. In all your work apply your knowledge as much as possible and as soon as possible.

34. Do not hesitate to commit to memory verbatim such materials as definitions of technical terms, formulæ, dates, or outlines, always provided, of course, that you also understand them.

35. When the material to be learned by heart presents no obvious rational associations, it is perfectly legitimate to invent some artificial scheme for learning and recalling it.

36. In committing to memory a poem, a declaration, or oration, do not break it up into parts but learn it as a whole.

37. In committing to memory, it is better to read aloud than to read silently, and better to read rapidly than slowly.

38. If your work includes attendance at lectures, take a moderate amount of notes during the lectures, using a system of abbreviations, and rewrite these notes daily, amplified into a reasonably compendious outline organized as suggested in Rule 32.

Conclusion.—As a summary of the facts presented in this chapter the following general statements from Watson[1] seem pertinent:

"1. The fact of diminishing returns from practice. Within certain limits, the less the frequency of practice the more efficient is each practice period.

"2. The less the number of habits formed simultaneously, the more rapid is the rise of any given habit. 1 is valid here also, apparently, regardless of the number of habits formed simultaneously.

"3. Again within certain limits, the younger the organism the

[1] Watson, J. B., *Psychology from the Standpoint of a Behaviorist*, p. 405.

more rapidly will the habit be formed. This generalization as yet has not been completely established.

"4. Word or other symbolic material which has to be learned to the point of errorless verbal reproduction, regardless of its length (within wide limits), should be learned by the whole rather than by the part method.

"5. The higher the incentive to the formation of the habit and the more uniformly this incentive is maintained, the more rapidly will the habit be formed."

References

BAIR, J. H. "The Practice Curve," *Psy. Rev. Mon. Suppl.*, No. 19, V, 1902.

BOOK, W. F. *The Psychology of Skill: with Special Reference to its Acquisition in Typewriting*. Univ. of Montana Publications in Psychology, Bull. 53, Psy. Series No. 1. Pp. 188.

BRYAN and HARTER. "Studies in the Physiology and Psychology of the Telegraphic Language," *Psy. Rev.*, IV (1897), pp. 27–53; VI (1899), pp. 345–375.

BUSH, A. D. "Tobacco Smoking and Mental Efficiency," *N.Y. Medical Jour.*, XCIX, 11 (Mar. 1914), pp. 519–527.

CAMERON, E. H. *Psychology and the School*. New York, Century Co., 1921. Pp. xiv+339.

CHAPMAN, J. C. "The Learning Curve in Typewriting," *J. Appl. Psy.*, III (1919).

DEARBORN, W. F. "Experiments in Learning," *J.E.P.*, I, 7 (Sept. 1910), pp. 373–388.

DODGE and BENEDICT. *The Psychological Effects of Alcohol*. Carnegie Institute of Washington, 1915, No. 232.

EBBINGHAUS, H. *Memory*. (Published 1885, translated by Ruger and Bussenius, 1913, Teachers' College, Columbia University.) Pp. 169.

EDWARD, W. G. *Improvement Curves in the Learning of Typewriting*. Toronto, Ryerson Press, 1923. Pp. 69.

FISHER and FISK. *How to live*. New York, Funk and Wagnall, 1926. Pp. xxviii+513.

FREEMAN, F. N. *How Children Learn*. Boston, Houghton Mifflin, 1917.

HAHN and THORNDIKE. "Some Results of Practice in Addition under School Conditions," *J.E.P.*, V, 2 (Feb. 1914), pp. 65–84.

HILL, REJALL, and THORNDIKE. "Practice in the case of Typewriting," *Ped. Sem.*, XX (1913).

HYDE and LEUBA. "Studies from the Bryn Mawr Coll. Psy. Lab. An Experiment in Learning to make Hand Movements," *Psy. Rev.*, XII (1905), pp. 351–369.

JOST, A. "Die Associationsfestigkeit in ihrer Abhängigkeit von der Verteilung der Wiederholungen," *Zeit. für Psy.*, XIV (1897), pp. 436–472.

KIRBY, T. J. *The Results of Practice under School Conditions*. T. C. Contributions to Education, Columbia University, 1913.

LAKENAN, MARY E. "The Whole and Part Methods of Memorizing Poetry and Prose," *J.E.P.*, IV, 4 (April, 1913), pp. 189–198.

LYON, D. O. "The Relation of the Length of Material to the Time taken for Learning, and the Optimum Distribution of Time," *J.E.P.*, V, 1, 2, 3 (Jan., Feb., Mar.), 1914.

MEUMANN, E. *The Psychology of Learning*. New York, Appleton, 1913. Pp. xix+387.

O'SHEA, M. V *Tobacco and Mental Efficiency*. New York, Macmillan, 1913.

PACK, F. J. "Smoking and Football Men," *Pop. Sci. Mo.*, LXXXI (Oct. 1912), p. 336.

PARKER, S. C. *Methods of Teaching in High Schools*. Boston, Ginn, 1915. Pp. xxv+529.

PECHSTEIN, L. A. "Alleged Elements of Waste in Learning a Motor Problem by the 'Part' Method," *J.E.P.*, VIII, 5 (May, 1917), pp. 303–310.

PECHSTEIN, L. A. "Whole *versus* Part Methods in learning Nonsensical Syllables," *J.E.P.*, IX, 7 (Sept. 1918), p. 381.

PYLE, W. H. *The Psychology of Learning*. Baltimore, Warwick and York, 1921. Pp. 308.

PYLE, W. H. "Concentrated *versus* Distributed Practice," *J.E.P.*, V, 5 (May, 1914), pp. 247–258.

PYLE and SNYDER. "The Most Economical Unit for Committing to Memory," *J.E.P.*, II, 3 (Mar. 1911), pp. 133–142.

RIVERS, W. H. R. *Influence of Tobacco and other Drugs on Fatigue*. London, Arnold, 1908.

RUGER, H. A. *The Psychology of Efficiency*. New York, Science Press, 1910.

SEATON, E. T. *Practice in Arithmetic*. Toronto, Univ. Press, 1924. Pp. 72

SPEARMAN, C. E. *The Abilities of Man; their Nature and Measurement*. London, Macmillan, 1927. Pp. viii+415+xxxiii.

STARCH, D. *Educational Psychology*. New York, Macmillan, 1927. Pp. ix +568.

STARLING, HUTCHINSON, MOTT and PEARL. *The Action of Alcohol on Man*. London, Longmans, Green, 1923.

SWIFT, E. J. "Studies in the Psychology and Physiology of Learning," *Amer. Jour. Psy.*, XIV (1903), pp. 201–251.

THOMSON, G. H. *Instinct, Intelligence and Character*. New York. Longmans, Green, 1925. Pp. 282.

THORNDIKE, E. L. *Educational Psychology*. II. *The Psychology of Learning*. New York, Teachers College, Columbia University, 1913. Pp. xi+452.

WATSON, J. B. *Psychology from the Standpoint of a Behaviorist*. Philadelphia, Lippincott, 1924. Pp. xvii+448.

WATT, H. J. *The Economy and Training of Memory*. London, Arnold, 1909. Pp. 128.

WHIPPLE, G. M. *How to Study Effectively*. Bloomington, Ill., Public School Publishing Co., 1926.

CHAPTER XII

THE PERMANENCE OF IMPROVEMENT: REMEMBERING AND FORGETTING

The Problem.—The conventional way of stating the problem of this chapter, such, for example, as may be found in chapters on Association and Memory in introspectionist psychologies, would be somewhat as follows: Memory, according to popular language, may mean impression, or retention, or recall, separately or collectively. But, technically, memory is limited by the psychologist to recall or recollection. This problem of recall, as Bergson in *Matter and Memory* points out, is not a simple one. There are really two distinct kinds of memory: first, the sort that consists of habit; and second, the sort that consists of independent recollection. In learning a lesson by heart, we are said to know it when we can "remember" it. This is an example of the first kind of memory, and simply means that we have acquired certain language habits. The second kind of memory is illustrated, say, by recalling what we had for breakfast this morning. This is the recollection of a unique event, and cannot be explained by habit.

The conventional psychology will then carefully explain that the psychology of memory has nothing at all to do with the first kind of memory, because that is nothing more nor less than habit; any discussion of memory must confine its attention to the second kind, namely, recollections of unique events. The problem of memory is to discover the way we recall these unique events. At this point a discussion of images will probably be introduced and the relations they bear to sensation and perception. The classification of persons into visiles, audiles, olfactives, gustatives, and tactiles, according to the dominant type of image used in remembering, may follow. Acute and interesting observations will undoubtedly be found, but the treatment is so highly speculative, and so little open to experimental investigation, that we gladly leave this aspect of the subject to the metaphysicians who revel in introspective orgies of this nature.

We shall confine our attention almost exclusively to the way in which memory as habit seems to work. More succinctly we shall define the problem of this chapter as the determination of (1) the factors which make for the retention of improvement due to the exercise of a function; (2) the rate at which the impairment of a function, following disuse, takes place; (3) the rate at which relearning, after complete or partial loss from disuse, takes place; and (4) the final product (if any) which may remain after prolonged neglect of a function. Restricting our inquiry to the preceding four questions and to such others as lend themselves to experimental inquiry, some dependable conclusions may be reached. In any case, the findings, both in the field of manual and of motor habits, unlike those from speculative introspections, are open to confirmation or rejection by other workers.

Factors influencing the Permanence of Habits.—The factors favourable to the initial formation of habits are also conducive to their permanency. Repetition keeps associations alive while disuse leads to their impairment. This is the well-known factor of *use* or *frequency*. The most permanent habits we have are generally those which have been most frequently exercised. It will be recalled that experiments with conditioned reactions showed that they were strengthened by exercise. It is from this principle of use that drill in the schoolroom receives its sanction. *Vividness* is another factor leading to permanence of improvement. The reason vivid initial impressions lead to such permanent conditioning is that *attention* is lent to an experience in proportion to its vividness. Sometimes indeed an experience may be so exciting emotionally that pathological conditions arise. We saw that " the burnt child dreads the fire " ; one experience was sufficient to cause a permanent learning. The reason children learn more quickly and more permanently from one teacher than another is partly by reason of the vividness of the presentations of the lessons. But vividness is a relative term. In order that mountains may appear high we must have the contrast of deep valleys. *Recency* is a factor almost constant in its effect. Of two events of equal significance the remoter one will likely be less well remembered. The reason for this is not known, but it is probable that the changes made in the nervous system gradually disappear in time. The traces left behind by experiences to-day are deeper than those of a year ago. We can recall what we had for breakfast this morning, but we cannot be sure of what we ate a year ago to-day. Teachers must review their school work because children forget so easily. Drills and reviews, it should be noted, involve both the factors of frequency and recency. Another factor, the *resultant satisfaction* (law of effect), is undoubtedly conducive to permanence of learning. Besides the biological significance of satisfaction, there is the fact, emphasized by the Freudians, that we tend to shun, to suppress the unpleasant. Jones goes so far as to say that all forgetting is due, in part, to suppression. If this be true, then forgetting is not a mere fading away, but a forcible ejection from the mind of unpleasant experiences. There is, however, one aspect of the law of effect which is frequently overlooked by teachers, namely, that the satisfaction which comes from completing a hard task is one of the greatest and purest satisfactions that life can offer. Interest and effort, as Dewey maintains, are frequently correlated. There are several other factors such as *primacy* (now disputed on experimental evidence), *the mood of the moment* (set) which deserve consideration, but need not detain us here.

Learning to Skate in Summer.—Ever since James made familiar to English-speaking peoples the German proverb, " We learn to skate in summer and swim in winter," there has arisen a belief in the necessity for incubation periods in learning. Book concluded :

" The increase in score by our memory series was due, so far as we could make out, rather to the disappearance with the lapse of time, of numerous psycho-physical difficulties, interfering associations, bad habits of attention, incidentally acquired in the course of learning, interfering habits and tendencies, which, as they fade, left the more firmly established typewriting associations free to act."

His conclusions are based on the following facts :

Tests.	1	2	3	4	5	6	7	8	9	10	Av.
Last Regular Practice Jan. 7–16, 1906 . .	1503	1509	1404	1572	1494	1436	1501	1455	1508	1698	1570
First Memory Test June 1–10, 1906 . .	1365	1421	1421	1433	1529	1443	1523	1504	1313	1472	1443
Second Memory Test June 1–10, 1907 . .	1390	1344	1345	1537	1681	1694	1634	1845	1761	1850	1611

The table shows that an actual gain in number of strokes (the work was measured in strokes, not words typed) was made in the average of the second memory test. However, careful examination of the " Last Regular Practice " series shows that most of the work was done on a plateau from which a vigorous end spurt raised the subject nearly 200 points. The practice of the first memory test probably had a considerable influence on the records of the second.

Anyhow, it is contrary to common sense as well as to the law of exercise to say that lack of practice strengthens associative bonds. Thorndike maintains:

"The doctrine is misleading, the real facts which in a measure excuse it being simple: (1) that an improvement of function may be masked by fatigue, so that disuse, involving rest, produces an apparent gain; (2) that an improvement in the *strength* of desirable bonds may be masked by a decrease in their *readiness*—a drop in interest, a 'going stale' as the athletes say—so that disuse, by doing more good to interest than it does harm to the strength of the bonds, produces an apparent improvement; (3) that unwise exercise of the function, as in worry and confusion or under misleading instructions, may form undesirable bonds, whose weakening by disuse improves the function." [1]

If it be remembered that every practice curve is a composite of positive improvement due to the practice and negative improvement due to fatigue, the latter eventually becoming so great as to overcome the positive improvement from practice, then Thorndike's first contention becomes self-evident. Rest removes fatigue and improves learning; there is, however, no consolidation of practice effects during the interval of no practice. The other two contentions are obvious and need no further discussion. We can, therefore, dismiss as unfounded the doctrine that we learn to skate in summer—that cessation of practice leads to improvement in learning.

The Rate of Forgetting.—Why is it that dancing, swimming, skating, bicycle-riding, once learned, are so permanent, while languages, history, and knowledge in general are so fugitive? The probable explanation is, first, that in the former activities certain native connections are largely drawn upon. The motions of swimming, dancing, skating, and bicycle-riding are not very far removed from movements that are perfectly natural to all of us. Secondly, each movement is over-learned to an enormous extent. The striking-out movement in skating must be performed hundreds of thousands of times by Canadian youths during a normal winter. On the contrary, language and all knowledge which has language as its basis, has to be "acquired" to a much greater extent than dancing or skating; there is less of a native basis for it, as it were. Further, the multiplicity of bonds in the language activities precludes the over-learning of any of them. In the Anatomy Course of the University of Toronto, it has been computed, the medical student has to learn 5000 new technical terms during his second year. How many of these can become over-learned? The same number of new words in a foreign language would certainly provide anybody with a good working vocabulary.

[1] Thorndike, E. L., *Educational Psychology*, II, p. 301.

The difference between the two sets of functions can be illustrated from the personal experience of the writer. Like most boys living in England in 1895, he learned to skate during the seven weeks of continuous frost which occurred at that time. A succession of mild winters prevented him from skating again until he came to Canada in 1913. The interval of eighteen years had caused some lapse in the learning, yet to all intents and purposes he began his skating in 1913 at the stage where he left off in 1895. But Danish, a language he learned to a fair extent during a two-months' sojourn in Denmark in 1906, seems almost to have disappeared completely. He cannot, for example, count up to ten in Danish, though he has been trying hard to do it during the past two or three minutes. That the language has not altogether disappeared, but has left some traces behind, would be shown by the greater ease of relearning it in comparison with the first learning.

Experimental Evidence in Rate of Forgetting.—Ebbinghaus was the first to conduct extensive experiments on the rate of forgetting (1885). He used the method of complete memorization, that is, he repeated his subject-matter (nonsense syllables) until he could reproduce them without error, without hesitation, and with the certainty of correctness. The number of presentations required for complete learning was the measure of the efficiency. He could not remember more than seven syllables after a single reading. It took 16 readings to memorize 12, 44 readings to memorize 24, and 55 readings to memorize 26 syllables. A list imperfectly learned on one day was perfected the next day more easily, and the time saved was roughly proportional to the number of readings on the first occasion. The rate of forgetting, measured by the time required to relearn a list which had once been perfectly known, was very much more rapid at first than later on.

This method of study has been improved by Müller and Schumann, who prepared lists of nonsense syllables of equal difficulty; and modified by Radossawljewitsch,[1] who demanded that the series be repeated twice correctly before the learning was considered perfect. The latter also used poetry as well as nonsense syllables.

Table XX gives data from four investigations into the permanence of learning in terms of the per cent. of time saved in re-learning.

[1] Radossawljewitsch, P. R., *Das Behalten und Vergessen bei Kindern und Erwachsenen nach experimentellen Untersuchungen.* (Das Fortschreiten des Vergessens mit der Zeit.) Leipzig, 1907.

Interval.	Percentage of time saved in relearning.				
	Nonsense syllables.			Poetry.	
	Ebbinghaus.	Radossawljewitsch.	Finkenbinder.	Radossawljewitsch.	Magneff.
5 mins.	—	98	—	100	—
20 „	58	89	—	96	—
60 „	44	71	73	81	—
480 „	—	47	65	58	—
525 „	36	—	—	—	—
1 day	34	68	58	79	67
2 days	28	61	56	67	43
3 „	—	—	52	56	65
4 „	—	—	—	54	48
5 „	—	—	—	56	—
6 „	25	49	—	42	45
7 „	—	—	—	50	61
10 „	—	—	—	—	50
12 „	—	—	—	—	40
13 „	—	—	—	30	59
14 „	—	41	—	—	25
16 „	—	—	—	—	44
21 „	—	38	—	48	—
25 „	—	—	—	—	—
30 „	21	20	—	24	50
120 „	—	3	—	—	—

TABLE XX.—Showing the permanence of ability to recite a series of nonsense syllables and selections of poetry.

Fig. 51 presents some of the facts in graphical form. On the whole, poetry is retained longer than nonsense syllables. This is to be expected. The remarkable fact about these results is that one-fifth of the nonsense material was retained over a period of 30 days and had not totally disappeared in 120 days. Even after twenty-two years, Ebbinghaus found some retention of poetry learned only once to the point of one perfect recitation, and never seen since. This lends some support to the contention that nothing learned is ever completely forgotten. Traces are left behind, which, even after a very long interval, facilitate the relearning. Another fact of practical import in the economy of learning is that the forgetting is extremely rapid in the earlier phases, after which the loss, though steady, is comparatively light. Teachers of the young should review material which has been memorized very soon after the learning, preferably at the end of the same day and certainly not later than the next day. A few relearnings quickly following the first learning will provide better results than practice deferred, say, a month or more.

The amount remembered depends upon the way the material is memorized. Witasek found active recitations of the matter to be memorized superior to passive reading of the presented lists. Gates confirmed these findings.[1] "One method consisted of reading and re-reading a list of 16 nonsense syllables (or a group

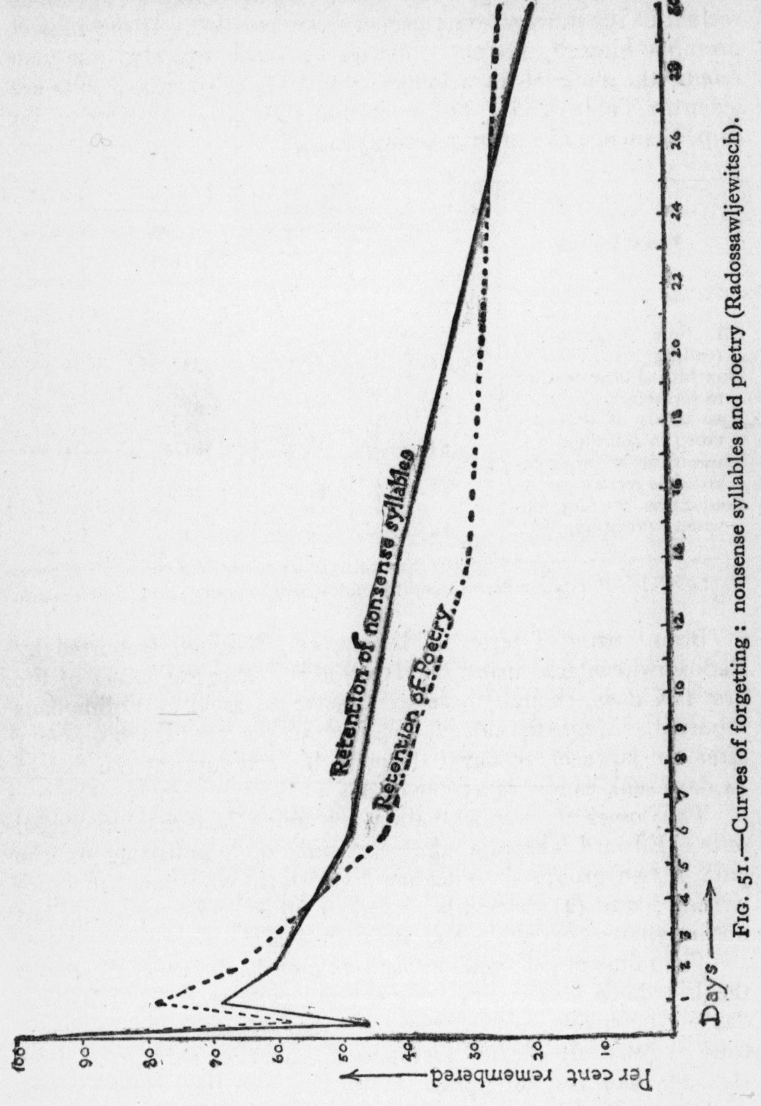

FIG. 51.—Curves of forgetting : nonsense syllables and poetry (Radossawljewitsch).

of five short biographies totalling about 70 words) without looking up from the paper. Another method consisted in beginning,

[1] Gates, A. I., *Psychology for Students of Education*, pp. 269–270.

early or late, to recite—that is, to attempt to recall when not looking at the material—prompting one's self speedily by glancing at the paper when unable to proceed." This second method is the one needed later in actual recall. Long before a list can be recited in its entirety some parts can be recalled. If the subject prompts himself, he not only learns more quickly, but also retains the material for a longer time. Gates's actual results are given in Table XXI. The recitation method is superior so far as permanence of learning is concerned.

Type of learning.	Sixteen nonsense syllables. Per cent. remembered.		Five biographies. Per cent. remembered.	
	Immediately.	After 4 hrs.	Immediately.	After 4 hrs.
All time devoted to reading	35	15	35	16
One-fifth of time devoted to recitation . . .	50	26	37	19
Two-thirds of time devoted to recitation .	54	28	41	25
Three-fifths of time devoted to recitation .	57	37	42	26
Four-fifths of time devoted to recitation .	74	48	42	26

TABLE XXI.—Recitation *versus* Reading methods of memorization (from Gates).

Bean,[1] using a series of letters, and Magneff (reported by Radossawljewitsch) using poetry, confirm the great losses of the first few days, though these were never so great as Ebbinghaus reported. Magneff, indeed, retained 50 per cent. of his poetry after the lapse of 25 days, although his retention at the end of 14 days sank as low as 25 per cent.

The losses in manual habits are much less than in verbal ones. Edward [2] reports the relearning of typewriting on the part of two groups of repeaters: (1) those who failed in typewriting; and (2) those who failed in other school subjects, but not in typewriting, at the end of the first year.

The midsummer vacation of three months intervened between the last day's typewriting of the first year's work and the first day's typewriting of the repeated year's work, during which time it was afterwards ascertained none of these particular students had had any practice on a typewriter. The courses

[1] Bean, C. H., *The Curve of Forgetting*. Archives of Psychology, No. 21 (1912).

[2] Edward, W. G., *Improvement Curves in the Learning of Typewriting*, pp. 52–54.

for both years were identical with reference to words, pages, budgets, length of periods, duration of course, etc., and the students were the same, but a year older. The only condition that differed in the work of the two years was the number of errors allowed per page. During the first year's work a maximum of three errors per page was allowed, while in the repeated year the same pages had to be done with no errors at all in order to be accepted. This higher standard of work with reference to errors would naturally tend to reduce the possible output of approved pages, but in spite of this fact it will be seen that even the repeaters who were plucked in typewriting the year before effected a remarkable increase in the number of pages typed, as compared with their previous year's record. In other words, the manual habit of typewriting exhibited a remarkable permanence. The figures are given in Table XXII.

	First Year Budgets.						Total pages.	Repeated Year Budgets.						Total pages.	Gain per cent.
Student.	I.	II.	III.	IV.	V.	VI.		I.	II.	III.	IV.	V.	VI.		
1. A. B.	3	6	6	6	3	3	27	9	6	9	8	7	3	42	55·55
2. H. C.	3	3	6	3	3	1	19	6	6	6	3	3	2	26	36·84
3. J. S.	3	4	3	5	3	1	19	3	3	7	6	3	2	24	26·31
4. H. C.	3	4	3	3	3	0	16	5	4	6	3	3	0	21	31·25
5. H. P.	4	3	6	3	3	3	22	10	16	11	4	3	3	47	113·63
6. M. I.	3	3	4	3	3	3	19	15	19	12	18	18	6	88	363·16
7. E. S.	3	4	4	3	3	2	19	12	28	8	5	6	2	61	221·05
8. S. R.	3	4	8	5	3	2	25	16	18	10	11	5	2	62	148·00
9. J. H.	4	3	4	3	3	3	20	18	11	11	10	3	3	56	180·00
10. J. M.	3	3	3	3	1	3	16	8	6	4	4	3	3	28	75·00
1. P. N.	4	6	8	6	3	6	33	24	18	15	18	15	3	93	181·81
2. I. T.	4	10	17	7	6	6	50	16	16	11	10	6	4	63	26·00
3. W. G.	3	4	13	7	3	3	33	13	15	13	13	6	2	62	87·87
4. E. M.	3	8	5	3	3	3	25	10	25	9	8	4	4	60	140·00
5. E. M.	8	10	9	5	4	4	40	13	22	14	12	6	2	69	72·50
6. K. C.	6	6	6	5	3	3	29	23	42	35	15	10	7	132	355·17
7. G. M.	4	6	4	3	3	3	23	9	19	10	6	3	4	51	121·74
8. E. V.	3	4	6	6	3	3	25	11	8	17	8	7	4	55	120·00
9. A. F.	3	9	9	8	6	4	39	4	28	13	9	6	5	65	66·66
10. V. S.	3	4	8	9	4	5	33	19	14	9	10	6	4	62	87·87
11. C. M.	3	5	6	4	1	3	22	21	6	10	10	1	3	51	131·81
12. E. S.	3	4	6	5	3	3	24	24	11	13	7	8	3	66	175·00
13. J. M.	7	8	20	13	6	6	60	30	23	36	16	21	8	134	123·33
14. R. C.	9	6	10	5	6	6	42	27	20	22	11	11	6	97	130·95
15. J. H.	6	5	3	8	1	3	26	17	11	27	18	6	6	85	226·92
16. C. S.	6	9	5	6	4	3	33	30	19	16	38	13	3	119	260·60
17. M. H.	7	7	8	12	3	3	40	22	13	9	9	6	6	65	62·50
18. W. S.	4	5	2	6	1	3	21	22	9	14	12	6	6	69	228·57
19. J. W.	4	2	7	10	1	3	27	16	11	18	9	3	3	63	133·33
20. M. B.	3	5	9	6	6	3	32	17	18	17	11	3	3	69	115·62

TABLE XXII.—Scores by pages in learning and re-learning typewriting. Upper 10, relearning of ten failures in typewriting; lower 20, relearning of failures in school subjects, but not in typewriting.

Edward's measurements (by pages) are admittedly crude, and he does not report the figures for the last budgets done in the previous school year. Nevertheless, his conclusions about the remarkable permanence of typewriting habits are confirmed by Book, Rejall, and others, whose work is reported very fully by Thorndike (*Educational Psychology*, pp. 310–322). For example :

> " Rejall tested the permanence of the ability to typewrite after an interval of three and a half years. In the last two weeks of learning, he wrote at a rate of 25 words per minute with 4 errors per hundred words copied ; in the memory test, he scored, in the first five days, 18·75 words per minute with 8 errors per hundred words, 18·9 with $7\frac{1}{3}$ errors, 21 with $6\frac{2}{3}$ errors, 22·1 with 5 errors, and 22·5 with $8\frac{2}{3}$ errors. On continuing the practice, five hours brought him to very nearly the same ability that thirty hours had been required to attain originally, his average score for the six days after five hours of relearning being 26 words per minute with $5\frac{1}{2}$ errors per hundred words."

Book and Swift also found typewriting habits to be permanent, but they are not so permanent as these workers are inclined to believe.

In relearning the juggling of balls, Swift, after four years of disuse, required slightly less than one-third of the time of the original to regain an equal degree of proficiency.

If any of the readers of this volume who learned when young to juggle three oranges at a time, to flip a coin up the sleeve, to balance a broom on the chin, or to perform sleight-of-hand tricks with cards will, at this stage, try them out to see if they can still be performed, he will be astonished at the relative permanence of the learning. Some loss in dexterity will be noticed, but compared with the losses found in Latin, French, and German learned about the same time, it is almost negligible.

In regard to manual habits, it might be fair to state that their permanence over periods ranging, say, from 5 to 10 years, is in the nature of 50 to 90 per cent. The losses from language habits during the same time closely approximates 100 per cent.

In arithmetic, the permanence of learning appears to be intermediate between strictly language habits, such as learning poetry, and strictly manual habits, such as skating and swimming. Kirby tested the losses in addition and division between June and September. He gave fourth-grade pupils sixty minutes of practice in addition and re-tested them with a fifteen-minute period in June, from three to twelve weeks after the last trial of the regular practice, and again in September after the long vacation. In addition, the sixty minutes of practice produced a gain of 15 examples ; the June test increased it to 17 examples ; the September test showed a fall to 10. But 20 to 45 minutes of practice brought it back to the June efficiency. In division, the gain from 60 minutes of practice was 35 examples ; the June test slightly increased the gain; September found it fallen to 17½ examples, but 15 to 35 minutes of drill brought it back to the June standard.

Permanence and Speed of Learning.—A number of workers (Norsworthy, Henderson, Lyon, and Pyle) have tried to discover the relationship existing between the speed of learning and retentiveness. Common opinion is that there is negative correlation between them; that so far as memory is concerned "slow and sure" is good advice. Yet in all the studies it was found that those who learned quickest retained the longest.

Miss Norsworthy found that the students in Teachers' College who learned the greatest number of words in a German-English vocabulary in a given time retained the largest percentage of what had been learned.

Henderson, testing students ranging from the elementary school to the university for connected trains of thought, discovered, incidentally, that those who learned quickest retained best.

Lyon [1] conducted an extensive series of experiments to discover the relationship between speed of learning and retentiveness. The material memorized included poetry, prose, nonsense syllables, words, and digits. Three methods of testing retention were employed: (1) the absolute amount retained; (2) the amount which could be reproduced after hearing the material read once again; (3) the amount of time taken to relearn the material. Judged by the first method the fastest learners retained all material longest—poetry, prose, words, nonsense syllables, and digits. Using method (2) the fastest learners were superior with all material except digits. With the third method as criterion the fast learners best retained logical material (poetry and prose), while the slow learners retained digits, words, and nonsense syllables longest. Lyon concludes: "Taking all three methods into consideration, we are entitled to say that with material that is logical in character, *those who learn quickly remember the longest.* With digits, however, we find the conditions, so far as method (3) is concerned, reversed, for here it is the quick learners who seem to forget the most."

Pyle found that subjects who could reproduce most of the 40 ideas in each of 21 pieces of prose of equal length, which had been learned the previous day, were the ones who had learned the material in the shortest time.

Using nonsense syllables, the same author found that those

[1] Lyon, D. O., *The Relation of Quickness of Learning to Retentiveness.* Archives of Psychology, No. 34, 1914.

who were quick in the first learning were also quick in relearning. With 2000 pupils, grades III to VIII, who had a piece of prose (Whipple's *Marble Statue*) read to them and were tested by two reproductions of it, immediately and a month afterwards, the Pearson coefficients of correlation between the first and second reproductions ranged from 0·50 to 0·80.

All in all, therefore, the evidence shows that facility in learning and tenacity in retention are positively correlated. This finding is to be expected from a consideration of intelligence test results; the child with a native intelligence sufficiently high to learn quickly will, by means of the same high native intelligence, retain the learning a long time.

As a matter of fact, James's contention that "no amount of culture would seem capable of modifying a man's general retentiveness" has withstood the shocks of experimentation to a remarkable degree. The methods employed in memorizing may be improved, but, at bottom, nature has the final say and the positive correlation between retentiveness and speed of learning is the result.

The Freudian View of Forgetting.—Like the introspectionists, the Freudians deal with that aspect of memory called recollection by Bergson, in contradistinction to that with which we have been dealing, namely, memory as motor habits, both manual and verbal. Viewing forgetting in its psychopathic forms, Freud enunciated his doctrine of *repression*. Repression is a biological function, a defence mechanism guarding the mind against the intrusion of experiences which would cause it pain or discomfort. Consequently the mind purchases peace by refusing to remember disquieting experiences. We remember our cheques, but forget our bills. We forget the names and the works of our rivals, but remember with gratitude those whose findings support our own. Charles Darwin naïvely remarked that he had to make a special note of observations which did not fit in with his theories, because they tended to slip his mind so easily. In the same category the Freudians place slips of the tongue, slips of the pen, and such-like temporary forgettings. There is a reason for the repression of every one of them, but it is frequently disguised from the forgetter.

According to the Freudians any healthy person will try to forget a poignant grief, say the loss of a loved one, where the loss is irreparable. "The dead are soon forgotten" seems a callous statement, but the fact that we can forget them prevents the living from becoming insane. James asks us "How long, O healthy reader, can you now continue thinking of your tomb?" (I, p. 421). Society also punishes the persons who forget its laws, and such punishment is regarded as just. We forget, so it is considered, because we do not want to remember; the forgetting is controlled by our own wills.

Such contentions are understandable, but when the Freudians explain the amnesia of early childhood, the forgetting of dreams and the like, by repression they are more difficult to follow. The phenomena of repression seem, to the non-Freudian, to be due to the non-exercise of the unpleasant. Most of the cases cited in their literature appear to be explained more rationally by the laws of exercise and effect. They are, however, to be commended for trying to collect factual data in a field that up to the present has been limited to introspections.

Memory and Language.—Quite as interesting as the Freudian theory of forgetting is Watson's theory which connects memory with language. We remember those things for which we made verbal associations at the time, and no others. There is no need, the behaviourist says, to invoke the aid of a censor, or even of imagery, to explain remembering and forgetting. For example, suppose you are asked to think about (call up in your mind, if you like) some well-known building. Can you count its windows, its columns, or its steps? You can if, when you examined the building, you said to yourself (thought it), "There are eight columns in front, five windows to the right of the doorway, six steps before the front door, etc.," but not otherwise. The so-called good visualizer is the one who talks most to himself when he sees things and, of course, remembers what he said. Even artists, who should be good visualizers, have to write such words as green, dark green, deep blue, and orange red on their pencil sketches of landscape in order that they may reproduce them afterwards in colour. They turn their observations into written language in order to be sure of them; only a Turner dare wholly rely on his memory of the sub-vocal observations made at the time of the sketch.

Watson believes that our inability to remember the experiences of the first three or four years of life is due to our lack of language at the time. As soon as language habits become functional we begin to remember events, that is, begin to be able to tell people about them. But we remember them in behaviour, in motor habits of the non-linguistic type. For example, a child of ten may not remember (in words) the dog which barked and frightened him when he was two years old, but his behaviour shows that he is still afraid of dogs. His nervous system still remembers, even though the experience cannot be couched in language.

Watson also maintains that the actions of glands and visceral muscles are seldom, if ever, associated with language, consequently they may influence conduct profoundly without affecting consciousness. In such cases the subject is unable to explain what is happening to him. This whole field of the relation of memory to language is an interesting one and should be investigated scientifically.

Over-learning.—Radossawljewitsch learned his nonsense syllables until he could say them twice without error; Ebbinghaus until he could just repeat them once. The former remembered more than the latter. If a subject practised his nonsense learning until he could repeat the series 1000 times without error, it is very probable that the permanence of the learning would be very marked. The series, in common parlance, would have been over-learned. The permanence of learning seems to depend on the degree of over-learning, on how strong the connections were at

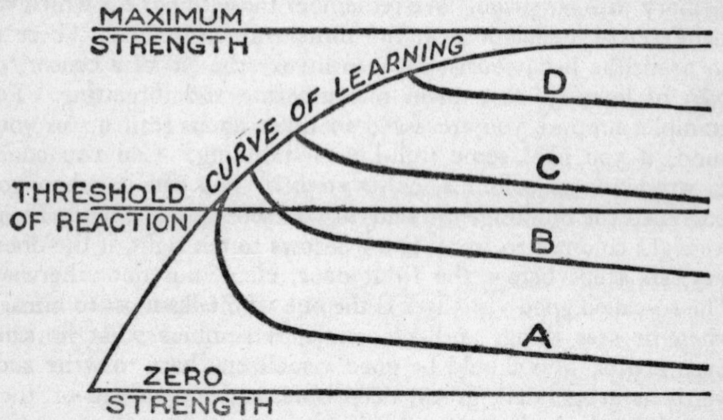

Fig. 52.—Curves showing the probable influence of disuse in the case of functions over-learned in various degrees. A shows the loss or forgetting when the function is barely learned. The initial loss is rapid and great, followed by a much slower rate of deterioration. B, C, and D show probable losses in functions which are over-learned slightly, considerably, and greatly respectively.

(*From Gates's "Psychology for Students of Education," by permission of The Macmillan Company, New York.*)

the beginning. If, in addition, nature has already formed some of the bonds, as, for example, in skating, dancing, swimming, and juggling, the rate of forgetting will be very slow. Fig. 52 (from Gates, p. 259) illustrates the probable influence of disuse in the case of functions over-learned in various degrees.

Some parts of school work must of necessity be over-learned. Writing is over-learned by all of us in the sense that we do so much of it that we never forget it. The A B C's, striking the bar in typewriting, the nursery rhymes of childhood, the simpler combinations in arithmetic, the commoner words in spelling, and the tune of "God Save the King" remain with us for life, largely because of their over-learning in childhood. Contrarily, the fugitive nature of the language and history of childhood is due to the fact that they are so frequently learned like nonsense syllables —to the point when they can just be reproduced and no more. The justification for making children learn some things so well that the practical limit almost coincides with the physiological limit, lies in the fact that permanence and over-learning are so closely related.

Paderewski staged a "come-back" to the concert hall because his previous over-learning enabled him to recapture his earlier skill with comparative ease. Robert Louis Stevenson observed of himself that no one had more certificates for less learning, by which he meant that he had forgotten things that he had known, but not things which he had over-learned. So it is with all of us. Few professors in universities could pass the examinations which gave them their B.A. degrees, but it is certain that they could regain the requisite knowledge more easily than they, as undergraduates, gained it in the first instance.

If these facts about over-learning be true, and if it be freely granted that only a relatively few branches and skills can be "over-learned" at one and the same time, then the selection by the school of those things which are to be learned to the limit must be made with the greatest care. Individual differences in the native capacities of pupils must receive appropriate recognition, and individual, as opposed to mass, instruction must receive more attention than has been accorded to it in the past.

Conclusion.—The following facts seem to be well established in connection with the retention of experience:

1. The rate of forgetting depends on the degree to which the material has been learned before the commencement of the period of forgetting. Over-learning makes forgetting slower.

2. Manual habits are retained longer than verbal habits.

3. Significant material, such as poetry, is retained longer than meaningless material, such as nonsense syllables.

4. The rate of forgetting depends on the method of learning, that is, on such factors as the amount learned at a time, on the concentration and distribution of practice, etc. Large amounts are more slowly forgotten than small amounts. Distributed practice is better for retention than concentrated practice. The recitation method of learning secures more permanent results than the reading method.

5. The permanence of improvement varies with the individual. Other things being equal, fast learners are slow forgetters.

6. Pleasant experiences are remembered longer than unpleasant

ones. This necessarily follows from the laws of exercise and effect, although, in psychopathic cases, it seems as if the Freudian doctrine of repression had a real basis.

7. We can never be absolutely sure that things, once learned, are ever completely forgotten. Some trace seems to be left behind which facilitates the re-learning even after a considerable interval. For practical purposes, however, we may conclude that disuse in time causes complete forgetfulness.

8. In linguistic habits the amount lost in the early stages of disuse is very great; after a few days the rate becomes slower and steadier. Re-learning is easier immediately after a cessation of practice than after longer intervals. New material should be reviewed not later than one day after learning.

9. There is no evidence for the belief that habits undergo incubation and improve after practice has ceased.

References

Bean, C. H. "The Curve of Forgetting," *Archives of Psychology*, No. 21.

Book, W. F. *The Psychology of Skill: with Special Reference to its Acquisition in Typewriting*. University of Montana Publications in Psychology, Bull. 53, Psychological Series No. 1.

Cleveland, A. A. "The Psychology of Chess and of Learning to Play it," *Am. J. Psy.*, XVIII (1907), pp. 269–308.

Ebbinghaus, H. *Ueber das Gedachtniss* (1885). Trans. by Ruger and Bussenius. Teachers' College, Columbia University (1913). Pp. 169.

Edward, W. G. *Improvement Curves in the Learning of Typewriting*. Toronto, Ryerson Press, 1923. Pp. 69.

Gates, A. I. *Psychology for Students of Education*. New York, Macmillan, 1924. Pp. xvi+489.

Holt, E. B. *The Freudian Wish and its Place in Ethics*. New York, Holt, 1915. Pp. 212.

James, W. *Principles of Psychology*, vol. i. New York, Holt, 1890 (1st ed.). Pp. xii+689.

Kirby, T. J. *The Results of Practice under School Conditions*. Teachers' College, Columbia University, Contributions to Education, 1913.

Ladd and Woodworth. *Elements of Educational Psychology*. New York, Scribners, 1911. Pp. xix+704.

Lyon, D. O. "The Relation of Quickness of Learning to Retentiveness," *Archives of Psy.*, No. 34, 1916.

Norsworthy, N. "Acquisition as related to Retention," *J.E.P.*, III, 4 (April, 1912), pp. 214–218.

Pear, T. H. *Remembering and Forgetting*. London, Methuen, 1922. Pp. xii+242.

Pyle, W. H. *The Psychology of Learning*. Baltimore, Warwick and York, 1921. Pp. 308.

Radossawljewitsch, P R. *Das Behalten und Vergessen bei Kindern und Erwachsenen nach experinentellen Untersuchungen* (*Das Fortschreiten des Vergessens mit der Zeit*), 1907.

RUSSELL, B. *The Analysis of Mind.* London, Allen and Unwin, 1921 Pp. 310.

SANDIFORD, P. *The Mental and Physical Life of School Children.* London, Longmans, 1913. Pp. xii+346.

STARCH, D. *Educational Psychology.* New York, Macmillan, 1927. Pp. ix+568.

SWIFT, E. J. "Memory of a Complex Skilful Act," *A.J.P.*, XVI (1905), pp. 131–133.

SWIFT, E. J. "Memory of Skilful Movements," *Psy. Bull.*, III (1906), pp. 185–187.

SWIFT, E. J. "Re-learning a Skilful Act; an Experimental Study in Neuro-muscular Memory," *Psy. Bull.*, VII (1910), pp. 17–19.

THORNDIKE, E. L. *Educational Psychology.* Vol. II. *The Psychology of Learning.* New York, Teachers College, Columbia University, 1913. Pp. xi+452.

WHIPPLE, G. M. *Manual of Mental and Physical Tests.* Baltimore, Warwick and York, 1st ed, 1910. Pp. xix+534.

CHAPTER XIII

CONTINUOUS PRACTICE: FATIGUE IN LEARNING

Fatigue and Boredom.—In the practice curve we do not measure the true efficiency due to practice, but a composite of improvement due to practice and loss of efficiency ensuing from fatigue. Similarly, in measurements of fatigue from continuous practice we do not measure loss of efficiency due solely to fatigue, but a loss resulting from fatigue, *plus* an amount due to the familiarization of practice. Measurements of fatigue during continuous practice are further complicated by the confusion of *fatigue*, which is the fact of decreasing competency to do work, with *boredom*, which is a lack of desire to do work, an aversion from it. Consequently there is no subject of investigation which has led to such inconsistent and often diametrically opposed results as that of fatigue. Indeed, as early as 1903, Ellis and Shipe were prepared to throw overboard all previous studies in fatigue and make a fresh start. Later workers have shown that a positive distastefulness for a task may go hand in hand with a high degree of efficiency in its performance. Boredom appears earlier than fatigue and increases at a more rapid rate, but is quite distinct from it. In this chapter fatigue will be regarded as increasing inability to do work, irrespective of subjective feelings (disinclination) on the matter.

The Physiology of Fatigue.—The experimental work on the physiology of fatigue centres around the three problems of fatigability of (*a*) muscle; (*b*) nerve-trunks; and (*c*) reflexes.

Muscle.—That the performance of muscular work leads to fatigue is common knowledge. If we lift a heavy weight above the head repeatedly, a state is soon reached when the muscles of the body refuse to obey the mandates of the will. Fatigue, as we say, has set in.

Mosso invented an instrument, called by him an ergograph, which measures and records the work done by a single or, at most, a few muscles of the body. In this instrument, the forearm and hand, together with all fingers except the middle one, are firmly fixed with the palm uppermost. The flexion of the free finger lifts a weight of 2 to 3 kilograms suspended by a string running over a pulley at the edge of the table, and the several lifts are recorded automatically on a rotating drum. From the use of the ergograph several interesting facts regarding muscle action have emerged.

(1) The fall in efficiency of muscular action is pronounced at first, then the rate slackens, and then speeds up once more until fatigue results.

(2) If a sufficient rest period, say 10 seconds, is allowed after each contraction, no fatigue occurs.

(3) A certain length of time, about two hours for the flexors of the fingers, is necessary for the recovery from fatigue.

(4) If after complete fatigue the subject makes abortive contractions, the period of recovery from fatigue is greatly extended.

(5) The amount of work a muscle can do and the rapidity with which fatigue sets in depend very largerly on the number of contractions, executed in a unit of time; the more rapid the contractions the less the total amount of work done and the fewer the contractions made before fatigue sets in.

(6) Whatever interferes with the removal of waste products or with the supply of food lessens the power of the muscle and hastens fatigue. Hence loss of sleep, hunger, anæmia, and dissipation lower the amount of work which can be done. On the other hand, improved circulation resulting from massage, better foods, and sugar solutions increases the muscular work.

(7) The fatigue of a certain set of muscles will decrease the amount of work which can be obtained from other muscles of the body, probably through the circulation of fatigue products in the blood. Through the same agency the nervous system becomes affected and mental fatigue follows.

(8) Sometimes mental work fatigues the muscles, but measurements are not consistent. In all measurements the subject is supposed to do his very best, but this supposition is not susceptible of objective verification.

(9) There is some confusion as to the effects of drugs—alcohol, nicotine, caffeine, etc.—upon muscular power. On the other hand, sugar, 30 to 40 minutes after its injection, improves the capacity for muscular work. Artificial removal of sugar from the body by drugs causes a large decrease in muscular power.

If experiments are conducted on a freshly excised muscle, say the leg muscle of a newly killed frog, stimulation of the attached motor nerve by an electric shock results in a contraction of the muscle. This contraction, as in ergographic experiments, can be automatically recorded. If another stimulus of the same strength is applied, say, one second after the first, the second contraction is a little higher than the first. Continuing these regular stimulations a staircase diagram is obtained, each contraction being greater than the preceding. This warming up indicates that the irritability of the muscle or its power to do work is increased by previous activity. There is, however, a limit to these successive increases. The maximum contraction is soon reached, becomes stationary for a time, and then falls off until complete fatigue is reached. The increased irritability in the early stages has been ascribed by Lee and others to the influence of the products formed by the activity of the muscle, since two of these, carbon dioxide and lactic acid in small amounts, have been found to increase muscular power.

Nerve-trunks.—Nerve-trunks are comparatively indefatigable ; indeed, under the ordinary conditions of stimulation a nerve fibre cannot be fatigued, as may be shown by the following experiment : If the " muscle-nerve preparation " described in the previous paragraph is stimulated at the rate of ten or twenty per second, while a " block " of the nerve (produced by cold or by the drug curare) is maintained, no contraction of the muscle takes place, although the nerve conducts as far as the point at which the block is applied. If, after stimulation for ten hours or more, the block is removed (by warming up or removing the effects of the curare), the muscle again contracts, thus demonstrating the extraordinary resistance to fatigue of nerve-trunks. We may, therefore, conclude that while muscle is easily fatigable, the main nerves of the body are practically unfatigable. The energy consumed by the impulse in its passage through the nerve must be exceedingly slight, but the fact that electrical and chemical changes take place shows that some work is done. Adrian, however, has shown that the impulse gathers energy from the nerve tissue as it passes along, leading to the all-or-none phenomenon, namely, that if the impulse passes at all, it does so in the strongest possible manner and that an increase in the strength of the stimulus does not increase the strength of the impulse.

Reflexes.—The physiology of the reflex has been worked out by Sherrington.[1] He found that " a spinal reflex under continuous excitation or frequent repetition becomes weaker, and may cease altogether." This fatigue of a reflex is not due to the tiring of the muscle, for the same muscle in a dog which refuses to respond, say, to a flexion-reflex will respond to a scratch-reflex. Nor, as we have seen, is it due to fatigue of the

[1] Sherrington, C. S., *The Integrative Action of the Nervous System*, pp. 214–223.

nerve-trunk for these are practically indefatigable. The seat of the fatigue must, therefore, be intra-spinal, probably at the first synapse. A spinal reflex recovers very quickly from fatigue, acting, in this respect, in marked contrast to muscle.

Further observations show that "when the scratch-reflex elicited from a spot of skin is fatigued, the fatigue holds for that spot but does not implicate the reflex as obtained from the surrounding skin." The reflex when tired out to stimuli at that spot is easily obtainable by stimulation two or three centimetres away. This is true of both mechanical and electrical stimulation. The explanation is that each sensitive area is connected through synapses of the spinal cord with a common nerve-trunk running to the muscle; if one synaptic connection becomes fatigued, the others are still fresh and may play their part in causing the reflex movement to take place.

A reflex movement of muscle, therefore, may have several receptors as the starting-point. The synaptic fatigue of the cord prevents a too prolonged continuous use of a common path and muscle by any one receptor. "It precludes one receptor from occupying for long periods an effector organ to the exclusion of all other receptors. It prevents long continuous possession of a common path by any one reflex of considerable intensity. It favours the receptors taking turn about. It helps to ensure serial variety of reaction. The organism, to be successful in a million-sided environment, must in its reactions be many-sided. Were it not for such so-called 'fatigue,' an organism might, in regard to its receptivity, develop an eye, or an ear, or a mouth, or a hand or leg, but it would hardly develop the marvellous congeries of all those various sense-organs which it is actually found to possess."

Of the three structures, muscles, nerve-trunks, and nerve-endings (synapses), the nerve-endings, therefore, are the most susceptible to fatigue. Like the fuses in an electric circuit they are the most vulnerable part of the system, but are also the most easily repaired.

Causes of Fatigue.—There are three main causes of fatigue:

(1) *The Exhaustion of the Energy-producing Compounds* in the body, especially in muscle fibres, and in the cell-bodies of neurons. The nutriment of the body, which is absorbed by the blood, is carried by this medium to all parts of the body and utilized in the building up of bodily tissues and in providing a store of energy in the form of highly complex, easily decomposable chemical compounds in the movement-producing cells of the body. Thus muscle cells are stored with a supply of such compounds. When a nervous impulse passes into the muscle a part of these compounds

breaks up, the rapid decomposition providing the energy for the contraction. In the same way a neuron, especially in the cell-body, contains a stainable material (chromophilic substance) which supplies the energy of the nervous impulse. If the stimulation of the muscle or neuron is prolonged, a stage is reached when the available supply of these compounds is exhausted. A state of fatigue is then reached and the parts affected will not function until rest has allowed more of these compounds to accumulate. In the muscle the time is prolonged; in the neuron extremely short. The exact chemical composition of these compounds is as yet unknown. They are, however, known to be exceedingly complex and to decompose with ease.

(2) *The Presence of Toxic Waste Products.*—When a muscle is exercised waste products or toxins are formed. These toxins are poisonous and their presence in quantity causes the symptoms of fatigue. That these waste products alone can produce fatigue was shown by Mosso, who injected the blood from a dog, excessively fatigued by electrical stimulation, into a normal dog and thereby caused symptoms of fatigue to appear in the second animal. Further, if a fatigued excised muscle is perfused (that is, washed by forcing a fluid through the blood vessels) with physiologic salt solution, the fatigue gradually disappears. The waste products are washed away. If a little dextrose is added to the salt solution, fatigue disappears more quickly, thus showing that fatigue is partly due to a lack of food material. The chief fatigue products are lactic acid, $C_3H_6O_3$; acid potassium phosphate, KH_2PO_4; and carbon dioxide, CO_2. The elimination of fatigue substances from the body is effected primarily by means of the circulation of blood and lymph, and secondarily by means of the lungs, skin, and kidneys. Injection of solutions of any of these fatigue substances into a muscle lowers its irritability. On the other hand, as we have seen, minute amounts of these waste products increase the excitability of muscle. The selfsame compounds, therefore, are responsible for both the increase and decrease of irritability, producing the staircase phenomenon as well as fatigue. But, as Sherrington has shown, it is the effect of waste products upon the synaptic nerve-endings which produces most of the observable phenomena of fatigue.

(3) *Lack of Oxygen.*—The decomposition of the energy producing compounds of the body cannot take place without the assistance of oxygen carried by the red corpuscles of the blood. The presence of oxygen is also necessary for conduction in a nerve. The removal of fatigue is certainly accomplished in part by oxidation; as a matter of fact the lactic acid is finally oxidized to CO_2 and water and eliminated by the lungs. Hence any

impairment of the oxygen supply, or, what amounts to the same thing, any increase in the amount of waste products needing oxidation, leads to fatigue. The primary phenomena of muscular exercise, namely, a quickening of respiration and an acceleration of the heart beat, are probably due to the body's increased need of oxygen. But this third cause of fatigue is not so important as the other two and is probably a resultant of them.

Remedy for Fatigue.—Nature's sovereign remedy for fatigue is sleep. In this state of rest, opportunity is given for replenishing the supply of energy-producing compounds and for the elimination of waste products by oxidation or otherwise. The taking of food, especially sugars, hastens recovery from fatigue, as do also certain stimulants such as tea and coffee. But if the fatigue is of a localized mental kind, such as is normally produced by school tasks, the remedy may be the substitution of another activity. Inattention (of children in school) is nature's way of changing a mental operation which has produced a temporary fatigue.

Book [1] secured data from students in the University of Indiana which showed "that some students need a great deal more sleep than others, either because they fatigue more easily and rapidly or because they are slow to recuperate, or because they have not formed the habit of getting proper rest while they sleep. These three factors in varying degrees may account for the fact that some students regularly take and apparently require more than twice as much sleep as others. No correlation was, therefore, found between the amount of sleep taken and the amount of work attempted or done. In fact, those who sleep the least seem to do the most work."

It is unwise, however, to allow children to drop a task the moment that boredom appears. As will be shown later, efficiency may still be high when boredom is great. But at present we do not know just how far we should train pupils to drive themselves. Habit undoubtedly plays a part, and longer tasks can be attempted after habituation.

Kinds of Fatigue.—Fatigue is usually divided into muscular fatigue, sensory fatigue, and mental fatigue. These divisions are artificial, for sense organs are connected to muscles *viâ* the central nervous system and it is impossible to say where the fatigue centres. Physiological experiments show that the chief seat of fatigue lies in the synaptic connections of the central nervous system, with secondary seats in sense organs and muscle plates. The peripheral ends of sensory neurons (sense organs) are

[1] Book, W. F., *How to Succeed in College*, 1927, pp. 73–74.

somewhat easily fatigued. We quickly become insensitive to odours and tastes, for example, owing to the fatigability of our olfactory and taste cells; and certain phenomena connected with vision have been attributed to the fatigue of the rods and cones of the retina. Common practice, however, distinguishes between mental fatigue and bodily fatigue. The former is ıeferred to the nervous system; the latter to the muscles. These two forms of fatigue are closely associated; it is impossible to experience either of them in a pure form. Especially does muscular fatigue, through its waste products, tend to pass over into mental fatigue. A twenty-mile tramp is not the best immediate preparation for hard intellectual work. Prolonged mental exercise may cause muscular fatigue, although it is difficult to demonstrate it.

Measurements of Mental Fatigue.—Much ingenuity has been displayed in measurements of mental fatigue. A tabulation of the methods which have been used most frequently, with a list of the workers who have used them, is attempted below:

I. Measurements of Mental Fatigue through its Influence on Organic Processes.

(*a*) *Changes in Pulse Rate.*

1. Davy, John, "On the Temperature of Man," *Phil. Trans.*, CXXXV (1845), pp. 319–349.
2. Mosso, A., *La fatica.* Eng. trans. by Drummond, 1904.
3. MacDougall, W., "The Physiological Characteristics of Attention," *Psy. Rev.*, 1896, pp. 158–160.
4. Vaschide, N., "Influence du travail intellectuel prolongé sur la vitesse du pouls," *L'Année Psychol.*, IV (1897), pp. 356–378.
5. Binet et Henri, *La fatigue intellectuelle*, Paris, 1898.
6. Larguier des Bancels, J., "Mesure de la fatigue," *L'Année Psychol.*, V (1898), pp. 191–195.
7. Gley, E., *Études de Psychologie, Physiologique et Pathologique.* Paris, 1903.
8. Benedict and Carpenter, *The Influence of Muscular and Mental Work on Metabolism and the Efficiency of the Human Body as a Machine.* Washington, General Printing Office, 1909.
9. Billings and Shephard, "The Change of Heart Rate with Attention," *Psy. Rev.*, XVII (1910), pp. 217–228.

(*b*) *Changes in Body Temperature.*

1. Davy, J. (See above.)
2. Lombard, *Experimental Researches on the Regional Temperature of the Head.* London, 1879.
3. Speck, "Untersuch über die Beziehungen der geistigen Thätigkeit zum Stoffwechsels," *Archiv. Exptl. Path. u. Pharmakol.*, XV (1881), pp. 87–88.
4. Larquier des Bancels, J. (See above.)
5. Gley, E. (See above.)
6. Benedict and Carpenter. (See above.)

(*c*) *Changes in Metabolism* (*respiration calorimeter*).

1. Speck. (See above.)
2. Atwater, Woods, and Benedict. U.S. Dept. of Agric. Office of Experimental Station, Bull. 44.
3. Benedict and Carpenter. (See above.)

II. Measurements of Mental Fatigue through its Influence on Motor Power and Reaction Time.

(*a*) *Muscular Efficiency* (*ergograph*).

1. Mosso, A. (See above.)
2. Kemsies, Fr., "Zur Frage der Ueberbürdung," *Deutsche Medizinische Wochenschrift*, XXII (July 2, 1896).
3. Thorndike, E. L., "Mental Fatigue," *Psych. Rev.*, VII (Sept. 1900), pp. 466–482.
4. Ellis and Shipe, "A Study of the Accuracy of the Present Methods of Testing Fatigue," *Amer. J. Psy.*, XIV (1903), pp. 496–509.
5. Keller, R., "Experimentelle Untersuchungen über die Ermüdung von Schulern durch geistige Arbeit," *Zeit. f. Schulhygiene*, X, 1897.
6. Keller, R., "Ueber den 40-Minuten-betrieb des Gynasiums und der Industrieschule in Winterthur," *Interl. Magazine of School Hygiene*, II, 1906.
7. Larquier des Bancels, J., "Revue des derniers travaux sur la technique de l'ergographe," *L'Annèe Psychol.*, VII (1902).
8. Bolton and Miller, "On the Validity of the Ergograph as a Measurer of Work Capacity," *Nebraska Univ. Studies*, 1904, 79, 128.
9. Marsh, H. D., "The Diurnal Course of Efficiency," *Arch. of Phil., Psy. and Sci. Method, Columbia Univ. Contrib. to Phil. & Psy.*, XIV, 3.

(*b*) *Muscular Strength* (*dynamometer*).

1. Loeb, J., "Muskeltätigkeit als Mass psychischer Tätigkeit," *Pfluger's Archiv. f. d. ges. Physiologie* 39, 1886.
2. Gineff, D., *Prüfung der Methoden zur Messung geistiger Ermüdung*, 1899 (Dissertation, Zurich).
3. Claviere, J., "Le Travail intellectuel dans ses rapports avec la force musculaire," *L'Annèe Psy.*, VII, 1901.
4. Claparède, E., *Experimental Pedagogy* (tr. Louch and Holman). London, Arnold, 1911.
5. Schuyten, M. C., "Comment doit-on mesurer la fatigue des écoliers," *Archiv. de Psychol.*, IV, 1905.
6. James, W., "The Energies of Man," *Philos. Rev.*, XVI (1907), pp. 1–20.

(*c*) *Motor Efficiency* (*tapping*).

1. Dresslar, "Rapidity of Voluntary Movement," *Amer. J. Psy.*, V (1892).
2. Stern, W., *Ueber Psychologie der individuellen Differenzen* (1900).
3. Lay, W., *Experimentelle Didaktik* (1893).
4. Wells, F. L., "A Neglected Measure of Fatigue," *A.J.P.*, XIX (1908), pp. 345–348. Other studies in
   A.J.P., XIX (1908), pp. 437–483;
   A.J.P., XX (1909), pp. 38–59;
   A.J.P., XX (1909), pp. 353–363.

(*d*) *Reaction Time.*

1. Bernstein, J. A., "Ueber die Ermüdung und Erholung der Nerven," *Archiv. g. Phys.*, XV (1877), pp. 289–327.
2. Bettmann, S., "Ueber die Beeinflussung enifacher Psychischer Vorgäge durch Körperliche und geistige Arbeit," *Psychol. Arbeiten*, I (1896), p. 152.
3. Ellis and Shipe. (See above.)

III. Measurements of Mental Fatigue through its Influence on the Sensitivity of the Skin, and by other Methods of the Psychological Laboratory.

(*a*) *Æsthesiometry.*

1. Griesbach, H., *Energetik und Hygiene des Nervensystems in der Schule*, 1895.
2. Griesbach, H., "Ueber Beziehungen zwischen geistiger Ermüdung und Empfindungsvermögen der Haut.," *Arch. f. Hygiene*, XXIV, 1895.
3. Keller, R. (See above.)
4. Wagner, L., "Unterricht und Ermudungsmessungen an Schülern des neuen Gymnasiums in Darmstadt." In *Schiller-Ziehen, Sammlung von Abhaudlungen aus dem Gebiet der pädogogischen Psychologie und Physiologie*, Heft 4, 1898.
5. Binet et Henri. (See above.)
6. Leuba, J. H., "On the Validity of the Griesbach Method of Determining Fatigue," *Psy. Rev.*, VI (1899), pp. 573–598.
7. Germann, J. B., "On the Invalidity of the Æsthesiometric Method as a Measure of Mental Fatigue," *Psy. Rev.*, VI (1899), pp. 599–605.
8. Gineff, D. (See above.)
9. Bolton, T. L., "The Reliability of Certain Methods for Measuring the Degree of Fatigue in School Children," *Psy. Rev.*, VII (1900), pp. 136–137.
10. Bonoff, N., "Étude médico-pedagogique sur l'esthesiometrie et la simulation a l'école," *International Mag. School Hygiene*, IV, 1907–1908.

(*b*) *Kinematometry.*

1. Meumann, E., *Psychology of Learning* (tr.), 1913.
2. Gineff, D. (See above.)

(*c*) *Algesiometry.*

1. Vannod, Td., "La fatigue intellectuelle," *Rev. Med. de la Suisse Romande*, XVII, 1897.
2. Swift, E., "Sensibility to Pain," *A.J.P.*, XI (1900), pp. 312–317.
3. Vaschide, N., "Les recherches experimentelles sur la fatigue intellectuelle," *Rev. de Philos*, V, 1905.
4. Binet, A., "Recherches sur la fatigue intellectuelle scolaire," *Année Psychol.*, XI, 1905.
5. Meumann, E. (See above.)

(*d*) *Liminal Values.*

1. Baur, A., *Das Kranke Schulkind*, 1902.
2. Seashore and Kent, "Periodicity and Progressive Change in Continuous Mental Work," *Psy. Rev. Monographs*, 1905.

IV. Measurement of Mental Fatigue through its Influence on the Efficiency of Mental Functions.

(*a*) *Questionnaire Studies.*

1. Galton, F., "Remarks on Replies by Teachers to Questions respecting Mental Fatigue," *Jour. Anthro. Instit.*, XVIII (1888–1889), p. 157.

(*b*) *Errors in Writing and Talking.*

1. Sikorski, J., "Sur les effets de la lassitude provoquée par les travaux intellectuels chez les enfants à l'âge scolaire," *Annales d'hygiene publique*, II (1879), pp. 458–467.
2. Burgerstein, L., "Die Arbeitscurve einer Schulstunde," *Zeit. f. Schulgesundheitspflege*, IV (1891), pp. 543–563.
3. Laser, H., "Ueber geistige Ermüdung beim Schulunterrichte," *Zeit. f. Schulgesundheitspflege*, VII (1894), pp. 2–22.
4. Ebbinghaus, H., "Ueber eine neue Methode zur Prüfung geistiger Fähigkeiten und ihre Anwendung bei Schulkindern," *Zeit. f. Psychol.*, XIII (1897), pp. 401–457.
5. Friedrich, J., "Untersuchungen ueber die Einflüsse der Arbeitsdauer und der Arbeitspausen auf die geistige Leistungsfähigkeit der Schulkinder," *Zeit. f. Psychol.*, XIII (1897), pp. 1–53.

(*c*) *Computation.*

1. Laser, H. (See above.)
2. Burgerstein, L. (See above.)
3. Bettmann, S. (See above.)
4. Holmes, M. E., "The Fatigue of the School Hour," *Ped. Sem.*, III (1895), pp. 213–234.
5. Thorndike, E. L., "Mental Fatigue," *Psy. Rev.*, VII (1900), pp. 466–489 and 547–579. Also *J.E.P.*, II (1911), pp. 61–80.
6. Ellis and Shipe. (See above.)
7. Rivers and Kraepelin, "Ueber Ermüdung und Erholung," *Psychol. Arbeit.*, I (1896), pp. 627–678.

(*d*) *Attention.*

1. Pillsbury, W. B., "Attention Waves as Means of Measuring Fatigue," *A.J.P.*, XIV (1903), pp. 541–552.

(*e*) *Memory.*

1. Ebbinghaus, H. (See above.)
2. Oehrn, A., "Experimentelle Studien zur Individualpsychologie," *Psychol. Arbeit.*, I (1889), pp. 92–151.
3. Amberg, E., "Ueber den Einfluss von Arbeitspausen auf die geistige Leistungsfähigkeit," *Psy. Arbeit.*, I (1896), pp. 300–377.

(*f*) *Completion.*

1. Ebbinghaus, H. (See above.)
2. Wiersma, E., "Die Ebbinghaus'sche Combinationsmethode,' *Zeit. f. Psy.*, XXX (1902), pp. 196–222.

(*g*) *Persistence of Visual Sensations, hitting at Moving Dots, and Cancellation.*

1. Bibliography in Offner, M., *Mental Fatigue* (tr. Whipple) Baltimore, 1911; Claparede, E., *Experimental Pedagogy*; and Thorndike, E. L., *Educational Psychology*, vol. ii.

V. Measurement of Mental Fatigue produced by Continuous Mental Work.

(*a*) *Mental Multiplication, Addition, etc.*

1. Thorndike, E. L. (See *J.E.P.*, above.)
2. Arai, Tsuru, *Mental Fatigue.* T. C. Contributions to Education, No. 54, 1912. Pp. 115.
3. Starch and Ash, "The Mental Work Curve," *Psy. Rev.*, XXIV (1917), pp. 391–402.
4. Reed, H. B., "Fatigue and Work Curve from a 10-hour Day in Addition," *J.E.P.*, XV, 6 (Sept. 1924), pp. 389–392.

Despite the above studies and hundreds of others which might have been included in the list, teachers are still without a reliable "measuring stick" for fatigue. The concept of fatigue is simple enough, but what constitutes the crux of its measurement is complete isolation. In chemical terms, it has never been isolated in a pure state; it is always contaminated with such factors as zeal, attention, determination, practice, and bodily state at the time of the investigation.

All indirect measures of mental fatigue by means of bodily changes have proved singularly unreliable and disappointing. We do not know whether or not we become warmer or colder, breathe faster or slower, or become stronger or weaker, as a result of mental fatigue. Thorndike, criticizing the use of physical fatigue as a measure of mental fatigue, states that it supposes the amounts of physical work are (1) functions of the central nervous system; and (2) dependent on such general factors as are at play in mental work and mental fatigue. Therefore (3) we may measure mental inability by physical inability. The first is not definitely proven. The second is mere assumption. The third is an hypothesis to be proved.

The methods which have employed instruments, like æsthesiometers, algesiometers, dynamometers, and so forth, have given equally conflicting results. With variations in mental fatigue, changes in the sensitivity of the skin to pressure and pain may take place, but nobody has yet succeeded in demonstrating concomitance between them.

Consequently, the only hope that is left is the direct measurement of the loss of efficiency of a mental function during its continuous exercise. Some experimental results will now be given.

Experimental Results.—Thorndike[1] was the first to employ mental multiplication (probably as pure a mental function as can be profitably employed) in the measurement of fatigue. The function studied was the mental multiplication of a three-

[1] Thorndike, E. L., "Mental Fatigue," *J.E.P.*, II, 2 (Feb. 1911), pp. 61–80.

place number by a three-place number, neither having any 0's or 1's among the digits. The subjects were sixteen students, and each was directed to obtain the answers in his head, and to write nothing down but the six-place answers as they were serially obtained. Each subject worked continuously on one day from four to twelve hours, broken only by a brief rest for luncheon. The next day they worked from one-half to an hour on the same task. The amount of fatigue was measured by the difference in the time required to do the same amount of work with the same accuracy at the end of the long fatiguing practice, and at the beginning of the test on the next day after the long rest. The increase of time required, with equal accuracy, at the end of the work-period over that at the beginning of the rest period in per cents. of the latter were, for the sixteen subjects, 45, 36, 197, 81, −9, −15, 14, 28, 68, 36, 55, 83, 152, 118, 5, and −39. In the case of the seven individuals who worked approximately seven hours, the average increase in time required (with allowance for accuracy) at the end of the work period over the beginning of the test next day was 54 per cent. But this should not be interpreted to mean that seven hours of mental work reduced the efficiency by one-half (see criticism of Miss Arai's experiment which follows).

The most extended investigation of fatigue by means of mental multiplication was made by Miss Arai,[1] a Japanese graduate student at Teachers' College, Columbia University, she herself being the subject. Miss Arai first practised herself in mental multiplication of pairs of four-figure numbers like

2645	8324	7954	5438
5784	7384	3528	2347

At first the numbers were multiplied mentally but with the original numbers in sight. The answer was written down as soon as it was obtained and the time recorded. This was repeated for each of the examples. As she became practised, the fluctuations of time for each example became less. The practice was continued until she became expert. Miss Arai then tried to fatigue herself by working from 1.46 p.m. to 10.08 p.m., with a stop between 6.32 p.m. and 7.41 p.m. for dinner. The results were disappointing, as the work did not prove difficult enough to produce fatigue.

The method was then varied. Instead of multiplying with

[1] Arai, Tsuru, *Mental Fatigue*. T. C. Contributions to Education, No. 54. New York, Columbia University, 1912.

the original figures in sight, she relied on memory for the figures and multiplied them mentally with closed eyes. When she forgot the original figures she looked at them again, but the time was counted from the beginning. This loss by forgetting, however, seldom occurred. After six practice experiments, she did mental multiplication on four successive days from about 11 a.m. to 11 p.m. without any interval for meals, 67 examples being done on each day.

Miss Arai also carried out other interesting fatigue experiments upon herself, such as memorizing German equivalents of English words, and translating Dewey's *Influence of Darwin on Philosophy and Other Essays* into Japanese. For the results of these later experiments the reader is referred to the original monograph.

In Table XXIII, Miss Arai's mental-multiplication results are averaged for each successive ten, except, of course, for the last group where there are only seven examples.

Averages of examples.	March 3, 1909. 11.02 a.m. to 11.07 p.m.		March 4. 11.12 a.m. to 10.52 p.m.		March 5. 10.08 a.m. to 10.55 p.m.		March 6. 11.15 a.m. to 11.27 p.m.	
	Time.	Errors.	Time.	Errors.	Time.	Errors.	Time.	Errors.
1–10	5.47	1·7	5.50	1·8	4.52	1·6	4.45	2·0
11–20	7.28	1·0	7.00	1·2	6.21	1·8	6.06	1·5
21–30	8.18	1·3	7.30	2·5	7.33	1·2	7.07	2·1
31–40	10.49	1·8	10.06	1·5	7.32	1·0	8.20	2·1
41–50	11.52	2·1	11.30	1·7	11.26	2·4	9.14	1·6
51–60	11.50	1·3	11.04	1·8	8.08	2·3	8.54	4·1
61–67	13.27	1·3	12.14	3·1	10.28	3·4	8.54	3·1
Averages .	9.47	1·5	9.13	1·9	7.55	1·9	7.45	2·3

TABLE XXIII.—Time taken and errors made per example by Miss Arai in multiplying mentally four-figure numbers by four-figure numbers in about twelve hours of continuous work.

Thorndike has worked up Miss Arai's original material in another way by combining time and errors into a single measurement. Combining the examples in groups of four, he added, for each wrong figure more than two in any answer, 3 per cent. of the time required for the four examples (that is, 12 per cent. of the time required per example) and for each wrong figure less than two in any example, he subtracted 3 per cent. of the time. His calculations are given in Table XXIV.

Examples in sets of four.	March 3.	March 4.	March 5.	March 6.	Average.
1–4	23·6	20·7	19·3	16·5	20·0
5–8	23·3	24·5	16·5	29·6	23·9
9–12	23·2	23·5	20·9	28·5	23·4
13–16	26·1	25·9	22·8	23·0	24·6
17–20	25·8	27·8	28·3	20·2	26·8
21–24	27·3	31·4	31·7	26·2	29·4
25–28	34·3	37·3	24·0	33·6	34·0
29–32	31·3	24·9	27·5	33·8	29·4
33–36	40·0	35·0	17·1	26·7	30·9
37–40	49·8	41·5	31·0	38·6	40·0
41–44	52·2	45·8	39·1	35·6	42·5
45–48	43·8	44·6	48·1	34·1	44·2
49–52	37·9	41·8	41·0	47·0	41·4
53–56	42·5	46·5	27·9	29·8	36·2
57–60	39·7	31·1	28·3	47·1	36·6
61–64	39·0	52·0	50·0	45·6	46·7
[1]65–67	62·1	44·4	49·1	32·9	47·1
First eight (1–8)	46·9	45·2	35·8	46·1	43·9
[1]Last eight (61–67)	101·1	96·4	99·1	78·5	93·8

TABLE XXIV.—Time required in minutes, with allowances for errors, for successive sets of four examples multiplied mentally by Miss Arai.

Probably the most remarkable result of this study is that Miss Arai, on each of the four days after twelve hours of the most fatiguing mental work that can be imagined, could still produce results. True, her efficiency declined on each of the days, but on the fourth less than on any of the other days. That fatigue resulted is shown (*a*) by the average increase of the time and (*b*) by the average increase in the number of errors.

But as Thorndike says:

"For a person to be able to multiply a number like 9263 by one like 5748 without any visual, written, or spoken aids, even in fifteen, or for that matter in a hundred and fifteen, minutes, implies a very high degree of efficiency. That a person can exert himself to the utmost at this very difficult work for ten or twelve hours without rest and still be able to do it, even if at the expense of twice or thrice as many minutes per example as at the beginning, means that the loss in efficiency by any absolute standard has been small. For Shakespeare to have required twice as long to write *Hamlet* as he actually did require would not have meant a loss of half the efficiency of the play-writing function! For Napoleon to have taken twenty instead of five minutes to plan a series of moves at Austerlitz would not have meant that his generalship was only one-fourth as efficient" (*Educational Psychology*, III, pp. 19–20).

He estimates that Miss Arai's efficiency during the last half-hours

[1] Scores of last 3 and last 7 adjusted to 4 and 8 respectively.

of each day was certainly not less than 75 per cent. of her initial efficiency.

Most of us would be bored to extinction if we were made to do such a task. As Miss Arai was interested and voluntarily undertook the work for the sole purpose of getting true fatigue curves, interest in the task, as well as remarkable will-power, carried her along to a successful completion. On March 3 she reports, "In the morning I felt very well. I did not have any special feeling of fatigue in the course of the experiment. Towards the end of the test, however, it was hard to keep the original figures and partial products in the mind, and I repeated the same products over and over again. Association became very slow and my mind wandered very much." Yet the errors made were actually fewer than at the beginning, although the time taken for each example was considerably increased. On March 4 she reports, "I feel excellent after the work and am not fatigued at all." On March 5, "This morning I did not feel so very enthusiastic about my experiments as I did yesterday. After work, I have a little headache and feel very weak." Yet by any test that can be applied, her actual efficiency on March 5 was greater than on March 4. So much for the value of introspections!

Miss Arai also persuaded eleven fellow-students to multiply mentally two-figure numbers by two-figure numbers for each of two periods of two hours separated by intervals ranging from 1 to 47 days. The averages of time per example for each successive ten minutes are given below:

	1	2	3	4	5	6	7	8	9	10	11	12
1st period .	98·7	97·7	95·9	99·3	101·4	76·2	94·8	96·4	92·2	95·9	86·4	74·7
2nd period .	69·9	65·5	70·4	74·1	67·3	76·5	68·5	79·8	72·4	65·3	73·2	69·4
Average .	84·3	81·6	83·2	85·2	84·4	76·4	81·7	88·1	82·2	80·6	79·8	72·1

The efficiency increased on the whole during the practices, since the time, after adding 10 seconds for each wrong figure, decreased from 84·3 to 72·1. Ten of the subjects were tested by ten-minute tests of the same function at the close of one or both periods after a rest of 10, 60, or 180 minutes. The ten-minute rest proved as good as sixty minutes, and the efficiency for all subjects improved on the average in the ratio of 121 to 100.

Starch and Ash,[1] as the task, used mental addition as described in Chapter XIII of his *Experiments in Educational Psychology* (1917 edition), where a partner announces a starting number consisting

[1] Starch and Ash, "The Mental Work Curve," *Psy. Rev.*, XXIV (1917), pp. 391–402.

of two digits. To this is added 6, then 7 to this new sum, and then 8 to that, then 9, and then again 6, 7, 8, and 9 in rotation. When the sum has reached 100 or more the hundreds digit is dropped and addition is continued with the two remaining digits. For example, if the number given by the partner were 80, then the consecutive sums would be 80, 86, 93, 101, 10, 16, 23, 31, etc. A new starting number is given every 30 seconds. The work was continued for two hours. The number of additions was only reduced from 14 to 13·4 and the number of errors did not increase.

The astonishing finding in all these experiments is that efficiency is decreased so slightly after prolonged periods of hard mental work.

Phases of the Fatigue Curve.—If uncomplicated by other factors, fatigue ought to cause regular decreases in efficiency. But on the contrary, quite apart from individual variations, the fluctuations of the fatigue curve are exceedingly irregular. Kraepelin, following Ebbinghaus, has analysed the fatigue curve and tried to reduce the chaos of the curve to a semblance of order. After examining a number of curves he concluded that the typical fatigue curve exhibited the following characteristics: (*a*) *An initial spurt.* This spurt (Antrieb) is due to will-power and interest. The subject starts the task with zest and enthusiasm, resulting in a rapid initial rise in the curve. (*b*) *A warming up, getting up steam* (Anregung). The initial spurt does not carry the subject very far; the subject has still to get into the real swing of the task. Hence the warming up, which occupies a considerable time, when the fatigue curve shows a steadily increasing efficiency. (*c*) *Familiarization* or *adaptation* (Gewöhnung). This is of a psychical rather than a physiological character. After the work has been going on for some time, the subject begins to see through it, to become familiar with its intricacies, which leads, together with the results of practice, to a fairly constant output of work. The curve, therefore, tends to remain fairly steady after the warming-up effects have disappeared. (*d*) *Spurts after fatigue and disturbance* (Ermüdungsantrieb and Störungsantrieb). However, the fatigue curve is never steady. It suffers from frequent depressions, due either to a temporary loss of interest or to distractions of some kind. At these points the curve takes sudden drops. The drops are always immediately followed by rises due to spurts. It is as if the subject, realizing that his work was waning, made renewed efforts to gain efficiency. (*e*) *End spurt* (Schlussantrieb). In spite of various spurts the subject declines in efficiency. There is the tendency towards a rapid rate of decline as the limit of endurance is approached. But the subject, realizing that the end is near, makes a last despairing effort, the result of which is a rise in the curve just before the end. Such a spurt may be compared with the fatigued horse which steps out better when nearing the stable. The end spurt is always followed by complete fatigue when all efforts to produce results are fruitless.

Thorndike [1] has subjected these findings of Kraepelin to a searching analysis. Taking all published data up to the year 1913, he has worked them over and failed to discover in them such phases as those described above. In other words, spurts, warming up, and adaptations, for the most part, are speculations rather than attested facts. Even such familiar expressions as "warming up" and "end spurt" have little experimental data to support them. If there is such a thing as warming up, it is accomplished very quickly, within a minute or so; and end spurts, where they occur, are characterized by such small increases as are represented by 2 to 4 per cent. As Thorndike states:

> "The most important fact about the curve of efficiency of a function under two hours or less continuous maximal exercise is that it is, when freed from daily eccentricities, so near a straight line and so near a horizontal line. The work grows much less satisfying or much more unbearable, but not much less effective. The commonest instinctive response to the intolerability of mental work is to stop it altogether. When, as under the conditions of the experiments this response is not allowed, habit leads us to continue work at our standard of speed and accuracy" (vol. iii, p. 69).

Chapman claims to have discovered evidence of an initial spurt when the work is calculated for such short intervals as two minutes, but his subjects only worked for sixteen minutes. It is conceivable that if the period had been several hours, then many two-minute periods would have been found that were just as productive as the first.

Reed,[2] using eight subjects, seven college students and himself, added five 2-figure problems from 7.30 in the morning to 5.30 in the afternoon, stopping 35 minutes at 12.15 for lunch. His results offered "no evidence either for initial or for end spurt, regardless of whether the intervals studied are one hour, ten minutes, or are one minute long."

In the same way a critical analysis of the data respecting the influence on the course of fatigue of such factors as age, sex, intelligence, season of year, time of day, day of week, position of body, and a score of others on which scattered data can be found, leads to conflicting and unsatisfactory conclusions.

[1] Thorndike, E. L., *Educational Psychology*, vol. iii, chap. iii.

[2] Reed, H. B., "Fatigue and Work Curve from a 10-hour Day in Addition," *J.E.P.*, XV, 6 (Sept. 1924), pp. 389–392.

Ventilation and Fatigue.—The effect of ventilation on mental efficiency is of more than academic interest to educators. Thorndike, McCall, and Chapman,[1] working under the auspices of the New York State Commission on Ventilation, carried out an elaborate series of tests upon the efficiency of students working under rigidly controlled experimental conditions. The sixty subjects were paid upon a commercial basis. The tests included colour-naming; cancellation of numbers; opposites; additions; mental multiplication of three-place number by three-place number; mental multiplication of a three-place number by two-place number; typewriting; grading specimens of handwriting; and grading English compositions. The conditions of the work-room were varied for temperature, relative humidity, movement of air, amount of CO_2, air supply per person, etc. Some of the conditions under which the subjects worked for four hours a day and for five consecutive days were worse than they would ever meet naturally. For example, working at a temperature of 86° F., a relative humidity of 80 per cent., with no circulation or change of air, is just about as strenuous a "climate" as can be imagined. Yet the results are positively startling:

"With the forms of work and lengths of period used, we find that when an individual is urged to do his best he does as much, and does it as well, and improves as rapidly in a hot, humid, stale, and stagnant air condition (86° F., 80 per cent. relative humidity, with no air or only recirculated air, and with no movement of air save what is caused by events in the room and, in the case of recirculation, by the recirculating force), as in an optimum condition (68° F., 50 per cent. rel. hum., 45 cu. ft. per person per minute of outside air introduced). . . .

"We find further that when an individual is given work to do that is of no interest or value to him and is deprived even of the means of telling how well he does do it, and is in other ways tempted to relax standards and do work of a poor quality, he still shows no inferiority in the quality of the product produced in stagnant air at 86°, 80 per cent. r.h. with 30 to 40 parts CO_2 per 10,000, he being subjected to this condition for 8 hours a day for four successive days, and tested on the second, third, and fourth days. There is some evidence that he spends more time on the work, but even this is not certain.

"Finally, we find that when an individual is left to his (or her) own choice as to whether he shall do mental work or read stories, rest, talk, or sleep, he does as much work per hour when the temperature is 75° as when it is 68°."

All of which shows that our ideas of mental fatigue need revising. Apparently we can, if we will, work as hard under

[1] Thorndike, McCall, and Chapman, *Ventilation in Relation to Mental Work*. T. C. Contributions to Education, No. 78, 1916.

adverse conditions of heat and humidity as under favourable ones. Even summer school in New York or Timbuctoo need not daunt us! What should be noted, however, is that these distressing conditions are uncomfortable, and if we subject children to them, the likelihood is that their attention will be distracted from work. At present, therefore, we shall be wise to make schoolroom conditions as comfortable as possible for the pupils, and especially should we pay attention to the circulation and movement of the air.

Fatigue in School.—From what has been said we should expect that so-called fatigue in school mainly resolves itself into boredom or lassitude. Measurements of the actual decreases in efficiency occasioned by the daily sessions in school show figures ranging from 1 to 5 per cent. instead of the 50 to 70 per cent. that many teachers suppose.

Winch [1] found that day workers attending evening schools, when tested with such tests as problem solving, computation, memorization, apparently lose one-sixth of their efficiency during the evening session. This is the greatest loss of efficiency shown by any study.

Thorndike [2] tested 240–700 pupils in the schools of Scranton and Cleveland and eliminated practice and novelty by never giving the same test twice. Using adding, multiplying, marking mis-spelled words on a page of print, memorizing lists of 10 digits, 5 nonsense syllables, 10 letters, and 6 simple forms, and testing the pupils at the beginning of the morning period and again at the end of the afternoon one, he found that they did substantially the same in the late afternoon as in the early morning. The results in percentages, counting the early morning tests 100, were as follows:

Multiplication: 99·3; mistakes 103·9.

Mis-spellings: Amount of page 99·0, words marked 105, words marked improperly 97·9.

Memorizing: All pupils 102.

Memorizing forms: 94·6.

Miss King tested 590 fifth-grade children at varying hours and obtained their total relative efficiency as follows:

9.30 a.m.	103
10.30 a.m.	98
11.30 a.m.	106
1.30 p.m.	92
2.30 p.m.	101

[1] Winch, W. H., "Some Measurements of Mental Fatigue in Adolescent Pupils in Evening Schools," *J.E.P.*, I (1910), pp. 13–22 and 83–100.

[2] Thorndike, E. L., "Mental Fatigue," *Psy. Rev.*, VII (1900), pp. 466–482 and 547–579.

These results, and also those obtained by Heck, Marsh, Ritter, Sikorski, and Friedrich, show that pupils, when given tests which interest them, do just about as well at the end of a school day as at the beginning. What troubles pupils in the afternoon is not fatigue, but boredom. If teachers could devise exercises for the afternoon sessions which enlisted the interest of their pupils, they would find that children could do them quite well, even though the tests were difficult.

Fatigue-Coefficients of School Subjects.—In elementary schools it is customary to place arithmetic in the first of the morning periods and to reserve such subjects as singing, shop-work and drawing for the afternoon periods. The theory underlying this arrangement is that arithmetic is more fatiguing than singing, and therefore ought to be taught when the pupils are freshest. As a matter of fact, we do not know the fatigue-coefficients of school subjects. German psychologists have attempted to find them, but their methods are unsound. Wagner, using the æsthesiometer, found, in the Gymnasium of Darmstadt, that the subjects could be arranged according to difficulty as follows:

Subject	
Mathematics (the standard)	100
Latin	91
Greek	90
Gymnastics	90
History and Geography	85
French and German	82
Natural History	80
Drawing and Religion	77

Kemsies, who used the dynamometer, found that gymnastics, given as a recreational treat, was the most fatiguing of all school subjects.

It is probable that the way subjects are taught has more effect than the content of subjects, some teachers being more fatiguing than others, or, at least, more boring. And it should be remembered that boredom may be just as effective in reducing the output of pupils as real fatigue.

Conclusion.—If this chapter proves anything, it is that the human body is awonderfully adaptive mechanism which, given a fair chance, will respond to demands made upon it in most surprising and gratifying ways. Mental fatigue, in the sense of loss of real efficiency, is difficult to achieve. There is little loss in efficiency after several hours of hard mental work. Unfavourable hygienic and other environmental conditions, at least for short periods of time, do not seriously reduce efficiency, providing we can ignore their obvious discomforts. Yet fatigue and boredom must have some biological significance. The most obvious explanation is that they serve as protective mechanisms. This seems to be true of the physiological aspects of fatigue, especially the fatigue of the synaptic connections of the central nervous system. But it may be, as Sherrington suggests, that fatigue also serves to give variety to behaviour, the unfatigued mechanisms getting a chance to act when the fatigued mechanisms cease to function. Even boredom may play a protective part by providing the preliminary warnings of the danger of excessive mental work. But as the facts of this chapter show, pupils and students are too prone to heed the first warnings. They might very well be encouraged to carry on, in the full knowledge that the first onset of boredom does not mean that their efficiency is hopelessly impaired.

References

ARAI, TSURU. *Mental Fatigue.* T. C. Contributions to Education, No. 54. New York, Columbia University, 1912. Pp. 115.

BINET and HENRI. *La fatigue intellectuelle.* Paris, Schleicher, 1898. Pp. 338.

CLAPARÈDE, ED. *Experimental Pedagogy and the Psychology of the Child* (tr. Louch and Holman). London, Arnold, 1911. Pp. viii+332.

EBBINGHAUS, H. " Ueber eine neue Methode zur Prüfung geistiger Fähigkeiten und ihre Anwendung bei Schulkindern," *Zeit. f. Psych.*, XIII (1897), pp. 401–459.

KRAEPELIN, E. " Die Arbeits curve," *Philos. Studien,* XIX (1902), pp. 459–507.

MARSH, H. D. "The Diurnal Curve of Efficiency." *Archives of Phil., Psy., and Sci. Methods,* No. 7. Columbia Univ. Contrib. to Phil. and Psy., XIV, 3.

MOSSO, A. *Fatigue.* Eng. tr. New York, 1904. Pp. 304.

OFFNER, M. *Mental Fatigue* (tr. G. M. Whipple). Baltimore, Warwick and York, 1911. Pp. viii+133.

SHERRINGTON, C. S. *The Integrative Action of the Nervous System.* New Haven, Yale University Press, 1923. Pp. xvi+411.

THORNDIKE, E. L. *Educational Psychology.* Vol. III. *Mental Work and Fatigue and Individual Differences and their Causes.* New York, Teachers College, Columbia University, 1914. Pp. x+408.

THORNDIKE, MCCALL, and CHAPMAN. *Ventilation in Relation to Mental Work.* T. C. Contributions to Education, No. 78. New York, Columbia University, 1916. Pp. 83.

WAGNER, E. *Unterricht und Ermüdung.* Berlin, 1898.

WHIPPLE, G. M. *Manual of Mental and Physical Tests.* Baltimore, Warwick and York, 1910. Pp. xix+534.

CHAPTER XIV

TRANSFER OF TRAINING: RECIPROCAL IMPROVEMENT IN LEARNING

The Problem.—The names given to the topic under discussion are numerous. Among them are to be found Mental Discipline, Formal Discipline, General Discipline, Formal Training, General Training, Transference of Training, Transfer of Training, and Reciprocal Improvement in Learning. The title selected for this chapter is, perhaps, as descriptive as any. The problem with which it is concerned, whatever its designation, is the following: How does the training of a specific function affect the efficiency of other mental functions? Does training or discipline acquired in one branch of learning carry over to other branches, both similar and diverse? If so, what is the extent of the transfer? Is the amount of transfer to one subject the same as to another? What is the mechanism of transfer? How does it take place?

More specifically we may ask if the reasoning power developed by mathematics will help us to reason better about such problems as Tariff *versus* Free Trade. Does the training in obedience that a pupil gets in school make him more amenable to the laws of the land or to the voice of his conscience? Is memory power so generalized that we are justified in spending considerable time and money on a course of memory training?

The belief in transfer is widespread. Laymen spend considerable sums on training courses for memory, will-power, initiative, and so forth. They want to become master-minds by short-cut methods. Nor are professional educators immune. Every course of study for elementary and secondary pupils is a testimony to the schoolman's belief in formal discipline. Especially do educators believe in the disciplinary virtues of Latin, mathematics, and grammar. These subjects are regarded as giving the pupil a desirable body of useful knowledge, and are also considered to be pre-eminent in strengthening the intellect.

Prior to 1900 the faith in formal discipline was announced unashamedly, but to-day, while the belief still affects our programmes of study, most educators are careful to disclaim such doctrines.

Thorndike, in 1903, collected quite a number of quotations from well-known authors which expressed the profoundest faith in the transfer of training. Excerpts from a few of these are given below:

> "Arithmetic, if judiciously taught, forms in the pupil habits of mental attention, argumentative sequence, absolute accuracy, and satisfaction in truth as a result, that do not seem to spring equally from the study of any other subject suitable to this stage of instruction" (J. Payne, *Lectures on Education*, vol. i, p. 264).
>
> "The value of the study of German 'lies in the scientific study of the language itself, in the consequent training of the reason, of the powers of observation, comparison, and synthesis; in short, in the upbuilding and strengthening of the scientific intellect'" (C. Thomas, *Methods of Teaching Modern Languages*, p. 27).
>
> "We speak of the 'disciplinary' studies—having in our thought the mathematics of arithmetic, elementary algebra, and geometry, the Greek-Latin texts and grammars, the elements of English and of French or German. . . . The mind takes fibre, facility, strength, adaptability, certainty of touch from handling them, when the teacher knows his art and their power" (W. Wilson, *Science*, Nov. 7, 1902).
>
> "Since the mind is a unit and the faculties are simple phases or manifestations of its activity, whatever strengthens one faculty indirectly strengthens all the others" (R. N. Roark, *Method in Education*, p. 27).

The teachers of Latin have been loath to accept the conclusions of the experimental investigations on the transfer of training, and as late as 1915 Lodge could write: "Far above every other subject it (Latin) trains (1) the process of observation, (2) the function of correct record, (3) the reasoning power and general intelligence in correct inference from recorded observation. To this should be added its great value in developing the power of voluntary attention" (Lodge, G., in *Principles of Secondary Education*, ed. P. Monroe, p. 388). The Classical Investigation under the chairmanship of A. F. West, which should have been a dispassionate inquiry into facts, degenerated into a disgraceful exhibition of special pleading.[1] Their report virtually suppressed certain important scientific investigations which did not support their prejudiced views.

[1] See especially West, A. F. (editor), *Value of the Classics*, Princeton University Press, 1917.

Psychologists themselves are not free from taint. Is not Stern's one of the most widely accepted definitions of intelligence that we have? "Intelligence is a general capacity of an individual consciously to adjust his thinking to new requirements; it is general mental adaptability to new problems and conditions of life." Here we have a belief that reactions and knowledge learned in one situation can be transferred to another. This paradox of teachers and psychologists inveighing against transference on the one hand, and tacitly accepting it on the other, must be resolved.

The difficulties with the transfer of training are exactly those which confronted us when we discussed heredity and environment. The Latinists point with triumph to the number of prime ministers and other notables who were produced by the Oxford "Greats." But may it not be a case of selection rather than of training? These were clever men who showed their cleverness not only in acquiring Latin for Greats, but also later in life in their various vocations. Latin was a selecter of these men; nature produced them. If science instead of Latin had been their traditional study, then science would have seemed to produce them. That cookery and carpentry do not seem to produce eminent men and women may be due to their poor selective qualities. Cookery and carpentry can, without a doubt, be done successfully at a lower mental age level than mathematics and Latin. In other words, more people can do cookery and carpentry well than Latin and mathematics. This is the justification of vocational trade schools for boys and girls of slightly inferior intellect. These children cannot succeed with the traditional professional curriculum of the secondary schools and universities, but they can succeed with the manual subjects of a trade school. This is not a plea for class distinctions, but a plain common-sense support of democratic education, where every child is given the best possible education he is capable of receiving irrespective of the wealth or poverty of his parents.

The problem of this chapter, therefore, is to try to resolve some of these difficulties. But before presenting the experimental evidence which denies the extravagant claims of many of the proponents of general training, a brief survey of the history of the doctrine will be given.

History of the Doctrine of Mental Discipline.—To the Greeks there could hardly have been a problem of transfer, since everything transferred. The mind (soul) was an indivisible whole, and everything that affected a part affected the whole, much in the same way as the whole of a gas balloon is affected by pressing in one side. Nevertheless, Plato subscribed to the doctrine that some subjects were more effective than others, " that where a ready reception of any kind of learning is an object, it will make all and every difference whether the pupil has applied himself to geometry or not " (Book VII, *Republic*).

The indivisible mind of the Greeks gradually became a mind divided into faculties. Thus great divisions arose such as memory, observation, judgment, reasoning, concentration, attention, quickness, etc., which stood for elemental abilities which are the same no matter what material they worked upon. Hence the faculty of memory enabled us to memorize everything, faces as well as words. Anything that was memorized strengthened memory as a whole. In the same way observation in general was improved by making any kind of specific observations. Doubt was first cast upon the unity of a faculty when at least one of them, memory, was seen to be composed of independent parts. In some illnesses or through accident one part of memory was retained and another part lost. Teachers, however, still believed in faculties and acted upon their belief. Children, for example, were given object-lessons in order to develop their powers of observation, and were made to attend to minute differences in grammatical construction so that their powers of attending to everything else might be improved. The truth of the doctrine was never questioned, yet careful observation for five minutes would have shown them its falsity. Darwin, for example, was one of the best observers of natural phenomena that ever lived, yet he tells us that as a young man he visited Wales without observing any of the abundant signs of glaciation. Visiting the country some years later, having in the meantime read Lyell's *Geology*, the marks of glaciation, such as perched blocks, scratched and rounded rocks, pot-holes, and the like, literally forced themselves on his attention. Even Darwin had not a faculty of observation but several powers of observation, each apparently independent of the others.

Thus the question stood when James, using himself as the subject, experimented on the training of memory.

" I have tried to see," he tells us, " whether a certain amount of daily training in learning poetry by heart will shorten the time it takes to learn an entirely different kind of poetry. During eight successive days I learned 158 lines of Victor Hugo's *Satyr*. The total number of minutes required for this was $131\frac{5}{6}$—it should be said that I had learned nothing by heart for many years. I then, working for twenty-odd minutes daily, learned the entire first book of *Paradise Lost*, occupying 38 days in the process. After this training I went back to Victor Hugo's poem, and found that 158 additional lines (divided exactly as on the former occasion) took me $151\frac{1}{2}$ minutes."

This result so astonished him that he suggests that fatigue may have hindered the second batch of Victor Hugo. Nevertheless, he persuaded four other persons to attempt similar experiments, with the result that three of them showed gains and one a loss. The gains and losses were very slight. (This experiment has since been repeated by Peterson with two subjects, one of whom showed a loss, the other a gain (*Psy. Rev.*, XIX (1912), pp. 491–2).)

After some rather dubious experiments by Gilbert and Fracker on transference in reacting to various sensory stimuli (1897), Thorndike and Woodworth enter on the scene. In their experiments they used an improved, though far from perfect, methodology, since the trained and untrained groups were not equated either for ability or preliminary skill. The object of the investigation [1] was the determination of the transference due to practice in estimating areas, lengths, weights, and in various forms of observation or perception upon slightly different forms. Thorndike has summarized the results in *Educational Psychology*, II, pp. 397–398, as follows:

"Individuals practised estimating the areas of rectangles from 10 to 100 sq. cm. in size until a very marked improvement was attained. The improvement in accuracy for areas of the same size but of different shape due to this training was only 44 per cent. as great as that for areas of the same shape and size. For areas of the same shape, but from 140–300 sq. cm. in size, the improvement was 30 per cent. as great. For areas of different shape and from 140–400 sq. cm. in size, the improvement was 52 per cent. as great.

"Training in estimating weights of from 40–120 grams resulted in only 39 per cent. as much improvement in estimating weights from 120–1800 grams. Training in estimating lines from 0·5 to 1·5 inches long (resulting in a reduction of error to 25 per cent. of the initial amount) resulted in no improvement in the estimation of lines 6–12 inches long.

"Training in perceiving words containing *e* and *s* gave a certain amount of improvement in speed and accuracy in that special ability. In the ability to perceive words containing *i* and *t*, *s* and *p*, *c* and *a*, *e* and *r*, *a* and *n*, *l* and *o*, mis-spelled words and A's, there was an improvement in speed of only 39 per cent. as much as in the ability especially trained, and in accuracy of only 25 per cent. as much. Training in perceiving English verbs gave a reduction in time of nearly 21 per cent., and in omissions of 70 per cent. The ability to

[1] Thorndike and Woodworth, "The Influence of Improvement in one Mental Function upon the Efficiency of other Functions," *Psy. Rev.*, III (1901). (1) Plan and Conclusions of Study, and Area Test, pp. 247–61 (May). (2) The Estimation of Magnitudes, pp. 384–95 (July). (3) Functions involving Attention, Observation, Discrimination, pp. 556–564 (November).

perceive other parts of speech showed a reduction in time of 3 per cent., but an increase in omissions of over 100 per cent.

They concluded that:

"Improvement in any single mental function need not improve ability in functions commonly called by the same name. It may injure it."

"Improvement in any single mental function rarely brings about equal improvement in any other function, no matter how similar, for the working of every mental function-group is conditioned by the nature of the data in each particular case."

"The general consideration of the cases of retention or loss of practice effect seems to make it likely that spread of practice occurs only where identical elements are concerned in the influencing and influenced functions."

James had gently disturbed people by his inadequate experiment. Thorndike and Woodworth, owing to the extended and careful nature of their experiments, cast a veritable bombshell into the educational camp. An age-long tradition was challenged. The educational world was immediately up in arms. Scores of experiments were designed to confirm or refute these findings. Some typical experiments will be synopsized later in this chapter. Suffice it to say at this point that Thorndike and Woodworth had given the doctrine of formal discipline, at least in its extreme forms, a death-blow. Discipline or transference there is, but it is much less than is usually supposed. Common sense ought to teach us that a thing so difficult to discover as transference can neither be so common nor so big as popular opinion believes it to be.

The Technique of Experimentation on Transfer.—For a perfect experiment on transfer four equivalent groups are essential. By equivalent groups we mean groups of pupils which are equal in number, similar in age, of same average I.Q.'s, same sex, same grade, same present ability in the function to be tested, and similar in any other trait as far as it is relevant to the experiment. Such equivalent groups are so difficult to obtain that most investigators are content if their groups are only approximately equal in some of the less essential qualities. Let us suppose that the experiment is to study the effect of memorizing digits on the memorization of poetry, and that we have obtained four equivalent groups: A, B, C, D. The groups A and C are "practice groups," since these are given a defined amount of practice in memorizing digits. B and D are the control groups, and are given no practice. All four groups are tested with poetry at the beginning and again at the end of the experiment, but with this difference—the initial and final test pieces for A and B are the reverse of those given to C and D. This ensures that if one of the test pieces is harder than the other, the averaging of results from the two pairs of groups will cancel out the error. Schematically, the arrangement is as follows:

Equivalent groups.	Preliminary poetry test.	Practice in memorization.	Final poetry test.	Gains (im provement).
A (Practice)	I	Memorizes digits	II	A over B
B (Control)	I	No memorization	II	
C (Practice)	II	Memorizes digits	I	C over D
D (Control)	II	No memorization	I	
			Average Gain	

The average gain, representing transfer effects, may be positive, zero, or negative, in which cases the training would be regarded as helpful, neutral, or hindering, respectively. Other details which should be noted are: (1) that the preliminary and final tests should not be too long; (2) that the practice periods should be adequate to produce effects; and (3) (very important) that the gains should preferably be computed in terms of the variabilities of the scores of the initial and final tests. For this purpose the standard deviation (S.D.) of the distributions is the best measure of variability to use.

Variations of this scheme are easily introduced. For instance, instead of a single preliminary or final test several may be used. Instead of allowing groups B and D to have no practice, practices with different material may be introduced. If the initial and final tests consist of well-standardized material with alternative forms, then groups C and D can be dispensed with.

As an illustration of a variation in technique we shall synopsize Gates's study of reading reactions.[1] The subjects were three classes at each of the levels, Grades III, IV, V, and VI, *i.e.* twelve classes in all, in the Horace Mann School. The preliminary and final tests, by means of which the amount of transfer was measured, consisted of the following seven tests:

1. Thorndike-McCall Scale for Ability to Understand Paragraphs.
2. Monroe's Standardized Silent Reading Test, Revised.
3. Courtis Silent Reading Test. Understanding of Paragraphs.
4. Courtis Silent Reading Test. Rate. Score is number of words read per minute.

[1] Gates, A. I., "A Critique of Methods of Estimating and Measuring the Transfer of Training," *J.E.P.*, XV, 9 (Dec. 1924), pp. 545–558.

5. Word Perception Test, consisting of twenty-four blocks of words, of which the easiest and hardest follow :

Hat	Sat Pot	Rat	Bat	Hat
Magnificent	Mountainous Distinction Magnifficant	Everlasting Magnificent Illustrious	Magnifersant Merchandise Measurement	Appointment Maggnifsunt Composition

The task is to select and underline the word in the group which is the same as the word in the margin. This test was constructed to measure the speed and accuracy of the mechanical operations of word perception. Score is number of exercises done correctly.

6. Cancellation of Unlike Groups of Digits. This test consists of rows of pairs of numbers, mainly five digits each. The task is to cancel each number which is not identical with the number with which it was paired. Score is the number of groups attempted minus three times the number of errors.

7. Picture-naming Test. A page containing clear outline drawings of seventy familiar objects, such as hat, watch, bite. The task is to write the names of the objects under the pictures as rapidly as possible. Score is number correct.

Tests 5, 6, and 7 form the basis of the analysis of the control group technique.

The three groups in each of the four grades were given the following training: Group I was taught by the Paragraph-Question method (P.Q.), which consisted in reading ten minutes daily as rapidly as possible mimeographed passages for the purpose of answering questions placed below, calling for the main ideas. Group II was taught by the Oral-Recitation method (O.R.), which consisted in reading materials from selected books for three minutes followed by two minutes' oral recitation ; then three minutes' reading and two minutes' recitation, a total of ten minutes daily, the same as the P.Q. group. The practice period covered a little more than a month, although the total number of days' work put in by all members of each group, because of absences, was usually less than twenty. Group III, the control group, was given no special training.

Improvement was computed in terms of multiples of the standard deviations of the distribution of ability in the initial tests. The gains from specific practice, results of all four grades combined, were as follows : P.Q. reading, scored in terms of number of questions correctly answered, 2·45 S.D. ; P.Q. scored in terms of number of lines read, 3·33 S.D. ; and the O.R. reading, scored in terms of number of lines read 4·63 S.D. The results are given in Table XXV and the interpretations in Table XXVI.

Tests.		Average S.D. gains.			Average S.D. gains minus control group gains.		P.Q. gains surpass O.R. gains by
		P.Q.	O.R.	Control.	P.Q.	O.R.	
Thorndike-McCall . .	Mean	0·72	0·55	0·27	0·45	0·28	0·17
	P.E.	0·035	0·047	0·030	0·047	0·054	0·073
Monroe Comprehension	Mean	0·76	0·56	0·31	0·45	0·25	0·20
	P.E.	0·054	0·082	0·072	0·078	0·109	0·133
Monroe Rate . . .	Mean	0·68	0·53	0·45	0·15	0·08	0·07
	P.E.	0·061	0·087	0·081	0·10	0·12	0·15
Courtis Comprehension	Mean	0·62	0·62	0·29	0·33	0·33	0·00
	P.E.	0·041	0·080	0·026	0·05	0·08	0·10
Courtis Rate. . . .	Mean	0·75	1·69	0·55	0·20	1·14	0·94
	P.E.	0·110	0·240	0·047	0·13	0·25	0·24
Word Perception . .	Mean	0·51	0·60	0·33	0·18	0·27	0·09
	P.E.	0·040	0·029	0·041	0·056	0·05	0·07
Picture naming (writing)	Mean	0·52	0·45	0·40	0·12	0·05	0·07
	P.E.	0·047	0·061	0·034	0·059	0·068	0·09
Cancellation. . . .	Mean	0·33	0·35	0·30	0·03	0·05	0·02
	P.E.	0·016	0·017	0·021	0·027	0·028	0·039

TABLE XXV.—S.D. gains for all grades combined, together with the P.E. of the Means (from Gates).

Results of specific training shown at top of each column with transfer values below :

P.Q. scored by number Q.'s correctly answered, average all grades=2·45 S.D.	P.Q. scored number lines read, comprehension disregarded, all grades=3·33 S.D.	O.R., scored by number lines read, comprehension disregarded, grades IV, V, VI=4·63.
Thorndike-McCall, scored as above, gain =9·45 S.D. or 18·4 per cent. of specific improvement.		Thorndike-McCall, scored by number Q.'s correct, results for same grades as above, gain =0·34 or 7·30 per cent.
Monroe Comprehension, scored as above, gain =0·45 S.D. or 18·4 per cent.		Monroe Comprehension, scored by number Q.'s correct, results for grades above, gain =0·14 S.D. or 5·2 per cent.
	Monroe Rate, scored as above, gain = 0·15 S.D. or 4·5 per cent.	Monroe Rate, scored as above, same grades as above, gain=0·00 S.D. or 0 per cent.

Courtis Comprehension, scored as above, gain =0·33 S.D. or 13·4 per cent.		Courtis Comprehension, scored by number Q.'s correct, same grades as above, gain=0·32 S.D. or 7 per cent.
	Courtis Rate, scored as above, gain=0·20 or 6·0 per cent.	Courtis Rate, scored as above, same grades as above, gain=1·03 S.D. or 22·2 per cent.
Average gain, comprehension measures=16·7 per cent.	Average gain, rate tests =5·25 per cent.	Gain, rate tests, Courtis only=22 per cent. Average gain, comprehension tests=5·2 per cent.

TABLE XXVI.—Results of Table XXV arranged to yield the fairest comparison of relative gains.

On the whole the P.Q. method of training children to read, in which practice is given in gaining meanings from what is read, produces better results so far as transfer values are concerned. But the transfer values, even when the practice is somewhat similar to the initial and final tests, are low. The variability of the figures also show that reading is not a unitary function, an ability to be learned in general, but a form of reaction in which the number of types to be acquired is great. And each one, in the main, has to be specially developed.

Some of the gains in reading tests are not all due to the training given in reading, but are partly due to general improvement from practice with tests. This is a real transfer and always makes the apparent transfer from training greater than it should be. Gates, by making these allowances for improvement in factors not intrinsically reading abilities, and measuring them by the Word Perception, Cancellation, and Picture-naming tests, showed that the transfer values shown in Table XXVI were all too high. The average gains, for example, of the first column by these allowances should be reduced from 16·7 to 12 per cent.

Gates also showed how the technique of partial correlations could be used in interpreting the transfer effects, but as this is somewhat removed from the main thesis of the chapter, the reader is referred to the original article.

Experimental Data on Transfer.—The number of experiments on transfer of training is very great. Before giving a general summary, a typical research in a selection of the fields which have been investigated will be described.

(*a*) *Cross Education.*—The term " cross education " was given by Scripture to the special transfer of skill from one side of the body to a symmetrical part on the other side. Training the left hand to grip more strongly, for example, leads to an increase in the strength of grip of the right. The subject has been investigated by Volkmann (1858, discrimination of two-point threshold); Fechner (1858, writing); Scripture (1894, speed, force, and accuracy of movement); Woodworth (1899, hitting a dot with pencil); Swift (1903, tossing balls); Starch (1910, tracing six-pointed star); and others.

Woodworth [1] practised his left hand in hitting a dot with a pencil and studied the effect it had upon the right. In terms of the errors made, the results were as follows:

	Hitting at a rate per minute of		
	40.	120.	200.
Left Hand: Before training	3·5	4·2	8·3
After "	0·4	3·8	7·2
Right Hand: Early test	3·1	3·9	7·1
Late "	0·7	3·8	6·6

There is an improvement of the right hand which is equal to about 50 per cent. of that of the left.

In cross education the transfer is not a general transfer to all parts of the body but a specific transfer to a symmetrical part of the body. Such transfer effects, of course, cannot be used in support of the doctrine of formal discipline, although the transfer from one side of the body to the other is always positive and always high, running in some cases to as much as 80 per cent. Woodworth was inclined to believe that the chief reason for his improvement was the training given to the eyes in fixating the point.

But it should be remembered that the same portion of the cerebral hemisphere (left for right-handed persons) is concerned with skilled movements from either hand. Since some of the neural connections from the left and right sides are different, the transfer is never perfect. If training of the right hand transferred to the right or left foot the argument for transfer would be strengthened, but even this result would have to be interpreted with caution, since there are so many avenues by means of which the transfer could take place.

(*b*) *Memory*.—The chief experiments on transfer of memory training have been those of James (reported earlier in the chapter);

[1] Woodworth, R. S., "The Accuracy of Voluntary Movement," *Psy. Rev. Mon. Suppl.*, No. 13.

Ebert and Meumann (1904, effect of training in memorizing nonsense syllables on other forms of memorization); Dearborn (1906, repetition of Ebert and Meumann's series without the intervening practice); Fracker (1908, memorizing the order of four different intensities of the same tuning-fork and finding amount of transfer in memorizing poetry, order of four greys, geometrical figures, two-place numbers and the like); Winch (1908, effect of memorizing poetry upon memorization of history and descriptions of places; 1910, effect of memorization of meaningful and meaningless materials upon meaningful material); and Sleight (1911). As Sleight's experiments are the most extensive and careful that have been made, we select them for a more extended mention.

Sleight [1] directed his attention to the problem of the effect of memorizing poetry, tables, and prose substance upon other forms of memorizing.

The first set of experiments had as subjects 84 girls in Standard VI (about Grade VII) of average age 12 yrs. 8 mos. These subjects were divided into four approximately equivalent groups. Group 1 was untrained, taking only the ten tests; Group 2 was trained in learning poetry such as *Hiawatha*, *Skylark*, and *The Cloud;* Group 3 was trained by learning multiplication, pence, and metric tables of all kinds, squares, vulgar fractions with their decimal equivalents, etc.; and Group 4 was trained with "prose substance"—scientific, geographical, and historical—by reading selections to them and having them write out the gist as well as they could remember it.

The series of ten tests included:

(1) Points in circles. Children reproduced the positions of points in a circle drawn on a card and exposed six times for one second. Each child, therefore, made six attempts.

(2) Dates. Dates and corresponding events were learned orally, then children wrote date when event was announced.

(3) Nonsense syllables. Eight syllables exposed singly in succession five times.

(4) Poetry. Stanzas of 8–12 lines were used.

(5) Prose. Short literary extract. Verbatim learning.

(6) Prose substance. Children wrote substance of a piece of prose read twice to them.

(7) Map test. Trained in location of names on a large mercator map and then marked places on their own smaller ones.

(8) Dictation. Continuous prose dictated in portions gradually increasing from 8 to 19 words.

[1] Sleight, W. G., "Memory and Formal Training," *Brit. Jour. Psy.*, IV (1911), pp. 386–457.

(9) Letters. Sixteen series of consonants gradually increasing from 4 to 8 letters were dictated.

(10) Names. Forty-four common Christian and surnames in combinations of 2, 3, and 4 were used.

These ten tests were given at the beginning, middle, and end of a period of training, which lasted for 720 minutes spread over six weeks.

The results are shown in summary form in Table XXVII.

Groups compared.	Points.	Dates.	Nonsense.	Poetry.	Prose verbatim.	Prose substance.	Map.	Dictation.	Letters.	Names.	Average.
Superiority of Group 2 (practised in poetry) over Group 1 (unpractised) . . .	21	19	66	−31	−14	−22	50	−31	−5	−3	9
Superiority of Group 3 (practised in Tables) over Group 1 . .	48	−12	85	−9	−5	7	1	−10	1	−14	5
Superiority of Group 4 (practised in prose substance) over Group 1 . . .	23	−12	8	0	21	31	13	0	−2	17	10

TABLE XXVII.—Superiority of the practised groups (2, 3, and 4) over the unpractised group (1). (Subjects, children, after Sleight.)

The second set of experiments was conducted with a group of women normal school students of average age 18–19. Six of the ten tests were given before and after the period of training. The summarized results are given in Table XXVIII.

Groups compared.	Tables.	Nonsense.	Poetry.	Prose verbatim.	Prose substance.	Letters.	Average.
Group 2 (practised in poetry) compared with Group 1 (unpractised) . . .	32	33	33	9	−7	−24	13
Group 2 (practised in Tables) compared with Group 1 . .	59	9	−27	−36	49	−3	8·5
Group 3 (practised in prose substance) compared with Group 1 . . .	−6	−62	−7	−17	52	27	−2

TABLE XXVIII.—Superiority of the practised groups (2, 3, and 4) over the unpractised group (1). (Subjects, women students, after Sleight.)

Tables XXVII and XXVIII show conclusively: (1) that training in one kind of memorizing may affect other kinds either favourably or unfavourably. Practice with prose substance, for example, greatly improved the learning of prose substance but affected adversely the learning of nonsense syllables; and (2) considering that the practice with the ten tests led to an average gain of 52 points (not shown in Tables) the transfer effects shown in the Tables (5, 9, and 10; average 8, in Table XXVII; and 13, 8·5 and −2; average 6·5, in Table XXVIII) are remarkably small.

In general it may be said that the transfer effects of memorization range generally between 5 and 15 per cent. Sometimes it is less than 5 per cent. and occasionally has turned out to be negative.

(*c*) *Sensori-motor Learning.*—The chief experiments on sensori-motor learning have been carried out by Bergstrom (1894, card-sorting); Blair (1902, succession of typewriter keyboards in which six of the keys had been changed from letters to symbols); Angell and Coover (transfer effects from card sorting to type-writing); Scholckow and Judd (1908, hitting target placed in water); Coover (1916, card sorting); and Webb (1917, transfer effects in learning mazes—rats and humans).

The experiment of Scholckow and Judd [1] represents a variation in transfer experimentation. They taught one group of boys the principles of refraction and left another group without such knowledge. They investigated the influence of this knowledge on learning to hit a target under water. The practice began with the target 12 inches below the surface of the water, which, later, was changed to 4 inches. The groups were equally slow in acquiring facility when the target was at a depth of 12 inches, but when the depth was reduced to 4 inches the group which had been given a theoretical explanation of refraction soon outdistanced the untutored group. As we shall see later in the chapter this experiment has influenced Judd's explanation of the mechanism of transfer.

(*d*) *Discriminative Judgments.*—Among the investigations of the transfer of improvement in situations involving discriminative judgment the best are those of Thorndike and Woodworth (1901, previously cited); Judd (1902, Müller-Lyer illusion); Bennett (1907, colours); Angell and Coover (1908, brightnesses); Kline (1909, effect of cancelling *e*'s and *t*'s on cancellation of nouns, verbs, prepositions, pronouns, and adverbs); Whipple (1910, visual perception); and Foster (1911, drawing objects and

[1] Judd, C. H., "The Relation of Special Training to General Intelligence," *Educational Review*, XXXVI (1908), pp. 28–42.

pictures presented visually for 10 to 60 seconds). Kline[1] found that practice in crossing out *e*'s and *t*'s on pages of prose hindered the cancellation of nouns, verbs, prepositions, pronouns, and adverbs. In other words, the general gain in efficiency from practice in eye-fixations, marking pages, and attention was more than offset by the confusion effects caused by the change of task. The average gains of the practised and unpractised groups were 1·8 and 3·3 respectively.

(*e*) *Neatness.*—This aspect of school work has been studied by Squire (1905, neatness in arithmetic papers to neatness in language and spelling papers); and Ruediger (1908, does ideal of neatness, brought out in connection with, and applied in, one school subject function in other school subjects?). Squire found that neatness developed in arithmetic did not transfer to language and spelling papers. Ruediger reported that an ideal of neatness seemed to transfer to some extent.

(*f*) *Grammar.*—This favourite of the formal disciplinarians has been studied by Hoyt (1906, grammar to composition); Briggs (1913, formal grammar *versus* work in composition on ability to check plurals, judge definitions, etc.); and Starch (1915, formal grammar and English usage). The general results may be summed up in Hoyt's words, "The teaching of grammar is of little avail in strengthening one's ability to use language." Starch, however, notices that "study of foreign languages materially increases a pupil's knowledge of English grammar but only slightly increases his ability in the correct usage of the English language."

(*g*) *Arithmetic.*—Transfer from training in arithmetic has been studied by Winch [1910, "rule examples" (chiefly computation) to reasoning in arithmetic]; and Starch (1911, mental multiplication upon other arithmetical processes). Starch[2] used eight subjects in his training group and seven in his control group. The practice consisted of multiplying mentally a three-figure number by a one-figure number, doing 50 problems a day for 14 days. His results are given in Table XXIX. The transfer effect was found to be about 26 per cent. of the gain in the practice series itself.

[1] Kline, L. W., *Some Experimental Evidence on the Doctrine of Formal Discipline*. Bull. of the State Normal School, Duluth, Minn., Feb. 1909.

[2] Starch, D., "The Transfer of Training in Arithmetical Operations," *J.E.P.*, II (1911), pp. 209–213.

Abilities tested.	Trained persons.	Untrained persons.	Differences.
Adding fractions	40	12	28
Adding three-place numbers . . .	49	10	39
Memory span for numbers . . .	−3	−2	−1
Subtracting numbers	58	35	23
Multiplying four-place numbers . .	53	29	24
Memory span for words	3	−5	8
Multiplying two-place numbers . .	47	10	37
Dividing three-place numbers . .	45	25	20
Average, exclusive of memory span .	49	20	29

TABLE XXIX.—Transfer of training from mental multiplication to other arithmetical operations (Starch).

(*h*) *Latin.*—Latin has been the subject of a large number of studies on transfer effects. Among them may be cited : Swift (1906, Latin *versus* German on progress in learning Spanish) ; Perkins (1914, the effect of emphasizing the derivation of English words from Latin upon the efficiency of Latin instruction) ; Harris (1915, effect of Latin on ability to spell English words) ; Partridge (1915, Latin on marks in English obtained in the Regents Examination) ; Starch (1915, Latin *versus* German on progress of students through the university) ; Starch (1917, Latin *versus* native ability on English composition) ; Dallam (1917, Latin on English) ; College Entrance Board Examinations (1917, Latin on rating in examination) ; Wilcox (1917, Latin *versus* school records before Latin was begun) ; Foster (1917, Latin on English spelling) ; Thorndike (1923, Latin *versus* non-Latin on knowledge of English) ; Thorndike and Ruger (1923, Latin *versus* non-Latin on growth in English) ; Briggs and Miller (1923, standards of English obtained in translations of Cicero) ; Coxe (1923, Latin on spelling of English words of Latin derivation) ; and Hamblen (1924, Latin *versus* non-Latin on knowledge of English ; also on effectiveness of emphasis on English words of Latin derivation).

The general trend of the findings, considering the common content of much of the English and Latin, is that the transfer is much smaller than the Latinists have claimed, the amounts almost invariably ranging below 20 per cent. Perkins [1] made a study of the effect of emphasizing the derivation of English words from Latin words in the instruction in Latin given to pupils of a commercial course. His two equivalent groups

[1] Perkins, A. S., " Latin as a Vocational Study in the Commercial Course," *Classical Journal*, X (1914), pp. 7–16.

were pupils in second year of Latin, and pupils in the second year of a modern language. The six tests used were spelling, use of words in sentences, definitions and parts of speech, meanings of words and spelling, excellence of vocabulary, and meanings of words and spellings. The results were as follows :

	Averages.	
	Latin per cent.	Non-Latin per cent.
Jan. and Feb., 1914.		
1. Spelling	82·5	72·6
2. Use of words in sentences . .	57·5	40·6
3. Definitions and parts of speech .	69·5	33·3
4. Meaning of words and spelling .	57·0	27·5
5. Excellence in vocabulary . . .	36·0	6·8
June, 1913.		
6. Meaning of words and spelling .	63·3	12·3
Averages	61·3	32·18
Difference	29·12 per cent.	

The difference is impressive. If, however, we turn to the examples of words used in the tests we find in (1) such words as valedictory, competition, occurrence, benevolence, and legible; and in (2) impediment, advocate, reference, anticipate, and subside. These words undoubtedly favour the Latin pupil although the words for (3) taken from *The Tale of Two Cities*, and those for (6) taken from Franklin's *Autobiography* and *Silas Marner* may not have done so. However, the lists used are not given. The real weakness of the investigation is failure to calculate improvement made on a second test when compared with the initial one. Moreover, equating pupils on scores in Latin and in a foreign language may not have secured truly equal groups, since the standards of the two examinations may have been, and probably were, different.

(*i*) *Geometry*.—The chief study in this field is Rugg's doctorate dissertation.[1] The subjects were 326 students in the College of Engineering of the University of Illinois. A group of 78 students in other colleges served as a control group. Five tests

[1] Rugg, H. O., *The Experimental Determination of Mental Discipline in School Studies*. Baltimore, Warwick and York, 1916.

were used: 1, arithmetic; 2, arithmetic; 3, imaging letters; 4, painted cube test; and 5, geometrical objects. Thus tests 4 and 5 were strictly geometrical, 3 was quasi-geometrical, and 1 and 2 were non-geometrical. The residual differences in the five tests between the training and control groups were: —1·10, 15·78, 19·4, 14·0, and 48·5 respectively. From which Rugg concludes:

> The study of descriptive geometry (under ordinary classroom conditions throughout a semester of 15 weeks) in which such natural and not undue consideration is given to practice in geometrical visualization as is necessary for the solution of descriptive geometry problems operates:
>
> (1) Substantially to increase the students' ability in solving problems requiring the mental manipulation of a geometrical nature, the content of which is distinctly different from the visual content of descriptive geometry itself.
>
> (2) Substantially to increase the students' ability in solving problems requiring the mental manipulation of spatial elements of a slightly geometrical character (point, line, and plane).
>
> (3) Substantially to increase the students' ability in solving problems requiring the mental manipulation of spatial elements of a completely non-geometrical nature (no lines or planes).
>
> (4) The training effect of such study in descriptive geometry operates more efficiently in those problems whose visual content more closely resembles that of the training course itself.

But it should also be noted that one-third of the students showed no transfer effects, and that the gain in the geometrical tests was four times greater than in the strictly non-geometrical ones.

(*j*) *Science.*—A very good study of transfer in power of observation in science to observation in general was made by Miss Hewins.[1] The subjects were 34 boys and 50 girls taking first year botany in high school. These were divided into two equivalent groups. The practice was confined to botanical observation and recording. The initial and final tests were partly biological, partly non-biological. The gains in scores are shown in the following table:

[1] Hewins, Nellie P., *The Doctrine of Formal Discipline in the Light of Experimental Investigation*, 1916.

	Biological tests.	Non-biological tests.
Practised Groups:		
Boys	8·06	8·97
Girls	6·41	6·20
Average	7·23	7·58
Unpractised Groups:		
Boys	3·03	5·37
Girls	−1·24	5·60
Average	0·89	5·48
Residual difference between practised and unpractised groups	6·34	2·10
Percentage gains	33·9	5·4

Median score in biological tests in Series I before practice	18·7
" " non-biological " " "	39·0

Making allowances for gains due to practice, the transfer effects are 5·4 per cent. for non-biological and 33·9 per cent. for the biological tests.

Summary of Experimental Findings.—An analysis of all the available material on transfer leads to the following conclusions:

(1) The transfer effect of training may be negative, zero, or positive. It is usually positive, but the amounts are usually much nearer to zero than to 100 per cent.

(2) If the transfer effect is considerable, it is invariably found that the contents (or methods of presentation) of the testing and training materials have many elements in common.

(3) There is little ground for the belief that the intellect secures an all-round training from the specific training of any part of it.

Thorndike's Crucial Investigation.—The rapid improvement of intelligence tests has enabled Thorndike to return to the problem of transfer, which, as we have seen, greatly interested him in youth. His studies, entitled "Mental Discipline in High School Studies," [1] have brought us nearer to a solution of the problem than any other. For his initial and final tests he used alternative forms of the I.E.R. Tests of Selective and Relational Thinking. For his practice series he used a year of normal schooling. Thus the children were unaware that they were acting as subjects.

[1] Thorndike, E. L., "Mental Discipline in High School Studies," *J.E.P.*, XV, 1 and 2 (Jan. and Feb. 1924), pp. 1–22, 83–89.
Broyler, Thorndike, and Woodward, "A Second Study of Discipline in High School Studies," *J.E.P.*, XVIII, 6 (Sept. 1927), pp. 377–404.

In tests made one year apart the subjects, of course, make higher scores at the second attempt than at the first. Some of this improvement is due to increasing familiarity with the tests, some to the studies that they had pursued in the interval. As these subjects had varied, Thorndike, by first equating pupils in initial attainments and then analysing out the contributions of each subject to any improvement which was found in the final scores, could calculate the transfer effects of any given study. For instance, if two pupils of equal initial ability studied subjects A B C D X and A B C D Y respectively, then the difference in the final scores could be attributed to the differing influences of X and Y. When several hundred students are found, who only differ by X and Y in their courses, the averaging of results gives a high degree of reliability to the findings.

For his subjects Thorndike used 8564 high school pupils in grades 10, 11, 12. Summarizing the study he states :

" Our procedure was to discover by a rough method certain studies which were of about average influence, and then to compare students who took any given study with students of equal intelligence who took one of these studies of average influence (or nothing) in place of it. For example, representing one of these studies of average influence by I, representing civics, economics, psychology, or sociology by II, representing biology or agriculture by III, representing arithmetic or bookkeeping by IV, and representing geometry, algebra, or trigonometry by V, we compared the gains of pupils taking I, II, III, and IV with the gain of pupils taking V, II, III, and IV. The influence of taking V is thus compared with the influence of taking I. . . .

" Our studies of ' about average influence ' (which were in fact a trifle below average influence) were business, drawing, English, history, music, shop, and Spanish. The symbol I represents any one of these.

" The difference in gain between a pupil taking a given subject and a pupil of the same sex and the same ability in the initial test of intelligence who took I or nothing in place of it, was as follows :

For arithmetic or bookkeeping	(IV)	+2·92
For chemistry, physics, or general science	(IX)	+2·64
For algebra, geometry, or trigonometry	(V)	+2·33
For Latin or French	(VI)	+1·64
For physical training	(T)	+0·66
For civics, economics, psychology, or sociology	(II)	+ ·27
For dramatic art	(D)	−0·29
For cooking, sewing, stenography	(VIII)	−0·47
For biology, zoology, botany, physiology, or agriculture	(III)	−0·90
For manual training	(M)	insufficient data

" The unit is a little over 4 per cent. of the average gain from the first test to the retest. It is about one-tenth of the difference between the gain in a year of an average white pupil in high school and the gain in a year of an average coloured pupil in high school in a western city. The superiority in gain due to taking the highest study over taking the lowest is thus about two-fifths of the superiority in gain during one year of the average white over the average coloured high-school pupil. Expressing the above differences as deviations from their own average we have :

For arithmetic or bookkeeping	(IV)	+1·94
For chemistry, physics, or general science	(IX)	+1·66
For algebra, geometry, or trigonometry	(V)	+1·35
For Latin or French	(VI)	+0·66
For physical training	(T)	−0·32
For civics, economics, psychology, or sociology.	(II)	−0·71
For dramatic art	(D)	−1·27
For cooking, sewing, stenography.	(VIII)	−1·45
For biology, zoology, botany, physiology, or agriculture . .	(III)	−1·88
For manual training	(M) ”	

These results are in pronounced opposition to the traditional view that mathematics and Latin train pupils to think better than other branches of the curriculum. Bookkeeping and science are much superior. But the transfer effect of any subject is quite small.

“ If,” as Thorndike states, “ our inquiry had been carried out by a psychologist from Mars, who knew nothing of theories of mental discipline, and simply tried to answer the question, ‘ What are the amounts of influence of sex, race, age, amount of ability, and studies taken, upon the gain made during the year in power to think, or intellect, or whatever our stock intelligence tests measure ? ’ he might even dismiss ‘ studies taken ’ with the comment, ‘ The differences are so small and the unreliabilities are relatively so large, that this factor seems unimportant.’ The one causal factor which he would be sure was at work would be the intellect already existent. Those who have the most to begin with gain the most during the year. Whatever studies they take will seem to produce large gains in intellect.”

In the second study an additional 5000 pupils were tested. Averaging the results of both studies in the order of subjects, we find :

Subject.		1922–23.	1925–26.	Average.
Algebra, geom., trig.	(V)	+2·33	+3·64	+2·99
Civics, econ., psy., sociol.	(II)	+0·27	+5·50	+2·89
Chem., physics, gen. sci.	(IX)	+2·64	+2·77	+2·71
Arith. and bookkeeping	(IV)	+2·92	+2·28	+2·60
Physical training	(T)	+0·66	+1·00	+0·83
Latin, French	(VIII)	+1·64	−0·07	+0·79
Cooking, sewing, stenog.	(VIII)	−0·47	+0·19	−0·14
Biol., zool., bot., phys., agric.	(III)	−0·90	+0·60	−0·15
Dramatic art	(D)	−0·29	−0·67	−0·48

The claims of mathematics are seemingly sustained, but Latin sinks in the scale. Combining the two we get 1·89, which is only 1·81 greater than the average of physical training (T), cooking and sewing (VIII), and dramatic art (D).

The transfer gains, however, play such a small rôle, when compared with the native intelligence of the pupil, that Thorndike is forced to the following conclusion :

"By any reasonable interpretation of the results, the intellectual values of studies should be determined largely by the special information, habits, interests, attitudes, and ideals which they demonstrably produce. The expectation of any large difference in general improvement of the mind from one study rather than another seems doomed to disappointment. The chief reason why good thinkers seem superficially to have been made such by having taken certain school studies, is that good thinkers have taken such studies, becoming better by the inherent tendency of the good to gain more than the poor from any study. When the good thinkers studied Greek and Latin, these studies seemed to make good thinking. Now that the good thinkers study Physics and Trigonometry, these seem to make good thinkers. If the abler pupils should all study Physical Education and Dramatic Art, these subjects would seem to make good thinkers. These were, indeed, a large function of the program of studies for the best thinkers the world has produced, the Athenian Greeks. After positive correlation of gain with initial ability is allowed for, the balance in favour of any study is certainly not large. Disciplinary values may be real and deserve weight in the curriculum, but the weights should be reasonable."

Theories of Transfer.—As a result of their experiments in 1901, Thorndike and Woodworth concluded "that spread of practice occurs only where *identical elements* are concerned in the influencing and influenced functions." Later, these identical elements were called identities of substance (matter) and identities of procedure (method). Geography helps history because maps are common to both. Addition improves multiplication because multiplication is largely addition. French helps German because the methods of study used in the two languages have the common element of hunting up words in a dictionary. Writing and spelling, learned in connection with any subject, transfers to all others in which writing and spelling are used. All study helps all other study in so far as it involves learning the habit of sticking to a task for an hour or two at a time. In this sense Bagley's third identity (ideal or aim) can be conceded. The ideal of work, for example, may transfer from the intellectual tasks of the winter time to the chores of wood chopping and painting boats which confront us in summer time at the country cottage.

This theory of identical elements is a perfectly reasonable one. Out of the millions of specific reactions, each with its specific connection in the nervous system, some of them are bound to be common to several situations. The greater the number of these common elements, the greater will be the transfer effect.

A second theory of transfer, stoutly maintained by Judd,[1] is that of *generalization of experience.* A few quotations will be given to show the trend of his argument.

" Trained intelligence is particular in its content but general in its method. It is characteristic of human thinking that wherever one encounters any phenomenon one tends to interpret it in terms of general categories."

" The human power of generalization is so intimately related to the evolution of language that the two cannot be thought of as existing separately. Words are records of generalization, and their use implies the power to apply to new experiences the established classifications expressed in language."

" The unfortunate effect of the use of such words as ' discipline ' and ' transfer ' is that prejudices have been created which in reality have no bearing on the main issue. The student of psychology should keep his mind fixed on the real problem and should use all these terms only in so far as they help him to formulate and answer the question : How does the education which the pupil receives in school affect his subsequent thinking and conduct ?

" If there is any one who asserts that mathematics or Latin or science will train the general powers of discrimination or observation or reasoning, that person is wrong. If, on the other hand, any one asserts that all training is particular, that the mind is made up of many independent special modes of thinking, that person is just as wrong as his opponent.

" There is no guaranty in its content that any subject will give general training to the mind. The type of training which pupils receive is determined by the method of presentation and by the degree to which self-activity is induced rather than by content. It is not far from the truth to assert that any subject taught with a view to training pupils in methods of generalization is highly useful as a source of mental training, and that any subject which emphasizes particular items of knowledge and does not stimulate generalization is educationally barren."

" A study of scientific methods powerfully reinforces the general concept of organization which is expounded by the *Gestalt* psychologists. ' Scientific method ' is a name for a mode of thinking which is so general that it becomes impossible to think of it as a single item of experience."

" When the ends thus described are attained, transfer of training, or formal discipline, has taken place because it is the very nature of generalization and abstraction that they extend beyond the particular experiences in which they originate."

[1] Judd, C. H., *Psychology of Secondary Education*, 1927, chap. xix.

At first glance the theories of Thorndike and Judd seem to be hopelessly at variance. Further consideration, however, shows that the identical elements in Judd's generalization may be the specific habits of language engendered by the process. Language is, *par excellence*, the medium by means of which knowledge can be transferred from one situation to another; it is the grand "short-circuiter" of learning. And the language need not be vocal; the sub-vocal variety used in thinking is just as effective.

For example, a teacher of mathematics in all kinds of mathematical situations—algebraic and geometrical problems—trains his pupils to ask themselves, "Is this a new problem? If it is, what must be done to turn it into a form with which I am familiar?" Every new problem must be twisted into the form of an old problem whose solution is already known; otherwise, it can never be solved. Now this generalization in the form of a language habit is applicable to every mathematical situation. It is the way that mathematicians are made. But a further step can be taken. The teacher may show that the principle—the new must always be solved or interpreted in terms of the old—is of universal applicability. In so far as this extension is made mathematics may be said to have a general disciplinary value far beyond the confines of the subject itself. Its disciplinary value, however, resides in the formation of specific language habits which have applicability to other, non-mathematical situations. Judd's generalization of experience, therefore, on analysis resolves itself into nothing more nor less than the formation of specific language habits having applicability to situations other than those in which they were learned. Since the effective use of language is limited to those who are intellectually endowed, the clever people, as Thorndike found, will benefit more from any kind of an education than those to whom this gift is denied.

Educational Implication of the Experimental Findings.—If the transfer effect or disciplinary value of a subject is as small as it has been proved to be, then curricula for schools will have to receive their sanction on other than disciplinary grounds. No longer shall we be able to introduce Latin, or mathematics, or science into the course of studies and defend our actions on disciplinary grounds. As a matter of fact, the great interest in curriculum study found on the North American continent was stimulated by the experiments on transfer. If transfer proves to be a broken reed, then studies whose content is socially useful must be emphasized. Hence the purging of courses of study of elements which were palpably unpractical and unsuited to present-day civilization. Hence the job analyses.

whose object was to determine the frequency of use in life situations of certain skills and forms of knowledge. If cube root is not used by one in a million once in a lifetime, it must be cast out of the course in arithmetic and something more useful substituted for it. This movement, which is leading to valuable improvements in curricula, may, however, go too far. Greek cannot be defended as a universal study on disciplinary grounds, but Greek culture has played such an important part in the history of mankind, that a few choice spirits should certainly be encouraged to study the language. A distinction should, therefore, be drawn between the common minimum which all should acquire, and the variations which can be superimposed on this minimum. Life is varied, and our schools, which are a part of this varied life, should reflect its richnesses. Not only do we require different types of schools, but also a variety of studies within these schools. Over-narrowness in types of school and subjects of study must be sedulously avoided. The preservation of a nice balance between minimum essentials and the variety which adds spice to life is the task of the administrator.

Secondly, experiments in transfer show that the transfer is greatest when common elements are involved. Man, through language habits, has developed a tool of transfer which is denied to all sub-human species. Judd's generalization of experience, as we have seen, is merely the acquirement of language habits. Hence the method of teaching children becomes of greater importance than the subjects used to teach them. Teachers should be trained to present their material in such a way that wide transfers of language habits are assured. The difference between good and bad teaching is a matter of method rather than content.

Thirdly, studies and methods of study may affect the emotional as well as the intellectual life of the pupil. Little is known about emotional spread—the effect of studies in interests, prejudices, attitudes, and ideals—but in the aggregate it is probably very great. As Thomson [1] pertinently remarks: "As a child grows up he develops ways of looking at the world, and ways of reacting to situations; he grows up into a conservative or a radical, a solicitor or a plumber, an atheist or a Wesleyan Methodist, a patriot or a cosmopolitan, and the difference between these are not merely differences in skill or in knowledge or in power of reasoning, not merely differences in the integration of knowledge into science, but also in the integration of the feelings and emotions into sentiments,"

[1] Thomson, G. H., *Instinct, Intelligence, and Character*, p. 147.

References

BALLARD, P. B. *The Changing School.* London, Hodder & Stoughton, 1925. Pp. xi+332.

BROYLER, THORNDIKE, and WOODWARD. "A Second Study of Mental Discipline in High School Studies," *J.E.P.*, XVIII, 6 (Sept. 1927), pp. 377–404.

GATES, A. I. *Psychology for Students of Education.* New York, Macmillan, 1924. Pp. xvi+489.

GATES, A. I. "A Critique of Methods of Estimating and Measuring the Transfer of Training," *J.E.P.*, XV, 9 (Dec. 1924), pp. 545–558.

HECK, W. H. *Mental Discipline and Educational Values.* New York, Lane, 1919. Pp. 147.

HEWINS, NELLIE P. *The Doctrine of Formal Discipline in the Light of Experimental Investigation.* Baltimore, Warwick & York, 1916. Pp. viii+120.

JUDD, C. H. *Psychology of Secondary Education.* Boston, Ginn, 1927. Pp. xiv+545.

JUDD, C. H. "The Relation of Special Training to General Intelligence." *Educational Review*, XXXVI (1908), pp. 28–42.

KLINE, L. W. *Some Experimental Evidence on the Doctrine of Formal Discipline.* Bull. of the State Normal School, Duluth, Minn., Feb. 1909.

MEUMANN, E. *The Psychology of Learning.* New York, Appleton, 1913. Pp. xix+393.

PERKINS, A. S. "Latin as a Vocational Study in the Commercial Course," *Classical Journal*, X (1914), pp. 7–16.

PYLE, W. H. *The Psychology of Learning.* Baltimore, Warwick & York, 1921. Pp. 308.

RUGG, H. O. *The Experimental Determination of Mental Discipline in School Studies.* Baltimore, Warwick & York, 1916.

SKINNER, GAST, and SKINNER. *Readings in Educational Psychology.* New York, Appleton, 1926. Pp. xxvii+833.

SLEIGHT, W. G. "Memory and Formal Training," *Brit. Jour. Psy.*, IV (1911), pp. 386–457.

STARCH, D. "The Transfer of Training in Arithmetical Operations," *J.E.P.*, II (1911), pp. 209–213.

STARCH, D. *Educational Psychology.* New York, Macmillan, 1927. Pp. ix+568.

THOMSON, G. H. *Instinct, Intelligence, and Character.* New York, Longmans, 1925. Pp. 282.

THORNDIKE, E. L. *Principles of Teaching.* New York, Seiler, 1906. Pp. xii+293.

THORNDIKE, E. L. *Educational Psychology.* Vol. II. *The Psychology of Learning.* New York, Teachers College, Columbia University, 1921. Pp. xi+452.

THORNDIKE, E. L. "Mental Discipline in High School Studies," *J.E.P.*, XV, 1 and 2 (Jan. and Feb. 1924), pp. 1–22, 83–98.

THORNDIKE and WOODWORTH. "The Influence of Improvement in one Mental Function upon the Efficiency of other Functions," *Psy. Rev.*, VIII (1901), pp. 247–261, 384–395, 556–564.

WOODWORTH, R. S. "The Accuracy of Voluntary Movement," *Psy. Rev. Mon. Suppl.* No. 13, 1899.

CHAPTER XV

THE MEASUREMENT OF IMPROVEMENT: EDUCATIONAL TESTS

The Problem Stated.—The teacher's task is to make certain changes (improvements) in pupils, chiefly changes in their knowledge, skill, and attitudes. When he wishes to learn if he has been successful or not he examines or tests them in some way. Sometimes his test is very informal, as when he questions the children orally; sometimes it is more formal, as when written replies are required. But whether formal or informal, the examination is designed to measure the changes, if any, that have been made in pupils by educational procedures. The success of the teacher is measured by his success in producing these changes; indeed, there is no other way by which his success can be measured. But some will object and say that the most important changes induced by education cannot be measured. The changes in character, for example, the most precious of all the changes, resist every attempt at measurement. While all this may in a way be granted, yet measurements of these elusive traits are continuously being made by teachers, only they are unreliable and unverifiable ones. Thus the teacher who says that character cannot be measured, will unhesitatingly affirm that Tommy is more truthful or more reliable than Johnny. And the person who says that Shakespeare is a better dramatist than Shaw has measured the dramatic abilities of these two persons in some way or other. Measures of this kind, which we call personal opinions, are always lacking in precision. The art of examining is to measure the changes more accurately and reliably. If the change is one of knowledge, as in learning geography and history, the object is to find out either how much the pupil knows, or how difficult a question he can answer. If the change is one in skill, as in arithmetic, writing, spelling, algebra, and typewriting, the object of the examination is to discover how well the pupil can do it. This may be done by discovering what standard of quality can be reached by the pupil, or how accurately and rapidly he can do it. If the change is one of appreciation or taste, as in literature and the other arts, the object of the examination is to learn to what extent these powers have been developed. Whatever their form, or by whomsoever given, examinations are designed to measure changes made in pupils. The more accurately, reliably, and economically this is done, the better is the examination.

Functions of Examinations.—Written examinations of the essay type fulfil three functions. They serve to measure more or less exactly the educational achievements of pupils. They act as incentives or motivating agents. They provide a training for the pupil in written composition.

The part that examinations play as incentives to effort on the part of teachers and pupils has been severely criticized, but incentives seem to be inseparable elements of any test. To know that one's knowledge or skill is to be judged from the results of a forthcoming examination stimulates both teachers and pupils to put forth their best efforts in teaching and learning. Public opinion at present demands that the tests be made. What should concern the examiner, whether he be a teacher or public official, is that the examinations are fair and properly conducted.

As a training in written composition, examinations of the essay type are undoubtedly valuable. The ability to make clear, unambiguous statements is a useful accomplishment for anybody, and written examinations undoubtedly develop this art. It may be questioned whether examinations develop this ability to as great an extent as composition lessons in class, but in any case, they certainly develop a facility in writing against time.

But it is as a measure of achievement that examinations must be judged. If this function is not fulfilled properly, they carry their own condemnation. The essay type of examination has been most severely criticized on the ground of unreliability of its measurements. Its inherent weaknesses have led to much experimentation with other forms of examinations, so much so, that the essay type is now generally referred to as the *old type* in contradistinction to the objective which is now termed the *new type* examination.

Types of Examinations.—Examinations are of many kinds. There is the *informal test* which the teacher conducts, usually orally, to find out how the pupils are progressing in a subject. Although weak and unreliable as a measuring instrument, it seems destined to have a long life in the class-room because of its convenience. Yet little or nothing has been done to improve the form of the informal test or to develop the principles which underlie its technique. The informal oral test, which is more of a teaching than a testing device, is being rapidly replaced by informal objective tests, whose items are prepared and accumulated by the teacher over a number of years. Through repeated use, the teacher can discover the relative value of each item and what started out as an informal may become in time a somewhat precise measuring instrument.

The more *formal examinations*, which are never oral, are of three main types:

(1) The essay type of examination.
(2) The standardized test or scale.
(3) The objective or new type examination.

These will now be given a somewhat extended analysis.

The Essay Type of Examination.—The essay type is the traditional type. Requiring the pupil to make his statements in clear, logical language, it fills a place that objective examinations can never fill. In asking pupils to "compare," "discuss," "explain," "give reasons for," etc., the essay type provides a valuable form of training which the newer forms of examination omit altogether. It is, however, difficult to evaluate. This difficulty arises from the fact that factors like composition, neatness, arrangement of subject-matter, spelling, and handwriting, besides actual knowledge of subject-matter, are introduced into the evaluation and make it unreliable. If any reader has doubts on this point let him try the following experiment: First mark a series of fifty papers of the essay type, putting the scores on a separate sheet. Two weeks later mark the papers again and compare the two sets of scores. If they are marked on a percentage system, they are sure to disagree; in fact, an examiner whose two sets of marks correlate as highly as 0·80 may consider himself better at his job than the average. But more objective evidence of unreliability can be adduced.

(*a*) In the English Department of the University of Toronto, the same subject was set for an essay in different years. An essay which had secured a mark of 80 in one year was copied by a student in another year and handed in as his work. The mark given to it the second time was 39.

(*b*) The writer, in his final examinations in psychology, has been in the habit of dividing the paper into two parts. One part consists of the usual type of question, the other a new type objective test. He was interested to discover the relative contributions of intelligence, ability in composition, and knowledge of subject-matter to the final mark given in the essay part of the examination. Using the technique of partial and multiple correlations and ending with the prophecy equation known as the regression equation, he found :[1]

$$x_1 = 1{\cdot}92x_2 + 0{\cdot}49x_3 + 0{\cdot}26x_4$$

where x_1=mark on essay type of examination,
x_2=composition,
x_3=knowledge of psychology,
x_4=general intelligence.

In other words, the best prediction that can be made for x_1, given x_2, x_3, and x_4, is obtained by weighing composition four times as heavily as knowledge of subject-matter. No doubt the reader will be feeling superior, and quite sure that his marks are not so insecure as the writer's appear to be. He is, however, advised to test himself out. His findings may be quite as disturbing as the writer's were. If the investigation had been extended to the influence of neatness, handwriting, and spelling on the final mark, it would, no doubt, have been found to be considerable for each of them. It may, therefore, be said without fear of contradiction that a score for an answer to an essay type of question is a composite of marks given for knowledge of subject-matter, composition, neatness, handwriting, spelling, and the like. It may be that this is what teachers think it ought to be, but if so, they should know what proportion is assigned for each element.

(*c*) It is the writer's custom, when trying to show his students the unreliability of subjective marks, to write a sample of handwriting on the blackboard and ask them to score it on a percentage basis. The lowest range of marks obtained in ten years is 45.

(*d*) State matriculation examinations are always carefully conducted, yet such things as the following are always cropping up :

After two weeks of examining, when a Physics paper was passed around and marked by the various associate examiners in Toronto, the range of marks was from 50 to 70, where 60 was the pass mark.

A paper in Honour Matriculation History was scored 50 (60 less 10 for misspellings) by the examiners. This paper was untidy, illegible, and badly spelled, yet as a history paper it had some merit. It was copied out in fair handwriting and the mistakes in spelling corrected, but all other mistakes were retained. The rewritten paper was again sent to the examiners and scored by them as a new paper. The mark given to it this

[1] See article, "The Use of Partial Coefficients of Correlation in Educational Research," a paper read at the meeting of the British Association for the Advancement of Science at Toronto, August, 1924. Printed in *The School*, Toronto, 1925, XIII, pp. 845–853.

second time was 70 (70 less 0 mistakes for mis-spellings). We can only conclude that the examiners were influenced in giving 10 marks less than it apparently deserved by its general untidiness and illegibility. They had, however, been instructed not to deduct marks for any of these extraneous factors except spelling, and for this a maximum of 10 marks was the limit.

Wood [1] studied the algebra and geometry examinations of the College Entrance Examination Board for June, 1921.

"About 400 algebra and an equal number of geometry papers selected at random were scored each twice independently by two different readers of the Board. The correlations between the first and second scorings were very high for both algebra and geometry, about 0·98 and 0·96. In spite of this almost perfect objectivity in the scoring, however, the reliabilities of the examinations themselves were very low. The correlation between random halves of the algebra examination was found to be only 0·61, and that between random halves of the geometry examination only 0·41. By the use of Brown's formula, the reliability of the whole algebra examination is estimated as not greater than 0·76, and that of the geometry examination as not greater than 0·58.

"The meaning of these reliability coefficients may be made clearer by consideration of an hypothetical case closely resembling the actual situation faced by the Board in giving college entrance examinations.

"Let us suppose that 10,000 candidates are tested with Form A of a given geometry examination whose reliability is about 0·60, and that 30 per cent. of the 10,000 fail. Now let us suppose that the same 10,000 are tested, with another equivalent geometry examination, say Form B, whose reliability is also 0·60, and which fails 30 per cent. of the candidates.

"If the reliability of the two forms of the examination were 1·00, the same 3000 would be failed by both forms; but with a reliability of only 0·60, the agreement on failures would be as follows in gross numbers:

Failed Form A. Passed Form B. 1279	Passed on both Forms. 5721
Failed on both Forms. 1721	Passed Form A. Failed Form B. 1279

"In other words, accepting the results of one examination as valid, which was done by the Board in 1921, another equivalent examination

[1] Wood, B. D., *Measurement in Higher Education*, Yonkers-on-Hudson, World Book Co., 1923, pp. 124–126.

would pass 1279 of the 3000 failed by the first, and would fail 1279 of the 7000 passed on into college by the first."

(*e*) Ruch [1] got 91 teachers to grade three answers to geography questions each on a scale of 20. The range for answer 1 was 2–20; for answer 2, 0–2; for answer 3, 20. Similarly, three entire history papers taken from a seventh-grade class in American history were mimeographed and sent to 115 teachers, who graded each on a scale of 100. The ranges were 70–100, 45–90, and 25–85.

These confirm the findings of Starch and Elliott, who found the range of marks for an English paper (142 examiners) to be 64–98; for a second English paper, 50–98; for a geometry paper (118 examiners), 28–92; and for a history paper (70 examiners), 43–90.

Illustrating this same point we have the following humorous incident told by Wood [2]:

"The facts of a subjective scale are well illustrated in the following anecdote concerning the grading of history papers by a group of college professors of history in the summer of 1920. One of the five or six expert readers assigned to a certain group of history papers, after scoring a few, wrote out for his own convenience what he considered a model paper for the given set of ten questions. By some mischance this model fell into the hands of another reader who graded it in a perfectly *bonâ fide* fashion. The mark he assigned to it was below passing, and, in accordance with the custom, this model was rated by a number of other expert readers in order to ensure that it was properly marked. The marks assigned to it by these readers varied from 40 to 90."

These vagaries of markings are not due to the incompetence of the examiners, but to the type of examination, the essay type, which was set. No mark that depends on the subjective judgment (opinion) of an examiner can ever be reliable. To get reliability the form of the examination must be changed. However, by the adoption of the following devices, the reliability of subjective markings may be increased:

(1) Get rid of the idea that 100 per cent. means perfection. It means exactly what the examiner thinks it means and nothing else.

(2) Get rid of the idea that a 60 per cent. pass mark is like a law of the Medes and Persians, which altereth not. It alters

[1] Ruch, G. M., *The Improvement of the Written Examination*, Chicago, Scott Foresman & Co., 1924, pp. 56–62.

[2] Wood, B. D., "Measurement of College Work," *Educational Administration and Supervision*, VII (Sept. 1921), pp. 301–304.

from hour to hour; and does not mean the same thing before lunch as after lunch. The pass mark in the United States is generally 75 per cent.; in Ontario 60 per cent.; but this does not mean that Ontario standards are lower than those of the United States. Hundreds of candidates in the Mathematical Tripos Examination at Cambridge University have been placed among the wranglers, although they made fewer than 10 per cent. of the marks on the whole examination. As a matter of fact, in the long history of this examination only one candidate has ever succeeded in making more than 40 per cent. on it.

(3) Mark about 20 papers. Select one of average value and use it as a standard, referring to it again and again. Arrange papers, as they are marked, above and below this standard, placing them in piles which differ from the piles above and below them by just perceptible differences in quality. Assign a mark (say 70) for the average paper and add (or subtract) two three, or four marks to each succeeding group, arranging the scale so that the total range is from about 50 to 90. Those below 60 fail. This is simply a device for turning a subjective mark into an objective one. In State examinations a similar result is achieved by setting up objective standards for each part of the examination. In the long run, it would be better to change the form of the examination to some objective type than to try to reduce the variability of the marks by any of these refinements.

A further criticism that may be levelled against the essay type of examination is that the standards, even in State examinations, vary from year to year. The results given below show the percentages of failure in Algebra on College Entrance Board examinations from 1916 to 1921.

Algebra.	1916.	1917.	1918.	1919.	1920.	1921.
Percentages of failure . .	61·8	36·7	25·3	61·3	26·1	28·5

Since the students from year to year would reach about the same level of achievement, these results show that there either was a variation in the difficulty of the examination, or that the standards of marking varied, or that both variabilities were present.

In universities the same variability of standards in essay type examinations is perennially present. Meyer found that the professors of Latin, elocution, and chemistry in the University of Missouri had never failed a single student in five years, while the Professor of English had failed 28 per cent. in the same period. Foster found that the Professor of Greek in Harvard gave 25 per cent. of the students A's, while the Professor of English, presumably teaching the same students, gave A's to

1 per cent. only. This variability would be measurably reduced if we set up a standard of distribution of marks which each teacher should try to approximate. Any of the following six distributions may be followed, but no teacher should be expected to do more than approximate any of them. The pass mark is assumed to be 50 per cent

Six Schemes of distributing Marks in Essay Type Examinations.

Marks.	Percentage obtaining marks.					
	I.	II.	III.	IV.	V.	VI.
Below 40			2	5	2	4
40–49	4	7	14	15	8	10
50–59	24	24	34	30	23	22
60–69	44	38	34	30	34	28
70–79	24	24	14	15	23	22
80–89	4	7	2	5	8	10
90–100					2	4
Percentage failing	4	7	16	20	10	14

So far the essay type of examination has been criticized because of the inability of the examiner to score the answers fairly. This unfairness creeps in because a rating based upon subjective opinion must be used. There is no escape from it only in so far as an "objective" technique of scoring is substituted for a subjective one. Since this substitution can never be made 100 per cent. perfect a certain unreliability always remains. But *a second weakness due to limited sampling* must be considered. The usual essay type of examination consists of five to ten questions, that is, of an intensive sampling of five to ten portions of the course of study. It is easily possible for a student to know a great deal about a given subject without being able to answer the particular sampling of it selected by the examiner. A second sampling by the same examiner may yield totally different results, because the second set of questions, as we say, "suits the student." This limited sampling of the traditional examination leads pupils and teachers to try to "spot" the questions. They know from experience that a careful study of the questions set in a subject over a period of ten years is very helpful, since examinations tend to become stereotyped. Examiners get into a rut and ask questions about the same parts of a subject time after time.

Ruch and Stoddard [1] have made clear some of the assumptions underlying examination construction of the essay type. The teacher should bear in mind that:

(1) Any examination is a limited sampling.

(2) The actual questions selected depend in part upon the teacher's point of view at the moment.

(3) The actual lot of questions drawn up will ordinarily yield a different average mark, a different range of marks, and different individual marks from those of a second set of questions by the same teacher at a different time, or by a different teacher handling the same course.

(4) If a teacher made up two sets of ten final examination questions and gave both examinations to the same class, the results, pupil by pupil, will not agree in their numerical statements or even in the rank orders of the pupils on the two examinations.

(5) Other things being equal, the longer the examination (in terms of numbers of questions or of actual working time), the more valid and reliable the results.

(6) The statement of a pupil's mark as 85 per cent. can at best mean merely that he answered 85 per cent. of the questions asked; never that he knows 85 per cent. of the subject, since he probably was not examined over more than 5 per cent. to 20 per cent. of the subject-matter.

(7) The possible errors in ascertaining the pupil's accomplishment by means of an examination will be further complicated by the personal equation of the reader of the paper.

(8) With a few-question examination, errors due to absences of the pupil from school, misunderstanding of the phrasing of a question, etc., will tend to be larger than in the many-question examination with its wider sampling.

The Standardized Test and Scale.—A standardized test, as its name implies, is one that has been standardized with respect to giving and scoring and for which representative norms of known accuracy and reliability have been secured. A standardized scale is used to describe a test in which the scale element, the measuring instrument used in describing the performance of pupils, is the characteristic and distinguishing feature. But the two terms, "test" and "scale," are used somewhat indiscriminately. It is usual to speak of handwriting and composition scales, but of history and geography tests. It should, however, be remembered that any good test is scaled accurately, that is, the increments of difficulty between two successive items of a test are equal at all parts of the scale.

The problem of representative norms is not an easy one

[1] Ruch and Stoddard, *Tests and Measurements in High School Instruction*, pp. 258–259.

First of all we should know what norms to secure. The most usual are those for age, grade, sex, and race. Age norms are better than grade norms, because age is a more constant factor than grade. Sex differences are usually so slight that in most subjects they can be neglected, but where there seems to be a constant difference, as in the superiority of boys over girls in history, separate norms must be secured. Race norms should be more frequently obtained than is now customary, since there is a considerable body of evidence indicating that different racial groups give different average results on tests. These results may be due to differences in opportunity or to real differences in native ability. It can also be shown that locality, motivation, methods of teaching and practice, affect norms. It is better, therefore, to obtain several sets of norms than a single set, but each of them should be as representative as possible. At present, it is futile to expect one set of norms to be applicable, say, to all pupils of the North American continent. In such subjects as the fundamentals of arithmetic, spelling, and reading, the norms of standardized tests may have wide applicability. In such subjects as history and geography their range of applicability is bound to be narrow.

A standard differs from a norm. It represents the score which a pupil is expected to make, while a norm is the median score that a sample group actually makes on a test. The standard to be set must take into account the whole programme of the pupil—at home as well as at school. Usually, however, the norm is considered as the standard to be achieved.

The New Type Examination.—The new type examination represents the teacher's attempt to rid his tests of the weak features inherent in the traditional examination. The new type test resembles a standardized test in its construction, but lacks its norms. It is essentially a classroom test devised by the teacher to measure the achievement of his pupils. Being a flexible instrument, it can be made to fit any school situation and its findings can be used for grouping pupils, for grading pupils and marking them, for finding the central tendency and variability of the group, and for diagnostic purposes. It is especially useful to the teacher who wishes to make a rapid survey of the work covered in a course. Of all the tests yet devised it best satisfies the criteria of validity, reliability, etc., which any good examination should satisfy.

The outstanding characteristic of the new type examination is that it is objective rather than subjective ; it is uninfluenced by the idiosyncrasies of examiners. This desirable state of affairs is reached—

(1) By having all answers to the questions (items) either right or wrong. Partial credits are never given.

(2) By drawing up directions for giving and scoring the test so carefully and explicitly that nobody can misunderstand them. No judgment need be exercised. In colloquial language, they are "fool-proof"; the wayfaring man, though a fool, need not err therein.

(3) By simplifying the marking of the test. Any normal child of twelve could score a new type test accurately if he were provided with the necessary directions and key.

(4) By getting rid of such disturbing factors as neatness of arrangement, quality of handwriting, skill in composition, spelling, and punctuation. The pupil is required to answer the test by merely underlining a phrase, writing a number or a word, or by stating a numerical result.

Other features of the new examination are the multiplicity of its questions. Instead of the 5 to 10 found in the traditional examination, the questions in the new type run from 100 to 200. These, of course, are necessarily brief, but they provide a more perfect sampling of the whole field than is possible when fewer questions are used. Since the amount of writing that the pupil has to do is reduced to a minimum, they usually take but a fraction of the time that the traditional examination consumes. A new type examination takes longer to prepare than an essay type, but it is scored much more rapidly. And best of all, it defeats the crammer, whether he be regarded as one who stuffs facts into the child, or as one who tries to anticipate the questions which will be set. The new type covers the whole course of study, and the only preparation that pays the candidate is a study of the whole course.

The questions in the new examination are usually arranged in order of difficulty and, as far as possible, the steps between successive questions are made equal. The test may be "timed," so that while the dullest pupil in the class can answer at least a few of the questions, the brightest cannot answer all of them. This gets rid of undistributed zero and undistributed perfect scores. Sometimes, however, no time limit is set, but in such cases the degree of difficulty of the hardest questions has to be very high.

Admittedly the new examinations suit knowledge subjects best. Facts are what it feeds upon. Skill subjects are less readily tested by the new examination; while the problem of testing æsthetic appreciation by means of new type examinations has never been squarely faced. It gives no practice in composition or in the organization of a field of knowledge. But it defeats the pupil who uses words to cloak his ignorance.

Forms of New Type Examinations.—A great many excellent forms of new type examinations have been evolved. Some of the commoner forms now in use will be described.

1. *True-False Test.*—This test, occurring in many varieties consists essentially of a number of statements some of which are false and some true. The candidate has to judge of the truth or falsity of each statement. Examples of the true-false test are given below:

A. Some of the following statements are *true*, some *false*. If the statement is true, the word *true* must be underlined; if false, the word *false*. If in doubt, omit the item. Do not guess.

1. Standard time is sun time . . . . True—False.
2. The earth turns on its axis from east to west . True—False.
3. At the North Pole every direction is south . . True—False.

B. This is a True-False paper. In the spaces in the margin below write *Yes* before each sentence you think is *right*, and *No* before each sentence you think is *not right*. Do your best and answer every statement.

...... 1. Iceland is larger than Greenland.
...... 2. Eskimos build their homes near the water.

C. Some of the following statements are true and some are false. When the statement is true, draw a line under *True*; when it is false, draw a line under *False*. Be sure to make a mark for every statement. If you do not know, guess.

1. The Catskill Mountains are in Maine . . . . True—False.
2. Sheffield is noted for its manufacture of cutlery. True—False.

D. About one-half of the following statements are true and about one-half are false. Mark each true statement with a plus sign (+) on the dotted line at the left of the statement. Mark each statement that is partly or wholly false with a zero (0) on the dotted line at the left of the statement. Do not mark statements which you do not know.

Mark the statements in order.
DO NOT GUESS. Guessing reduces your score.
Ask no questions.

...... 1. Eskimos are dark-skinned people.
...... 2. Greenland has a warm climate.

E. If the following questions can be answered by *Yes*, underline *Yes*; if by *No*, underline *No*. Do not guess; omit the questions you cannot answer.

1. Is Canada north of the equator? . . . . . . Yes—No.
2. Does the River Mackenzie flow into Hudson Bay? Yes—No.

Since this form of test, (E), obviates the necessity of putting false statements before the pupil (a procedure that is considered unpedagogical by some authorities), it has been considered a good form. However, there is no evidence to show that the wrong statements are stamped in when the pupil is told that some of the statements are false and that the task is to mark those which are.

The wording of the items of a True-False test calls for care. The following rules from Weidemann [1] seem admirable:

(*a*) Avoid long statements.
(*b*) Avoid ambiguous statements.
(*c*) Avoid trivial statements.
(*d*) Avoid suggestive statements.
(*e*) Put statements positively when possible.
(*f*) See that one statement does not answer the preceding one.
(*g*) Avoid dependent clauses (especially those which determine the truth or falsity of the statement).
(*h*) Avoid compound sentences containing two separate ideas, either of which may be false. If either half of a compound sentence is false, the whole item must be considered false.

In constructing the True-False test Russell [2] recommends the following procedure:

1. First make a series of true statements covering the subject-matter concerned.
2. Arrange these statements in chance order by drawing numbered cards, previously shuffled, from a hat. The item whose number is drawn first becomes the first of the series; that drawn second, the second of the series, etc.
3. Make the statements true or false in accordance with some chance method. Toss a coin. If heads turns up, allow the statement to remain true; if tails, turn the true statement into a false one. Do this for all the statements.

Several vexed problems arise in connection with the true-false test. The most insistent of these is connected with the element of chance which enters into the test. Shall pupils be instructed to guess or not to guess? The experimental evidence on the whole is in favour of instructing the pupils *not to guess*. Since chance may still enter into the score, shall the number of right responses be counted, or shall the formula Rights *minus* Wrongs be used to determine the score? Again, on the whole, the evidence seems to point to the Rights *minus* Wrongs as the correct procedure, although a good case can be made out for the method which simply uses the number of right responses. Apparently no great harm is done if either method is employed. The pupils are arranged in the same order by both methods,

[1] Weidemann, C. C., *How to Construct the True-False Examination*, p. 78.
[2] Russell, C., *Classroom Tests*, chap. iii.

although the scores determined by "number right" are consistently higher than those determined by the R—W method.

It should be noted, however, that the R—W method will only correct perfectly for a group whose scores are averaged. It may still fail to be fair for a single individual, since his "luck" may be "in" or "out" for any given test. But if an individual's scores in several tests be averaged, the element of luck is compensated for automatically. Nobody is "lucky" or "unlucky" all the time.

2. *Multiple Choice or Multiple Response Tests; and Best Answer of Judgment Tests.*—The following are samples of these tests:

A. Underline the word that makes the correct answer.

1. Venice is a city of
   Greece, Italy, France, Switzerland.
2. Coffee is an important export of
   Brazil, France, South Africa, Peru.

B. Each of the following statements can be completed by any one of the four numbered words. But one of these only is the best or truest answer. Find the best answer and place its number in parentheses to the right.

1. Canada imports most from
   (1) England, (2) Germany, (3) United States, (4) Japan (   ).
2. At noon in London, England, the time in Toronto is
   (1) 7 a.m.; (2) 5 p.m.; (3) 7 p.m.; (4) 5 a.m. . . (   ).

C. Read each question and select the *best* answer to that question. Record the *number* of the best answer on the dotted line at the right.

1. A poem with symbolic characters is a(n)
   (1) Limerick, (2) epic, (3) lyric, (4) elegy, (5) allegory. ......

D. Below are a number of incomplete statements which may be completed by any one of three possible answers. Only one answer is scientifically correct; the other two are partly or entirely incorrect. Study each statement and then make a cross (x) in front of the *best* answer.

1. The chief function of the red blood corpuscles is the
   ...... Destruction of disease germs in the blood.
   ...... Carrying of oxygen to the tissues.
   ...... Carrying of food materials to the tissues.
2. Nitrogen is made available for plant use by
   ...... Bacteria in the soil.
   ...... The chlorophyll of the leaves.
   ...... The cambium layer of the stem.

The element of chance is not so conspicuous as in the true-false test. If four or more choices are allowed, chance plays a comparatively insignificant part in determining the score and usually need not be considered. If fewer than four choices are given, the score may be determined by using the following general formula:

$$\text{Score}=\text{Rights}-\frac{\text{Wrongs}}{N-1}$$

where N is the number of responses presented.

In constructing this type of test the following rules should be observed:

(*a*) None of the choices should be made too obviously incorrect.
(*b*) In general, from four to seven choices should be allowed.
(*c*) The position of the correct answers should be determined by lot, by drawing numbers from a hat.
(*d*) Arrange the test, if possible, so that the answers are numbers placed in parentheses to the right of the questions. This makes for the quickest form of scoring yet discovered.

3. *The Completion Test.*—This test consists of a number of statements from which words have been omitted. The pupil is instructed to supply the missing words.

Examples of such tests are given below:

A. In the paragraph below write in the words that have been left out. Try to find the word for each blank that makes the best sense.

The peculiar properties possessed by the radioactive elements, their ability, for example, to affect a —— plate wrapped in —— paper, or to cause air to become a —— of electricity, or to make certain minerals —— in the dark, was early found to be due to the fact that they emit invisible —— or radiations.

B. In each blank insert the proper *word* which will make the statement complete and true.

1. Czechoslovakia is a —— in Europe.
2. Chicago is a great packing-house centre because it is in the —— belt.

It is impossible to make this form of test absolutely objective. For example, the first blank of test A above may be filled by "sensitive" or "photographic," but "photographic," being a better answer, should receive a higher score than "sensitive."

4. *The Matching or Association Test.*—The essential feature of this test is the arrangement of two sets of associated facts in chance order in parallel columns. The object of the test is to match or pair the items correctly.

A. Number each of the topics in Column B with the corresponding number in Column A, so as to show by pairs which are the most closely associated.

Column A.		*Column B:*
1. Boyle's law.	( )	Limestone.
2. A mixture.	( )	Maple syrup.
3. A solution.	( )	Gunpowder.
4. A compound.	( )	$P \times V = \text{constant}$.

B. In the left-hand column is a list of causes. In the right-hand column is a list of results. Take your pencil and draw a line connecting each cause with the proper result.

(*a*) The Mackenzie Rebellion.	(*a*) Canada under British Rule.
(*b*) United Empire Loyalists.	(*b*) Lord Durham's Report.
(*c*) Fall of Quebec to Wolfe.	(*c*) Union of Upper and Lower Canada.
(*d*) Lord Sydenham as Governor-General.	(*d*) Family Compact.

C. From the list at the right select the names of three persons who were prominent in each of the following periods. Write their numbers in parentheses under the name of the period in which they were prominent.

(*a*) Discovery and exploration.	(1) Brock.
( ) ( ) ( )	(2) Champlain.
(*b*) War of 1812.	(3) Macdonald.
( ) ( ) ( )	(4) Brown.
(*c*) The Struggle for Confederation.	(5) Jacques Cartier.
( ) ( ) ( )	(6) La Salle.
	(7) G. E. Cartier.
	(8) Laura Secord.
	(9) Brant.
	(10) Tecumseh.
	(11) Papineau.
	(12) Simcoe.

Usually not more than 10–15 items should be included in each column. If phrases or extracts are used in one of the columns, a better type of examination is produced.

5. *Arrangement Test.*

A. Arrange consecutively by numbers in parentheses according to size the following breeds of poultry. Begin with the smallest.

( ) The Cochin.	( ) The Wyandotte.
( ) The Brahma.	( ) The Leghorn.
( ) The Bantam.	( ) The Minorca.

B. Indicate the chronological order (the time order) in which the following men lived by placing a figure (1) in parentheses before the individual who lived first, a figure (2) before the individual who lived second, and so on through the list.

( ) Champlain.
( ) Sir Wilfrid Laurier.
( ) Jacques Cartier.
( ) Sir John A. Macdonald.
( ) Montcalm.
( ) Frontenac.
( ) Egerton Ryerson.
( ) John Cabot.
( ) Governor Shirley.
( ) Simcoe.

6. *Analogies, or Mixed Relations Test.*

A. Fill in the blank space so as to make the best analogy.
1. Hydrogen : 1 : : Nitrogen : ——
2. Sulphuric Acid : H_2SO_4 : : Hydrogen Sulphide : ——
3. Oxygen : Water : : Sulphur : ——

7. *Recall Test.*

A. Write a word or short phrase on each blank line which will make each statement true.
1. The inventor of the cotton gin was ——
2. Darwin was one of the world's greatest ——

8. *Similarities Test.*

Find the way in which the first three things on a line are alike. Then look at the five other things on the same line and draw a line under the one which is most like the first three.

1. Red, yellow, green — rose, paper, grass, soft, blue.
2. Coal, tar, soot — crow, hot, water, fire, syrup.

9. *Classification Test, or Cross-out Test.*

In each line cross out the word that does not belong there. Cross out just *one* word in each line.

1. Primrose, Violet, Edith, Ernest, Sarah.
2. Red, rose, yellow, green, blue.

Additional benefits accrue when several kinds of tests are combined to form a battery. In constructing a battery the time to be devoted to each test must be predetermined. Experiments have shown that high school pupils on the average can answer 10–15 true-false items per minute; 6–10 recognition items per minute; and 4–8 recall items per minute. Items requiring thought require longer time. Consequently, a battery where equal times are given to each unit will have tests with widely varying numbers of items. The weighting to be given to each test should then be determined. This is usually done by calculating the variabilities of scores on each test, and giving weights inversely proportionate to the variabilities. But in ordinary school tests it is sufficiently accurate for all practical purposes to assign one mark for each item of the test, the final score in the test being the sum of the scores obtained in each of the constituent tests.

Advantages and Disadvantages of New Type Examinations.—The most obvious advantage of the new type examination is that it can be scored objectively. The unreliability of the traditional examination in this regard is noteworthy. Secondly, it can be scored very rapidly and economically, thus compensating for the additional trouble that it gives in preparing it. Thirdly, the new type examination, owing to the great number of its items, is more comprehensive than the traditional one; the sampling is fairer and defeats the crammer. Fourthly, the pupils can be given their marks with assurance; the scores cannot possibly reflect any favouritism or bias on the part of the teacher. Fifthly, the new type examination puts a premium on thinking. Having little writing to do, the pupil can concentrate on the solution of the problems. Sixthly, it defeats the pupil who writes around a question instead of on it.

The disadvantages are: (1) the new type examination places a premium on factual knowledge; (2) it does not give the pupil an opportunity of organizing his thoughts and expressing them in good style; (3) it probably does not measure up to the ways in which knowledge will be actually used so well as the traditional examination; (4) it induces guessing and the examiner cannot tell where knowledge stops and guessing starts. The corrections made for guessing are fair when the average scores of a group are considered, but may be unfair to any individual.

Summarizing the evidence, we can say that the advantages of the new type test far outweigh its limitations. These limitations may be overcome, in part, by the retention of the essay type for such purposes as it can adequately fulfil. The conspicuous weakness of the latter in regard to the reliability of its scores should cause teachers to pay more attention to this aspect of the subject. Otherwise the virtues it possesses (in that it makes pupils organize their thoughts) will continue to be swamped by the vices of its unreliability.

Criteria of Educational Tests.—The criteria which are used to judge the goodness of educational tests are the same as those that we applied to the intelligence test, namely, validity, accuracy, reliability, objectivity, economy of time and effort, and satisfactoriness of norms.

Validity.—A test is perfectly valid when it measures exactly what it aims to measure. A geography test, therefore, is perfectly valid when it tests achievement in geography. In so far as a pupil's score on a geography test is affected by his handwriting, neatness, and spelling, it loses validity as a test for geography. In the same way, a good examination in arithmetic will test arithmetic, but will not test intelligence, neatness, or anything else, unless these are genuinely correlated with the ability under consideration.

Validity is easy to describe, but difficult to secure. All teachers when marking a traditional examination, say, in history, are unconsciously influenced by the neatness of the arrangement of the answers, the quality of the English composition, the excellence of the spelling, and the legibility of the handwriting. These extraneous factors may be sufficiently important to merit serious consideration, but in so far as they enter into the scores given for the test, the examination loses validity as a test in history.

Validity is enormously increased by the new type forms of examination, since most of these factors are automatically excluded by the form of the test. But a new type alone does not ensure validity. Something more is needed. The sampling, though large, may be inadequately done, with the result that the test is only a fair measure for a part of the subject. The selection of materials, therefore, must be fair. If one wishes to construct a test valid over a wide area, then adequate samplings of material must be drawn from every section of the area. In history, for example, the various texts in use must be weighted and drawn upon for items in proportion to the frequency of their use. And what applies to texts as a whole applies also to their separate chapters and topics. Those more frequently dealt with and at greater length must receive more consideration than those which are treated more summarily by the authors. According to Symonds,[1] six distinct methods or criteria have been employed in the choice of material for standardized tests. These are: (1) the criterion of social usefulness; (2) the criterion of errors; (3) composite of text-books (illustrated above); (4) the composite of requirements in the course of study; (5) the composite of teachers' examinations; and (6) the judgments of experts. If each of these is adequately met, the test is assured of a high degree of validity.

Accuracy.—A test is perfectly accurate when the units of measurement are wholly appropriate and are absolutely equal at all points of the scale. In obtaining equality of units on his handwriting scale, Thorndike used the principle of just observable differences of quality, and secured the average judgments of

[1] Symonds, P. M., *Measurement in Secondary Education*, chap. xiv.

40 competent persons in this regard. For most subjects the scales have been derived from the percentages of pupils passing on each item. The scaling of a test is a difficult operation. The method which uses the variability of scores as a unit is the one most commonly employed.

Reliability.—A test is perfectly reliable when two applications of the equivalent tests to the same pupil yield identical scores. The test is tested for reliability by (1) giving the same test after an interval great enough to eliminate the memory effect and correlating the two sets of scores (a poor method); (2) by breaking it up into chance halves and correlating the two scores; and (3) by correlating the two scores obtained from equivalent forms of a test given to the same pupils.

No test, however, is ever perfectly reliable, and for obvious reasons. Any test is but a sample of the total field measured, whether it be addition in arithmetic, spelling, or a portion of history or geography. Furthermore, the pupil taking the test is a variable factor. His attention may wander, he may become fatigued or bored, or his health may vary. In general, however, the reliability of a test is increased by making it more objective, that is, by reducing the personal equation of the examiner; by increasing it in length and especially by increasing the number of items of the test; by using finer units in the scale by which the test is scored; and by keeping as constant as possible the conditions under which the test is taken.

Objectivity.—A test is perfectly objective when two examiners using equivalent tests upon the same pupils secure identical scores. A fatal weakness of the traditional examination is that it cannot be made objective. The personal element in the judgment of the examiner cannot be eliminated. Even in new type examinations for writing, drawing, literature, and composition, perfect objectivity cannot be achieved. In arithmetic, history, geography, and factual subjects in general, a very high degree of objectivity can easily be attained. While true-false, multiple choice, matching and some other forms of tests may reach perfect objectivity, recall and completion tests can never be made perfectly objective. Since objectivity reduces the sources of variability, it tends also to make a test more reliable.

Economy.—The chief factors influencing the economy of an examination are the ease of its administration and scoring, and the lowness of its printing or reproduction costs. The scoring costs may be considerably reduced by using easily scored forms in the construction of the test. By the same token an economical test is usually a reliable one.

Norms.—As we have previously stated, age norms for

elementary pupils are of more general usefulness than grade norms. Percentile norms and scores based upon the standard deviation as a unit of variability (such, for example, as McCall's T score), while less familiar than age and grade norms, are far more scientific. As they become better known to teachers, they will become increasingly appreciated.

The Accomplishment Quotient or Ratio.—The interpretation of scores made by a pupil is not the least important of the duties of an examiner. In tests for intelligence the score obtained in a Binet test (the mental age) was interpreted by means of the intelligence quotient. In the same way educational quotients may be obtained for each educational test. The educational quotient is obtained by the formula:

$$EQ=\frac{EA}{CA}$$

where EQ=Educational quotient
EA=Educational age
CA=Chronological age

If a pupil of 10 years of age makes a score in arithmetic as high as that of pupils whose average age is 11, he has an EQ of 110. This pupil, however, may be of high intelligence, let us say, of 12 years of mental age. Other things being equal, he should have an educational age of 12 years in all subjects. In order to find out if he is working up to the level of his mentality the concept of the Accomplishment Quotient has been introduced. The relationships of the AQ to other measures are seen in the following equations:

$$AQ=\frac{EQ}{IQ}=\frac{\frac{EA}{CA}}{\frac{MA}{CA}}=\frac{EA}{MA}$$

when AQ=Accomplishment quotient
EQ=Educational quotient
IQ=Intelligence quotient

Applying the formula, we find the pupil's AQ to be 92. In other words, he is not doing so well in arithmetic as his intelligence would lead us to expect, although he is doing better in this subject than boys of the same average age as himself.

Since the AQ discounts intelligence, it is a true measure of a pupil's merit. If a pupil works according to the degree of his native ability, his rating by the AQ will not fall below 100, no matter what his IQ may be. The brighter pupil has to do more to get the AQ rating than the duller one. In the same way, the AQ is an excellent measure of a teacher's efficiency. If the average AQ of a class in a subject is below 100, then the teaching and not the intelligence of the pupils can be held to blame.

It should be noted, however, that, in order to measure the AQ accurately, standardized tests with reliable age norms are essential. The AQ cannot be obtained from the measures of a new type test casually devised by a teacher as part of his teaching programme for the year.

Uses and Results of Educational Measurements.— Educational tests are of little value unless the marks are put to practical use. According to Symonds,[1] measurements are being used for the following purposes:

(1) To inform pupils of their achievement.
(2) As incentives to study.
(3) To promote competition:
  (*a*) Between groups;
  (*b*) Between individuals;
  (*c*) With one's own record.
(4) To determine promotion.
(5) To diagnose weak spots in the pupils' achievement.
(6) To determine the quality of instruction.
(7) To determine admission to the High School.
(8) To place a pupil in school.
(9) To determine admission to college.
(10) To provide reports to parents.
(11) To determine credits, honours, etc.
(12) Educational and vocational guidance.
(13) To rate teachers.
(14) To predict a pupil's success.
(15) To study the efficiency of a school.

It is obvious that if the measurements are inaccurately made these functions will be inadequately fulfilled. Indeed, grave injustice may be done. That the unreliability of teachers' measurements are contributing to grave injustice, ample evidence has been adduced in the preceding sections of this chapter. Fortunately, a happier state is being rapidly reached. Teachers are more critical of their examinations than was formerly the case, and are endeavouring to make them fairer by adopting some of the measures for improvement previously discussed. Yet we cannot fail to be disturbed at such findings as those of Wood [2] and MacPhail,[3] who discovered that a special intelligence

[1] Symonds, P. M., *Measurement in Secondary Education*, pp. 1 and 2.
[2] Wood, B. D., *Measurement in Higher Education*, p. 85.
[3] MacPhail, A. H., *The Intelligence of College Students*, p. 151.

test given to college freshmen was more predictive of success in college than either a state matriculation examination or the marks they had been given throughout their secondary school careers.

Wood found that an intelligence test taking 3½ hours to administer is predictive of success in college to a slightly greater extent than the Regents' examination of New York State, and to a much greater extent than secondary school marks.

The coefficients of correlation between two-year scholarship scores in Columbia College and the scores in three different criteria for admission are given below:

	r
(1) Thorndike Intelligence Scores	0·672
(2) Regents' Examinations	0·644
(3) Secondary School Marks	0·262

The results from Brown University, where the entering students are given both the Thorndike Test and the Brown University Test, confirm the findings from Columbia College. MacPhail concluded that "The high school principal's estimate of a student is of very little value in indicating what the student will accomplish in college. Neither do these general estimates show any relation to the students' intelligence as measured by the Brown and Thorndike tests, nor do they constitute reliable indices of the students' rank in high school at graduation."

Much, therefore, remains to be done. But the happiest augury is that teachers are realizing their imperfections in the field of measurement. This, together with the very practical help that is being given to them by expert workers in the field, will undoubtedly lead to rapid improvement.

References

Ballard, P. B. *The New Examiner*. London, Hodder & Stoughton, 1923. Pp. 269.

Burt, C. *The Distribution and Relations of Educational Ability*. London, P. S. King, 1917. Pp. xiii+93.

Burt, C. *Mental and Scholastic Tests*. London, P. S. King. Pp. xv+432.

Chapman, J. C. "Individual Injustice and Guessing in the True-False Examination," *Jour. Appl. Psy.*, VI (Dec. 1922), pp. 342–348.

Foster, W. T. "Scientific *versus* Personal Distribution of College Credits," *Pop. Sc. Mo.*, LXXVIII (Apr. 1911), pp. 388–408.

Holzinger, K. J. "On Scoring Multiple Response Tests," *J.E.P.*, XV (Oct. 1924), pp. 445–447.

Laird, D. A. "A Comparison of the Essay and the Objective Type of Examinations," *J.E.P.*, XIV, 2 (Feb. 1923), pp. 123–124.

MacPhail, A. H. *The Intelligence of College Students*. Baltimore, Warwick and York, 1924. Pp. viii+176.

McCall, W. A. *How to Measure in Education.* New York, Macmillan, 1922. Pp. xii+416.

McCall, W. A. *How to Experiment in Education.* New York, Macmillan, 1923. Pp. xiv+281.

Meyer, M. " The Grading of Students," *Science*, vol. xxviii (April 21, 1908), pp. 243–252.

Monroe, De Voss, and Kelly. *Educational Tests and Measurements.* Boston, Houghton Mifflin, 1924, 2nd ed. Pp. 521.

Monroe and Souders. *Present Status of Written Examinations and Suggestions for their Improvement.* Bull. No. 17 (1923), Bureau of Educational Research, University of Illinois, Urbana, Ill.

Odell, C. W. (1) *Educational Tests for Use in High Schools, Second Revision.* (2) *Educational Tests for Use in Elementary Schools, Second Revision.* University of Illinois, Urbana, Ill. Bulletins Nos. 48 and 49 of the Bureau of Educational Research, College of Education.

Paterson, D. G. *Preparation and Use of New Type Examinations.* Yonkers-on-Hudson, World Book Co. Pp. vi+87.

Paterson, D. G. " Do New and Old Type Examinations Measure Different Mental Functions ? " *School and Society*, XXIV (Aug. 21, 1926), pp. 246–248.

Reed, H. B. *Psychology of Elementary School Subjects.* Boston, Ginn, 1927. Pp. x+481.

Remmers, H. H., *et al.* " An Experimental Study of the Relative Difficulty of True-False, Multiple Choice, and Incomplete-Sentence Types of Examination Questions," *J.E.P.*, XIV (Sept. 1923), pp. 366–371.

Ruch, G. M. *The Improvement of the Written Examination.* Chicago, Scott Foresman & Co., 1924. Pp. 193.

Ruch and De Graff. " Corrections for Chance and ' Guess ' *versus* Do not Guess Instructions in Multiple-Response Tests," *J.E.P.*, XVII (Sept. 1926), pp. 368–375.

Ruch and Stoddard. " Comparative Reliabilities of Five Types of Objective Examinations," *J.E.P.*, XVI (Feb. 1925), pp. 89–103.

Ruch and Stoddard. *Tests and Measurements in High School Instruction.* Yonkers-on-Hudson, World Book Co. Pp. xix+381.

Ruch *et al. Objective Examination Methods in the Social Studies.* Chicago, Scott Foresman & Co., 1926. Pp. 126.

Russell, C. *Classroom Tests.* Boston, Ginn & Co., 1926. Pp. 346.

Symonds, P. M. *Measurement in Secondary Education.* New York, The Macmillan Co., 1927. Pp. xvii+588.

Weidemann, C. C. *How to Construct the True-False Examination.* T. C Contributions to Education, No. 225. Bureau of Publications, Teachers College, Columbia University, N.Y., 1926. Pp. 118.

Wood, B. D. *Measurement in Higher Education.* Yonkers-on-Hudson, World Book Co., 1923. Pp. xi+337.

CHAPTER XVI

IMPROVEMENT IN SPECIAL SUBJECTS

A. The Acquirement of Language Habits

Analysis of the Problem.—Although many animals have powers of communication by means of one which may be regarded as primitively linguistic, man alone is possessed of articulate language or speech. Speech, therefore, and the related habits of reading and writing constitute the main behaviour differences between man and brute. In the sub-vocal movements of articulate speech, thinking is chiefly carried on, and memory consists mainly of language recall. The theory which maintains that we cannot remember the events of early life because they happened in our pre-linguistic stage of development, and consequently were not associated with speech, is finding increasing favour among psychologists.

Language also is the chief medium of social heredity. Oral language annihilates space, for it enables us to project ourselves outwards and to break down barriers existing between persons at a distance. Written language enables us to annihilate both space and time. Theoretically, every thought of the past which was committed to writing can be utilized by us to-day. In the early history of mankind the transmission of thoughts was imperfect and unreliable, but with the invention of writing, the accuracy of the records was immeasurably increased. To-day, without this social inheritance, civilization, as we know it, would be an impossibility and even our very existence would be menaced.

In the study of the acquirement of linguistic habits by children, four main problems arise :

1. Understanding the mother tongue when it is spoken—the development of responses to oral speech.

2. Use of the mother tongue in speech—the acquirement of oral language habits.

3. Understanding the mother tongue when it is written or printed—the art of reading.

4. Use of the mother tongue in writing—the acquirement of habits involved in writing, spelling, composition, grammar, and punctuation.

Normally, the acquisition of language habits in children is in the order given above. A baby, for example, understands or responds to oral language before he can use it, and reading generally develops ahead of writing. Throughout life, however, language habits, just like our manual habits, are in a state of flux. Words are learned and lost again, with the gains on the whole outnumbering the losses until senile decay sets in. But it would be a mistake to suppose that we have a single vocabulary. We have several, depending upon the use to which we put language. Most people, for example, have a bigger reading vocabulary (3, above) than writing (4) or speaking (2) vocabulary; and most people can understand more words, both in writing and speech, than they can themselves use in these activities.

Linguistic Development of the Pre-School Period.—Language habits prior to entry into school are mostly those concerned with oral language. These habits are elaborations of inherited behaviour patterns. But we must not fall into the error of thinking that it is the ability to use a specific language, say English or Chinese, which is inherited. What we inherit is a capacity for *language*, not for *a language*, and the particular direction the development takes is dependent upon environment. A child of English-speaking parents reared from infancy in a French-speaking family will have French for its mother tongue, while English will be regarded and learned as a "foreign" language.

The inherited behaviour patterns involved in language learning are very numerous and quite widespread. The whole body is used in speech, glandular as well as muscular systems, but the neuro-muscular system in the head, neck, and chest is the most important. More specifically, the movements of the diaphragm, the lungs and muscles of the thorax, the muscles of the larynx, pharynx, nose, palate, cheeks, tongue, and lips co-operate in the production of every spoken word. These basic movement patterns are innate, but the co-ordinations evolved from them give us the various words of our own language as well as those of others.

Understanding of words develops before their use in speech. The baby, however, does not understand words as we do. When he retrieves a ball in response to "Fetch the ball, baby," he understands just to the extent he responds or does, and no more. Certainly the first responses of children are not to words as such, but mainly to different gestures, intonations, grimaces, and pantomime. The truth of this is seen when the statement "Ah! you are a naughty boy!" is made to a baby with a calm voice and smiling face. The baby's normal response is a smile or chortle. But tell the baby that he is a "sweet little angel" in a gruff voice and with a frowning face, and the result is a terrified squall. Even adults "understand just as much as they do," and no more. The meanings which words have for us parallel our responses to them. We "mean" what we "do"; meaning develops contemporaneously with doing.

In the use of language, the first eight months of life, or thereabouts, are generally regarded as a pre-linguistic stage. The cries of the first month are almost undifferentiated, although observant mothers and nurses can distinguish the cry of pain from that of hunger, and even, in some cases, between the cries representing different degrees of discomfort.

The earliest sounds are the "a" sounds in all its variations—a, ab, uä, rah, ma, yah. The easiest consonants are m, p, t, and d. These become attached to the primordial "a" and we get such words as "mama," "dada," "papa," "tata," etc. Since the otherwise meaningless sound "mama" is the first to bear any resemblance to ordinary speech, the mothers of practically all nations have appropriated this word as a pet name for themselves.

When words really begin to come, they come with a rush. Several investigations of the growth of vocabulary up to five or six years of age have been made, and they all show its astonishing rapidity. Even when we discount the fact that these reports invariably represent cases of very superior vocabularies (proud parents only report abnormally good ones), the rate of increase still remains remarkable. The following tables, constructed by Waddle,[1] give the salient facts:

Average Vocabularies at Different Ages (Waddle).

Age.	No. of cases.	Average No. of words.	Extremes.	
			Least.	Greatest.
1 year	10	8·9	3	24
2 years	20	528·0	115	1127
3 "	8	1407·0	681	2282
4 "	6	2171·0	1020	3915
5 "	1	6837·0		
6 "	1	3950·0		

[1] Waddle, C. W., *Child Psychology*, p. 166.

Parts of Speech in Child Vocabularies (expressed in percentages).

Cases.	Age.	Total average vocabulary.	Nouns.	Verbs.	Adj.	Adv.	Pron.	Prep.	Conj.	Inter.
10	1	8·8	65·3	6·9	5·1	12·8	0	0	0	9·8
20	2	528	58·9	20·8	9·8	4·9	1·9	1·4	0·2	1·9
8	3	1407	55·6	23·1	10·8	5·1	2·2	1·4	0·6	0·9
6	4	2171	53·6	25·0	12·0	5·1	1·4	1·0	0·7	0·9
1	5	6837	56·8	19·3	21·8		2·2			
1	6	3950	48·0	24·0	10·0	3·4	0·9	0·6	0·2	0·5

The above vocabularies refer to the words actually used by children at the stated ages. Their understanding vocabularies would probably be much greater. The Stanford-Binet has norms for the number of words understood at various ages. The words are regarded as being understood when they can be defined, however simply. Terman's norms are given below:

Stanford-Binet Vocabulary Norms (Terman's).

Year.	Definitions.	Words.
8	20	3,600
10	30	5,400
12	40	7,200
14	50	9,000
16 average adult	65	11,700
18 superior adult	75	13,500

We shall, therefore, not be far from the mark if we regard the normal child on entering school as knowing the meaning of about 2000 words, of which number he can probably use half in his oral speech.

Reading

The Nature of Reading.—From a sociological point of view reading (with writing) is important because it enables the race to transmit its acquired experience in an easily accessible form; from a psychological point of view it represents the technique we adopt to get responses of meaning from an arrangement of certain highly artificial symbols we call the alphabet. This latter point of view, namely, that the final end of reading is the comprehension of what is read, was lost sight of for many years. Reading in the elementary school meant oral reading. If a pupil could read aloud, giving due emphasis to the pronunciation and articulation of the words and to the modulation of his voice, he satisfied all demands. Any test applied to him showed that he could read. That the pupil might be merely pronouncing

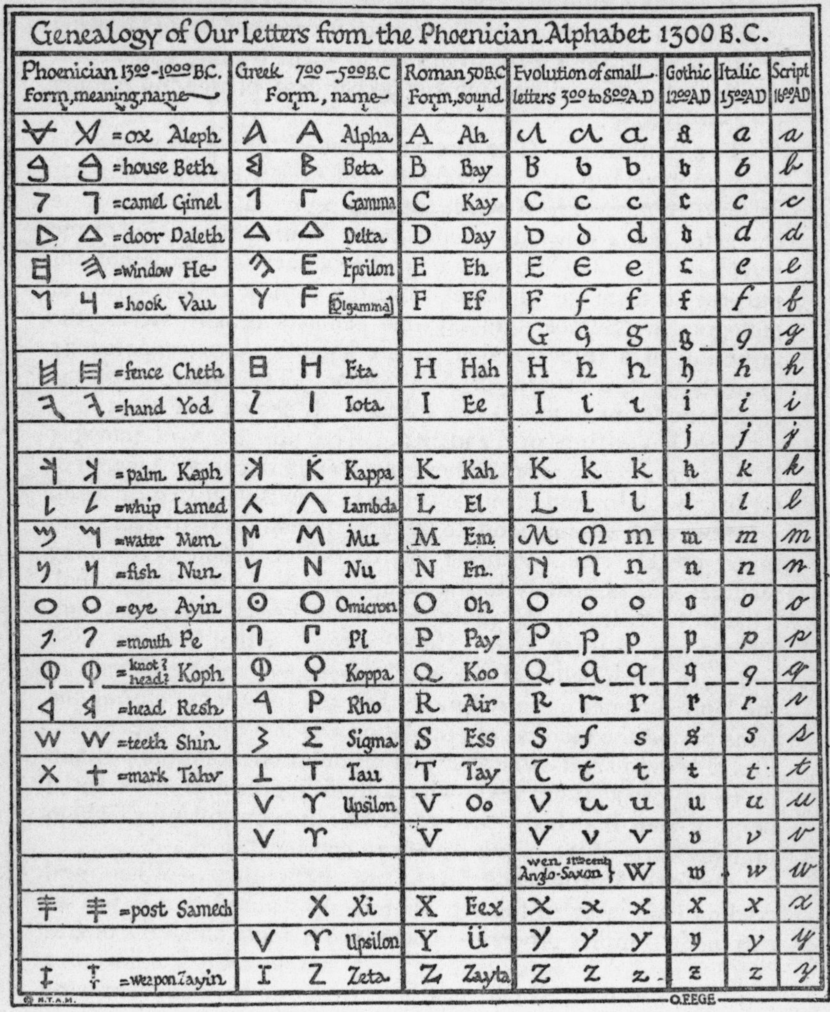

Genealogy of Our Letters from the Phoenician Alphabet 1300 B.C.

Phoenician 1300–1000 B.C. Form, meaning, name	Greek 700–500 B.C. Form, name	Roman 50 B.C. Form, sound	Evolution of small letters 300 to 800 A.D.	Gothic 1200 A.D.	Italic 1500 A.D.	Script 1600 A.D.
=ox Aleph	A A Alpha	A Ah	a a a	a	a	a
=house Beth	B Beta	B Bay	B b b	b	b	b
=camel Gimel	Γ Gamma	C Kay	C c c	c	c	c
=door Daleth	Δ Δ Delta	D Day	D d d	d	d	d
=window He	E Epsilon	E Eh	E e e	e	e	e
=hook Vau	Y F (Digamma)	F Ef	F f f	f	f	f
			G g g	g	g	g
=fence Cheth	H Eta	H Hah	H h h	h	h	h
=hand Yod	I Iota	I Ee	I i i	i	i	i
				j	j	j
=palm Kaph	K Kappa	K Kah	K k k	k	k	k
=whip Lamed	Λ Lambda	L El	L l l	l	l	l
=water Mem	M M Mu	M Em	M m m	m	m	m
=fish Nun	N Nu	N En	N n n	n	n	n
=eye Ayin	O Omicron	O Oh	O o o	o	o	o
=mouth Pe	Γ Pi	P Pay	P p p	p	p	p
=knot? head? Koph	Φ Ϙ Koppa	Q Koo	Q q q	q	q	q
=head Resh	P Rho	R Air	R r r	r	r	r
=teeth Shin	Σ Sigma	S Ess	S ſ s	s	s	s
=mark Tahv	T Tau	T Tay	T t t	t	t	t
	V Υ Upsilon	V Oo	V u u	u	u	u
	V Υ	V	V v v	v	v	v
			wen 11th cent. Anglo-Saxon W	w	w	w
=post Samech	X Xi	X Eex	x x x	x	x	x
	V Υ Upsilon	Y Ü	y y y	y	y	y
=weapon Zayin	I Z Zeta	Z Zayta	Z z z	z	z	z

© N.T.A.M. O. EGE

FIG. 53.—Evolution of the alphabet (chart by Ege).

(By kind permission of N. T. A. Munder Co., Baltimore, publishers of "The Story of the Alphabet" and "Pre-alphabet Days.")

the words without comprehending their meaning, very much in the same fashion as a beginner in German might read a difficult passage in that language and be totally ignorant of what it was all about, nobody apparently discovered. The teacher's point of view was that if a child could pronounce the words, he could, *ipso facto*, understand them. Silent reading, which could not be tested by any known device, was regarded either as an extra-curricular activity or as solely a matter for the home. The swing of emphasis in the school from oral to silent reading is a step in the right direction, since probably 99 per cent. of all adult reading is silent reading.

The Alphabet.—The discovery that all the words which the human tongue can utter are composed of a relatively small number of unit sounds, each of which can be represented by a separate character, was a slow and painful one. Neither the genius of the Egyptians nor the Chinese managed to achieve it. It is not our purpose to trace the alphabet from the earliest known forms of pictographs. Suffice it to say that scholars usually ascribe the invention of a true alphabet, where sounds are represented by symbols, to the peoples of Asia Minor. The evolution of the alphabetic forms in use to-day is succinctly shown in Fig. 53.

The Invention of Printing.—The utilization of movable letters in printing marks another great step in the upward march of civilization. Instead of single copies laboriously written by hand, printing enabled mankind to secure thousands of copies with much greater ease. Printing led to the extension of teaching facilities and ultimately to the compulsory and free state school. This in turn, led to the multiplication of books, magazines, and newspapers of every kind. Judd[1] estimated that between 1880 and 1910 the number of issues of newspapers and periodicals in the United States increased more than 500 per cent. During the same period the increase of population was less than 100 per cent. Probably similar, if somewhat less pronounced, conditions obtain in many other countries. The astonishing fact from a social point of view is that the percentage of illiteracy still runs so high in many parts of the North American continent.

Factors influencing Reading Efficiency.—When oral reading held sway in the schools nobody realized that it was an extremely complex process. Those who thought about the matter at all regarded it as a comparatively simple compounding of a few basic habits, in which voice culture played the dominant part. Some glimmering of the truth appeared when a clear distinction was drawn between oral and silent reading, but it was experimentation, beginning with the objective recording of eye-movements, that opened the eyes of educators to the real complexity of the problem. The analysis of reading ability has never been satis-

[1] Judd, C. H., "Relation of School Expansion to Reading," *Elementary School Journal*, XXIII (Dec. 1922), pp. 253–266.

factorily made, but some of the factors which have been studied by psychologists are listed below :

1. Hygienic factors.
    (*a*) Those usually beyond the control of the teacher.
        (1) Size and kind of type.
        (2) Uniformity of length of lines.
        (3) Kind and colour of paper.
        (4) Spacing of words and lines.
        (5) Illumination of classroom.
    (*b*) Those usually within the control of the teacher.
        (1) Posture of pupil during reading.
        (2) Method of holding book.
        (3) Breathing habits in oral reading.
2. Reading material.
    (1) Extent of vocabulary used.
    (2) Difficulty of vocabulary used.
    (3) Sentence structure and style.
    (4) Appeal which the subject-matter makes to the interest of pupils at given stages of intellectual development.
3. Eye-movements.
    (1) Number of fixations per line in oral and in silent reading.
    (2) Duration of fixations in oral and silent reading.
    (3) Interfixation movements.
    (4) Regressive or refixating movements. (Rhythm of movements.)
    (5) Return sweeps.
4. The eye-voice span in silent and oral reading.
5. Perceptual processes.
    (1) Span of clear perception.
    (2) Recognition span in oral and silent reading.
    (3) Rate of recognition in oral and silent reading.
    (4) Rate and accuracy of pronunciation in oral reading.
    (5) Recognition of letters, words, and phrases.
6. Rate of oral reading.
    (1) With different types of material.
    (2) According to purpose for which it is done.
7. Rate of silent reading.
    (1) With different types of material.
    (2) According to purpose for which it is done.
        (*a*) For pleasure (or the story).
        (*b*) For study (ability to answer questions on it).
        (*c*) For general drift (skimming).
        (*d*) For paraphrase.
        (*e*) For organization of thought of selection.

8. Comprehension in oral reading.

9. Comprehension in silent reading.

10. Vocalization (inner speech) in silent reading.

11. Vocalization in oral reading and the formation of linguistic habits.

12. Intelligence of pupil. Correlations with various measures of ability in reading.

13. Individual differences.

(1) Diagnosis of defects in oral reading.

(*a*) Mispronunciations.
(*b*) Repetitions.
(*c*) Insertions.
(*d*) Omissions.
(*e*) Substitutions.

(2) Diagnosis of defects in silent reading.

(*a*) Overpotency of words.
(*b*) Neglect of key words and sentences.
(*c*) Wrong relations.

14. Appreciation.

(1) Of the beautiful (æsthetic and literary values).
(2) Of humour.
(3) Of social values.
(4) Of the intellectual or thought elements.

The above is a somewhat formidable list, but when we look into the literature of the subject, we find that, except in the case of linguistic habits in oral reading (expression) and of appreciation, somewhat reliable objective measures of most of the factors have been made. In one of them, eye-movements, the measurement has, indeed, been most precise.

Measurements of Reading Abilities.—By far the most important measurements made of reading abilities are those connected with standardized tests and with eye-movements. Brief descriptions of these will now be given.

(*a*) *Measurement by Means of Standardized Tests.*—Reading tests are designed to measure the *products* of reading instruction; they tell us whether or not the teacher has succeeded in his task, but only by inference do they inform us about the effectiveness of the means he employed. The abilities for which tests have been devised are listed below:

1. Accuracy of word recognition (vocabulary tests)—Haggerty Primary Reading Vocabulary Scales; Pressey Attainment Scale (Grades 1 and 2); Thorndike Visual Vocabulary Scales; Thorndike Test of Word Knowledge; Holley Sentence Vocabulary Scale.

2. Rate and accuracy of oral reading—Gray's Oral Reading Check Tests (Individual).

3. Rate of silent reading.
   (*a*) Amount read in a specified time—Brown Silent Reading Test; Fordyce Scale for Measuring Achievements in Reading; Courtis Silent Reading Test No. 2; Burgess Picture Supplement Scale for Measuring Ability in Silent Reading.
   (*b*) Time taken to read fixed amount—Gray Silent Reading Test.
   (*c*) Rate plus Comprehension—Monroe Standardized Silent Reading Tests, Revised; Gray Silent Reading Test; Burgess Picture Supplement Scale for Measuring Ability in Silent Reading.

4. Comprehension of silent reading.
   (*a*) Deleting incorrect words—Chapman-Cook Speed of Reading Tests.
   (*b*) Completion test—Stanford Achievement Test.
   (*c*) Following directions—Burgess Picture Supplement Scale; Kansas Silent Reading Test; Monroe Standardized Silent Reading Tests, Revised; Haggerty Silent Reading Scales, Sigma 1 and 3.
   (*d*) Answering questions—Haggerty Silent Reading Scales; Thorndike-McCall Reading Scales for the Understanding of Sentences; Monroe Silent Reading Tests; Courtis Silent Reading Test No. 2; Thorndike Scale, Alpha 2.
   (*e*) Reproductions—Gray Silent Reading Test; Brown Silent Reading Test; Monroe Standardized Silent Reading Tests.
   (*f*) Selecting central idea—Woody Silent Reading Test.

Obviously no single test measures all aspects of reading ability; nor would all that have been devised measure every aspect. Tests for measuring skimming ability and ability to summarize (obviously useful reading accomplishments) are still lacking. Certain tests have diagnostic values, but on the whole most of the tests give little information about the actual elements which entered into the final score. Moreover, such tests as we have do not yield comparable scores, since (1) they make different demands on the experience and knowledge of the pupil; (2) they differ in subject-matter; (3) they differ in complexity; and (4) they are scaled differently.

(*b*) *Measurement by means of Eye-movements.*—The investigation of reading ability by means of the muscular movements of the eyes is a triumph of objective psychology. Although the eyes in reading had moved in a succession of jerks ever since man began to read, introspective observations had failed to note them. Apparently they still remain a closed book to introspective analysis, for although we know them to be jerky, subjectively they appear to be regular and rhythmical sweeps. Eye-movements were first observed to be jerky about the middle of the nineteenth century, but it was Javal who first succeeded in recording them in 1879. Various experimenters—Delabarre, Erdmann, Dodge, and Huey—devised methods for recording the movements automatically, but few reliable results were obtained until the Chicago school of workers—Judd, Schmidt, Gray, and Buswell—perfected an apparatus for recording them photographically on a moving picture film.

The apparatus now used enables a strong beam of light to be reflected first to the cornea from silvered glass mirrors, and then from the cornea through a lens to a film moving in a vertical plane. So long as the eye-ball remains stationary the film record is a vertical line, but with movements of the eye, the line shifts to the right or left. If the light is intercepted with the prong of an electrically driven tuning-fork, with a vibration rate of 25 per second, the solid vertical line becomes a series of dots, each representing exactly $\frac{1}{25}$ of a second. The extent of the movement and the duration of the pauses are both accurately registered, and these, in turn, can be keyed with the reading material. If, further, during oral reading a synchronous dictaphone record is made, most interesting material for scientific interpretation is obtained.

Figs. 54 and 55 are reproduced from Buswell's researches.[1] The short vertical lines crossing the lines of print indicate the eye-fixations or pauses in the eye-movements when reading takes place. The serial numbers above the vertical lines indicate the order of the pauses; the numbers below the verticals give the duration in twenty-fifths of a second.

Of these two records Buswell writes (p. 1):

"In the silent reading of an easy paragraph, Barbara, a first-grade pupil, read at a rate of 39·6 words per minute, while Miss W., a college senior, read at a rate of 369 words per minute. A further analysis of the records of these two readers shows that the first-grade pupil has a very narrow recognition span, making an average of 21·3 fixation pauses per line, while the college student has a very wide span, requiring only 3·6 fixations per line. The first-grade pupil was not sure of her recognition of words even after her eyes had fixated upon them, and consequently found it necessary to make an average of 6·8 backward,

[1] Buswell, G. T., *Fundamental Reading Habits: A Study of their Development*, pp. 2 and 3.

or refixating, movements per line. The college student, however, did not make a single backward eye-movement in reading the entire paragraph. A further difference between the habits of these two readers can be seen in the duration of their fixations. In spite of the fact that the first-grade pupil had a very narrow recognition span, she

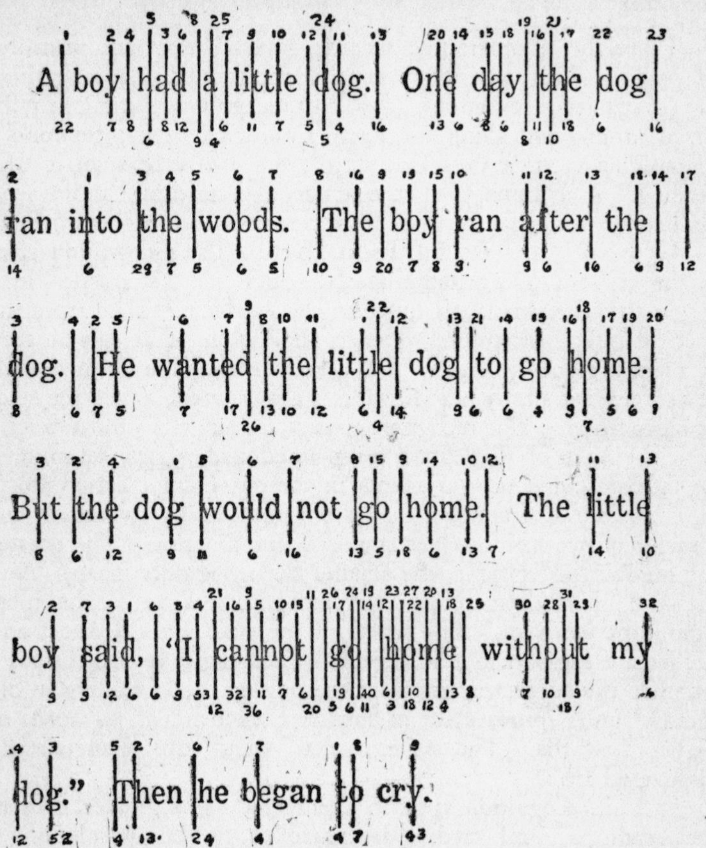

FIG. 54.—Showing eye-movements of an immature reader (Grade I, A) (Buswell).

In Figs. 54 and 55 showing records of eye-movements the positions of the eye-fixations are indicated by the short vertical lines drawn across the lines of print. The serial numbers above the verticals indicate the order of the pauses; the number at the lower end of each vertical indicates, in twenty-fifths of a second, the duration of the fixation.

required an average of 11·7 twenty-fifths of a second per fixation pause to get a clear perception of this small unit of material; while the college student recognized a much wider unit in an average fixation time of 8 twenty-fifths of a second. The record of the first-grade pupil gave clear evidence of periods of mental confusion, but that of the college student was perfectly regular throughout. . . .

"The cases just described illustrate the wide difference between the reading habits of the beginner and the mature reader. The task of the school is to convert the habits of the one into those of the other."

From the photographic records, several important measures of reading ability can be accurately determined. Among these are (*a*) span of recognition ; (*b*) rate of recognition ; and (*c*) rhythmical progression along the line. Combined with synchronous dictaphone records they give us (*d*) the eye-voice span in oral reading. A summary of the chief experimental findings in connection with each of these four measurements is given below :

Growth of the Recognition Span.—The recognition span is the amount of printed material which can be grasped in a single attention span. It must be clearly distinguished from the span of clear perception, which is the amount that can be seen at a single glance. The span of clear perception is given to each of us, once for all, by heredity and is always greater than the span of recognition. The recognition span corresponds almost exactly with the span of perception for printed material as determined by tachistoscopic measurements in the psychological laboratory. It is measured from eye-movement records by averaging the number of eye-fixations per standard line of print. The greater the number of fixations, the smaller the recognition span. As a measure of reading ability, the recognition span is the most significant we have. The width of the span gives a direct and immediate measure of the fluency of reading. It also discloses whether the subject is grasping the passage he is reading in big thought units (phrases) or in smaller elements such as words or parts of words. The salient facts about the span already discovered are :

1. The recognition span in silent reading is greater than in oral reading. Oral reading is controlled by the articulation of speech units, which results in an appreciable narrowing of the recognition span. Silent reading is controlled by meaning. Meaning is obtained frequently in large units (phrases). These large units cause the number of fixations to be fewer than in oral reading.

2. The size of the recognition span depends upon the type of reading material. It is as easy to perceive complete words as it is to perceive the separate letters of which the words are composed. Meaningful material results in larger recognition units than nonsensical material. Fiction requires fewer fixations than blank verse, French grammar, or algebra, but a mathematician

may read algebraic material, with which he is thoroughly familiar, in greater units than he reads the less familiar French grammar.

3. The recognition unit varies with the purpose of the reading. It is shorter when we read for purposes of study than when we read for pleasure.

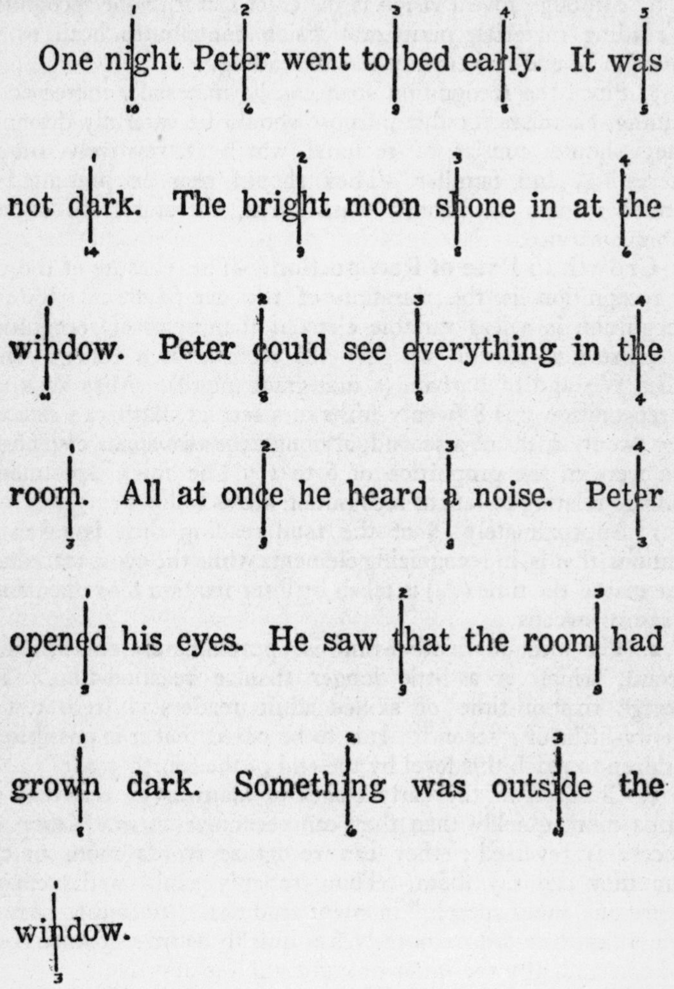

One night Peter went to bed early. It was
not dark. The bright moon shone in at the
window. Peter could see everything in the
room. All at once he heard a noise. Peter
opened his eyes. He saw that the room had
grown dark. Something was outside the
window.

FIG. 55.—Showing eye-movements of a mature reader (College Senior) (Buswell).

4. In elementary school pupils the curve of average growth in span of recognition reveals three definite tendencies :

(*a*) a very rapid growth during the first four school years ;

(*b*) a plateau extending from the fifth grade to the end of the first year of high school;

(*c*) a second gain made during the middle high school years.

5. The recognition span apparently does not vary with the size of type ordinarily used.

6. Although foveal vision is the chief factor in the recognition of reading material, peripheral vision contributes both to the direction of eye-movements and to reading.

7. Since the recognition span can be materially increased by training, exercises for this purpose should be carefully designed. They should consist of material which is relatively simple, interesting, and familiar. They should also be presented in natural reading situations; flash cards, therefore, are of very dubious service.

Growth in Rate of Recognition.—The measure of the rate of recognition is the duration of the eye-fixations. Rate of recognition is a less variable element than span of recognition. In a previous section we gave the records of a college senior (Miss W.) and of Barbara (a first-grade pupil). Miss W.'s rate of recognition was 8 twenty-fifths of a second, Barbara's rate was 11·7 twenty-fifths of a second, although the two spans of recognition were in the proportion of 6 to 1. The chief experimental findings relating to rate of recognition are as follows:

1. Approximately $\frac{12}{13}$ of the total reading time is taken by fixations, that is, in recognizing elements while the eye is stationary. The rest of the time ($\frac{1}{13}$) is taken by inter-fixation movements and in return sweeps.

2. The limit of fixation-time is approximately one-fifth of a second, which is a little longer than a reaction-time. The average fixation-time of skilled adult readers is from 5 to 6 twenty-fifths of a second. It is to be noted that it is possible for children to reach this level by the end of the fourth grade.

3. Children in the early stages of learning to read can say words more quickly than they can recognize them. Later, the process is reversed; they can recognize words more quickly than they can say them. This probably explains the clipped nature of "inner speech" in silent reading. We cannot possibly pronounce the words to ourselves as quickly as we recognize them, and consequently the inner pronunciation is abortive.

4. The rate of recognition improves more rapidly and for a shorter period of time than the span of recognition. But—

5. Rate of recognition and span of recognition correlate rather highly; both are expressions of increased facility in reading.

Growth in Rhythmic Progression along the Line.—An excellent objective measure of rhythmic progression along the line in reading is the number of regressive movements made by the eyes. The immature reader, chiefly through mental confusion, oscillates back and forth along the line; the trained reader's eye progresses along the line with a rhythmic swing. Besides mental confusion, other factors operating to produce regressive movements are (*a*) imperfect return sweep of the eye from the end of one line to the beginning of the next; (*b*) over-reaching the

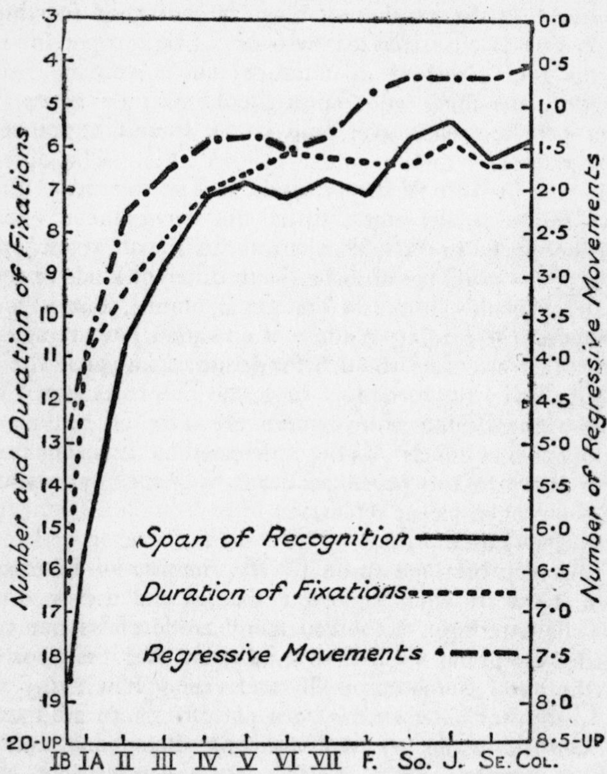

FIG. 56.—Growth curves of span of recognition (number of fixations), duration of fixations, and regressive eye-movements in silent reading (after Buswell).

recognition span; (*c*) lack of word knowledge on the part of the reader; (*d*) difficulty of the material; and (*e*) the attitude of the reader to the material. The number of regressive movements decreases in silent reading from 5 to 1·5 per line between the first and fourth grades. Thereafter, the rate of progress is slower. Regressive movements never disappear; college students average 0·5 per line. In oral reading the regressions are slightly more numerous than in silent reading, but there is little real difference between them.

Buswell made a careful study of growth in silent reading ability as measured by the fundamental habits of recognition span, rate of recognition, and rhythmic progression along the line. Fig. 56 gives a graphical representation of his averages from the first grade of the elementary school to the first year of college.

Interpreting the graphs, we may say that good fourth-grade silent reading is characterized by 6 or 7 fixations per line, each averaging $\frac{1}{5}$ of a second in duration, and involving less than 2 refixations per line; good adult silent reading exhibits 5 or 6 fixations per line, each averaging $\frac{1}{5}$ of a second, and involving about 1 refixation in the course of two lines. The difference between them is comparatively small, and should cause teachers to have serious misgivings. Either the technique of teaching reading seriously breaks down after the fourth grade, or the energies of the pupil are absorbed with different kinds of reading material. Probably both factors are operative, but it is very probable that the reading of adults is on such a low average plane of ability that attention to such fundamental habits as the three discussed above would lead to very marked improvement. There are well-authenticated cases where the rate of reading light literature, such as novels, has been increased by conscious practice from 30 pages to 120 pages per hour, without any measurable loss of comprehension or retention.

The Eye-Voice Span.—The eye-voice span in oral reading is the distance best measured by the number of letter-spaces between the word which the eye is fixating and the word which the voice is uttering. Some rough indication of its size can be obtained by slipping a piece of cardboard over the book from which the pupil is reading orally and seeing how many words he can read after his view has been cut off. Accurate measurements can be made by synchronizing dictaphone and eye-movement records. From the two, the eye-voice span at any given moment may be found.

The eye-voice span in silent reading is the distance between the word which the eye is fixating and the word which the voice is silently uttering in the form of "inner speech." This span cannot be measured accurately, but some idea of its size may be obtained from eye-movement records taken from reading material containing confusion words, which can be pronounced correctly only when the eye is several words ahead of the voice. Thus in the sentence "There were tears in her eyes and tears in her dress," the confusion word *tears* can only be pronounced correctly provided the eye has reached the words "eyes" and "dress" respectively.

When children read word by word, the eye-voice span is approximately zero; the eye and voice are at the same point. This leads to a jerky, unintelligent method of reading. With increasing facility the eye-voice span lengthens and the words are grouped into meaningful units before they are pronounced. The eye-voice span, therefore, provides a valuable measure of maturity in reading.

The eye-voice span on the average increases with school grades and with the quality of the reading. The growth, however, is very irregular and some elementary pupils have longer eye-voice spans than adults. The span is wider in reading easy, familiar material than in reading difficult, unfamiliar material. As a matter of fact the span immediately contracts whenever an unfamiliar word is encountered. The length of the span varies with the position in the sentence, but has little relationship to the position in the line. Buswell [1] found that the span at the beginning of a sentence, when a pause is generally made in oral reading, was greater than at the end by 46 per cent.; and greater in the centre than the end by 23 per cent. The actual span-averages for the beginning, middle, and ends of sentences, measured in letter-spaces, were 15·9, 13·9, and 10·9 respectively.

Good readers have wider spans than poor readers, as may be seen from the following summaries of Buswell:

Average Eye-Voice Span by Grades (Buswell).

Subjects.	Grade.						Average for all grades.
	II.	III.	IV.	V.	VI.	VII.	
Good readers .	11·0	13·2	13·9	16·8	11·9	15·9	13·8
Poor readers . .	5·4	10·3	6·1	9·7	11·2	9·4	8·7
Good and poor .	8·2	11·8	10·0	13·3	11·6	12·7	11·3

In High School, twelve good readers and twelve poor ones had spans of 15·2 and 11·2 respectively.

The rate of reading and the eye-voice span increase together, but a negative correlation is found between the eye-voice span and the number of regressive movements per line.

There is a close relationship between the eye-voice span and the grasp of the meaning of what is read. Meaning is partially grasped through perception (eye) but is completed through

[1] Buswell, G. T., *The Eye-Voice Span in Reading*.

pronunciation (voice or inner-speech). Beginners in reading see, pronounce, and understand the word at about the same time. Mature readers, with restricted inner speech in silent reading, mainly grasp the meaning with the eye but fill it out with the voice. Immature readers are more dependent upon pronunciation for meaning, as may be seen by the large amount of vocal movements (lips and tongue) they use when reading silently.

Other Factors in Reading Ability.—Certain other factors entering into reading should be mentioned. These are:

(*a*) *Vocalization or Inner Speech in Silent Reading.*—By inner speech is meant the movements of the general musculature of articulation—tongue, lips, throat, vocal cords—which accompany or closely follow visualization in silent reading; it is the silent or internal pronunciation of words which accompanies silent reading. The retention of inner speech by man to-day is probably due to the fact that oral speech played a dominant rôle for such a long time in the history of the race. Immature readers are dependent on silent pronunciation for meaning. With skilled readers, inner speech becomes slurred and clipped, but it is demonstrably present in most, if not all, reading and thinking. Some quick readers, however, claim that they are "eye-readers" and secure meaning without the aid of inner speech. Inner speech retards the rate of silent reading. Any teaching device which increases the rate of reading automatically decreases the amount of inner speech that accompanies it. Inner speech, however, is essential for the proper appreciation of the rhythmical qualities of poetry.

(*b*) *Precision of Recognition.*—As a result of his measurements of the perceptual abilities of children, Gates,[1] using such materials as digits, letters, and drawings, concluded that there was no general perceptual ability, but many relatively specific abilities for specific items. Huey showed that mature readers did not see every detail of words, but that they read them, as it were, from the cues given by the ghostly outlines of their form, in which the letters with loops and tails played the more important part. Accuracy of recognition in reading is a relative affair; even good readers may confuse words that are similar in form. The difficulty of securing printed matter free from typographical errors is a testimony to the customary inaccuracies of our recognition. With oral reading the inaccuracies can be easily recorded. They may be classified as non-recognition, total mis-pronunciations, partial mis-pronunciations, omissions, substitutions, repetitions, and insertions. Precision of recognition is aided by the context.

[1] Gates, A. I., *Psychology of Reading and Spelling*, pp. 20–37.

Phonetic drills are the best known school device for increasing the accuracy of recognition, but these may be carried on so long that word-sounding takes the place of comprehension as the final aim of reading. With silent reading, the diagnosis of inaccuracies is more difficult. However, as Gates has demonstrated, tests which diagnose each specific difficulty can be constructed.

(*c*) *Return Sweeps*.—Little reliable data have been secured on the growth of accuracy of the return sweeps of the eyes as they pass from the end of one line to the beginning of the next. Accuracy is improved by printing the lines farther apart.

The Hygiene of Reading.—Considering the amount of time spent by moderns in reading, the hygiene of the process should receive more consideration than is now given to it. Such elements as size, form and thickness of type, spacing of type, the length of the printed line, the colour of the ink, and the colour and gloss of the paper are important enough to deserve further experimental investigation. All authorities are agreed that the blackest of ink on the whitest of unglazed paper should be used in printing so as to produce the greatest contrast without any reflection. The lines should not exceed 3·5 to 4 inches in length and the left- and right-hand margins should be regular. A plain style of type should be used with the vertical strokes of the letters thick enough to stand out clearly. The size of the type and its spacing are the most important elements. The British Association Committee on the Influence of School-books upon Eyesight recommended (1913) that the following minimum requirements with regard to type should be met by all school texts:

Minimum Requirements for Size of Type.

Age of reader.	Minimum height of face of short letters.	Minimum length of alphabet of small letters.	Minimum inter-linear space.	Maximum No. of lines per 100 mm. of 4 inches.	Maximum length of line.
Under 7 years	3·5 mm.	96 mm. or 272 pt.	6·5 mm. or 18 pt.	10	—
7–8 years	2·5 mm.	72 mm. or 204 pt.	6·0 mm. or 11 pt.	15	100 mm. or 4 in.
8–9 „	2·0 mm.	55 mm. or 156 pt.	2·9 mm. or 8 pt.	20	93 mm. or 3⅝ in.
9–12 „	1·8 mm.	50 mm. or 143 pt.	2·4 mm. or 7 pt.	22	93 mm. or 3⅝ in.
Over 12 years	1·58 mm. or $\frac{1}{16}$ in.	48 mm. or 133 pt.	2·2 mm. or 6 pt.	24	93 mm. or 3⅝ in.

1 inch=25·4 mm. 1 point=$\frac{1}{72}$ inch=0·353 mm.

A very satisfactory test for a combination of size of type

and spacing is that devised by Cohn. This consists of a square hole of 1 cm. side cut in a piece of cardboard. When the bottom of the square is placed just above a line of print, not more than two lines should be visible within the square. About one-half of present-day school texts fail to reach Cohn's standard.

The Pedagogy of Reading.—In connection with the pedagogy of reading we may usefully discuss such questions as (*a*) the aim of reading; (*b*) the selection of materials for reading; (*c*) the methods of teaching reading to beginners and to older pupils; (*d*) individual differences in reading ability and remedial treatment.

(*a*) *The Aim of Reading.*—The aim of reading is to get information and enjoyment from the printed page. There are many kinds of information and enjoyment, and each may be sought for many purposes. But whatever nature of the printed material or the purpose for which it is used, ability to read implies a certain mastery of comprehension and a certain amount of speed. Comprehension and speed are the two factors which govern the amount of information and enjoyment that a person gets from his reading.

In addition to the ultimate aim expressed above, many specific aims which govern the instruction and practice at various stages of progress can also be listed. Among them are:

1. Development of a broad recognition-unit, as measured by the average scope of eye-fixations.

2. Development of habits of quick recognition, regardless of the size of the unit, as measured by the duration of the fixation process.

3. Development of precision of recognition, as measured by errors in oral reading, or mistakes in comprehension in silent reading.

4. Development of a rhythmic progression in reading, as measured inversely by regressive eye-movements.

5. Development in accuracy of return sweeps, as recorded by eye-movements from line to line.

6. Development of a wide eye-voice span, measured as described in a previous section.

7. Decrease in vocalization in silent reading, measured by decrease in number of incipient articulatory movements.

8. Development of the total rate of reading, as measured by standardized rate tests for reading.

9. Development of ability to interpret the meanings of sentences and paragraphs, as measured by standardized comprehension tests for reading.

10. Development of ability to appreciate the artistic and

literary values of literature, as judged by the books children select for voluntary reading.

(*b*) *The Selection of Materials for Reading.*—Whatever material is selected should be within the scope of the child's experience and should appeal to his interests. Gray [1] summarizing the studies made on the nature and content of reading materials, states:

"The most important conclusions of the investigations to which reference has been made follow: (1) The religious element in readers which held a pre-eminent place in 1750 has practically disappeared. (2) The literary ideal seems to dominate most sets of readers to-day. (3) There are noteworthy changes in the specific nature of the content from the lower grades to the upper grades. There are wide variations, however, in the emphasis placed on different types of content at each level of advancement. (4) A very critical attitude towards the content of readers has developed, as illustrated in the study of the nature element in first-grade readers, the duplication of material in second-grade readers, and the disappearance of social-science content in eighth-grade readers. (5) Desirable and undesirable qualities of reading material are clearly distinguished as a result of Uhl's study. The fact is also emphasized that informational material proves very interesting if appropriately written. . . .

"Furthermore, there is greater need at present of experimental studies to determine the characteristics of desirable and undesirable reading materials than of tabular studies of selections or types of content in current use."

Uhl [2] found that among the undesirable qualities most frequently occurring in the reading material of the elementary school were "over-maturity," "too difficult," "lack of action or plot," "unreal," "depressing," "monotonous," "not well told," and "too long or scrappy." The desirable qualities most eagerly sought by teachers and students were, in the order of preference: (1) dramatic action, adventure and heroic; (2) interesting action (not dramatic); (3) humour; (4) fairy and supernatural; (5) interesting characters, home life or child life; (6) interesting problems or character study; (7) kindness and faithfulness; (8) about animals and personification; (9) availability for dramatization; (10) interesting repetition; and (11) interesting information.

Children, as judged by their independent reading, appear to know what kind of books they want to read. Dunn found that they had a decided preference for prose. Uhl found less dislike for poetry than Dunn or Jordan. Boys like adventure

[1] Gray, W. S., *Summary of Investigations Relating to Reading*, p. 184.

[2] Uhl, W. L., *Scientific Determination of the Content of the Elementary School Course in Reading*, 1921.

stories, girls fiction. Interest in fiction increases rapidly from nine to eighteen years of age in the case of both boys and girls. The sexes are alike " in their failure to choose to any large extent books on science, information, travel, biography, history, and magazines on humour and nature " (Jordan). Uhl, however, attributed the lack of interest in informational material to the fact that most of it was written for adults rather than for children. He found that " newer types of informational material prove very successful and provide content which has ample social justification." The preferences of children are also affected by the physical make-up of the book (Bamberger); by the reading ability of the child (Green); and by teachers' preferences (Wightman).

Miss Green,[1] through class discussion, got children to state the principles they would use in selecting books for their reading lists. The children concluded that:

> " A book, to be on our lists, must be about something we want to know about. It must be written in words we can understand. If it tries to state facts, they must be accurate. If it tells a story involving what is true to life, the story must not be so overdrawn as to be ridiculous. It must become more interesting as the story proceeds. It must be told in good English."

Before reading selections can be regarded as satisfactory, their vocabularies should be tested for appropriateness to the age of the children for whom they are intended. The range of vocabularies in different reading materials is surprisingly wide. Selke and Selke found 1636 different words in twelve primers, the range in different books being from 157 to 630. Only 38 of the 1626 were found in all twelve books. Packer studied ten first readers and found 3541 different words. Of these, 2048 occur four times or less. In ten second-grade readers Housh found a range from 1198 to 1910, with 419 words common to all ten readers. Since Thorndike made his extensive word count in reading material and embodied it in the famous " Word List," a means of checking vocabularies has been to hand. If too many words from the upper part of the list are included, the material should be rejected or modified.

West, as the result of his researches into bilingualism in Bengal, is of opinion that modification by simplification is the proper solution. He does not hesitate to modify classical English stories by substituting synonymous words of greater for those of lesser frequency. According to the number of substitutions, he

[1] Green, Jenny L., " When Children Read for Fun," *School and Society*. XVII (April 7, 1923), pp. 390–392.

obtains material of known vocabulary levels. The method is also applicable to foreign language selections; by substituting common words for uncommon ones, they can be brought within vocabulary ranges appropriate to any given stage of intellectual development of pupils.

(*c*) *Methods of Teaching Reading.*—In the development of reading ability of children, five fairly distinct stages can be recognized. These are:

1. A pre-reading stage in which preparation for reading is made by extending the vocabularies of children and giving them a greater command of oral English. This stage concerns the home, the kindergarten, and the early part of the first grade.

2. The initial stages of reading instruction. It may be termed a pre-primer stage, since instruction must largely depend, not on books, but on blackboard and chart reading. Primarily early first-grade work.

3. A book-reading stage when rapid progress is made in the fundamental attitudes, habits, and skills of reading. This stage includes phonetic analysis as well as intelligent interpretation. It is essentially the period when the fundamental habits or tools of reading are finally mastered. Towards the end of the period the emphasis shifts from oral to silent reading. This stage normally extends from the latter part of the first grade to the end of the third or fourth.

4. The stage of wide reading. This is largely the stage of silent reading, and includes the use of arithmetical, historical, and social as well as literary material. The aim of the teaching is the enrichment of experience and the cultivation of proper attitudes and tastes. This stage extends to the end of the sixth grade.

5. The stage leading to maturity, when habits, attitudes, and tastes are refined by placing the pupils in contact with a wide selection of literary and informational material. In this stage the reading of foreign languages, of mathematical and scientific material is introduced. It extends through the junior and senior high schools and is not even completed by a college course.

The methodology of the first three stages has been worked out more fully than the later stages. It is generally agreed that in the first or pre-reading stages the pupil must be placed in command of a big speaking vocabulary by means of carefully motivated exercises. Anything that leads to spontaneous speech, marked by ease and freedom, is to be encouraged.

In the second or blackboard stage the transition is made from the child's oral command and auditory recognition of portions of the English language to the recognition and understanding of the same portions when seen in print. For beginners, reading is not so much a matter of extracting meanings from printed words as of attaching known meanings to unfamiliar sets of visual symbols. Action words and games written on the blackboard or printed on charts provide the first reading material. This is usually followed by the reading of well-known rhymes. At all times the necessity for creating correct attitudes, for using meaningful content, for stimulating the desire to read and for analysis of the reading material should be borne in mind. The technique has been carefully worked out by kindergarten-primary teachers and need not be elaborated here.

In the book-reading stage the pupils are first stimulated to find out all about the pictures in the book. Care is taken to direct their attention to specific places in the material where they can find out about the pictures. Drills are relegated to a separate period. The children are encouraged to read page after page to find out all about the story. If children are told the first few stories and helped with the new words, fluency and coherency are encouraged.

Phonetic analysis is next begun. The differences between the advocates of the "look-and-say" and the "phonic" methods have been resolved. It is now clearly recognized that the child must be given command of a technique which will enable him to become an independent reader, and that instruction in phonetic analysis which is too prolonged develops a word-sounding rather than an interpretative attitude. It is also agreed that phonetic instruction should be given in a separate period to protect the sight-reading period from interfering attitudes. Although we cannot be dogmatic about any given system of phonetics, the following principles seem to be sound: (1) Derive the sounds by analysis of well-known words; (2) teach the easy sounds first; (3) teach the most useful sounds first; (4) use a "system" in teaching. Haphazard work in phonetic instruction is worse than useless; it may be positive hindrance to the pupil.

At the end of this third stage of reading, the pupil is usually fairly mature in regard to such fundamental habits as span of recognition, rate of recognition, rhythm of reading, eye-voice span, vocalization, etc. While judgment about the relative merits of methods employed should be held in suspense until more scientific evidence accumulates, the following questions, which Buswell thinks the teacher of reading might well ask himself, are so sane and timely that they are here reproduced:

1. What kind of an attitude toward reading do my pupils have? Do they consider reading as a process of gaining meaning or of

pronouncing words? When, according to my method, should I expect a correct reading attitude to be attained?

2. Do my pupils' eyes follow the printed lines in regular order as they read? Do they depend upon their perception of the words or their memory of the story for their meaning?

3. Are their habits of word-recognition satisfactory for their stage of development? Are they able to master a new word by the method of phonetic analysis? When, in my method, should children be able to do this?

4. Is the span of recognition of my pupils developed up to the average for the grade? Do the pupils see words and phrases, or is their recognition unit smaller than a single word? Do they make many or few eye-movements in reading a single line?

5. Do they have habits of quick perception or are they slow in recognition? Can they read from flash cards when presented at a rapid rate?

6. In observing their eye-movements can I detect many backward, oscillating movements, or is there regularity of fixation along the lines?

7. Do my pupils give evidence of fusing their words into large units of meaning, or do they read in a mechanical word-by-word manner? Does the rhythm of their oral expression display a recognition of thought units?

8. Does my method provide any specific exercise for deficiencies in these elements?

The methods for the fourth and fifth stages, extending from the middle of the elementary school to the university, are essentially the natural developments of those in the third stage. Phonetic analysis for English words is dropped, but it may be introduced in a more elaborate form when modern languages are studied. Oral reading, except in so far as it is concerned with appreciation, especially in poetry, sinks in importance, while silent reading achieves a dominance of position that it never afterwards loses.

(*d*) *Individual Differences and Remedial Treatment.*—Wide individual differences in reading ability appear among pupils no matter how carefully they have been taught or by what method. If pronounced subnormalities appear, they should be critically investigated and the difficulties diagnosed. That this is no easy matter can be seen from Gray's [1] list of the causes of difficulty. This list includes inferior learning capacity, congenital word-blindness, poor auditory memory, defective vision, narrow span of recognition, ineffective eye-movements, inadequate training in phonetics, inadequate attention to content, inadequate speaking vocabulary, small meaning vocabulary, speech defects, lack of

[1] Gray *et al.*, *Remedial Cases in Reading: Their Diagnosis and Treatment*, 1922.

interest, guessing, and timidity. Reading tests will show whether or not a pupil is below average in general reading ability, in rate, and in comprehension of reading, but for diagnostic purposes such information as can be got from a study of eye-movements and other detailed methods of analysis is essential. Gray made use of three general steps, namely, a study of the child's physical and pedagogical history, a preliminary diagnosis of reading accomplishment by means of standardized reading tests, and a more detailed analysis of reading difficulties through the use of informal tests.

After the difficulty has been diagnosed, appropriate exercises to remedy it must be devised and given to the pupil. Exercises for increasing the span of recognition, the accuracy of recognition and interpretation are now well known, but remedial treatment at present is in its infancy. However, the extreme complexity of the reading process is now widely recognized, and some progress has been made in the solution of its problems. Indeed, the progress in the last decade has been more than encouraging, and for this we are deeply indebted to the Chicago school of workers.

Spelling

Importance of Spelling.—Spelling became important only when language became fixed in writing and bound down by printing. The writers in the pre-printing period spelled very much as fancy dictated, and even Shakespeare spelled his name differently at different times in his life. The production of the first English dictionary by Dr. Samuel Johnson in 1755 did more than anything else to standardize English spelling. That it is still in a fluid condition can be seen by comparing a number of different dictionaries. The Oxford English Dictionary, the work of two generations of eminent scholars, is the chief British authority for spelling; while Webster's Dictionary is generally regarded as the standard for American spelling. The non-phonetic character of English spelling is a great drawback to the more extended use of the language in foreign countries, and constitutes a problem of the first magnitude in schools where English is the mother tongue. So difficult is our spelling, that even the best speller among us knows how to spell only a mere fraction of the total words in the language.

Psychological Basis of Spelling.—Spelling is a sensori-motor habit acquired by repeated motor reactions to certain sensory stimuli. The arousal may be due to a sound stimulus, as when the teacher says spell "hippopotamus." In free composition the arousal may be due to the memory of a word which fits a felt meaning. Thus in writing about the animals of Africa we may want to say: "The large animal that lives in the rivers of Africa is called the—crocodile. No, crocodile won't do: hippopotamus, that's it!" So consent is given to the writing of hippopotamus, and the writing takes place automatically, provided the spelling is known. In writing the word, or in spelling it aloud, the conventional order of the letters must be known. This knowledge is obtained by seeing or hearing the letters in a given order and by thinking, speaking, or writing them in the order in which they are seen or heard. As in all habits, repeated practice is necessary before the bonds are firmly established. In free composition, spelling is almost wholly given over to the kinæsthetic system. We spell at the ends of our fingers, as it were; the writing of one letter being the stimulus for the next letter in the word.

What Words to Teach.—Since it is impossible for pupils to learn to spell every word in the language, the first thing to be settled is what words we should teach them to spell. The older spellers seemed to be built on the plan that the hardest words that could be found in the dictionary should be taught, and spellers containing 20,000 to 30,000 difficult words were not uncommon. The simple, common-sense answer that we should teach the words that will be most frequently needed in writing never seems to have occurred to the earlier compilers of spelling-books. This criterion of selection, namely, that we should choose the words which are of most permanent value in writing done in school and in life outside the school, may be supplemented by others. For example, we should teach words which are also of permanent value in reading both in and out of school; which are most frequently used by children in speech; which are phonetic; and are easiest to spell.

Fortunately Horn [1] has done for spelling what Thorndike did for reading by his *Teacher's Word Book*. He has tabulated, from a count of over 5,000,000 words, the 10,000 which occur most frequently. While including several investigations of other workers, he added several special ones of his own. The final list was derived from the following:

1. Anderson, W. N., *Determination of a Spelling Vocabulary based upon Written Correspondence*. University of Iowa Studies in Education. Vol. II, No. 1, Iowa City.
2. Ayres, L. P., *The Spelling Vocabularies of Personal and Business Letters*. New York, Russell Sage Foundation.

[1] Horn, E., *Ten Thousand Words most commonly used in Writing*. Monograph, State University of Iowa. A brief description of it is given in the *Third Yearbook of the Department of Superintendence*, chap. iv; and first 3000 words are to be found in the *Fourth Yearbook of the Department of Superintendence*, chap. vi.

3. Clarke, W. F., "Writing Vocabularies," *Elementary School Journal*, XXI, pp. 349–351.

4. Cook and O'Shea, *The Child and His Spelling*. Indianapolis, The Bobbs-Merrill Co.

5. Crowder, Cora, *A Study of the Spelling Vocabulary of Representative Businesses of St. Paul and Minneapolis*. Master's Thesis, University of Minnesota.

6. Curtis, Ethel, *A Study of the Correspondence of a Single Individual over a Period of Eight Years* (unpublished).

7. Horn, E., "The Spelling Vocabularies of Bankers' Letters," *English Journal*, XII, 6.

8. Houser, J. D., "An Investigation of the Writing Vocabularies of Representatives of an Economic Class," *Elementary School Journal*, XVII, pp. 708–718.

9. Nicholson, Anne, *A Speller for the Use of Teachers of California*. Sacramento: California State Printing Office.

10. Horn, E. The following special investigations:
   (*a*) Vocabulary of Business Letters.
   (*b*) The Vocabulary of Letters written by Literary Men.
   (*c*) The Vocabulary of Correspondence of a Personal Nature.
   (*d*) The Vocabulary of Letters of Application and Recommendation.
   (*e*) The Vocabulary of Material contributed by Laymen to Newspapers and Magazines.
   (*f*) The Vocabulary of Minutes, Sets of Resolutions, and Reports of Committees.
   (*g*) The Vocabularies of Excuses written by Parents to Teachers.
   (*h*) The Personal Correspondence of College Students at the University of Iowa.

This list renders obsolete all counts previously made; it will in turn be rendered obsolete by additional counts which may subsequently be made. But it is the best available at present. If from it are selected the first 3000–4000 words, sufficient basic words for the elementary grades will be included. Words of local value may be added if deemed necessary. Thus the correct spelling of Toronto, Ottawa, and Winnipeg should be known by Canadian children, but they need not necessarily be learned by pupils of the United States.

The Placement of Words in Grades.—Having got the 3000–4000 words which are to be taught during the elementary school course, the next step is to assign them to grades. The placement is most scientifically made by first finding the percentages of children in the various grades who spell each of the words correctly. This gives a list of words from the easiest to the most difficult. The number to be taught in each of the grades can only be guessed at the present time. If, however, the opinions of competent teachers were averaged, a more reliable division would be obtained. The thing to remember is that the spelling of a word should be taught when the child needs to use it in writing and in reading.

The Teaching of Spelling.—The earlier psychology of spelling was certainly false. It assumed that spelling was a method of memory supported by certain rules, and this led to a false pedagogy of the subject in which lists of isolated words from a spelling-book played a conspicuous part. Memory has comparatively little to do with it. Business men who dictate all their letters to stenographers do not forget how to spell. Rules also play a minor rôle in spelling; indeed, there are only one or two rules without numerous exceptions, and these cover but a score or two of words out of the 400,000 or more composing the English language. Maturity is the greatest single factor in learning to spell. Age alone gives acquaintance with words and the practice that is necessary for correct spelling. The natural ability to perceive minute differences in words also plays an important part. Some people apparently are born without this ability. Since they do not see that " accommodation " has two *c*'s and two *m*'s they have difficulty in spelling it correctly. Apparently about 3 per cent. of pupils are so badly handicapped in this way that they will always need the special attention of the teacher. Intelligence is also a factor, but the correlations between intelligence and spelling scores are low, certainly not greater than 0·40 or 0·50.

The learning of spelling obeys the general laws of learning laid down in a previous chapter. The golden rule is to keep as many methods of ingress going as possible. Thus children should write the words singly and in sentences, spell them aloud, and write and whisper them simultaneously. The formation of numerous bonds will lead to the recall of one of them when the others, perhaps, have temporarily disappeared. We saw that " Teach when the need arises " was a good rule. This leads to every teacher being necessarily a teacher of spelling. The teacher of high school mathematics who fails to teach his pupils to spell " isosceles " or " parallel " has failed in his duty. Frequency and vividness are important elements. Frequent reviews—monthly, weekly, and possibly daily—are indispensable. Vividness is obtained by stimulating the closest possible attention to the words, and to the parts of the words that most frequently occasion difficulty. Thus in teaching pupils to spell " separate " and " receive," the " pa " and the " ei " should be emphasized. Incentives such as spelling-bees and graphs of class and individual progress should be freely used. The words to be taught in a given lesson should be grouped according to a " common difficulty " principle. Homonyms should not be taught until both words of the pair appear in the child's vocabulary. Lastly, no word should be taught unless its meaning is known, for only those words whose meanings are known can be used correctly in composition.

Suzzallo and Pearson[1] present the following excellent procedure for class teachers:

(*a*) Write the new word in its normal form on the blackboard.
(*b*) While writing it, pronounce it distinctly.
(*c*) Develop the meaning orally, either by calling on the pupil for a sentence using the word, or by giving, yourself, a sentence, or by defining the word.
(*d*) Show the syllables into which the word is divided.
(*e*) Have the pupils write the word on practice paper several times, spelling it quietly as they write.
(*f*) Allow the class a moment in which to look at the word again, then close the eyes and try to visualize it.
(*g*) Provide plenty of opportunities for drill.

To the above may be added the following:

1. Insist upon careful spelling in all written work.
2. Teach the pupils how to use the dictionary and require them to use it.
3. Do not waste time in teaching words that the pupils can spell already. Give them a preliminary test of the words which it is proposed to teach.
4. Do not require a pupil to write a word ten, fifteen, or twenty times mechanically.
5. Do not call attention to the wrong form. For example, never say, "Do not use two *l*'s in until." Say rather, "Notice the one *l* in until."

The pupil should also be taught to study by himself. Horn gives the following rules for children who have learned to write (second grade and above):

1. The first thing to do in learning to spell a word is to pronounce it correctly. Look at the word. Say it. Look at each part as you say it again. Then say the letters.
2. Close your eyes. Say the word. Then try to remember how it looked in your book as you say the letters.
3. Open your eyes and look at your book to see if you said the letters aright.
4. Now try to write the word without looking at your book. Then look at your book to see if you spelled it right. If you did not, go through the first three steps again. If you spelled it right, cover the

[1] Suzzallo and Pearson, "Comparative Experimental Teaching in Spelling," *T. C. Record*, XIII, vol. i.

word with your hand so that you cannot copy, and write it again. If you spelled it right this time, write it one more time.

5. If all three trials are right, you may say that you have learned the word for the day. If you make a single mistake, begin with step one and go through each step again.

It seems to be established conclusively that fifteen minutes daily is ample time if the methods followed are good ones. More time than this has not been shown to be more productive of power.

Testing Spelling.—For testing pupils formally use either—(1) Ashbaugh, E. J., *The Iowa Spelling Scales*, Bloomington, Ill., Public School Publishing Co.; or (2) Buckingham, B. R., *The Buckingham Extension of the Ayres Spelling Scale*, Bloomington, Ill., Public School Publishing Co.

Test the pupils at the beginning and end of the term or year. The initial test will show which pupils are poor spellers and need remedial treatment. The difference between the two scores shows the improvement the pupils have made in spelling.

In addition, the words taught in each lesson should be tested to see if the pupils have learned them correctly. The errors made in spelling are either chance errors (slips of the pen) or errors due to ignorance. Errors of the first kind should be corrected by the pupil before he hands in his paper. Errors of the second kind should be corrected by re-teaching the words. Apparently girls are better than boys in spelling; only about one-third of the boys do as well as one-half of the girls.

Handwriting

History of Handwriting.—In the evolution of language, writing developed contemporaneously with reading. Writing began with the drawing of pictures such as a circle to represent the sun, a canoe to represent an actual canoe. These ideograms, as they are called, always represented concrete things and were intelligible to everybody, whether he understood the writer's language or not. Later, the ideograms became symbolic, as when the Indian drew a pipe to represent peace and a bird with extended wings to symbolize haste. These were understood only by the initiated. Even to-day the Roman numeral I is a picture of one finger and V a representation of the hand with its five fingers. The next step was to combine ideograms to express ideas. Thus the Chinese ideogram to represent coward is formed by combining the two representing heart and white (white-hearted). Working in this way the Chinese elaborated signs for 40,000 words—a cumbrous system and a terrible strain on the memory. The great step in the development of writing came when conventionalized ideograms were taken to represent sounds instead of things (phonograms). A simplification was at once obtained when the phonogram was made to represent a syllable instead of the entire word, and eventually an alphabet was arrived at when the sign symbolized one of the elementary sounds into which the syllable could be resolved. Although all alphabets are ultimately derived from Egyptian hieroglyphs, through the Semites, Greeks, and Romans, the Egyptians themselves never progressed to the discovery of a true alphabet. Alphabetic writing dates back about 7000 years.

To-day, handwriting is rapidly giving way to machine-writing, and the time may come when the school will provide the pupil with a typewriter instead of a pen. That time is far off, so the teaching of handwriting still remains one of the major pedagogical problems.

The Problem of Handwriting.—Psychologically, the problem of handwriting is the discovery and development of muscular habits which will result in legible, speedy, and æsthetic handwriting with the least expenditure of time and energy. In tabular form the problem is stated below:

	Secured by
A. Legibility.	1. Spacing of words. 2. Spacing of lines. 3. Slant of writing. 4. Form and size of letters. 5. Regularity of letters and slant. 6. Absence of flourishes.

	Secured by
B. Speed.	1. Ease of movement. 2. Rhythm of movement. 3. Slant of writing. 4. Size of letters. 5. Continuity of letters. 6. Method of holding pen and placing paper. 7. Kind of pen and paper.

	Secured by
C. Æsthetic Appearance.	1. Form of letters. 2. Regularity of writing.

Legibility.—The most important factor in writing is legibility. If writing is illegible it defeats its own end. Typewriting is rapidly taking the place of handwriting chiefly because it is more legible, but also, of course, because it is more speedy. Contrary to general opinion, the spacing of words has more to do with legibility than any other single element. Words insufficiently spaced seem to make one continuous word and the writing is very difficult to decipher. Flourishes at the beginning and the end of a word are to be deprecated chiefly because they interfere with proper spacing. Words in a sentence should be spaced about $\frac{1}{4}$ inch, roughly the width of the letter "m." Next in importance is the spacing of lines. These should be wide enough to prevent the serious overlapping of loops and tails. Spacing of lines is usually in hands other than the teacher's, but those responsible for the purchase of writing-books should see that the spacing is adequate, and that it is greater for younger than for older pupils. The slant is important. Vertical writing is more legible than slanting writing, but a compromise has to be made, since slanting writing is more speedy than vertical. The form of letters used in the "script" writing of England and the "library" hand of North America leads to legibility, but here again speed has been sacrificed for legibility. The compromise of a fairly well-rounded letter found in a good "running" hand is generally regarded as satisfactory. The size of letters in writing is important. Finger movements lead to small writing and consequent loss of legibility. Large writing, however, is slower than small writing owing to the greater distance the pen has to cover. Lastly, legibility is dependent upon the regularity of the writing. It is a well-known fact that writing composed of imperfectly formed letters, if regular in form and slant, can usually be read with ease.

Speed.—Speed of handwriting has too frequently been sacrificed to quality. It is true that greater speed is frequently purchased at an undue sacrifice of quality, but, on the other hand, quality is just as frequently secured at the cost of speed. What the teacher should strive for is a reasonably fair quality written at the highest speed that is consistent with the maintenance of the desired standard. Practice in speed writing, therefore, should form part of the regular writing programme of the upper grades.

The handwriting movement is probably the most important factor in speed. The commonest movements can be classified into five groups :

1. Free arm movement.
2. Arm movement with rest.
3. Finger movement.
4. Wrist movement.
5. Combined arm and finger movement.

The free arm movement, used only in blackboard writing, is probably the best to begin with. The finger movement is generally condemned as being too productive of writer's cramp.

The wrist movement is non-fatiguing, but it is not easy to achieve proficiency with it. There remain, then, the arm movement with rest, and the combined arm and finger movement. For writing on paper, it is probably best to start pupils with the arm movement as used in North America. The trouble with this movement is that it runs contrary to the native movements of our very flexible fingers. It is, therefore, very difficult to keep pure. In the opinion of the writer, no great harm seems to be done if pupils as they grow older are allowed to combine some finger movements with those of the arm. This combination is a natural one, and there are few adults, indeed, who do not use some form of finger movements in their writing. This is as far as we can go at present, although later researches might cause a modification of this opinion.

Speed is increased by rhythm of movement. Counting by the pupil as he writes, which Freeman strongly recommends, or even writing to the beat of a metronome or to a gramophone record, is probably useful. Writing movements in the first and third quadrants are speedier than those in the second and fourth. Writing with a backward slant, therefore, is to be deprecated. Writing with a forward slant of 45 degrees is quickest, but somewhat illegible. The best authorities, therefore, recommend a slant of not less than 10 degrees from the vertical and not more than 30 degrees. Small writing is speedier than large writing. It is also less legible. Since writing naturally tends to become smaller with age and with the increase of finger movements, it is best to start with fairly large writing and allow it to decrease slowly in size with age. Care should, of course, be taken to prevent it from becoming too small before the adult stage is reached. Script writing is slower than continuous writing, hence the beautiful legibility of script writing has to be sacrificed to speed. The current method of holding the pen, now universally taught, is conducive to a high degree of speed. Paper smooth enough and pens broad enough to prevent sputtering also add to speed.

Æsthetic Quality.—Everybody agrees that writing should be as beautiful as possible, but, in the past, teachers were far more concerned with beauty than with legibility and speed. They taught pupils as if every one of them were going to produce manuscripts which would rival those written by the old monks. This is now seen to have been a mistake, although the tails to the final *s* and other letters are a relic of the old tradition.

Teaching of Handwriting.—The aim of writing should be to render automatic the recording of thought. This can be accomplished only when both the spelling and various writing movements have been made habitual. Three well-defined stages can be distinguished in the perfecting of handwriting—immature, intermediate, and mature. The following table exhibits the variations in control, attention, pressure, and rhythm as the habit develops from the immature writing of the child to the automatic writing of the literate adult.

Stage of development.	Control.	Attention.	Pressure.	Rhythm.
1. Immature (beginners).	Visual.	Forms of strokes and letters.	Even throughout.	None.
2. Intermediate.	Kinæsthetic or muscle sense.	Mainly to meaning.	Unevenly distributed.	Appears.
3. Mature (adult).	Automatic.	Entirely to meaning.	Unevenly distributed.	Marked.

It is to be understood, of course, that when we speak of the automatic control in adult writing, we do not mean that the eyes have no work to do. Even a practised writer finds it difficult to write with his eyes shut. The eyes in mature writing play an important part in (*a*) keeping alignment; (*b*) keeping uniformity in size of letters; and (*c*) keeping uniformity of spacing.

Since writing should be a help rather than a hindrance to thought, practice in writing should, as far as possible, take the form in which the pupil expresses his own thoughts in writing while thinking. This is practice in free composition. Only too frequently the child is told to think about his writing, when, as a matter of fact, he should be forgetting that he is writing at all. We do not tell a child to think about adding 2 and 2; we try to make it so automatic that 4 is obtained without any thinking. This stage of writing is a fairly late one in the development of writing habits, but some teachers seem to forget that it is the ultimate goal. They hinder development by keeping the pupil on too childish a plane.

Writing is dependent upon the organization of a complex set of habits out of innumerable inherent movements. Writing, therefore, tends to become individual in character, because the basic elements of arm and finger movements, which go to its make-up, are individual. The pressure of a writing system may disguise this individuality for a time, but as soon as control by the teacher is relinquished, individuality begins to assert itself. Not only is this true of individuality, but the two sexes also tend to write differently. Apart from the immature form of childhood, writing may be said to be either masculine or feminine in character. Competent judges can distinguish sex in handwriting correctly between 60 and 70 per cent. of the times, some 10 to 20 per cent. more frequently than is required by chance. Some males write a feminine and some females a masculine hand, but, in general, each sex tends to keep to its own type.

Measurement of Handwriting.—In 1910 Thorndike constructed a "graphometer" or scale which could be used to measure merit in handwriting. It was admittedly rather a crude device, but historically interesting, since it was the first instrument for measuring school products ever constructed. The scale consists of samples of handwriting graded from zero (no merit) to eighteen (the highest merit), although the worst sample actually found in the scale is rated four. The grading was secured by taking the consensus of opinion of a number of competent judges. The sample to be judged is compared directly with the scale and is rated by the number of the standard it most closely approximates in merit.

Thorndike's efforts have been imitated by many workers, but in spite of all the researches upon measurement in handwriting, the various handwriting scales, like the numerous composition scales, still remain more or less scientific toys to be used on special occasions only. The various scales are of limited applicability owing to the fact that each style of handwriting demands a separate scale. Nevertheless, the Ayres scale (Gettysburg Edition) and others have been shown to have a remarkably wide range of applicability, owing to the fact that the samples in them are from systems in wide use.

Most scales can be used to measure (*a*) legibility (or quality) and (*b*) speed. Freeman's five analytical scales rate handwriting from the standpoints of uniformity of slant, uniformity of alignment, quality of line, letter-formation, and spacing.

The use of handwriting scales has demonstrated the futility of securing excessively high degrees of quality at the expense of low rates of speed. The following standards of attainment in speed and quality show the averages for the North American continent. By reference to them the teacher can discover whether his pupils are up to the average or not.

Standards of Attainments in Writing (*Starch*).

Grades.	I.	II.	III.	IV.	V.	VI.	VII.	VIII.
Speed (letter per minute)	20	31	38	47	57	65	75	83
Quality (Thorndike scale)	6·5	7·5	8·2	8·7	9·3	9·8	10·4	10·9
Quality (Ayres scale) .	—	27	33	37	43	47	53	57
Quality (Starch scale) .	8	9	9·7	10·3	10·9	11·4	12·0	12·5

It is generally agreed that for eighth-grade pupils, proficiency in writing greater than that represented by a speed of 83 letters per minute and a quality of 11 on the Thorndike scale or 60 on the Ayres scale is not desirable. This standard of handwriting satisfies the demands of business firms and social correspondence. Any higher quality is mainly concerned with æsthetic qualities rather than legibility. If, therefore, children have reached the minimum standard for quality, they may well be given exercises for improving speed. Experience shows that quality tends to deteriorate as speed increases. The art of teaching handwriting in the higher grades is to secure increase of speed without undue sacrifice of quality. It should be pointed out, however, that practice in handwriting should be specifically devoted to handwriting and not to the making of elaborate pen patterns so frequently found in writing systems. The amount of transfer from movement patterns to handwriting is too small to make such exercises profitable.

We shall not refer to other aspects of language-teaching such as composition and grammar. While objective investigations in these branches are not as numerous as in the ones we have chosen for illustration, those which have been made, apply the same general methods, namely, the acquisition of objective data uninfluenced by subjective opinion.

References

AYRES, L. P. *A Scale for Measuring the Handwriting of School Children.* New York, Russell Sage Foundation, Bull. No. 113, 1912. Pp. 16.

AYRES, L. P. *A Measuring Scale for Ability in Spelling.* New York, Russell Sage Foundation, 1915. Pp. 58.

BALLARD, P. B. "Silent Reading," *Jour. of Experimental Pedagogy*, V (March, 1920), pp. 174–178.

BROOKS, F. D. *The Applied Psychology of Reading.* New York, Appleton, 1926. Pp. xvii+278.

BROWN, H. A. *The Measurement of Ability to Read.* Concord, New Hampshire, State Department of Public Instruction, 1916. Pp. 56.

BUCKINGHAM, B. R. *Spelling Ability: Its Measurement and Distribution.* Teachers' College, Columbia University, 1913.

BURGESS, M. A. *The Measurement of Silent Reading.* New York, Russell Sage Foundation, 1921. Pp. 163.

BUSWELL, G. T. *An Experimental Study of the Eye-Voice Span in Reading.* Suppl. Educl. Monog., No. 17. Chicago, University Press, 1920. Pp. xii+106.

BUSWELL, G. T. *Fundamental Reading Habits: A Study of their Development.* Suppl. Educl. Monog., No. 21. Chicago, University Press, 1922. Pp. xiv+150.

DEARBORN, W. F. *The Psychology of Reading.* New York, Science Press, 1906. Pp. 136.

DEPARTMENT OF SUPERINTENDENCE YEARBOOKS. National Educational Association, Washington (especially 3rd to 6th). Washington, 1923 to date.

DOCKERAY, F. C. "The Span of Vision in Reading and the Legibility of Letters," *J.E.P.*, I, 3 (March, 1910), pp. 123–131.

FREEMAN, F. N. *The Handwriting Movement.* Suppl. Educl. Monog., II, No. 3. Chicago, University Press, 1918. Pp. xvi+169.

FREEMAN, F. N. "The Scientific Evidence of the Handwriting Movement," *J.E.P.*, XII (May, 1921), pp. 253–270.

FREEMAN and DOUGHERTY. *How to Teach Handwriting.* Boston, Houghton Mifflin, 1923. Pp. v+305.

GATES, A. I. *The Psychology of Reading and Spelling.* Teachers' College Contributions to Education, No. 129. New York, Teachers' College, Columbia University, 1922. Pp. viii+108.

GATES, A. I. *The Improvement of Reading.* New York, Macmillan, 1927. Pp. xii+440.

GRAY, C. T. *Deficiencies in Reading Ability.* Boston, Heath, 1922. Pp. xiv+420.

GRAY, W. S. *Summary of Investigations Relating to Reading.* Chicago, University Press, 1925. Pp. vii+275.

GRAY, KIBBE, LUCAS, and MILLER. *Remedial Cases in Reading: Their Diagnosis and Treatment.* Suppl. Educl. Monog., No. 22. Chicago, University Press, 1922. Pp. viii+208.

GREEN, JENNY L. "When Children Read for Fun," *School and Society*, XVI (Nov. 25, 1922), pp. 614–616; and XVII (April 7, 1923), pp. 390–392.

HAGGERTY, M. E. *The Ability to Read: Its Measurement and some Factors conditioning it.* Indiana University Studies, IV, No. 34. Bloomington, Indiana, 1917. Pp. 64.

HAGGERTY, M. E. *Educational Achievement. Rural School Survey of New York State, Ithaca.* New York, 1922. Pp. 223.

HAMILTON, D. E. *The Psychology and Pedagogy of Handwriting.* Toronto University Press, 1920. Pp. 108.

HOLLINGWORTH, LETA S. *The Psychology of Special Disability in Spelling.* New York, Teachers' College, Columbia University, 1918. Pp. vi+105.

HORN, E. *A Basic Writing Vocabulary.* Iowa City, University of Iowa, 1927. Pp. 225.

HUEY, E. B. *The Psychology and Pedagogy of Reading.* New York, Macmillan, 1908. Pp. xvi+470.

JUDD, C. H. *Genetic Psychology for Teachers.* New York, Appleton, 1903. Pp. xiii+329.

JUDD and BUSWELL. *Silent Reading: A Study of Various Types.* Suppl. Educl. Monog., No. 23. Chicago, University Press, 1922. Pp. xiv+160.

JUDD *et al.* *Reading: Its Nature and Development.* Suppl. Educl. Monog., II, No. 4. Chicago, University Press, 1918. Pp. xiv+1922.

MONROE, W. S. *A Critical Study of Certain Silent Reading Tests.* Univ. of Illinois Bull. Vol. XIX, No. 22. Urbana, Illinois, 1922. Pp. 52.

MONROE, DE VOSS, and KELLY. *Educational Tests and Measurements.* (Rev. Ed.) Boston, Houghton Mifflin, 1924. Pp. xxvii+521.

MUTT, H. W. "Rhythm in Handwriting," *Elem. School Jour.*, XVII (Feb. 1917), pp. 432–445.

NATIONAL SOCIETY FOR THE STUDY OF EDUCATION YEARBOOKS (especially 16th to 26th). Bloomington, Illinois, Public School Publishing Co., 1899 to date.

O'BRIEN, J. A. *Silent Reading.* New York, Macmillan, 1921. Pp. xiv+290.

O'Brien, J. A. *Reading: Its Psychology and Pedagogy.* New York, Century Co., 1926. Pp. xxviii+308.

Parker and Temple. *Unified Kindergarten and First-Grade Teaching.* Boston, Ginn, 1925. Pp. xv+600.

Pearson, H. C. "Experimental Studies in the Teaching of Spelling," *T. C. Record*, XIII, 1912, pp. 37–66.

Pearson, H. C. "Experimental Studies in the Teaching of Spelling," *T. C. Record*, XIII, 1 (Jan. 1912), pp. 37–66.

Pintner, R. "Inner Speech during Silent Reading," *Psy. Rev.*, XX (March, 1913), pp. 129–153.

Reed, H. B. *Psychology of Elementary School Subjects.* Boston, Ginn, 1927. Pp. x+481.

Ruediger, W. C. *The Field of Distinct Vision.* Columbia Univ. Contributions to Phil., Psy., and Education, XVI, No. 1. New York, Science Press, 1907. Pp. 68.

Rugg, H. *A Syllabus of the Course in the Psychology of the Elementary School Subjects.* New York Bureau of Publications, Teachers College, Columbia University. Pp. 110.

Schmidt, W. A. *An Experimental Study in the Psychology of Reading.* Suppl. Educl. Monog., I, No. 2. Chicago, University Press, 1917. Pp. iv+192.

Smith, F. "The Psychology of Adult Reading," *School World*, XIV (Nov. 1912), pp. 404–408.

Starch, D. "A Revision of the Starch Writing Scale," *School and Society*, X (Oct. 25, 1919), pp. 498–499.

Starch, D. *Educational Psychology.* New York, Macmillan, 1927. Pp. ix+568.

Stone, C. R. *Silent and Oral Reading.* Boston, Houghton Mifflin, 1922. Pp. 306.

Suzzallo, H. "The Teaching of Spelling." *Teachers College Record*, XII, 5 (Nov. 1911). Pp. 72.

Thompson, Mary E. *Psychology and Pedagogy of Writing.* Baltimore, Warwick and York, 1911. Pp. 123.

Thorndike, E. L. "Handwriting," *T. C. Record*, X, 2 (March, 1910).

Thorndike, E. L. *The Teacher's Word Book.* New York, Teachers College, Columbia University, 1921. Pp. vi+134.

Thorndike, E. L. "Reading as Reasoning: A Study of Mistakes in Paragraph Reading," *J.E.P.*, VIII, 6 (June, 1917), pp. 323–332.

Tidyman, W. F. *The Teaching of Spelling.* Yonkers-on-Hudson, World Book Co., 1926. Pp. ix+178

Uhl, W. L. *The Materials of Reading.* Boston, Silver Burdett, 1924.

Uhl, W. L. *Scientific Determination of the Content of the Elementary School Course in Reading.* Univ. of Wisconin Studies in the Social Sciences and History, No. 4. Madison, Wisconsin, 1921. Pp. 152.

Valentine, C. W. "Experiments on the Methods of Teaching Reading," *Jour. Exper. Pedagogy*, II (June, 1913), pp. 99–112.

Winch, W. H. "Further Experimental Researches on Learning to Spell," *J.E.P.*, V, 8 (Oct. 1914), pp. 449–460.,

Woody, C. "Measurement of a New Phase of Reading," *J.E.R.*, VIII (Nov. 1923), pp. 315–326.

Zirbes, Laura. "Diagnostic Measurement as a Basis for Procedure," *Elem. Sch. Jour.*, XVIII (March, 1918), pp. 505–522.

CHAPTER XVII

IMPROVEMENT IN SPECIAL SUBJECTS

B. The Acquirement of Skill in Arithmetic

The Problem.—The subject of arithmetic is selected for special consideration, because more investigations have been made upon it than on any other branch of the curriculum, with the possible exception of reading. Similarly to reading, arithmetic was formerly regarded as a comparatively simple subject, both in regard to content and to the methods of teaching it. Experimental researches have revealed it as an extraordinarily complicated subject about which dogmatism is absurdly out of place. Some basic questions which might be asked about it are : (1) What constitutes arithmetical ability ? Into what specific elements can it be analysed ? (2) What arithmetic should be taught to pupils, and at what stage of their intellectual development ? (3) How should arithmetic be taught ? Specific questions which may be asked under this heading are exceedingly numerous and range in magnitude from " should deductive or inductive methods of teaching be followed ? " to " should pupils be taught to add upwards or downwards ? " (4) How may arithmetical ability be tested, and what are the major findings of such standardized tests as have been constructed and used ?

The Constitution of Arithmetical Ability.—On analysis, arithmetical ability is found to be very complex. Even if it be limited to the abilities usually developed among elementary school pupils, we find the following main subdivisions :

(*a*) The meanings of numbers.

(*b*) Knowledge of the Hindu-Arabic system of decimal notation, that is, the ability to read, write, and speak numbers.

(*c*) Knowledge of common measures for lengths, areas, volumes, and money.

(*d*) Ability to perform the four fundamental operations—addition, subtraction, multiplication, and division—with integers, small fractions, decimals, denominate numbers, and money.

(*e*) Knowledge of terms, language, symbols, and diagrams used in elementary arithmetic.

(*f*) Application of the above to the solution of simple problems of common occurrence in industrial and business life, involving areas, volumes, per cents.

Each of the above, however, may be subdivided *ad infinitum*. Thorndike, for example, has analysed for us the bonds or steps necessary in simple two-column addition of integers. Besides the multitude of bonds connected with the recognition, writing, and naming of numbers, and the learning of all the addition combinations to 9+9, etc., the addition of integers involves the following processes or minor functions, each of which is psychologically distinct, and requires separate educational treatment:

(1) Learning to keep one's place in the column as one adds.

(2) Learning to keep in mind the result of each addition until the next number is added to it.

(3) Learning to add a seen to a thought-of number.

(4) Learning to neglect an empty space in the columns.

(5) Learning to neglect the 0's in the columns.

(6) Learning the application of the combinations to higher decades may for the less gifted pupils involve as much time and labour as learning all the original addition tables. And even for the most gifted child the formation of the connection " 8 and 7=15 " probably never quite ensures the presence of the connections " 38 and 7=45 " and " 18+7=25."

(7) Learning to write the figure signifying units rather than the total sum of a column. In particular, learning to write 0 in the cases where the sum of the column is 10, 20, etc. Learning to carry also involves in itself at least two distinct processes, by whatever way it is taught.[1]

As a second illustration of the complexity of arithmetical ability, we shall cite Clapp's study of the relative difficulty of number combinations [2] as determined by the frequency of errors made by 7000 pupils from Grades IV to VIII inclusive. The lists are as follows:

(*a*) *Additions from most to least difficult.*

8+5	4+6	8+0	2+4	4+1
7+9	7+6	1+0	3+0	3+1
5+8	7+4	5+2	4+5	4+0
9+7	9+8	4+2	0+8	1+8

[1] Thorndike, E. L., *The Psychology of Arithmetic*, p. 52.

[2] Clapp, F. L., *The Number Combinations, their Relative Difficulty and the Frequency of their Appearance in Text-books*. Bulletins Nos. 1 and 2. Bureau of Educational Research, University of Wisconsin, 1924.

6+8	3+7	1+2	6+0	9+9
6+9	9+0	5+3	8+3	7+7
5+7	2+6	0+3	8+2	2+0
7+8	9+3	0+5	6+4	6+1
8+7	0+6	5+1	1+4	5+4
9+6	6+5	7+0	9+1	3+3
5+9	3+8	0+7	5+0	1+1
8+9	3+4	0+1	6+6	9+2
8+6	3+9	7+2	3+2	8+8
4+7	2+3	1+9	4+3	1+3
7+5	3+5	0+5	1+5	1+6
4+9	6+3	8+1	7+1	1+7
9+5	7+3	6+2	2+9	2+1
9+4	2+7	0+4	2+5	2+2
6+7	8+4	3+6	2+8	5+5
5+6	4+8	0+2	4+4	0+0

(*b*) *Subtractions from most to least difficult.*

14−9	11−4	8−3	7−2	7−1
13−4	11−6	7−0	12−6	4−3
16−9	16−8	12−9	10−7	5−5
14−5	18−9	10−5	8−6	8−4
17−9	11−9	10−6	11−2	6−5
15−9	11−7	8−0	10−1	9−8
17−8	13−6	2−0	6−2	4−4
15−7	15−8	9−7	10−2	9−1
13−9	8−5	9−4	7−6	9−9
13−5	11−5	4−0	9−5	5−3
16−7	11−8	3−0	8−7	5−4
13−7	9−2	5−0	4−1	1−1
13−8	10−3	9−6	2−2	8−1
11−3	10−9	8−2	7−5	4−2
14−6	14−7	10−4	6−4	6−6
12−3	12−4	8−8	6−1	3−3
15−6	10−8	9−3	2−1	3−2
14−8	7−4	7−3	5−2	7−7
12−5	12−8	6−0	6−3	5−1
12−7	1−0	9−0	3−1	0−0

(*c*) *Multiplications from most to least difficult.*

7×0	9×6	4×8	6×4	7×1
0×5	6×9	3×8	1×2	8×2
0×7	7×9	4×6	6×5	3×2
0×1	7×8	5×8	2×6	3×1
4×0	6×8	3×9	3×6	6×1
0×8	8×6	7×7	8×3	1×8
0×2	4×9	3×7	6×2	1×4

0×4	4×7	5×7	3×5	2×9
2×0	1×1	5×9	8×1	2×1
0×6	8×9	9×5	1×9	1×6
9×0	9×4	7×3	4×3	1×5
8×0	7×4	9×9	5×5	2×2
0×3	7×6	7×5	3×3	9×2
6×0	8×8	4×5	9×1	2×8
0×9	8×5	3×4	7×2	1×4
3×0	8×4	2×4	2×7	2×5
9×7	9×8	4×2	2×3	1×3
5×0	9×3	5×3	4×1	5×1
1×0	5×6	6×6	4×4	1×7
8×7	6×7	6×3	5×2	0×0

(*d*) *Divisions from most to least difficult.*

2÷2	45÷9	18÷9	27÷3	49÷7
9÷9	30÷6	16÷8	16÷4	40÷8
28÷4	3÷1	4÷1	7÷1	72÷8
1÷1	35÷7	20÷4	12÷4	18÷6
36÷4	18÷3	6÷1	40÷5	24÷3
8÷8	7÷7	32÷8	21÷7	72÷9
3÷3	5÷5	35÷5	21÷3	20÷5
6÷6	4÷4	27÷9	30÷5	8÷2
56÷8	63÷9	5÷1	12÷3	12÷2
54÷6	0÷5	0÷3	15÷5	15÷3
9÷1	0÷9	64÷8	12÷6	14÷2
24÷6	54÷9	48÷8	36÷6	10÷5
0÷1	0÷2	0÷4	16÷2	6÷2
6÷3	0÷7	0÷6	14÷7	81÷9
32÷4	0÷8	42÷7	24÷8	9÷3
18÷2	8÷1	36÷9	48÷6	10÷2
8÷4	45÷5	28÷7	24÷4	25÷5
56÷7	42÷6	63÷7	2÷1	4÷2

These lists, comprising 390 basic bonds in the fundamental operations with integers, seem to give undue prominence to the number of elementary habits which have to be formed by pupils before they may be regarded as facile in arithmetic. As a matter of fact they grossly under-state the number. No mention, for example, is made of addition combinations in higher decades, of linguistic habits necessitated by arithmetic, of habits of eye-movements during arithmetical operations, of tables of lengths, areas, volumes, and money which even very elementary arithmetic involves, etc. If these were included, the number of separate habits, instead of being 390, would run into many thousands. And it must be remembered that these habits are, for the most part, quite specific, showing little or no transfer from one to the other. Children, for example, cannot transfer their knowledge of 9+7 to 19+7 and higher decades without specific guidance.

A third illustration of the complexity of the problem is given in Buswell and John's investigation entitled *Diagnostic Studies in Arithmetic*.[1] They employed three methods of analysis, namely, (1) a study of eye-movements made in adding columns of digits ; (2) a time analysis of the four fundamental operations ; and (3) detailed diagnoses of individual cases in which specially prepared charts were used.

Eye-movement records of pupils, made while they added columns of figures, were found to be as sure an index of their maturity in arithmetic as the corresponding records for reading were of their maturity in reading. The durations in arithmetic are longer than in reading, many of them running to 100 twenty-fifths of a second and over, but the records indicate clearly where mental confusion occurs and what fundamental habits of computation still remain to be mastered. The number of separate eye-movement habits is shown to be very great.

An analysis of the time shows the relative difficulties of bonds. For example, the percentage of the total time taken in adding a column composed of the following figures, 4, 9, 3, 2, 0, 4, 4, 2, 0, 1, 3, 8, 4, was, for each bond listed, as follows :

	Per cent. of total time (average).
9+4	10·0
13+3	10·1
16+2	8·3
18+4	11·3
22+4	8·6
26+2	7·1
28+1	7·4
29+3	17·3
32+8	13·5
40+4	6·0

Similar variations in time were found for combinations in subtraction, multiplication, and division.

The results of the detailed diagnoses reveal that a lack of knowledge of the fundamental combinations is the most potent of all the factors which lead to error in arithmetic. In the summaries printed below only the ten most frequently listed habits are given in each case :

[1] Buswell and John (Miss Leonore), *Diagnostic Studies in Arithmetic*. Chicago, 1926.

Frequency of Habits in Addition (Buswell and John).

Habit.	Grade.				Total.
	III.	IV.	V.	VI.	
1. Errors in combinations . . .	81	103	78	58	320
2. Counting	61	83	54	17	215
3. Adding carried number last . .	39	45	45	26	155
4. Forgot to add carried number .	37	38	34	17	126
5. Retraced work after partly done.	26	34	39	22	121
6. Added carried number irregularly	26	30	28	18	102
7. Wrote number to be carried. .	34	25	18	12	89
8. Carried wrong number . . .	28	19	26	14	87
9. Irregular procedure in column .	16	29	23	18	86
10. Grouped two or more numbers.	25	22	21	16	84

Frequency of Habits in Subtraction (Buswell and John).

Habit.	Grade.				Total.
	III.	IV.	V.	VI.	
1. Errors in combinations . . .	62	75	69	40	246
2. Did not allow for having borrowed	19	50	57	36	162
3. Counting	43	44	39	10	136
4. Errors due to zero in minuend .	25	39	26	15	105
5. Said example backward . . .	21	38	29	12	100
6. Subtracted minuend from subtrahend	47	33	12	4	59
7. Failed to borrow, gave zero as answer	21	20	14	4	59
8. Added instead of subtracting .	18	9	19	1	47
9. Error in reading	14	5	13	10	42
10. Used same digit in two columns.	18	15	3	4	40

Frequency of Habits in Multiplication (Buswell and John).

Habit.	Grade.				Total.
	III.	IV.	V.	VI.	
1. Errors in multiplication combinations	36	59	60	41	196
2. Error in adding the carried number.	6	40	58	45	149
3. Wrote rows of zeros	2	33	40	34	109
4. Errors in addition.	5	31	41	21	98
5. Carried a wrong number. . .	5	28	40	22	95
6. Used multiplicand as multiplier	18	33	23	15	89
7. Forgot to carry	10	30	27	22	89
8. Error in single zero combinations, zero as multiplier . .	11	20	23	27	81
9. Errors due to zero in multiplier.	5	26	30	17	78
10. Used wrong process	18	22	16	10	66

Frequency of Habits in Division (Buswell and John).

Habit.	Grade.				Total.
	III.	IV.	V.	VI.	
1. Errors in division combinations .	35	55	59	42	191
2. Errors in subtraction	4	25	47	37	113
3. Errors in multiplication . . .	1	20	48	36	105
4. Used remainder larger than divisor	1	17	39	29	86
5. Found quotient by trial multiplication	1	8	49	24	82
6. Neglected to use remainder with example.	5	27	25	13	70
7. Omitted zero resulting from another digit	0	20	22	24	66
8. Used wrong operation . . .	17	17	24	6	64
9. Omitted digit in dividend . .	4	15	27	18	64
10. Counted to get quotient . . .	5	25	24	4	58

Further evidence of the extreme complexity of arithmetic could easily be adduced, but enough has been said to show that its processes are almost endless in number and variety. The teacher's problem is to identify the separate elements, to devise economical ways of teaching them to children, and to arrange the elements in such a way that each receives an adequate amount of practice. Above all, he should teach in such a manner that the pupils start each new habit in the right way and do not drill themselves on uneconomical procedures.

The Course of Study in Arithmetic.—Out of an endless amount of arithmetical material the selection of that which will prove most profitable to the pupil is far from easy. Three principles of selection in curriculum making have been widely employed. These are:

(1) The principle of historical continuity. In brief, this principle states that the life of a people is continuous. If, in the past, an educational instrument has proved its value in the training of citizens, it should be discarded with caution and only when a demonstrably superior instrument can be substituted for it. Through the natural conservatism of the teaching profession (some would call it mental laziness) this principle has been overworked in curriculum making. Materials have been retained long after their usefulness has disappeared. And when challenged to give reasons for their actions, teachers have fallen back on "formal training"—a phrase which, like charity, covers a multitude of sins. In no subject has the historical argument been used so persistently as in arithmetic. Pupils still work examples in Archimedes' problem about three pipes, A, B, and C, filling a

cistern, although to-day we use only one pipe but make sure that it is big enough. They still work examples in Venetian alligation, although we neither mix metals nor tea by that method. Teachers have heeded the German proverb, "Take care that you do not throw away the baby with the water from the bath," to such an extent that they have not even changed the water for the next baby. The claim of history is a perfectly valid one, but we should never forget that we live in a dynamic, not a static world.

(2) The second principle, though widely used, has no scientific justification, since it adds nothing new towards the elucidation of the problem. This is the principle of average current selections. The theory is that by taking a large number of courses of study and finding the average of the whole in regard to subjects taught and time allotted to each subject, a perfect curriculum will be obtained. What such a principle of selection does is not to produce a *new* course of study, but to show the variability of an old one from the average of the whole. It may show that 100 school systems devote an average of 55 minutes per day to arithmetic and that some of them assign as few as 20 minutes, while others give as many as 110 minutes to this subject. But it does not show that 55 minutes is right and that 20 and 110 are wrong, or, indeed, whether arithmetic should be taught or not. It is an excellent device for reducing variability, but useless as a principle of selection.

(3) The third principle of selection is that of life's demands or of current social usages. This is sometimes spoken of as the "job analysis" method, since the method invoked for the discovery of social practices is that of analysing the activity of various groups of the world's workers. Thus if it were desired to find out what arithmetic should be taught in school, the best way is to go to the carpenter, the mechanic, the business man, etc., note what arithmetic they actually use in their various jobs and count the frequencies of the different arithmetical operations. The arithmetic course would then be planned to meet the widest needs. The flaw in the argument is that a purely ephemeral phase of activity may be so pronounced at any given period that a course of study designed to meet it would be obsolete before it got under way. A second caution needed is that mere frequency is an insufficient criterion. A course of study should reflect the highest attainments and permanent values of life ; the job analysis should be confined to the activities of the worthier members of the population. But the principle is sound in that it demands a curriculum suited to the life lived to-day rather than to that lived by distant ancestors. If a judicious combination of the historical and current social usages is made, an excellent curriculum results.

And as we have previously mentioned, the sheer inertia of schoolmen will keep as much of the historically valuable element as is good for us. The curriculum of the school always remains a generation behind the times, so there is little danger of the radicals among us overdoing things.

Before the principle of current social usage received such wide recognition, several attempts to purge the course of study in arithmetic of outworn topics were made. Jessup was an early leader in the movement. By directing the attention of school superintendents to the problem by means of a questionnaire he discovered the percentage among them who were in favour of the elimination of certain topics which invariably found a place in the course of study in arithmetic. As a result, he found [1] the majority of them in favour of the elimination of the following topics, or at least in having less attention devoted to them: alligation, unreal fractions, furlong, quarter, progression, dram, apothecaries weight, compound proportion, discount, surveyor's tables, cube root, troy weight, annual interest, paper folding, G.C.D., foreign money, complex fractions, partnership, reduction, L.C.M., rood, metric system, aliquot parts, cases in per cent., longitude, and time. This was before the War. If a similar inquiry were now made, very few would be in favour of the elimination of the metric system because of the increasing use made of it in industry. This is an excellent illustration of the necessity of going somewhat slowly in the making of changes. We must be sure that the tendencies studied are permanent rather than transitory elements in our changing civilization.

Thorndike has gone a step further. In addition to pointing out the old and useless elements in the course of study, he has listed a number which should find a place.[2] Among the wasteful or harmful bonds he lists:

(1) Arbitrary units in place of practical ones.

(2) Multiples of 11.

(3) Abstract and concrete numbers. "In all computations and operations in arithmetic, all numbers are essentially abstract and should be so treated. They are concrete only in the thought process that attends the operation and interprets the result."

(4) Least common multiple. Any convenient common multiple is the one to use and teach.

(5) Greatest common divisor. "In reducing fractions to lowest terms the pupil should divide by anything that he sees that he can

[1] Jessup, W. A., 'Some Eliminations in the Content of Arithmetic as a Factor in the Economy of Time," *Proceedings and Addresses of the N.E.A.*, LI (1913), pp. 464–468.

[2] Thorndike, E. L., *The Psychology of Arithmetic*, pp. 75–95.

divide by, favouring large divisors, and continue doing so until he gets the fraction in terms suitable for the purpose in hand."

(6) Rare and unimportant words.

(7) Misleading facts and procedures. "If a duck flying three-fifths as fast as a hawk flies 90 miles in an hour, how fast does the hawk fly?"

(8) Trivialities and absurdities. "A certain school has 14 rooms, and an average of 40 children in a room. If every one in the school should make 500 straight marks on each side of his slate, how many would be made in all?"

(9) Useless methods. "I wish to give 25 cents to a group of boys and find that it will require $2·75. How many boys are in the group?"

(10) Problems whose answers would, in real life, be already known. "The Canadian power canal at Sault Ste. Marie furnished 20,000 horse-power. The canal on the Michigan side furnished $2\frac{1}{2}$ times as much. How many horse-power does the latter furnish?"

(11) Needless linguistic difficulties. "If Fred had 6 chickens, how many times could he give away 2 chickens to his companions?"

Among the desirable bonds now often neglected are the following:

(1) Numbers as measures of continuous quantities. The number 3 should be connected with the idea of 3 inches (a portion of continuous length), 3 lbs. (a portion of continuous weight), etc., and not merely with three discrete things like 3 persons, 3 marbles, etc.

(2) Additions in higher decades.

(3) Uneven divisions.

(4) The equation form.

(5) Addition and subtraction facts in the case of fractions. Halves and thirds as sixths, etc.

(6) Fractional equivalents. Much used reductions should be firmly connected with the situations where they are needed.

(7) Protective habits in multiplying and dividing with fractions. Multiplying has been associated with getting larger, and division with getting smaller, hence the difficulty of $\frac{1}{4} \times 4$ and $4 \div \frac{1}{4}$ when met with for the first time.

(8) "Per cent. of" means "hundredths times." Five per cent. of=0·05 times.

(9) Habits of verifying results. Addition, by adding columns separately and adding sums so obtained; division, checked by multiplication; subtraction by addition; multiplication, by division or by reversing multiplier and the multiplicand.

When the course of study has been selected, it is necessary to secure adequate practice for the pupil in each of the bonds we desire him to form. Drill has been frequently shown to be the most important factor in securing facility in arithmetic. The amounts of drill provided in any text for each of the bonds of the four fundamental operations can easily be calculated. The counts which have been made show that, very frequently, the easier bonds are given far more practice than the difficult ones. Thorndike,[1] after a very extensive count, commented on the general situation as follows :

" In general, it is the fact that we use text-books in arithmetic with very vague and erroneous ideas of what is in them, and think they give much more practice than they do give.

" The authors of the text-book as a rule also probably had only very vague and erroneous ideas of what was in them. If they had known, they would almost certainly have revised their books. Surely no author would intentionally provide nearly four times as much practice on 2+2 as on 8+8, or eight times as much practice on 2×2 as on 9×8, or eleven times as much practice on 2−2 as on 17−8, or over forty times as much practice on 2÷2 as on 75÷8 and 75÷9, both together. Surely no author would have provided intentionally only twenty to thirty occurrences each of 16−7, 16−8, 16−9, 17−8, 17−9, and 18−9 for the entire course through Grade VI ; or have left the practice on 60÷7, 60÷8, 60÷9, 61÷7, 61÷8, 61÷9, and the like to occur only about once a year !

" Tables II to VII (not reproduced here) show that even gifted authors make instruments for instruction in arithmetic which contain much less practice on certain elementary facts than teachers suppose and which contain relatively much more practice on the more easily learned facts than on those which are harder to learn.

" How much practice should be given to arithmetic ? How should it be divided among the different bonds to be formed ? Below a certain amount there is waste because the pupil will need more time to detect and correct his errors than would have been required to give him mastery. Above a certain amount there is waste because of unproductive over-learning. If 668 is just enough for 2×2, 82 is not enough for 9×8. If 82 is just enough for 9×8, 668 is too much for 2×2."

Having decided on the topics which are to be included, and secured adequate practice for each of the bonds we desire pupils to form, the problem of dividing the material among the various grades still remains. The principle to be observed here is that whatever is selected should suit the pupil's stage of intellectual development.

Children on entering school have numerous number concepts. They know " two," for example, because they have used two knives, two forks, two spoons, and eaten two apples or two sweets. They probably know from their counting games that 6 is one bigger than 5 since 6 always follows 5 in counting. But this does not mean that formal arithmetic should be begun in the

[1] Thorndike, E. L., " The Psychology of Drill in Arithmetic ; The Amount of Practice," *J.E.P.*, XIII, 4 (April, 1921), pp. 183–194.

kindergarten, although kindergartners make out a good case for number teaching through concrete objects. Ballard,[1] however, maintains that number training on young children is a waste of time. Taylor [2] found that children in a New York City school who omitted arithmetic in the first grade and devoted the time to reading did just as well at the end of the second grade as those who had taken it. Haggerty [3] concluded that it is best to begin arithmetic in the second grade. There are, however, many factors entering into the problem. And since there is no indubitable evidence, we may agree with the bulk of teachers who believe that concrete number work may begin in the kindergarten or first grade and that the introduction of the text-book may be profitably deferred until the second or third grade.

Although, as we have seen, a great deal of scientific evidence has been accumulated in regard to the relative difficulties of arithmetical operations, nothing seems to have been done with it in respect to placement of arithmetical material within the grades. At present the situation is chaotic. The " Commission on Length of Elementary Education," 1927, states, " The commission found the reports on the curriculum very difficult to assemble in any adequate fashion. The reports which came on blank No. 4 (information with regard to grade placements and time allotments) were so uncertain in their estimates of grade placements and of the time devoted to individual items that the effort to tabulate the data was abandoned." The best estimate of current practice which can be made is that:

(*a*) Forty-five addition combinations are completed in Grade II.

(*b*) Multiplication tables are completed by Grade IV.

(*c*) Long division is taught in Grade IV.

(*d*) Addition and subtraction of fractions are taught in Grade V.

(*e*) Multiplication and division of fractions are taught in Grade V.

(*f*) Decimals are taught in Grade V or VI.

(*g*) Tables of weights and measures are taught in Grade VI.

(*h*) Percentage is taught in Grades VI and VII.

Further work needs to be done. The present placement of topics is empirical and there is no assurance that the plans now in

[1] Ballard, P. B., *The Teaching of Mathematics in London Public Elementary Schools*. Special Reports on Educational Subjects, 26, London, England; Board of Education, 1912.

[2] Taylor, J. S., " Omitting Arithmetic in the First Year," *Educational Adminis. and Supervision*, II (Feb. 1916), pp. 87–93.

[3] Haggerty, M. E., " Arithmetic: A Co-operative Study in Educational Measurements," Indiana Univ. Studies, No. 27. Indiana University Bull. XII, 18, pp. 385–507.

use are scientifically valid in regard to their arrangements of the various topics of the course.

Methods of Teaching.—The main problem of general method in arithmetic centres around the question, "Shall arithmetic be taught inductively or deductively?" The older text-books in method assumed that methods in arithmetic were the very antithesis of those employed for natural science. Whereas in science one proceeded from a number of particular examples and finally reached a generalization or law, in arithmetic the process was reversed—one started with the law or principle and by deductive reasoning worked back to the solution of the particular example. In deductive teaching of arithmetic, explanation to the pupil meant showing him how a particular process followed from general definitions and principles. This theory of method in arithmetic has been squarely challenged by Thorndike, who maintains that arithmetical operations are mainly a series of inductive processes and must be taught as such. Children should be taught to see how a particular operation gets the result that they want.

For example, the older texts started the topic of multiplication, by definitions of multiplication, product, multiplicand, and multiplier. The operation of multiplication was explained in terms of units, tens, etc. The inductive process explains the operation in some such fashion as the following:

A class is provided with 72 pads of paper, 96 sheets in a pad. How many sheets of paper did they have?

Here is a quick way to find out.

```
  96
  72
----
 192
672
----
6912
----
```

Think "two 6's=12." Write the 2 under the 2 of 72 in the ones column. Remember the 1.

Think "two 9's=18. 18 and 1=19." Write the 19.

Think "seven 6's=42." Write the 2 under the 7 of 72 in the tens column. Remember the 4.

Think "seven 9's=63. 63 and 4=67." Write the 67.

Add. Remember that the 672 counts 6720 in adding.

Objection may be made that children taught this way do not understand what they are doing. True, some of them do not, but the same pupils would never understand what they were doing after many explanations by the deductive method. They would follow the specific instructions blindly. Only the brighter pupils would see through the difficulties. In careful inductive teaching, pupils can be led up to useful generalizations. Take the following introduction to the addition of mixed numbers found in the Knight, Studebaker, and Ruch Arithmetics as an example of what child-en can be taught to find out for themselves.

Practice in Adding Mixed Numbers

(A Study Period)

Study these examples before the oral recitation begins. Be ready to answer any question your teacher may ask.

See if this example is done correctly.

1. Add:

$$\begin{array}{r} 3\frac{3}{4} \\ 4\frac{7}{8} \\ 4\frac{1}{2} \\ \hline \end{array}$$

First add the fractions. The denominators must all be 8; so we get:

$$\begin{array}{c} \frac{6}{8} \\ \frac{7}{8} \\ \frac{4}{8} \\ \hline \frac{17}{8}=2\frac{1}{8} \end{array}$$

Now we must add $2\frac{1}{8}$ to the whole numbers, thus:

$$\begin{array}{l} 3 \\ 4 \\ 4 \\ 2\frac{1}{8} \\ \hline 13\frac{1}{8} \text{ answer.} \end{array}$$

Did we forget to change the improper fractions?

Did we forget to add the whole number part of $2\frac{1}{8}$ to $\begin{array}{c}3\\4\\4\end{array}$?

2. See if this is right:

Add:

$$\begin{array}{r} 2\frac{2}{3} \\ \frac{1}{4} \\ 2\frac{8}{12} \end{array} \qquad \text{(Work } \begin{array}{c} \frac{8}{12} \\ \frac{3}{12} \\ \frac{8}{12} \\ \hline \frac{19}{12}=1\frac{7}{12}) \end{array}$$

The answer is $5\frac{7}{12}$. How did we get $5\frac{7}{12}$ instead of $4\frac{7}{12}$?

Remember about improper fractions in results.

Remember about carrying the whole part of the mixed number that is the sum of the fractions.

3. Are these done correctly?

A.	B.	C.
$2\frac{2}{3}$	$4\frac{1}{2}$	$4\frac{2}{3}$
$\frac{1}{2}$	$3\frac{4}{5}$	$2\frac{1}{2}$
$3\frac{1}{6}$	$2\frac{4}{10}$	$4\frac{3}{12}$
$6\frac{1}{3}$	$10\frac{7}{10}$	$11\frac{5}{12}$

Rules for adding mixed numbers. Study the example below. How would you do the addition?

$$\begin{array}{r} 4\frac{1}{2} \\ 3\frac{3}{8} \\ 2\frac{1}{4} \\ \hline \end{array}$$

In examples like the one above, it is wise to use the following rule: Add the fractions by themselves. Then add the whole numbers. Never forget to add the sum of the fractions to the sum of the whole numbers.

The special methods for arithmetic are almost as numerous as the specific bonds to be taught. They may, however, be grouped about the subdivisions listed earlier in the chapter under the heading, "The Constitution of Arithmetical Ability." Many excellent texts have been written on methods in arithmetic which illustrate the wisdom of first analysing the situation into its specific bonds and then making provision for drill in each of them.

Monroe [1] undertook to collect all the principles of method which are justified by scientific studies. The statements of principles without the accompanying comments are as follows:

1. In teaching the number concept, which is fundamental in arithmetic, purposeful experience with concrete objects should be provided. Counting and measuring are two of the most fruitful forms of experience.

2. In general, the meaning should be taught before the word or other symbol is given to the child. This applies to the number symbols 1, 2, 3, 4, etc., and to the technical words of arithmetic, such as "add," "subtract," "foot," "yard," "pound," "gain," "how much," and the like.

3. Learning tables is a matter of memorizing, and the rules for memorizing apply.

(*a*) The child should understand the meaning of the combinations which he is memorizing.

(*b*) Attentive repetitions are necessary to fix the associations in learning the tables. These repetitions may be given either in isolated drill or in the use of these number facts in the doing of examples.

(*c*) For permanent memorizing (which is desired in this case) the repetitions of drill must be carried beyond the point where immediate recall is just barely possible.

(*d*) The learning should be done under some pressure or concentration.

[1] Monroe, W. S., "Principles of Method in Teaching Arithmetic, as Derived from Scientific Investigation." Fourth Report of the Committee on Economy of Time in Education, pp. 78–95. *Eighteenth Yearbook of the National Society for the Study of Education, Part II.* Bloomington, Illinois; Public School Publishing Co., 1919.

(*e*) Memorize the number of facts in groups, not one fact at a time.

4. In learning the tables, the different combinations are not equally difficult, and the number of repetitions of the several combinations should correspond to the degree of difficulty, the most difficult receiving the largest number of repetitions.

5. The actual degree of difficulty of a combination to any one child is an " individual peculiarity." This condition makes it necessary to supplement class drills by provisions for individual practice.

6. In addition and multiplication both forms of each combination should be taught.

7. In column addition, grouping digits to make 10 or some other convenient number is not helpful. A variety of procedure is to be expected, and the best results are obtained when pupils are urged to work rapidly but are allowed to choose their own methods.

8. The Austrian, or additive, method of subtraction is not superior to the " take away " method.

9. In " borrowing," it is better to increase the subtrahend by one than to decrease the minuend.

10. The Austrian, or multiplicative, method of division is superior to the direct-association method of division in the initial stages of learning.

11. The Austrian method of placing the decimal point in the division of decimals is more efficient than the traditional method.

12. Most errors belong to recurring types. The most frequent of these types should receive special emphasis so that they can be eliminated.

13. Pupils should be taught to use an abbreviated phraseology.

14. After the initial stage of practice, drill upon the fundamental combinations should be given by means of examples.

15. The period of practice should be from 10 to 15 minutes.

16. Children's knowledge of their previous performances, combined with the desire to surpass those records, is the greatest factor contributing to improvement.

17. A preliminary practice at the beginning of a recitation serves as a " mental tonic."

18. In the operations of arithmetic, emphasis should be placed upon rapid work rather than upon accuracy. (Thorndike disputes this.)

19. Pupils belonging to the same class have been shown to differ widely in achievement. This condition makes it necessary to provide for individual instruction.

20. Arithmetical abilities are specific, and explicit training must be provided for each one.

21. The development of the abilities of a pupil to do different types of examples is frequently not uniform. To meet this situation, diagnosis and corrective instruction are required.

22. Arithmetical study and practice which is motivated by " practical " problems produces results superior to those secured by using the problems in the text-book.

23. Systematic measurement of the results of teaching by standardized tests produces a higher degree of efficiency.

24. Pupils need to be taught the meaning of technical terms that are used in the statement of problems, as a prerequisite for reasoning in solving problems.

Teaching children to solve problems in arithmetic occasions teachers more distress than any other portion of the subject. The difficulties met with are due to the failure to realize that thinking, which is necessary in the solution of problems, is nothing more nor less than particular forms of language habits. As Thorndike [1] says:

"Reasoning or selective, inferential thinking is not at all opposed to or independent of the laws of habit, but really is their necessary result under the condition imposed by man's nature and training. A closer examination of selective thinking will show that no principles beyond the laws of readiness, exercise, and effect are needed to explain it."

Correct thinking and reasoning in arithmetic are secured in the same way as correct habits are secured in any other form of learning. The fact that the habits are largely linguistic should not blind us to the fact that success with them is the potent factor leading to further exercise.

Newcomb [2] reports an ingenious plan for improving the ability of pupils in solving problems. Each pupil for a period of six weeks was required to solve his problems on separate problem-solution sheets, the headings of which only are reproduced below:

PROBLEM-SOLUTION SHEET

"Logical Reasoning Results from Correct Thought Habits."

1. Read the problem over carefully and thoughtfully.
2. State what is given.
3. State what is to be found.
4. Write down the processes you will use.
5. Write the approximate answer.
6. Solve the problem in the space below.
7. Check. Does your answer seem reasonable?

The progress made by pupils whose thoughts were thus directed, compared with those in control classes, was remarkable. The experiment classes made an average gain of 22·8 per cent. in speed and 5·5 per cent. in accuracy in the Stone Reasoning Test

[1] Thorndike, E. L., *The Psychology of Arithmetic*, p. 190.
[2] Newcomb, R. S., *Modern Methods of Teaching Arithmetic*, chap. xvi.

compared with an average of 5·1 per cent. in speed and 2·7 per cent. in accuracy for the control classes. The summing-up of the author is:

"The final results secured through the experiment classes, when examined from any angle, show appreciable superiority over the records made by the pupils of the control classes. While the method has been used in altogether too few classes to warrant a general acceptance of the plan, the results secured are sufficient to commend it for trial to all teachers who are experiencing difficulties in teaching pupils how to solve problems."

Measuring Arithmetical Ability.—In general, the observations previously made regarding the excellences and defects of standardized tests apply also to those in arithmetic. Scores in standardized tests are records of performance under given conditions. They are not measures of ability, although ability may be inferred from them. Tests tend to measure products in a lump; they give little information about the working of the pupils' minds. However, from the very nature of written arithmetical work, a better partial diagnosis of difficulties encountered by the pupils can be made with arithmetic tests than with those in other subjects. But the fact remains that it is the median class score which is mainly sought, since this is a very reliable measure of the work of a school. By comparing this score with that obtained in other schools, and with the general median and standard scores, pupils and teachers can estimate their progress accurately. There is abundant evidence to show that this knowledge stimulates pupils to do better work in arithmetic. Schools which employ standard tests as a regular part of their programme improve the work of their pupils in larger measure and more rapidly than schools which do not use them.

Standardized tests in arithmetic may be divided into two main groups—the formal tests for computation and the tests for ability to solve problems. It is not our purpose to describe any of the tests in detail. Information about them can be easily obtained from any of the standard works on educational tests and measurements.

The results of tests show that, on the whole, speed and accuracy are positively correlated, but there are quite a number of cases where slowness has been accompanied by accuracy, and high speed with a very low degree of accuracy. Most tests are measures of both rate and accuracy. Courtis and Thorndike's formula for combining them into a single composite score has not met with general acceptance.

Other findings reported by Buswell and Judd[1] and other writers are:

(*a*) Long vacations are followed by large losses in efficiency in arithmetic, short vacations by less loss.

(*b*) The correlations between different arithmetical operations are high, which seems to point to a general psychological factor which can be described as arithmetical ability. The majority of workers, however, find that arithmetical abilities are highly specialized.

(*c*) Scores in tests of intelligence show low correlation with those in arithmetic tests (0·41).

(*d*) There is a striking parallelism between scores made by parents and children in the same arithmetic tests, indicating that arithmetical ability has possibly an hereditary basis.

(*e*) Children vary their methods of performing a given arithmetical operation. This variation in procedure may be a cause of the variability in their test scores.

(*f*) The correlation between oral and written work is high (0·60).

(*g*) Sex differences in arithmetic are rather small. Boys usually make better scores in the reasoning problems and girls in computations, but the differences are not large enough to justify segregation for purposes of instruction.

(*h*) Speed and accuracy increase with age, with grade, and with the amount of intelligence.

(*i*) Variability in scores increases with age. This means that the differences between individuals tend to grow larger as the individuals themselves grow older. The increased differentiation demands a corresponding increase of differentiation in the education then provided.

(*j*) The overlapping of grades in arithmetic scores is quite as great as the overlapping of the ages of the pupils composing them. The cure for this state of affairs is the reclassification of the pupils.

(*k*) The four fundamental processes show low correlations with arithmetical reasoning (0·28 to 0·36).

Remedial Measures for Special Defects.—A good diagnostic test will reveal many of the errors made in computation but no test yet devised will reveal the details of the operations used in the solution of problems. And in cases of special difficulty, nothing but a detailed analysis of the pupil's mental processes will show the teacher the kind of remedial measures he needs to use.

Take the following case cited by Buswell and John[2]:

"Kurt was a bright boy in the third grade who had received his previous instruction at home and who entered school for the first

[1] Buswell and Judd, *Summary of Educational Investigations relating to Arithmetic*, pp. 56–57.

[2] Buswell and John, *Diagnostic Studies in Arithmetic*, p. 2.

time in this grade. He experienced many difficulties with both addition and subtraction. Some of his difficulties were of a peculiar type, especially those relating to his reading of numbers. In the example, 58 minus 4, he read the 58 as 85, then counted back to 81, and wrote the answer 18. He was very frequently confused by 6's and 9's, not being sure which was 6 and which was 9. In the example, 79 minus 3, he said '67,' both inverting and reversing numbers. He counted back '67, 57, 47,' stopped, and wrote the answer 74. In the next example, 98 minus 5, he read the 98 as 86 and then began to count back as follows: '86, 76, 66.' When he reached 66, he said 'Oh no,' and counted as follows: '86, 85, 84, 83, 82.' He reversed the answer and wrote his answer as 28. In the case of the example 89 plus 7 he said, '89, 99, 100, 102, 103, 104, 105,' and wrote 105 as the answer. In adding 53 and 8, he said, '53 and 8 is 43, no, 53, 63, 73, 83, 93. Well, I don't know which number this is (pointing back to the 53). Is it 50 or 30?' He then counted '54, 55, 56, 57, 58, 59, 60.' In writing the final answer, he reversed the digits and wrote 06."

Kurt's case is admittedly exceptional. He might have been a mirror-writer. He certainly needed instruction in the veriest elements of number reading and computation. He needed drill with combinations in order to get rid of his uneconomical habit of counting. Nothing but a fresh start from the beginning would be of much use with a pupil whose knowledge of fundamentals was so lamentable.

With a pupil who gets 324 as the answer to 43×8, and 4905 as the answer to 705×7 the defect is the simple and obvious one of forgetting to carry. Special drill on this would remedy the defect.

Examination of the frequency of errors in subtraction, multiplication, and division occurring in 812 test papers in the Courtis Standard Research Test, Series B, revealed the following in the order mentioned:

Subtraction: Borrowing, combinations, omissions, reversion, left-hand digit, 7−0=0, etc.

Multiplication: Tables, addition, cipher in multiplicand.

Division: Remainders too large, multiplication, subtraction, last remainder 0 and 0 in quotient, multiplicand longer than dividend, failure to bring down all of dividend, failure to place all figures in the quotient, failure to bring down correct digit, cipher in quotient.

Such knowledge as the above is excellent for showing the teacher where stress should be placed in his teaching, but after the limits of improvement have been reached by the pupils through class instruction, individual difficulties still remain to be diagnosed and remedied.

References

BALLARD, P. B. "The Teaching of Mathematics in London Public Elementary Schools." *The Teaching of Mathematics in the United Kingdom*, Part I, pp. 3–30. Special Reports on Educational Subjects, 26. London, England, Board of Education, 1912.

BROWN and COFFMAN. *The Teaching of Arithmetic.* Chicago, Row Peterson, 1925. Pp. 391.

BUCKINGHAM, B. R. "Mathematical Ability as related to General Intelligence," *School Science and Mathematics*, XXI (March, 1921), pp. 205–215.

BURT, C. *The Distribution and Relations of Educational Abilities.* London, P. S. King & Son, 1917. Pp. xiii+93.

BUSWELL and JOHN. *Diagnostic Studies in Arithmetic.* Suppl. Educl. Monog., No. 30. Chicago, University Press, 1926. Pp. xiii+212.

BUSWELL and JUDD. *Summary of Investigations relating to Arithmetic.* Suppl. Educl. Monog., No. 27. Chicago, University Press, 1925. Pp. vii+212.

CLAPP, F. L. *The Number Combinations: Their Relative Difficulty and the Frequency of their Appearance in Text-books.* Bureau of Educational Research. Bulletins Nos. 1 and 2. Madison, University of Wisconsin, 1924. Pp. 20 and 126.

COBB, MARGARET V. "A Preliminary Study of the Inheritance of Arithmetical Abilities," *J.E.P.*, VIII, 1 (Jan. 1917), pp. 1–20.

GARFINKEL, M. A. "The Effect of the Summer Vacation on Ability in the Fundamentals of Arithmetic," *J.E.P.*, X, 1 (Jan. 1919), pp. 44–48.

HAGGERTY, M. E. *Arithmetic: A Co-operative Study in Educational Measurements.* Indiana Univ. Studies, No. 27. Bull., vol. xii, 18, pp. 385–507. Bloomington, 1915.

HAGGERTY, M. E. (ED.) *Studies in Arithmetic.* Indiana Univ. Studies, No. 32. Bloomington, Indiana University, 1916. Pp. 110.

HOWELL, H. B. *A Foundation Study in the Pedagogy of Arithmetic.* New York, Macmillan, 1914. Pp. xii+328.

JESSUP and COFFMAN. *The Supervision of Arithmetic.* New York, Macmillan, 1916. Pp. viii+226.

KNIGHT, LUSE, and RUCH. *Problems in the Teaching of Arithmetic: A Syllabus for Discussions on Important Aspects of Elementary School Arithmetic.* Iowa City, Iowa, Iowa Supply Co., 1924.

KNIGHT, RUCH, and LUTES. "How shall Subtraction be Taught?" *J.E.R.*, XI (March, 1925), pp. 157–168.

McLELLAN and DEWEY. *The Psychology of Numbers.* New York, Appleton, 1895. Pp. xiv+310.

MERTON, BANTING, BRUECKNER, and SOUBA. "Remedial Work in Arithmetic. The Problem of the Elementary-School Principal in the Light of the Testing Movement." Pp. 395–429. *Second Yearbook of the Department of Elementary School Principals.* Washington, N.E.A., 1923.

MONROE, W. S. "Principles of Method in Teaching Arithmetic, as derived from Scientific Investigation." Fourth Report of the Committee on Economy of Time in Education, pp. 78–95. *Eighteenth Yearbook of the National Society for the Study of Education. Part II.* Bloomington Illinois, Public School Publishing Co., 1919.

MONROE, DEVOSS, and KELLY. *Educational Tests and Measurements.* Boston, Houghton Mifflin, 1924. Pp. xxvii+521.

NEWCOMB, R. S. *Modern Methods of Teaching Arithmetic.* Boston, Houghton Mifflin, 1926. Pp. xv+353.

OSBURN, W. J. *Corrective Arithmetic.* Boston, Houghton Mifflin, 1924. Pp. x+182.

REED, H. B. *Psychology of Elementary School Subjects.* Boston, Ginn, 1927. Pp. x+481.

RUGG, H. *A Syllabus of the Course in the Psychology of Elementary School Subjects.* New York, Teachers' College Bureau of Publications, Columbia University, 1926. Pp. 110.

SMITH, D. E. *History of Mathematics.* I. Boston, Ginn, 1923. Pp. xxii+596.

STONE, C. W. *Arithmetical Abilities and some Factors determining them.* Columbia Univ. Contributions to Education. T. C. Series, No. 19. New York, Teachers' College, Columbia Univ., 1908. Pp. 102.

SUZZALLO, H. *The Teaching of Primary Arithmetic.* Boston, Houghton, Mifflin, 1911. Pp. xii+124.

TERRY, P. W. *How Numerals are read : An Experimental Study of the Reading of Isolated Numerals and Numerals in Arithmetic Problems.* Suppl. Educl. Monog., No. 18. Chicago Univ. Press, 1922. Pp. xiv+110.

THORNDIKE, E. L. *The Psychology of Arithmetic.* New York, Macmillan, 1922. Pp. xvi+314.

THORNDIKE, E. L. *The New Methods in Arithmetic.* Chicago, Rand McNally, 1921. Pp. viii+260.

TRABUE, M. R. *Measuring Results in Education.* New York, American Book Co., 1924. Pp. 492.

WILSON, G. M. *A Survey of the Social and Business Usage of Arithmetic.* T. C. Contributions to Education, No. 100. New York, Teachers' College, Columbia University, 1919. Pp. vi+64.

WINCH, W. H. "'Equal Additions' versus 'Decomposition' in Teaching Subtraction: An Experimental Research," *Jour. Exper. Pedagogy*, V (June and Dec. 1920), pp. 207–220, 261–270.

WOODY, C. *Measurements of Some Achievements in Arithmetic.* T. C. Contributions to Education, No. 80. New York, Teachers' College, Columbia University, 1920 (revised). Pp. 78.

APPENDIX A

SOME BIBLIOGRAPHICAL MATERIAL

The Technical Journals.

A LIST of the more important technical journals in Education and Psychology is given below :

1. *American Journal of Psychology.* Cornell University, Ithaca, New York. Quarterly. Price $6.50. Editors, M. F. Washburn, K. M. Dallenbach, M. Bentley, and E. G. Boring. General and experimental, together with articles of theoretical and academic interest. Some experiments relating to educational psychology.

2. *American Journal of Sociology.* University of Chicago Press, Chicago, Ill. Bi-monthly. Price $4.00. Editors, E. Faris, R. Park, and others. Frequently contains material in social psychology.

3. *Biometrika.* Printed at the University Press, Cambridge, for the Galton Eugenics Laboratory, University College, London. One volume of about 400 pages issued annually. Subscription price is 44*s.* per vol. (including packing and postage). Single numbers 16*s.* net. Editor, Karl Pearson, assisted by Egon S. Pearson. Contains highly technical but foundational material for education and biology along biometric lines. The same agencies also publish the Drapers Co. Research Memoirs, and the Eugenics Laboratory Publications—Lecture Series, Memoir Series, Technical Series, and Questions of the Day and of the Fray.

4. *British Journal of Psychology.* Issued in two sections—a general section and a medical section—the latter now entitled the *British Journal of Medical Psychology.* British Psychological Society, Cambridge University Press, London, Fetter Lane, E.C.4. Quarterly. Editor, F. G. Bartlett. Experimental studies, many of them in the field of education.

5. *Educational Administration and Supervision.* Warwick & York, Baltimore, Md. Monthly, except June, July, and August. Price $3.00. Edited by Bagley, Bode *et al.* Contains original investigations and general discussions in the field of administration, supervision, and teacher training.

6. *The Educational Record.* The American Council on Education, Washington, D.C. Quarterly. Price $2.00. Editor, C. R. Mann. Deals especially with selection of freshmen in colleges, and examinations in colleges and universities.

7. *Educational Research Bulletin.* Bureau of Educational Research, Ohio State University, Columbus, Ohio. Fortnightly, except during June, July, and August. Free to teachers in Ohio and to selected

research workers. Editor, B. R. Buckingham. Practical problems dealt with from standpoint of research.

8. *Elementary School Journal.* Department of Education, University of Chicago, Chicago, Ill. Monthly, except July and August. Price $2.50. Editors, Staff of School of Education. General, with technical articles on psychology of elementary school subjects.

9. *Forum of Education.* Longmans, Green & Co., 39 Paternoster Row, London. Three issues—February, June, and November. Price 5*s*. Editor, C. W. Valentine. General and technical articles, but less technical than *J.E.R.*

10. *Journal of Abnormal and Social Psychology.* Boyd Printing Co., Albany, New York. Quarterly. Price $5.00; foreign $5.25. Editor, Morton Prince. Chiefly technical and psychiatric investigations.

11. *Journal of Applied Psychology.* Indiana University Press, Bloomington, Indiana. Quarterly. Price $5.00. Editors, J. P. Porter and W. F. Book. Popular applications to industrial, educational, and other fields.

12. *Journal of Comparative Psychology.* (Replaces *Journal of Animal Behaviour*, and *Psycho-Biology.*) Williams & Wilkins Co., Baltimore, Md. Bi-monthly. Price $5.00. Editors, Knight Dunlap and R. M. Yerkes. Investigations on animal learning.

13. *Journal of Educational Method.* Bureau of Publications, Teachers' College, Columbia University, New York City. Monthly, except July and August. Price $3.00. Editor, J. F. Hosic. Title indicates scope, but the project method receives greatest emphasis.

14. *The Journal of Educational Psychology.* Warwick & York, Inc., Baltimore, Maryland. Nine issues per year. Price $4.00 per year. Harold Rugg, Chairman of the Board of Editors. The articles are technical and devoted primarily to the scientific study of problems of learning and teaching.

15. *Journal of Educational Research.* Public School Publishing Co., Bloomington, Ill. Ten issues per year. Price $4.00 per year. Editor, B. R. Buckingham, Bureau of Educational Research, Ohio State University, Columbus, Ohio. Less technical than the *J.E.P.*

16. *Journal of Experimental Psychology.* Psychological Review Co., Princeton, N.J. Bi-monthly. Price $5.00. Editor, Madison Bentley. Reports of laboratory experiments.

17. *Journal of General Psychology.* Clark University, Worcester, Mass. Quarterly. Price $7.00. Editor, Carl Murchison. General, experimental, and clinical.

18. *Mental Hygiene.* National Committee on Mental Hygiene, Inc., Publication Office, 372–374 Broadway, Albany, New York; Editorial Office, 370 Seventh Avenue, New York City. Quarterly. Price $3.00. Editor, Frankwood E. Williams. Problems and researches in mental hygiene and personality adjustments. Practical.

19. *The Pedagogical Seminary and Journal of Genetic Psychology.* Clark University, Worcester, Mass. Quarterly. Price $7.00. Editor, Carl Murchison. Primarily devoted to psychology of childhood. Articles frequently long reports of comprehensive investigations.

20. *Personnel Journal.* William & Wilkins, Baltimore, Md. Bi-monthly. Price $5.00. Editor, V. Bingham. This is the official organ of the Personnel Research Federation and it publishes researches pertaining to personnel in many fields.

21. *Progressive Education.* Progressive Education Association, Washington, D.C. Quarterly. Price $2.00. Editor, Gertrude Hartman. The activities of Experimental Schools.

22. *Psychoanalytic Review.* Psychoanalytic Review, 3617, 10th St. N.W., Washington, D.C. Quarterly. Price $6.00. Editors, W. A. White and S. E. Jelliffe. Discussions and reports of cases by psychoanalysts of various schools.

23. *Psychological Abstracts.* Psychological Review Company, Princeton, N.J. Monthly. Price $6.00. Editor, W. S. Hunter. Abstracts of most of important articles appearing in other periodicals. Best journal to read in order to keep in touch with the whole field of psychology.

24. *Psychological Bulletin.* Psychological Review Company, Princeton, N.J. Monthly. Price $5.50. Editor, S. W. Fernberger. Summaries of current literature upon given fields and topics. Place now largely filled by " Psychological Abstracts."

25. *Psychological Clinic.* Psychological Clinic Press, Philadelphia, Pa. Nine numbers per year without fixed dates. Price $2.50. Editor, Lightmer Witmer. Some contributions on child development and hygiene.

26. *Psychological Index.* Psychological Review Company, Princeton, N.J. Price $2.00 per year. Editor, W. S. Hunter. Covering foreign and American publications, it lists under topical classifications all the psychological literature of the year. Supplements Psychological Abstracts.

27. *Psychological Review.* Psychological Review Company, Princeton, N.J. Bi-monthly. Price $5.00. Editors, H C. Warren and J. B. Watson. Theoretical and philosophical discussions of various psychological points of view.

28. *The School.* Ontario College of Education, University of Toronto, Toronto 5. Monthly, except July and August. Price $1.50. Editor, W. E. MacPherson. Occasional research articles in experimental education.

29. *School Review.* Department of Education, University of Chicago, Chicago, Ill. Monthly, except July and August. Editors, Staff of School of Education. Secondary education, frequently from the standpoint of experimental research. Price $2.50 ($2.80 in Canada).

30. *School and Society.* Science Press, Grand Central Terminal, New York City. Weekly. Price $5.00. Editor, J. McKeen Cattell. One article in each number on educational research and statistics.

31. *Teachers' College Record.* Teachers' College, Columbia University, New York City. Eight issues per year. Price $2.50. Managing Editor, Clyde J. Tidwell. General topics. Summarizes the T. C. doctorate dissertations.

32. *Training School Bulletin.* The Training School, Vineland, N.J. Monthly (10 numbers). Price $4.00. Editor, E. R. Johnstone. Psychology and training of defectives.

Bulletins and Monographs.

1. *Archives of Psychology.* Columbia University P.O., New York. Published without fixed dates. Price $5 00. Editor, R. S. Woodworth. Each number a single experimental study.

2. *Comparative Psychology Monographs.* Williams and Wilkins, Baltimore. Published without fixed dates. Price $5.00. Editor, K. Dunlap. Each number a single research.

3. *Contributions to Education.* Teachers' College, Columbia University, New York City. About 250 volumes in series, practically all of them doctorate dissertations in education.

4. *Department of Superintendence Yearbooks.* The National Education Association of the United States, 1201 Sixteenth Street N.W., Washington, D.C. The fifth yearbook was dated 1927. Prices vary. The topics dealt with are the status of the superintendent and various studies of the curriculum.

5. *Educational Psychology Monographs.* Warwick & York, Baltimore, Maryland. Nearly 100 titles at varying prices.

6. *Genetic Psychology Monographs.* Clark University, Worcester, Mass. Monthly. Price $7.00. Editor, Carl Murchison. Extended studies in genetic psychology.

7. *National Society for the Study of Education Yearbooks.* Public School Publishing Company, Bloomington, Ill. The 26th Yearbook was dated 1927. Each one is issued in two parts and deals with a single topic—curriculum studies, learning in the school subjects, certification of teachers, school supervision, rating of teachers, school surveys, minimal essentials and measurement, industrial and agricultural education, etc.

8. *Psychological Monographs.* Psychological Review Company, Princeton, N.J. Published without fixed dates. Price $6.00 per volume. Editor, R. Dodge. Each issue one or more researches.

9. *School Efficiency Monographs.* World Book Co., Yonkers-on-Hudson, New York. A series devoted to practical experiments and investigations in education.

10. *School and Home Monographs* now issued as the *Journal of Educational Research Monographs.* Public School Publishing Co., Bloomington, Ill.

11. *Supplementary Educational Monographs* published in conjunction with the *Elementary School Journal* and *The School Review*, University of Chicago Press, Chicago, Ill. Issued irregularly about 6 to 10 times a year. Price varies. Scientific studies on learning in the various subjects, especially reading. Other quantitative studies. Mostly doctorate dissertations in the School of Education of the University.

12. *University Series.* Many State universities are now issuing at irregular intervals bulletins, contributions, and monographs, some of which are in the field of educational psychology. Typical series are :

(*a*) Ohio State University Studies. Contributions in Principles of Education ; and Bureau of Educational Research Monographs. Ohio State University, Columbus, Ohio.
(*b*) University of Illinois, Urbana, Ill.
(*c*) State University of Iowa, Iowa City, Iowa.
(*d*) The University of Wisconsin, Madison, Wis.
(*e*) The University of Minnesota, Minneapolis, Minn.
(*f*) The University of Delaware, Wilmington, Delaware.
(*g*) The University of Pennsylvania, Philadelphia, Pa.

Other Bibliographical Material

Most of the above journals review books in each issue. The *Journal of Educational Psychology* prints each month an annotated list of articles in educational psychology appearing in other magazines. The United States Bureau of Education publishes *The Monthly Record of Educational Publications*—an annotated bibliography of practically all articles, books, monographs, and reports dealing with education.

APPENDIX B

A GRAPHICAL METHOD OF ESTIMATING "R" FOR SMALL GROUPS[1]

A GRAPHICAL method of calculating the coefficient of correlation would be a distinct advantage if in addition to producing the required result—a value of r—it would present a picture which would help to interpret the result. The only graphical method that appears to be in use is the one described by Rugg (p. 246 of *Statistical Methods*). In this the two sets of data are plotted as abscissæ and ordinates, and each pair of measurements is then represented by a point. The result is a scatter-diagram, which while it does undoubtedly present a picture of the facts, is not of very great assistance in interpreting them. The method of computation of r from this scatter-diagram as suggested by Rugg, appears to be a far more laborious task than the straight mathematical calculation.

It is possible to make a far more obvious pictorial representation of the facts, if instead of using abscissa and ordinate, we erect two vertical scales along which the two ranges of measurements are laid out. The scale does not matter so long as we set the total ranges of the two measures to occupy roughly equal distances along the vertical scales. It is also preferable to have the median points roughly opposite each other. Taking now the individual pairs of measures, a pair showing mark 63 in Test A and 55 in Test B, could be represented by a line drawn from point 63 on the A scale to point 55 on the B scale, and so for each of the other pairs.

From this completed diagram, a slight study will show any marked tendency, such as a tendency to bunch together on Test A or to spread out on Test B. Or it may reveal an upward trend in marks from Test A to Test B. In addition to these trends the graph may show an

[1] I am indebted to one of my former graduate students, Professor S. D. Holmes of Mount Allison University, for the material of Appendix B. While the method described is admittedly of quite restricted use in the classroom, its merits as a teaching device are such as to warrant a description.

Since the above was written, Symonds, in his *Measurement in Secondary Education*, has described a method of illustrating the value of r similar to the one used in this Appendix, but he has not carried the work as far as the derivation of a formula.

even distribution throughout both ranges or it may show a skewed distribution. All of these may prove useful in reading and interpreting results.

There is, however, an additional use for the diagram, and that is, in estimating the coefficient of correlation. An example of perfect positive correlation, where the highest mark in one test coincides with

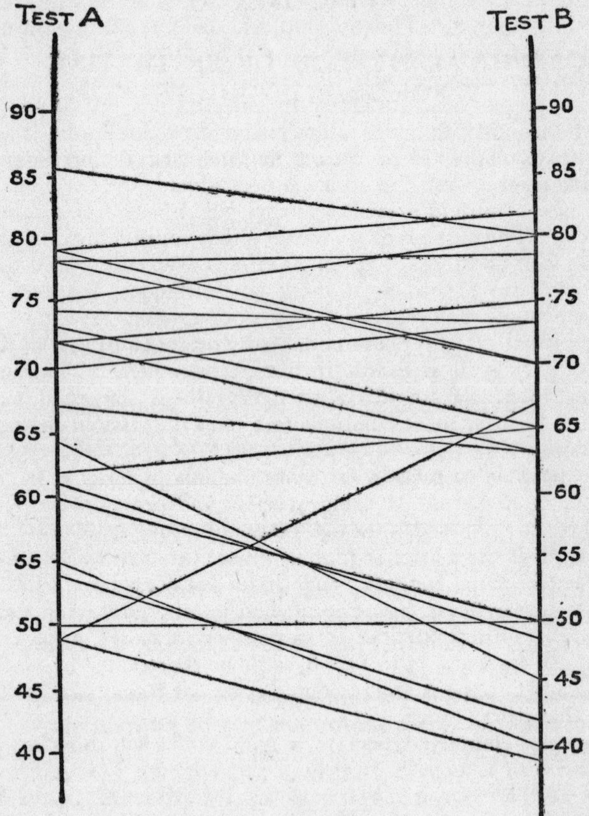

FIG. 57.—Correlation chart showing marks on two tests by a class of twenty-four pupils.

the highest in the other, and so on regularly throughout the distribution, would in this diagram be shown by a series of parallel lines like the steps of a ladder. Perfect negative correlation (the highest marks in one test accompanied by the lowest in the other) would be represented by a series of lines all intersecting in a common centre. No correlation (r=0·00) would be an irregular jumble of horizontal and sloping lines, as if by the operation of pure chance. A casual study of the figure might enable one to estimate roughly the degree of correlation and also to form a concept of its nature, but it appears that it can do more than that.

Since perfect positive correlation shows no intersections at all, and perfect negative correlation shows the maximum number of intersections, it might be possible that the laws of chance would operate to show a direct relationship between number of intersections and degree of correlation. Observation of a number of cases seems to show that there is a direct relationship, and that by counting the number of intersections we can estimate *r*.

A concrete example will illustrate. Twenty pairs of measures plotted out gave a count of thirty-six intersections. It is possible to find the maximum number of intersections of twenty lines. Two lines can cut once. Three lines can cut in three places, four lines in six places, and so on.

Lines.	Intersections.
2	1
3	3 or $1+2$
4	6 or $1+2+3$
n	$1+2+3++++(n-1)$ or $\frac{n(n-1)}{2}$

Twenty lines can then intersect in $\frac{20(19)}{2}$ or 190 places, and 190 intersections would represent perfect negative correlation, or 95 intersections would represent zero or no correlation.

r value	$-1·0$	0	$+0·5$	$+1·0$
Intersections	190	95	47	0

The thirty-six intersections which our twenty lines display would fix *r* at a point $\frac{36}{190}$ of the distance from $+1$ to -1, or $\frac{36}{95}$ of the distance from $+1$ to 0. A value of *r* can be found then by the formula $1-\frac{36}{95}$ of $1=0·62$.

Letting X stand for the number of intersections, and N for the number of cases (*i.e.* lines), the formula may be generalized :

$$r=1-\frac{X}{\frac{N(N-1)}{4}} \text{ or } 1-\frac{4X}{N(N-1)}$$

The results of fifteen applications of this method and the corresponding results from the same data calculated out by the Pearson method are tabulated below.

		Calc.	Graph.
Test A with Test B.	Class 2A 24 pupils.	0·34	0·33
	„ 2B 29 „	0·60	0·56
	„ 2C 21 „	0·52	0·52
	„ 2D 21 „	0·49	0·45
Test C with Test D.	„ 2A	0·67	0·66
	„ 2B	0·58	0·58
	„ 2C	0·59	0·61
	„ 2D	0·24	0·24

Test E with Test F.	Class 2A	0·37	0·44
Test G with Test H.	„ 2A	0·32	0·30
Test J with Test K.	„ 2D	0·21	0·18
Test L with Test M.	„ 2A	0·89	0·81
	„ 2B	0·88	0·84
	„ 2C	0·90	0·73
	„ 2D	0·85	0·75

These results show a very considerable degree of reliability except in the last group, and but for those exceptions we might be justified in accepting the direct relationship between the number of intersections on the diagram and the degree of correlation. An examination of the data shows a peculiarity existing in those groups which show the widest discrepancy. In each case there are two or more individuals whose marks lie completely isolated from the rest of the class, either above or below. Apparently these isolated cases, because they are so far separated from the class medians, weight the results very heavily. For example, in the last group, Class 2C shows a calculated coefficient of 0·90. The elimination of three cases, two at the top and one at the bottom, from the calculations, reduces the coefficient to 0·78, which more closely approximates the graphical value of 0·73. In the same group in Class 2A, the elimination of two outlying cases from the calculation reduces the coefficient to 0·85 which again comes much nearer to the graph result, and so far each of the other inconsistent results. Two views can be taken to these facts. It may be said that the graphical results are useless because the Pearson method of calculation by convention determines what we call the coefficient of correlation, and that methods which do not produce the same answers are not true methods of finding r values. On the other hand, it might be said with some measure of truth, that there may be some doubt cast on a method wherein the elimination of three cases from twenty-one can change a result from 0·90 to 0·78. Obviously the graphical method and result is not affected at all by the outlying measures if they lie so far from the group as to make no intersections, and the value of the method then hinges on the decision whether the determined coefficient should or should not be so heavily weighted by a few outlying measures.

Summing up, it would appear that this method may be useful in determining certain features of correlation data, such as range, distribution, upward or downward tendencies, or any marked abnormalities, all of which can be determined by inspection. As a method of finding r, it has the advantage of being non-mathematical and possibly faster than calculation. For an evenly distributed group it is accurate enough over the whole range from 0 to 1·00, and for groups varying in size. For very large groups it becomes too laborious, but groups of the size of the average class can be handled readily. For groups which show an uneven distribution, it may disagree with the calculated result, but for such groups it gives the correlation value of normally distributed cases and disregards exceptional measures.

INDEX